SELF-CONSCIOUSNESS

SELF-CONSCIOUSNESS
HUMAN BRAIN AS DATA PROCESSOR

MASAKAZU SHOJI

SELF-CONSCIOUSNESS
HUMAN BRAIN AS DATA PROCESSOR

iUniverse books may be ordered through booksellers or by contacting:

iUniverse
1663 Liberty Drive
Bloomington, IN 47403
www.iuniverse.com
1-800-Authors (1-800-288-4677)

ISBN: 978-1-5320-9390-6 (sc)
ISBN: 978-1-5320-9392-0 (hc)
ISBN: 978-1-5320-9391-3 (e)

Library of Congress Control Number: 2020902030

Print information available on the last page.

iUniverse rev. date: 02/24/2020

CONTENTS

PREFACE

The progress of natural science in the twentieth century led to the explaining of many mysteries of the physical world. The areas left unresolved are now limited to several domains of basic physics, chemistry, and biology. Many of the remaining hard mysteries such as the nature of time, the behavior of the quantum world, and the structure and history of the universe are all related to the way the human mind looks at mysterious objects. Then the basic problem is how to interpret our self-conscious mind by using our own mind. This is the subject of this book, titled *Self-Consciousness*.

The study of the human mind, the domain of psychology, is still at the level of descriptive science as biology was before Charles Darwin and Gregor Mendel and as geology was before Alfred Wegener. Any research effort to create a theory of self-consciousness is taboo to the rigidly institutionalized scientific community. Their view is that the state of self-consciousness cannot be observed objectively and that subjective observations of the mind by the person doing the observing disqualify as a scientific evidence. Yet practically any evidence of natural science has been gained by self-conscious observers, and given this fact, such evidence is not free of at least some subjective bias. Because of this, I believe there is no reason to ostracize self-consciousness research. When the human mind looks at nature's mysteries, the biological machine that exists in the human mind is observing the operation of nature working as a lifeless machine. Then we must know how our brain works as a machine to recognize the operation of nature. Finding such knowledge of how the human brain works is what I desire to accomplish in *Self-Consciousness*.

That said, self-consciousness is certainly an awkward subject of study since it does not belong to any classical, well-established scientific discipline carrying historically established rules of study. Yet this remote boundary region is practically covered in its entirety by information science. Then isn't it rational to explore the area by using information science, especially its practical embodiment, that is, the emerging systems science? This area of science is now rapidly growing and is ready to take on the challenge. The objection that evidence obtained subjectively disqualifies as material for scientific study is not valid in information science.

I have a background working in this subject. I started my scientific career in solid-state physics and have worked in integrated circuits, digital circuit theories, and microprocessor design. Since my youth, my hobby was electronic circuit building. Electronic circuits are curious objects that do not work like mechanical machines. They have their own character. This feature matches well with the brain, which is a huge neuron-based circuit.

Since my childhood, I have had an introverted character. Seeing daydreams, phantoms, and ghosts was a regular experience for me as a preteen in the time of World War II. Since that age, I had a habit of looking into my own mind and asking myself, "What is going on in my mind on such occasions when I see unusual images?" Almost regularly I go into introspective observation of my own mind. This history of myself and my technical background has been combined to make this work possible.

In my two previously published books (*Neuron Circuits, Electronic Circuits, and Self-Consciousness* [Vantage, 2009], and *Self-Consciousness: The Hidden Internal State of Digital Circuit* [iUniverse, 2013]), I explored human self-consciousness by reverse engineering my own brain using the conceptual design method and created a manageably simple mechanical model of the brain. Various modes of the model's operation revealed many convoluted features of self-consciousness. The design of such a complex system was never complete, and I kept upgrading the model all the time, deriving more conclusions from the model. This book, *Self-Consciousness*, is the summary of all my works. I was motivated to write it by my own mysterious experience in my youth, on which I have worked all throughout my life.

ACKNOWLEDGMENTS

Although the subject of this work falls into the boundary region of physics, systems science, and psychology, the study of the human mind covers the entire domain of human activity. So, I owe very much to many great teachers and mentors. I am forever grateful to these people who made my work possible throughout my life. I regret that what I accomplished is so little. My life appears like a desert river in Central Asia: its upstream is a spectacular flow from the Kunlun Mountains that carries jade rocks down, but it flows into the desert and dries up in debris. I apologize to my great teachers and mentors for my incapability.

Yet it is my consolation to remember such a spectacular upstream. The earliest of my mentors was Mr. Oyamada Tokio, my primary schoolteacher during World War II, who taught me to think everything by using my own mind as I describe in section 5.14. Mr. Goto Yasuo, my high school teacher, opened my eyes to philosophy and the humanities and encouraged me to study such subjects along with natural science. Professor Kure Moichi of the University of Tokyo, whose Greek and Latin classics seminar opened my eyes to human antiquity, motivated my lifelong interest in mythology and made me a devoted pagan. This led me to Jungian psychology, which became one basis of my study. Professor Shimoda Koichi, my physics professor, gave me an excellent basic physics education, and later he was my ScD thesis advisor. Professor Herbert Kroemer published a paper on negative mass amplifier that inspired me to continue the work in semiconductors throughout my life. Later he gave me such strong encouragement on my Gunn effect work. That was the brightest point of my technical life.

Professor Aldert van der Ziel was my PhD thesis advisor. I write about him in section 4.36. He was the teacher who decided my entire life's direction. I cannot overstate how much I owe him. Dr. William Shockley was my mentor for the first several years at Bell Telephone Laboratories, Murray Hill, New Jersey. He showed me how to approach the problems in solid-state physics. In him, I saw real examples of how bright the power of human thinking is, as I describe in section 4.27. Professors Kathryn Josserand and Nick Hopkins guided me to over sixty ancient Maya sites and advised my study in the connection between the Maya and Moche cultures as I describe in section 4.41. Native American anthropological study was one of the bases of this study of the human mind.

My teachers up to my high school period implanted in me a wide, unbiased view of human culture across the entire world. Professors and mentors of my undergraduate, graduate, and postgraduate periods showed me that they were truly interested in their subjects of study. I inherited their spirit. I remember the words of the now forgotten economist Thorstein Veblen, who held *idle curiosity* as the highest human value. My work is a product of my idle yet genuine curiosity disconnected from secular success that I inherited from my mentors.

As for my immediate family, my uncle Tsurukichi Shoji introduced me, when I was a preteen, to the emerging field of electronics. My father, Tsunetsugu Shoji, introduced me to the Chinese classics, which set my lifelong philosophical basis in Taoism. My sister, Shigematsu Yoshiko, followed up my mythology study as I describe in sections 2.07 and 6.08. Ancient mythology and history were another basis of my study of the human mind throughout the entire history of the world. Finally, but most importantly, my wife, Marika, a psychologist, read my manuscript, commented on it, and corrected the English. Because of these teachers, mentors, and family members, I was able to build my basic thought, not only on my professional background involving physics, electronic circuit theory, and systems science, but also on the psychology, mythology, and ancient history of the New World and the

Old World. I am grateful to all for giving me lifelong inspiration to continue this work since my early age.

The text of *Self-Consciousness* was edited by an excellent developmental editor of the publishing company iUniverse.

CHAPTER 1

BASIC FEATURES OF SELF-CONSCIOUSNESS

1.01 Overview

A seventeenth-century French philosopher wrote, "A human being is only a stalk of reed, the weakest in the world, but it is a thinking reed." In the twenty-first century, the most relevant word in this short aphorism is the conjunction *but*. The word reflects Blaise Pascal's hope for the future of humanity, anticipating the newly arrived period of the Enlightenment. Now, 350 years since that time, it is sadly realistic to replace *but* with *because*. Since we humans think, we destroy each other more effectively than people did during Pascal's seventeenth century. Because we think, we fear more for ourselves and our future than the simple seventeenth-century peasants did. Phrases such as "Jesus is coming again" or "Nam Amitabha Buddha" are no more than religious institutions' commercials. The priests and adherents repeat the words, but no one really counts on what they are expecting to happen. Like the huge French-Swiss particle accelerator that breaks a proton into numerous *components* and scatters them all over, social humans collide hard and destroy themselves, smashing each other to pieces.

So what is finally left for a person after his or her breakdown? What remains is a person's broken self-consciousness. As humans are broken down, what remains is our own injured mind. "What is my self-consciousness?" This question can no longer be kept behind the doors of religious institutions or within philosophers' coffee rooms. This is a serious question for everyone. It is an especially serious question at present, when we are heading for another dark age. Just look around the world. The human mind's blindness is everywhere; violent nationalism is emerging even in the West. The last dark age was not global. There were bright lights in China, in the domain of Islam, and in the cultural centers of the New World. In China, there was the literature and poetry of Tang and Soong; in the Islamic world, high technology; within the Maya civilization, advanced astronomy; and in the Moche civilization, beautiful arts. This time, in a globalized world, there is no special place on the earth. A Marco Polo of the twenty-first century has nowhere to revitalize his mind.

Since human society has been pulverized, we live the same solitary lives as our ancestors roaming around the African Great Rift Valley. Human self-consciousness developed in them in a harsh natural habitat where ferocious carnivorous animals and natural forces threatened their fearful lives. Our ancestors were literally weak, and they existed like the stalk of a reed. We share many experiences with them now in the social habitat we live in. It was the sense of fear that set the basic tone of self-consciousness. Now fear comes more from other humans than from nature. Darwin's idea that competition among the same species is more intense than that from among different species cannot be more real in the twenty-first century. To set fear as the focal point of self-consciousness is rational, natural, and necessary. This is the starting point of my study.

Fifty years after the philosopher of the reed aphorism died, another philosopher was born in the same country, France. A brave man of his time, Julien O. de La Mettrie had enough courage to tackle this same problem with his clear and unbiased mind. He was lucky in his life to be under the protection of history's great king, and one of the most enlightened, Friedrich der Grossen. I wish to track de La Mettrie's footsteps, not under the aegis of the great king, but as the weak stalk of a reed. This is all I can hope for as the last light of enlightenment is now dimming because of the return of violent religious and ideological fever in the twenty-first century's brutal globalized mass society.

I am eager to inherit de La Mettrie's clear thinking applied to the complex, mysterious, and convoluted human mind while living in the brutal mass society of the twenty-first century. Here, derailed democracy and bankrupt capitalism have destroyed all the great traditional values. The thinking totora reed does not stand on the pure water from the Andean glacier but in the middle of debris scattered by a dried-up yellow river in the barren highland desert. What is a dark age? It is a time when a pessimistic mind sees everything more clearly and rationally than an optimistic mind.

1.02 Self-Consciousness

What is self-consciousness? It is the state of mind that knows itself and its world. This is a curiously metaphysical definition, one that does not sound right to natural scientists. If any definition fails to create a clear image of the object, it leads to confusion as I show later in section 6.03. Self-consciousness requires a different definition. The right way to define it is to track its origin. Because, as I have observed, animals of successively lower evolutionary levels (apes, dogs, rats, turtles, frogs, and fish) show accordingly simpler self-conscious features, we can reach the origin of self-consciousness and identify the reason for its emergence. Yet there is a well-publicized objection to this approach, stating that we can never understand the mind of a bat. Here I smell the homocentric thinking of the Dark Ages returning.

First, I believe that humans are nothing special at all in the universe. As a natural scientist, I strictly adopt this Copernican canon that has been established in modern science since the Renaissance period. The reemergence of homocentric thought is a sure sign of the withering human imagination.

Second, along with any other feature of the human body and its functions, the human mind must have developed by evolution, at least until the geologically recent past of the Middle Paleolithic period.

Self-consciousness's role in evolution must be to satisfy the naturally set objective of maximizing the chance of survival at the minimum cost. For this objective, Darwin highlighted adaptive changes and not progress or specialization. This naturally set objective had been working until the emergence of modern humans by creating a more and more complex and sophisticated brain and its operational modes. Therefore the development of self-consciousness must have been continuous up to the Paleolithic period, from the remote geological past, even before the emergence of our close relatives, mammals. We should be able to understand the mind of a bat and should be able to understand a bat's self-consciousness according to the perspective of evolutionary history.

I define self-consciousness as the evolutionarily acquired capability to thrive in an animal's or human's habitat at the minimum cost. Here I add two realistic generalizations, namely that the habitat includes the animal society since the emergence of mammals and the evolutionary mechanism has gradually changed since then, from Darwinian to Lamarckian (this term is defined more precisely later).

Tracking the development process is most effectively carried out by conceptually designing the brain and body structure. Study of a complex system like the brain using this method had not been attempted until the last half of the twentieth century, when complex data processor designs became the routine work of systems engineers. My work relies on this new method of understanding, namely, conceiving and designing a complex brain by way of the top-down design method (section 6.11).

Study of self-consciousness by this method has one distinct feature of the traditional analysis used by philosophers. I focus on the most basic characteristics of self-consciousness, such as recognition of common images, acquisition of their meaning, manipulation of the images for one's life's purposes, and determining the action to be taken after having processed the images. Philosophical study of the human mind focuses on the mind's high-end capability, such as language and symbolic thinking. I show, by constructing the simplest basic functions in the model of the brain, that high-level capability can be synthesized by these combinations in the same way a computer program works (section 4.08). Yet there is a significant difference between the two: the

4

self-conscious brain is a composite of an unconscious data processor and its active and conscious administrator, which I call the SELF. Survival in the natural habitat was ensured by such composite capabilities acquired by evolution, and we create all the great cultural products by using the capabilities.

1.03 Background of Self-Consciousness

What is self-consciousness? This question has been asked since antiquity by philosophers of the East and the West. The Eastern and the Western philosophers reached diametrically opposite conclusions. In the East, philosophers focused on the basic characteristics of the human mind, and they concluded that there was nothing that makes the human mind special or different from that of animals. In the West, the philosophers focused on the highest capabilities of the human mind and declared that it is special and unique in the universe as a gift of God.

This Western view was challenged since the beginning of the Enlightenment period by the materialists such as de La Mettrie, which was followed by the development of the natural sciences, especially by Darwin's evolution. The Eastern view, less systematic but more realistic, was never challenged by Eastern philosophers. As Western culture dominated and Eastern society was exploited in the colonial period, many Eastern thinkers suffered from a sense of defeat and were silenced.

To break from this stalemate, we need a new approach. First I must allow the full infusion of modern natural science to the basically rational Eastern model of the human mind. In so doing, we must choose the proper level of the model's complexity to deal with the mind's complexity. I feel that the Western high-level approach of philosophers and theologians tends to become hand-waving. What I mean by hand-waving is that the thoughts are not based on the model of the brain's operation. The lowest-level approach to modern neuroscience is solid and reliable, but the extremely complex structure of the human brain and mind prevents a perspective, thereby ending up with the scientists seeing the trees but not the mountain. Since self-consciousness is a robust mental phenomenon, there must be quite a simple mechanism creating it. The right approach is to study the mechanism of self-consciousness from the perspective of modern systems science. This allows us to choose the proper level of the model's complexity and to study the brain and body together. I designed the model based on rational observations and assumptions, and then I improved it, step by step, while clarifying its modes of operation. Mine is a model-based study that explains and then predicts the features of human self-consciousness. The conclusions can be checked by human psychological phenomena, which will enable us to see if they are valid and realistic or not. Given this, my approach satisfies the natural sciences' criteria of falsifiability proposed by Karl Popper.

The work I present in *Self-Consciousness* relies on systems science, built on the thought of traditional Eastern philosophy. By this approach, my work exposes some dark sides of human self-consciousness. The driving force of evolution was development of adaptation mechanisms to the habitat, not creation of genius or sainthood. Evolutionary development did not lead humans to God but to a robust survivor. We began with the weakest animals who took refuge under the cover of the reed and then became the thinkers to philosophize the reeds.

1.04 Eastern and Western View of the Human Mind

Emerging from different historical and cultural backgrounds, philosophers of the East and the West had quite different views of humanity. In the West, they held the belief that humans are God's creation and set them at the highest position next to God. In the East, some thinkers declared, metaphorically, that humans are worms germinated between heaven and earth, which never raised anyone's eyebrows.

Reflecting this cultural difference between East and West, the views on the human mind are diametrically opposite. When the storm of evolution raged in the West, there was only admiration for Darwin by the Eastern thinkers. I am frequently asked by Japanese people about the Monkey Trial (some local school district prohibited teaching evolution in school, and any teacher who taught it was indicted). They are dismayed and wonder why the world's most industrialized society, the U.S., hosted such a circus.

The Western view is that every human has a soul, the substance of each person's existence. The person's soul recognizes his or her world and exercises his or her free will. However, there is no mechanical model of the soul. Then where can I start? Modern neurophysiology sets the seat of self-consciousness in the old evolutionary brain areas. This conclusion conforms well with the Eastern view.

The Eastern view is that such substance as a soul does not exist. Since the text that declares this view most clearly, the Pannya Paramita Fridaya Sutra, is not widely known outside the Buddhist cultural zone, I provide its dramatic beginning:

"Avalokiteśvara Bodhisattva, when he was in deep meditation [he, not more commonly she], clearly recognized that the five basic elements of the human soul are all lacking substance. ... Then, humans can be free from all fears and sufferings."

The five basic elements are (1) phenomenon and its image, (2) reception of the image, (3) identification of the image, (4) action to respond to the image, and (5) recognition of the causal consequence of the image. This sutra continues to state that since there is no substance to the human mind, what humans sense as life's suffering also has no substance.

This sutra emerged near the beginning of the common age among the Mahayana Buddhist philosophers. In its detailed and precise observation of the human mind, this sutra must represent the thought of a thinker who looked into his own mind as a humble, unbiased, and critical observer and came to the conclusion that has held for two thousand years in the East. This thought can be used as the starting point on which a detailed natural scientific theory, based on the mechanical model of the human brain, can be built. This model holds that humans do not have such substance as a soul. Then the basic objective of a scientific study is to make a model of the human brain, to show how it works, to check if the model is consistent with the Eastern viewpoint, and then to show how the brain's activity creates a *mirage* called the soul.

As the practical starting point, the previously quoted sutra points out two features of the human self-conscious mind:

(1) The self-conscious soul, whose carrier is the SELF, which appears to exist in the human mind, is a mirage. The sense of its existence is created by the activities of the brain.

(2) Our human mind engages with life's fear and suffering, and that determines the features of our self-consciousness. Humans struggle to find a way to free themselves of fear.

Scientific study of self-consciousness begins with the critical evaluation of the two points and their further elaboration. In the East, study of human self-consciousness has entailed the recognition of fear and suffering in the human being's daily life. The same feature is observed in all animals. This view has been criticized as the remains of ancient animistic religions of the East. This is nonsense, that disregards the origin of self-consciousness in evolution.

Before Mahayana Buddhists, the Taoist philosophers thought of how self-conscious humans sense, recognize, and understand objects in nature. They arrived at an important conclusion, namely that humans understand any object by becoming it. This is the first significant step toward understanding self-consciousness directly, which I elaborate on in the anthropomorphic sense in section 4.22. The Buddhist and Taoist conclusion is definite, rational, and consistent with the scientific observation of human self-consciousness as I show in this book, *Self-Consciousness*.

A crucial feature of the Eastern philosophers is that they looked at self-consciousness directly without assuming something more mysterious like a soul. I adopted this feature as the starting point of my self-consciousness research. A particularly significant feature is inclusion of the body in the study of the mind. Sometimes the body becomes the dominant factor. Our body is not the humble slave of the holy soul. The pair interacts and creates self-consciousness.

1.05 Self-Consciousness and Subconsciousness

The modern history of self-consciousness research has suffered from the peculiar culture of Western academia. Western academics hold the belief that no theory can be built on any subjectively observed evidence. This belief effectively ostracizes self-consciousness research from mainstream academia. From my viewpoint, this is strangely biased thinking. I must ask why the legal academics hold that a human witness is more credible than material evidence? What is acceptable as *objective* seems to depend on the academic culture.

Yet I believe that observation of the human mind must be made bias-free. Any person whose social prestige or power can be affected by exposing his or her mind cannot easily explore the character of his or her own mind. Socially, high-prestige psychology professors are persons of this type. This leads to an inevitable conclusion: self-consciousness research does not belong to academia but to *literates* like British scientists of the nineteenth century, who did not earn their living in their profession. I consider myself as one of the twenty-first century's literates.

Yet there is another, similarly strange culture belonging to psychoanalysis. Psychoanalysts treat mentally suffering patients and focus on the person's subconscious, which drives self-consciousness from behind. Can the subconscious be observed more objectively than self-consciousness by any means? I suspect that this disconnect is the result of institutionalization of the profession. Like no-man's-land, self-consciousness study was marginalized. I wonder if this is a healthy state of the science of the human mind.

Psychoanalysis now has a hundred-year of history, and it has created many concepts. Yet the relation among the concepts has never been clearly explained. The relation of the concepts can be visualized by a model, but there are few dynamic models shown in the books published by prominent psychoanalysts. I assembled their concepts' relation in a model as shown in figure 1.05.1. The model does not explain the dynamic relationship of the various concepts. Ego is the explicit manifestation of the mind, and there is the mind's center that controls the ego from the background.

9

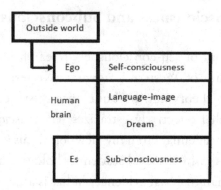

Figure 1.05.1 Structure of the human mind

So, I am not convinced by the psychoanalytical line of thought. Do lower-level animals like apes and canines have subconsciousness? What sort of subconsciousness do these animals have?

From these observations, I am skeptical of the theory that makes subconsciousness the centerpiece of the theory of the workings of the human mind. To explain self-consciousness by way of the subconscious is to explain a mystery by putting forth something that is more mysterious. I try to explain the psychological features presently ascribed to subconsciousness as a special *failure* mode of the operation of self-consciousness (section 3.29). Then I become able to set up a mechanical model in which the two can coexist consistently.

1.06 My Position in Self-Consciousness Study

Every self-conscious person feels that there is an elusive, hard to explain, but undeniably real master in his or her mind, a master that knows him and the world. This self-conscious subject, the SELF, is the brain's activity, which is observable only by the person himself. Such an existence, not accessible by any other independent observer, has been excluded from the scientific research of mainstream academia. At first sight, this might appear as a respectable tradition. Yet, on second thought, I realize that this is really a prejudiced opinion. Many objects of natural science, including small objects such as elementary particles, can never be observed without using delicate and often prohibitively expensive equipment that can be built only in one location in the world. There is no particle accelerator except the LHC in CERN, by which we can observe the Higgs boson. If the objectivity criterion is strictly applied, the boson is real only in France and Switzerland? Before getting into such absurdity, we must evaluate sensitivity, precision, and honesty of self-observation once again.

I believe that the damage done by stiff adherence to rigorism is especially intensely felt in psychology. Psychologists adopted systems science's black box approach. They consider a mouse to be a black box, and they subject the animal to various conditions to see its response. I support their adoption of a systems science approach, but systems science is much richer than offering only the black box concept. All of systems science's methods should be used to crack the mystery of human self-consciousness.

I stepped into this forbidden territory of academia because I had a strong personal need to satisfy my lifelong curiosity. Since I am a strongly introverted character, I have tried to observe my own self-conscious mind since my youth, and I have gained confidence in my introspective observations as a reliable method of getting objective evidence of the nature of my self-conscious mind. For this method to work, the report of introspective observation must be made bias-free. I am not socially successful, I am not confident, and I am an anxiety-ridden, depressive character, but to expose that character in my work does not compromise my self-esteem or social position. I highlight fear as the driving force creating the human mind. This feature is common to all life.

I published my work in two books (*Neuron Circuits, Electronic Circuits, and Self-Consciousness* [Vantage, 2009], and *Self-Consciousness, the Hidden Internal State of Digital Circuit* [iUniverse, 2013]). In this book, *Self-Consciousness*, I summarize all my past works since my youth and place proper weight on each. I show how the sense of the SELF (itself), the sense of space (world), and the sense of time (history) emerge. I show how intelligence developed from self-consciousness and how the SELF struggles to explain mysteries that it cannot understand. Anything that is not comprehensible is fearsome, so the SELF works hard to find an explanation. Mild fear creates idle curiosity, from which many valuable cultural products have emerged.

I am a firm believer of Darwin's theory of evolution by natural selection. From this firm belief, my self-consciousness must have been evolved from the prototype of the lower-level animals that are our ancestors. Then I believe that my fellow humans' self-consciousness must have general and basic similarities to mine. So I have the confidence to assert that the basic character and operational modes of my self-conscious subject SELF must be common to all humans, at the least in their most basic features. Furthermore, by observing animals, I believe that they have a basically similar, although not fully developed, self-consciousness as humans. So the superior human self-conscious mind should be able to understand the mind of a bat.

My belief in the human mind's evolutionary development is that the human brain and its operation were optimized by the trial and error process of evolution, which is exactly parallel to that of the development of the modern data processor. Yet evolution is extremely unpopular in the U.S. According to a 1999 poll, only 18 percent of Americans believe that evolution is the only explanation of human ancestry.[1] This is a mystery—and what is its cause? One obvious reason is that many elementary- to middle-school-level children live in urban, artificial environments. They never see the workings of the evolutionary force of nature. If I closely observe the natural world around me, I find that the evidence of evolution is literally everywhere.

I will provide an example. I joined the technical staff of Bell Telephone Laboratories, Murray Hill, New Jersey, in 1965. Bell Labs in the 1960s was the top center of electronics research and was well funded by AT&T and the government. Surrounded by green nature and wide lawns, I took thirty-minute walks after lunch. I love to make a wreath of dandelion flowers. To make a wreath, I need many

---

[1] John Grant, *Discarded Science* (Wisley, UK: Artists and Photographers Press Ltd., 2006).

flowers having long stems. In the 1960s and 1970s, I could not find any such flowers. At that time, AT&T maintained the top research center in the best condition, so the facility department mowed the extensive lawn so frequently that the subspecies of dandelion having long flower stems had no chance to survive.

Yet from the time of the Reagan administration in the 1980s, basic science research funding declined drastically, and the effect showed in the schedule of the facility's maintenance. They did not mow the lawns frequently enough, so the dandelion subspecies having longer flower stems, which is ecologically better adapted (since the seeds can be scattered over a wider range), took advantage and dominated the population. From the 1990s onward, I was able to make long wreaths of dandelion flowers to amuse secretaries. In just ten short years, natural selection allowed the population of the better-adapted subspecies of dandelion to dominate. When I see such clear evidence, I cannot help but believe in evolution by natural selection.

What developed in the human mind by evolution is self-consciousness, which senses, operates, and manipulates images that are qualitative, or digital information. Then it is not surprising that the brain is similar to the modern data processor. However, we can observe its function only from the inside of the brain. A digital data processor has an interesting character: two processors having different internal logic circuits behave in exactly the same way if they are observed in the system. If company B second-sources the processor originally produced by company A, the internal circuit, and even the logic circuit, of the two processors can be different. Then, if a system model that reproduces the same internal function as a human brain is built, it is the same as a human brain, functionally speaking. By observing the model's operation, we can explain human self-consciousness. Generally speaking, in a digital system, including the human brain, two systems having different circuits can function exactly the same way. If we were to make a model of the human brain, it would not be necessary to make an exact copy of the actual brain. This feature is very important, and it allows us to study brain's function by designing a model. That is my basic assumption in this work. There can be many small varieties of such a model that reflect the individual's character. To build such a model, it was necessary to observe my own mind bias-free and to reflect my observations onto the brain's model. That is what I have done in my work.

1.07 Introspective Observation of the SELF

Self-consciousness is an abstract concept. Its carrier, the elusively existing SELF, is at least an identifiable holder of self-consciousness accessible by the human senses. It is easier to focus on an object that can be sensed directly.

To gain insight into the character of the SELF, introspection is practically the only way. Introspection is the observation of my own mind by myself by isolating myself from the outside as in yoga or Zen meditation. In Zen meditation, a problem such as "What were you before your parents were born?" is given. Instead of attempting to answer such a question, I try to look into my own mind's activity, either leaving it as it is or conditioning myself, sometimes to quite an unusual condition. I look into my own mind in all possible circumstances, even when I am heavily stressed by an unexpected disaster and when I am free from any worry. Such observation is possible because my brain is able to maintain memories of the recent past, at least for several seconds to a few minutes, accurately. I am able to find the state of my mind right before the moment I asked the question "What is going on here?" One important feature of introspection is that, along with the observation of the images that emerge, I observe the bodily senses associated with the images, such as a cold spike on the back, an uncomfortable feeling in the lower body, or a slight pressure of the eyelids indicating eye movement. These are crucial pieces of information that determine the interaction between the brain and the body.

By repeating such observations, I can find the significant character of my SELF. At the moment I ask the question, my SELF exists. Yet a moment before asking, such may not be the case. This is so even if I am fully awake but in an indifferent state. Once I traveled from California to Chicago by train. While I was watching the monotonous countryside of the American Midwest, I asked the question, and I found I'd had no SELF before that moment. The unending view of farms, pastures, remote hills, and the occasional church was not interesting to my mind and body, so my SELF had no role to play. Yet it emerged at the moment of the question. Before my SELF emerged, the scene of the Midwest was seen by nobody. As soon as my SELF emerged, the SELF saw the landscape. Emergence of the SELF changed me from a passive nobody to an active observer. The SELF emerges at a moment's notice by sensing a change in the state of myself, by either external or internal access. The SELF is executing its task, that is, to watch my brain and body lest there be risk to my life.

From introspection of myself amid various circumstances, I have learned that my SELF's existence is not all-or-nothing. My SELF is associated with subjectively felt intensity. If the intensity is zero, my SELF does not exist. The intensity is high if the incoming image indicates a high impact on my life. Therefore I conclude that the SELF plays the role of sentry guard of my life, and the SELF's emergence is often associated with the sense of surprise or even fearful shock.

When my SELF suddenly emerges, there is always some associated bodily sense. In a fearful incident, I feel a cold flash run down my spine, followed by a strong heartbeat. When I am ashamed, I feel uneasiness in my lower body. On any occasion of my SELF's emergence upon hearing good news, I unconsciously raise my arms to express my thanks to my protector deities, in the same way many Greek sculptures are posed. When witnessing great human accomplishments, I shed tears. On such an occasion, my SELF is the master of my emotions. Intensity of the bodily sense is the sensation, which is always associated with the SELF. Here is a crucial feature of sensation: it is sensed only by my body, and it is impossible to transfer this sense to any other person. In my brain and body, any analog (or quantitative) information can be sensed only by the body, and the bodily sense is quite accurate, but this cannot be expressed by a number. So it is impossible to transfer this sense to another person. This feature is different from the images that can be communicated to other people.

My SELF can emerge at a moment's notice, but the moment may have some delay time. If I suddenly realize that I have made a mistake that would have some consequence (such as making mistake on an examination), I instantly feel my SELF and become fearful. When I had an auto accident, there was a short yet recognizable delay time between the point I lost control of the car and the point when I sensed fear. If my SELF is excited from the inside, the delay time is shorter than the excitation from the outside. The signal from the outside must be recognized as a risk before the sense of my SELF emerges.

The human brain is a signal processor, and it needs time to recognize any risk. The human brain is not an instantly responding machine. This feature of the self-conscious brain, more than anything else, convinces me that we humans are machines, since a machine is a system that executes a causal sequence of action. These observations and other evidences are enough to build up a rational mechanical model of my brain in the later part of *Self-Consciousness*. The SELF is associated with images from inside or from outside, and some images may demand action. Sometimes in introspection, the SELF carries no image or is looking for a specific image, but it is always associated with the bodily sense of sensation.

A method of *introspective observation* has been recently applied to test complex data processors. A small-scale self-test circuit is designed in the chip, and after the chip's overall integrity is ensured, the self-test circuit is activated in order to test the inaccessible parts of the processor. This testability issue is perhaps the closest contact point of systems science and psychology. I have been curious if any test engineer has ever come over to the side of psychology.

What is the substance of sensation? When I feel sensation, my brain and body are in an alert state, which consumes more energy than when my brain and body are in an indifferent state or a sleep state. The brain uses extra energy to maintain the state with the SELF. Sensation is the rate of the extra energy usage by the brain in order to accomplish its mission to protect the body. That is why the heartbeat and breath rate increase as the SELF emerges.

1.08 Dominance of Body or Brain

In the brain-body interaction structure, the interface region of the two is crucial to the determination of the self-conscious state since the area's activity controls the level of sensation. The question is, which of the two, the brain or the body, is dominant at the interface region? The relation is determined by genetics and by one's life experiences at an early age, when the structure is built. If the body is dominant, the value judgment of any image is subjective as shown in figure 1.08.1(a). Some images are preferred by the SELF because such images induce a comfortable bodily feeling. Other images are tolerated as inevitable. From the preferred and retained images, many more images are created internally, and the person is enriched but is polarized. The person produces imaginative, unique, unconventional, or often odd products or ideas. The person is generally not a conforming or popular character, living in his or her own world. The person is an introvert.

If the brain is dominant, the person tries to extend his or her world outside and tries to take in more and more images. The images stay in the brain in a much less organized fashion than in an introverted character. Yet the brain-dominant person has some images common to anyone who comes into contact with him or her. This person has a lot of common sense, he or she is popular, many find it easy to accept and trust him or her, but this person is not unique and is not especially creative. He or she is an encyclopedist at the time of enlightenment and not an idealist philosopher. The person is an extrovert as shown in figure 1.08.1(b). There are more extroverts than introverts in modern society because of the increased accessibility of information (section 4.38).

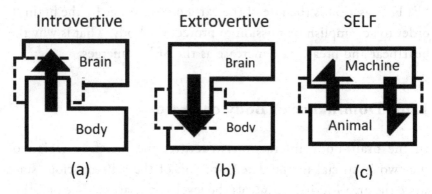

Figure 1.08.1 Brain-body interface

Being an introvert or extrovert is the most basic characteristic of a person. It is surprisingly difficult for a person of the one type to understand a person of the other type, and such misunderstanding is the source of many personal conflicts. The barrier is higher than any religious, cultural, or racial barrier, but this point is not properly appreciated. One well-documented historical case is the conflict between the two psychoanalysis giants, Sigmund Freud, an extrovert, and Carl Jung, an introvert. I am able to accept Jung's mysticism quite naturally. In my youth, I aspired to be a mythologist and ancient historian like Jung. I observed several cases showing that youths who are fascinated by such subjects are usually deeply introverted. Although a Greek, my wife does not have as strong an interest in Greek mythology as I do. She has lot of common sense and is popular. I have seen daydream images of gods and goddesses in many holy ancient sites in the world. From the Freudian viewpoint, this is abnormal. Jung had such experiences in his life.

In figure 1.08.1(c), the brain is shown as a machine, and the body is represented as an animal. The character of the person is set by the dominant side. Then how can the machine and the animal join and make a self-conscious human? To combine them, an interface, shown by the dotted box, is required. It is this interface that creates the SELF and determines the basic character of the individual. The machine part takes the outside object's images in, compares them with the existing images, and identifies them. Along with image identification, the combination (brain and body) is able to execute action directed by the images. Since the machine can identify objects, it must have an extensive memory of many objects' images and the logic to compare the incoming image with the existing images. While this machine works, it is not aware of itself. To make this system one step closer to being self-conscious, a scoring capability must exist in the interface. This scoring capability evaluates the performance of the machine. Then, as the machine works, it knows how well it has performed vis-à-vis the life objective.

The living organism detects the state of the habitat and makes best use of it. To do this, the animal part must provide the machine part the performance scoring standard. This is the core value of any self-conscious system. The interface relays the core value from the animal (body) to the machine (brain) by specifying the action's image. The combined system acquires the life's objective. To meet the objective, the interface directs the machine part to execute the required action. It does so by selecting the action images stored in the machine and letting the machine send these images out in order to execute the desired action. The machine part observes its execution, and the interface relays the score to the animal part. This combination acquires capability of recognition of the meaning of any image by sending the image out and observing the effect. Image input-output is done to recognize the meaning of the image by experience.

This is the image-sensing and image-understanding capability, executed by the joint operation of the machine part and the animal part. In this way, the combination acquires an image-sensing capability and the will to execute the action directed by the image, and knows the life's needs and objective. The combination determines the character.

19

If the animal part enforces a strong and unique value system, then an introvert's character emerges because many unique images are created internally. If the machine part is allowed to operate freely, then an extrovert's character emerges because his images are from the outside and are common among many individuals. Images of an extrovert's character originate from the outside, and they are taken in, memorized, and displayed either internally or externally. Images of the introverted character are built up internally, and they emerge by the person's motivation. Such images are often frightening, but some others are unique, positive images carrying high human values. This is the occasion when an introvert feels meaning in life. Figure 1.08.1(c) is the most basic block diagram of the human brain and body that will be upgraded to the next-level model in section 1.20, and then to the final functional model in section 2.14.

1.09   Brain's Data-Type Images

Another obvious conclusion of introspective observation is that my brain is engaged with information proper to each sense of the body. Images of visible objects are at the top of the list, followed by sounds, words, and statements of language, some representing abstract images such as the sense of taste and the smell of food, drink, medicine, and so on; the sense of contact with the body; and the sense of hot or cold, or of pain. I call all this information, recognized by self-conscious SELF, *internal images*. We are so used to remembering beautiful flowers, pretty young women, pleasant music, impressive dance performances, and the nice meal of a few days ago. These internal images are quite real, and we are able to explain them quite accurately.

When the SELF exists, the current internal image is associated with a certain level of bodily sense characterizing the relevance of the image, that is, sensation. If no sensation is felt, then SELF does not exist. Even if the SELF does not exist, images may still enter from the outside, but these are not sensed. Images from the outside may come in without leaving any effect on the current state, except for the last one, which may wake the SELF up. A self-conscious state is a composite of the level of sensation and the internal image characterizing the present state. An obvious, yet often not seriously recognized fact is that humans live in the physical world by feeling sensation and live in the image or information world by seeing images. Both worlds are equally relevant and important to life. If this key point is missed, a useless debate emerges, such as if gods exist or not. Gods do exist in the image world and do not exist in the physical world.

Images make sense and become useful only if they are connected to other images. If an image is presented without any reference or context setting, it makes no sense and no impact. How images are connected determines the character of a person. If the connection among the images is not tight, an image memory is not formed securely (section 2.06). Image memory is a multidimensionally connected web. Neuron circuits supporting an image have the capability of connecting images A and B in various ways: bidirectionally, unidirectionally, exclusively, and with various degree of closeness. As a whole, the image world has as much variety as our physical world, maybe even more.

Here a question may arise: What are the images of a blind person? My answer is that a blind person internally senses an image in the same way as any person who has sight. This is because an image is coded as the directive of bodily action as I discuss in sections 2.12 and 2.13. To say this simply, a blind person can still draw a simple image like a circle or triangle by moving his finger and then feeling the image.

Close observation of the self-conscious state indicates that there is a certain set of images that directly affect the body and that create the bodily sense with heightened sensation. These are abstract images sensed by the body, such as fear, anxiety, worry, or anger, all of which induce a certain bodily sense. A concrete object's images can be connected to such abstract images that determine the sensation. A sharp knife's image creates the sense of fear because of possible injury. This connection controls the brain-body relationship.

The image's capability as the working data of self-consciousness offers a special convenience. Images of action can be tested internally so that workable and unworkable actions can be determined. A workable image can be sent out to the actuator, such as a finger or the vocal cords, and accomplish the current SELF's objective. This is the way self-consciousness serves the welfare of our lives and avoids self-destructive action under normal conditions.

1.10   Human Images of Gods

The psychological nature of the images and their volume both depend on the person's character and life. If the person is an introvert, then unique, unconventional, and often negative images dominate. An extrovert's images are usually popular and positive but lack novelty and are often banal. Either way, images that affect the character the most are images of human beings and of the deities because humans are social animals created by evolution and their fellow members' images carry the most significant impact. Images of one's own family, friends, teachers, and mentors are the principal human images that build up one's personal history. Images of persons of the opposite gender are dear because of attraction and, most of the time, because there is less chance of competition in secular life. In the image world, this gender asymmetry created a difference in the character of the deities.

For Polish Catholics, Madre de Dios ascended to the position of a goddess, and in Mahayana Buddhism, Avalokiteśvara (female) is most widely worshipped. The Maya goddess Ixchel and the Aztec goddess Xochiquetzal are their New World versions. Why? The struggle for survival in our competitive society creates stressful life. The fearful SELF desires a compassionate companion in this lonely, miserable life and emotional support to deal with the hardships. These spiritual companions began to take on the image of real persons who carry female virtues or have the personality of merciful goddesses. These are the images of deities of solitary persons in modern society as pointed out by Mircea Eliade. They are created in the desperate human mind out of emotional necessity. These deities take on human form so that they can communicate emotionally. Yet they keep their original archaic character in the shadows; they are definitely different from the persons we interact with in secular life, and they carry the pristine human moral values of a respectable character, often quite stern.

Yet the images of the objects that affected human life in a devastating way were the origin of gods and goddesses. Fearsome images of sickness; discomfort, such as pain; extreme temperature; terrible natural forces; and predators, including other humans, are most archaic since their effects were direct and deadly. Among them, the powerful natural forces affecting life were deified in the earliest period, and many of them took on the image of a brutal animal or monster such as a dragon. Those fearful deities emerged in the earliest period from the most basic sense of fear. Then, as human society reached the level of having some control over the forces of nature, the original thunderstorm god in the image of a ferocious heavenly snake took on a milder animal or human form called a totem.

When my wife and I visited Japan, we went to the Fushimi Inari shrine in Kyoto. There, my Greek wife was astounded to see an old woman praying to a horse head. This deity is the *horse head* Avalokiteśvara, and its origin was as follows: Avalokiteśvara became a horse and helped workers in their excruciating work. In another Shinto shrine, the back walls are open, and behind we see pristine green mountains. Those are totems of mild deities. For example, Artemis's totem is a deer, and now the almost forgotten totem of Jesus is a fish.

Study of the history of religion reveals the evolution of the image of humans and of deities since the Upper Paleolithic period. The image started as a ferocious, all-subjugating animal or monster and developed into a fearsome god carrying a human image. Then the god's character softened to become accessible. For instance, Apollo was originally a fearful god of sickness but gradually changed to a mild cultural god. At this stage of history, our ancestors began to think that the relation between humans and deities was reciprocal, that is, that humans could offer tributes to the deities to soften their temper. This is not a bribe indicating deterioration of religious moral value; rather it is a progression of human thought, namely that the relationship should be bidirectional. Types of offerings changed from human life, to animal life, to foods or flowers, and then to honorable acts. Ancient legends tell us how wise heroes led such a change.

At this stage, God's character made a philosophical turn to become the abstract, almighty, and invisible god by attaching to him too much theology. God became ruler of the entire universe and, as its inevitable consequence, lost contact with secular human life. Then, finally, images of secular compassionate goddesses emerged.

The interesting phase is when human society reached the level of providing resources to keep institutionalized priests and theologians. They changed the god's character. God became too great and powerful to be relevant to human life and human thoughts. The Great Sun Buddha in esoteric Mahayana Buddhism is such a deity. Even in the Japanese pantheon, there is such a god, Amenominakanushi, whose name simply means the *lord at the center of heaven*. He has no myth attributed to him and no shrine. In complex, fearful human life, these super great deities lost direct human contact. Instead, more humane, benevolent deities took over. They are the Madre Dios and Avalokiteśvara. Humans want companionship with their deities, not for the deity to be a judge, an attorney, a prosecutor, or a ruler. This trend will most likely continue since modern society has become more brutal than ancient societies because of severe competition. As this trend continues, humans exercise their will more freely than before, yet behind their confidence, a dark shadow of fear of the unknown lurks. Predator animals and brutal natural forces have been replaced by greedy financial institutions and brutal rulers. Religion will never die, but humans need proper deities. Gods and humans jointly evolve.

1.11   Archetypal Images

There are certain archaic mythological images deep in the mind of humans whose emergence alters one's entire perspective of life. One such image is death and resurrection of a hero or heroine, widely narrated across the ancient world. Many such images involve the story of a tragic death to which an entirely new meaning is given. Stravinsky's *Spring Festival* shows such a pagan ritual: a maiden dances until she dies, to resurrect the goddess of spring. Anyone who attends such a ritual is filled with the emotion pertinent to the tragic fate of humans left alone in an ever destructive, cruel world. Then the event's image makes a sudden turn, and what appeared to have been a futile death reveals a high human value. Such images turn the human mind upside down and create new courage for people to continue on with their hard lives.

Since my youth, I sensed, deep within in my mind, that humans have made no essential progress since the Neolithic age, and we are repeating the same mistakes because of our blind ego and superstition. Dark clouds loom on the horizon of the future of humanity, such as destruction of pristine nature by way of economic greed. Eventually we will all perish by our own folly. Yet to live in such a world decently and bravely shows a tragic beauty that touches the deepest chord of the human soul.

This archetypal scenario acquired a real image when I visited the ancient Moche site of El Brujo, on the northwest Pacific coast of Peru, and saw what happened there. The archaeologist I met there, who heard that I was researching the cultural interaction between the Maya and the Moche, kindly showed us the remains of the queen just discovered in the huaca (pyramid): her dress, her royal scepter, and her military crown. She ruled the area in about AD 400, the middle classical period of the Maya. Seeing her painfully yet gracefully dead face hiding her tortured mind, I was shocked. Humans keep making the same mistake over and over again, on an ever increasing scale, finally reaching global proportions. May we be directly heading to the last day of our existence? Right after seeing the queen's remains, her simple yet elegant dress and royal scepter, I went up to the top of the huaca. There, while looking out at the shining Pacific beyond, I saw her last moment in a shocking daydream.

El Brujo is a Moche city-state in the area where the oldest South American civilization emerged. From the top of the huaca, Huaca Prieta, once considered the oldest site of the New World, and the vast expanse of the southern Pacific stretching to the horizon are both visible. Different from in Mesoamerica, the gravest disaster of coastal South America was, and still is, the sudden onset of too much rain caused by El Niño. Dark clouds on the horizon are a sure sign of an approaching disaster.

In my daydream, the time went back sixteen hundred years. The young queen, only twenty-eight years old, stood on the plaza at the top of huaca, and in front of her, several shackled and heavily sedated victims were crouching. The queen looked at the dark clouds on the Pacific horizon and the victims alternately and was hesitant to issue the sign to begin the sacrificial ritual. Her regent, staring at the growing and approaching dark clouds, was getting nervous and sent a sign to the queen. Behind her, the face of the ferocious decapitator god stared at the half-unconscious victims menacingly.

The queen was still hesitant. Not only did she feel pity for the victims, but also she had deep doubts: Will this sacrifice really appease the god and save her people from a disaster? She remembered her mother did all this but could not save the people. Finally, as the clouds approached the coast, the regent demanded for the queen to issue the order. In deep doubt, she did so. The executioner decapitated the first victim with a huge crescent bronze knife with one stroke. Blood spraying upward from the headless body hit rain and splashed all over the queen's feet. The queen was now only half conscious, and as she issued the next order, she felt dizzy and fell over the next victim. The executioner's knife barely missed her chest but still cut her artery, and the blood of the victim and that of the queen mixed and flowed away. The rain was now a torrent, and I could no longer see the queen. That evening, the rain ended. They found that the queen had fallen down on the image of the decapitator god and was not alive. It was a disaster. Yet the people thought that the queen had offered herself to the god.

Otherwise, it could have been much worse. Everyone kneeled to her and touched her body.

I returned to reality and saw the shining Pacific waves. I was absorbed in a thought: *Are we doing any better than this? Are our rulers more humane and thoughtful than this queen? Haven't we offered thousands of human sacrifices to the brutal God of modern ideology?* The future of humanity is under the dark clouds the queen saw over the Pacific. More than anything else, we must not have any illusions concerning the idiotic blindness of humans revealed in history, and we should not have any unrealistic expectation or hope for the future.

Why did the Moche bury their queen with such respect? Because she was a decent and compassionate woman. So they looked at the queen, who could not deliver what they wanted, with high respect and heavy hearts. That is why sixteen hundred years later, I was able to see her with utmost compassion and respect. I was motivated to draw her portrait. She now sits on my desk. This Moche queen is one of the most respected woman of New World antiquity, showing the dark sides of humanity so clearly. I am firmly convinced that humans have made no essential progress since the Neolithic age (The Moche civilization actually existed during the Bronze Age, but the Maya at that time were still in the Neolithic age). By the Enlightenment period following the Renaissance, humans reached the acme. Modern mass society, which lacks self-criticism, will ultimately bring us down, and this time there might not be any archaeologist to reconstruct what happened and no visitor to acquire such a moving archetypal image after humankind's last day on earth.

1.12 Self-Conscious Being in Habitat

Humans and animals live in their habitat, a complex system consisting of lifeless, living, and competing individuals. Development of the habitat's state is a complex mixture of predictable states, interspersed in mostly chaotic states. So, self-conscious humans and their habitat are both complex and unpredictable. The basic point I wish to make here is that for any self-conscious being, prediction of the future is practically impossible. For any being to survive in such a habitat with a minimum of comfort is a hard uphill battle. As for competition among humans, we fight hard to get the same rewards. We compete, and there are winners and losers. The chance of becoming a winner is minimal because there are so many competitors. Every social reform, such as the socialist revolution, has failed. The socialist revolution failed because none of the socialist leaders were decent human beings. We must accept the brutal fact of social Darwinism, of which Darwin himself was terrified. A monarchy holds one king or queen. Present democracy, lacking self-criticism, has created hundreds of kings and queens who exploit the others.

The twentieth-century development of physics showed that the future state prediction of a multibody, strongly interacting system is basically impossible. In spite of that, development of the physical sciences since the seventeenth century has created a widespread misbelief that the future state of any system is predictable if a better model and more powerful analysis method are available.

It is very easy to see why the future is unpredictable, but strangely no such explanation is widely distributed, nor is such an explanation accepted by many social scientists. Even a simple multibody system is unpredictable beyond a certain limit. A system's state goes from a quasi-predictable state to a chaotic unpredictable state, and no model can predict a definite future. Why does such a feature emerge in complex systems? Because a strong contact-based interaction of the components, which may be called *generalized collision* of the elements, takes place in a complex system. The easiest way to see this effect is to consider a solar system schematically shown in figure 1.12.1. To the one-planet solar system, meteorite M invades and collides with planet P by a slightly different path, A or B. The meteorite may be trapped by the solar system if path A is taken, but if M takes the only slightly different path B, it is deflected and exits the solar system.

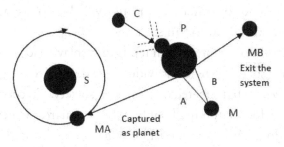

Figure 1.12.1 Collision of a meteorite

As is seen from this figure, only a small difference in the state of M creates a vastly different future state. Every time a collision takes place, the future uncertainty increases. Another possibility is that comet C may crush planet P and become part of it. Either way, the future is unpredictable.

The concept of collision can be generalized to include any strong, contacting interaction of elements of the many-body system. Natural processes such as a bird pecking bugs, a tornado blowing houses down, or frost killing tropical plants are generalized collisions. Collision occurs in the human brain as well, between a pair of images, very much the same way as in the solar system, a political system, or an economic system. As element's collision repeats, the future state becomes less and less predictable, and the system soon develops into a chaotic state where no more prediction is possible.

Both the world and the human brain go through a collision randomization process. Total chaos and semi-orderly state development mix unpredictably. In the semi-orderly state, a feature that is advantageous for life may emerge. For a basically chaotic system to change into a semi-orderly state for some time, the system must go into a quasi-periodic state. That includes several different internal periods, such as the earth year and lunar month, making a simple integer ratio. Then the beings learn how to deal with the periodic changes. Self-consciousness developed in such an environment, while experiencing the habitat's chaotic development. Self-consciousness takes advantage during the semi-orderly period, and it maximizes the chance of survival in the chaotic state by whatever means available. If we are not self-conscious, we cannot survive in such a world.

Human-to-human interaction tends to display chaotic uncertainty, especially in a society where individual freedom is the highest value. This ideology is what created the present society. Freedom carries a self-destructive force as pointed out by John Maynard Keynes, Friedrich Hayek, and José Ortega y Gasset. Ortega pointed out that freedom has quality, and this quality must be strictly maintained. There is no mechanism in mass society that prevents deterioration of the quality of freedom. In a free society, no one can order others to behave. That is why decent, well-behaved people dream not in an entirely free society but in a more orderly one, like the Inca Empire. The Inca ruled most of Andean South America by very severe rule, but there was no corruption in their rule. These *noble savages*, as once they were called, were more civilized than we are. In my college days in the 1950s, this view, first having emerged at the time of the Enlightenment, still remained, and I read many quotations from the early travelers and historians. Since then, this view has subsided in the emerging mass society. But since I visited the Andean highland and heard what the *paisanos* said, I believe in such a peaceful utopia. Such a rule never suppresses the free human spirit. Those who demand unlimited freedom cannot focus on anything to make a better future for humanity.

In our modern society, human-to-human relationships are more complex and harder to predict than human-to-habitat relationships. This is because other humans are the components of the habitat, and each has his or her own particular image of the habitat in his or her brain. Because of this convoluted structure, human-to-human relationships become human to multiply superposed habitats, which are impossibly unpredictable.

1.13 Evolution of Self-Consciousness

The human brain and body are the product of evolution. Primitive life-forms such as microbes are simple self-replicating machines. Their energy management is executed by chemical processes. Although simple, this function is the predecessor from which the sense of sensation later emerged. At this level, life depended entirely on the habitat, and the adaptive strategy of life-forms was facilitated by an enormous multiplication capability. As multicellular animals emerged, they were able to take some action to adapt to the habitat. They acquired sensors in order to detect the body's state of energy management and the external state of the habitat, and the actuators to take action for survival. The internal-state sensors provided information that provided the sense of sensation in the later stage of evolutionary development, and the external sensors went through a long history of development to provide the sense of images and image recognition capability.

As the sensors and the actuators are connected, reflex functions to defend the body emerged. After that, the animals acquired memory to retain the once experienced event. The memory kept the experience of the event. As the animals became aware of the development of the habitat using the image memory capability, conditional reflex emerged: the well-known experiment of Pavlov's dog salivating after hearing the bell. It was the conditional reflex that had infinite potential for later development. By conditional reflex, the action of the animal was executed consciously, and recognition of the cause made the animal aware of the effect. Along with this development, the energy management capability developed from the archaic distributed function over the entire body to the central control by way of the liver, heart, and gills/lungs. This central control provided a clear sense of sensation. Thus the pair of the basic information of image and sensation established a firm root in animal evolution.

Sensation associated with a simple image of the bodily sense was the prototype of emotion. Emotion developed further, and from that self-consciousness emerged. This development was effected to improve the image acquisition, image processing, and future prediction capability. The architecture of the image sensors and analyzers at this level and above are basically the same as that of humans. Bats, cats, and rats see the same images as humans see. Since we all share the same mechanism of sensation, humans and animals share the same image-sensation pair in their minds. Darwin's theory of evolution led, as its consequence, to the state that all humans are equal. Then why is there interracial bias among people in the present world?

This is because the evolutionary mechanism of humans changed from Darwinian to Lamarckian (a precise definition of this term is provided at the end of this section) since the Paleolithic period, and as its consequence, we inherited certain bias from our ancestors. Among all humans in the world, there is absolutely no difference in their innate wisdom, intelligence, and self-consciousness. Racial bias emerged because the new evolution mechanism effected the inheritance of the conscious mode of action and thinking and accumulated such acts and thoughts. Once free from this social bias, and after regaining natural human feeling, emotional relationships among people of different races from different parts of the world are absolutely smooth. Do we really know this simple fact by real personal experience? Unfortunately not all of us do.

From my youth I have admired the ancient culture of Native Americans and have studied particularly the Maya culture. I have visited Mesoamerica often for cultural study. I became friendly with many Maya folks and was happily surprised to discover how similar we really are, even if we have been separated since the Upper Paleolithic period. Our personal relationships are completely smooth, even with regard to very subtle emotional shadows that emerge in basic human relations. I tell a very lovely story of an event I experienced in the Maya site of Uaxactun.

When our tour group visited the Jaguar's Temple, a mother and her small daughter were selling local dolls. I like ethnic dolls. I wanted to get one, but I knew I had no space in the suitcase to carry such a large and delicate doll back home. So, I handed a twenty-quetzal bill to the mother. She handed me two dolls. I returned one, held the other to my chest, and then handed it to the small daughter, Antonia, saying, "My present." I didn't want to make them feel like beggars. From the mother's countenance, I immediately saw that she understood what I meant. Not only the mother, but also little Antonia, as she stretched out her small hand. I took her hand and walked the rocky trail with her down to their home. Later, I was asked by a travel mate why I just didn't hand over the money. I smiled and did not answer. This small lovely incident shows that empathy between the Maya mother and daughter and me is closer than that between two individuals from the same U.S. society.

The human evolutionary development mechanism has now changed from Darwinian to Lamarckian, the latter once having been the alternative to the former. A human child is born more prematurely than any wild animal and goes into a well-protected life in which the social culture is infused. This change began already a long time ago. From the time of the emergence of mammals, a certain social structure had emerged within the animal kingdom. The primitive society of humans and animals carried culture along with it, and everyone in it had to obey certain rules. The most significant rule is the system of rank. A rank system is clearly recognizable from the society of macaque monkeys to that of high-prestige aristocrats. Equality is not the virtue that emerged from evolution. In human society, hereditary monarchy lasted much longer than democracy since democracy produced many kings instead of one, and they all exploit the rest.

When I mention Lamarckian evolution in *Self-Consciousness*, I do not mean the genetic variation caused by acquired character as was postulated originally. I mean that the acquired character is transferred to the next generation by teaching and learning. This is particularly so in humans, since newborn human babies are more premature than any other animals and go through a long learning period.

1.14   Reflex, Emotion, and Self-Consciousness

The SELF is regarded as the holy master in the human mind that exercises free will and creativity, according to the philosophers of the West. Thinkers of the East regard the SELF as a weak and erratic tenant of the body that must go through a long journey to reach enlightenment. This latter viewpoint anchors the SELF to the body. Many of the body's instinctive demands on the SELF do not have high human value and often risk both body and mind. Modern neurophysiology supports the connection of the SELF to the body by assigning the *seat* of self-consciousness to the evolutionarily old area of the brain.

From the most primitive multicellular animals, evolution took three steps forward. The first phase of development was a simple, mechanical reflex function of the body, such as moving the body away from an object touching its surface. In this phase, there is no identifiable predecessor to the SELF, except for the sense of energy management, which developed later into sense of sensation. By the end of this phase, conditional reflex emerged, and the neural hardware carrying out this function gathered at the most protected area of the body, the head.

The second phase of development covers the period from this archaic stage to the emergence of mammals during the earth's middle age, when the developing central nervous system created the large neural aggregate, the brain, where the impact of the incoming images for the welfare of life was evaluated. Animals acquired simple image manipulation capability, and the image-sensation combination emerged as the basic information structure to control the action of the body. This combination is the emotion, the early form of self-consciousness. Emotion is loaded heavily by the body's image. To exercise emotional action, the image and sensation are correlated by the brain. The brain processes them together, maintaining proper balance. The impact of this development is that action is not all-or-nothing but is graded depending on the animal's needs. This is because the image is associated with an analog parameter, namely, sensation. This development allowed the animal to engage with its habitat to the most advantageous degree. The historical development of the animal's self-consciousness weighs heavily on the primitive level. Much of our present capability owes to our very remote animal ancestors.

The last step began at the end of the earth's middle age and continues to the present day by the emergence of mammals. During this period, the evolving brain acquired the capability of recognizing the development of the internal state and of the external world. Mammals developed their self-consciousness from the predecessor, reflex and emotion, while still retaining them in their base. At this evolutionary level, the naturally acquired behavior of taking care of their young proliferated to cover the group members. Their emerging social life created the emotional need to avoid solitary life.

Since humans carry the base of the two previous phases, reflex and emotion, they often disregard the welfare of the human race as a whole and set the individual's benefit first. That is why some individuals exercise brutal acts on other human beings without hesitation. Yet in the other extreme, emotional acts such as benevolence and compassion provide benefits for all. Acts based on emotion are intense, and their consequences are either a big positive or a big negative. Self-consciousness is, in a way, a diluted version of emotion. The acts driven by it are moderate or sometimes lukewarm. The two early developments share a similar feature: from reflex to emotion, the animal's reflex was graded by sensation, and from emotion to self-consciousness, the animal's emotion was graded by intelligence.

The evolutionary development of the brain structure matches the development of self-consciousness. An animal requires for its life maintenance the basic controller, a combination of hindbrain and spinal cord. On this basis, the developing brain acquired the structure called the reptile complex, which enables stereotyped action. Above this level, the limbic system was added, which enables instinctive action for survival and reproduction, and the sense of emotion at the later levels. On the limbic system, the neocortex was added to create the self-conscious brain. This development matches what I have described.

From the present stage, where do we go? The animals that are likely to survive the humans' last day are still at the stage of lowest-level mammals. The habitat earth will revert to what it was at the end of the Mesozoic era, and another seventy million years or so is required to re-create humanlike beings. Since the mammal's body structure has been set, what would emerge should look similar to the present humans. This much is reasonably certain to expect. But how about the mental character of such creatures? That is uncertain. Seventy million years is a long time, but the sun and the moon will still be there to delineate day and night.

1.15 Emergence of the Objective

An objective is an image that sets the direction of the mental or physical activity of the SELF to reach the desired internal or external state. An objective creates a sequence of imagined or selected action images to bring the desirable state to reality. This is not a purely mental function; execution of an action requires determination to maintain the course of action by way of physical and mental strength. Objectives demand not only mental activity but also physical work. Most objectives require action by the body.

Acquisition of objectives is considered by philosophers to be a signature of the sacred soul. Objectives cover a wide range of human desires, not only to bring about life comfort and welfare but also to satisfy vanity or even beastly desires. Spectacular edifices and monuments are often created to satisfy the vanity of the rulers at any one time. Moral or humane objectives usually have very low priority. An objective's origin is consistent with this feature.

Objective setting is not the special capability of the human mind. It has its origin in evolutionary history. The objective was set naturally by the mechanism of evolution to direct the species to thrive in the natural habitat. This *objective* actually did not emerge but was an essential feature of evolution, since those who did not adopt it perished. Over the long course of evolutionary history, the strategy to accomplish the objective changed significantly. At the beginning of evolution, the strategy of small animals was to make as many descendants as possible and disperse them over a wide range. This strategy became increasingly handicapped as animals developed.

As the animals' size increased, their lives became less vulnerable to changes in the habitat and to predators. Yet large size has its own vulnerability as I discuss in section 5.17. Up to the level of reptiles, the animals' strategy was more biological than mental. At the level of mammals, the newborn babies were weak and required care and protection. They were still weak for some time in the postweaning period. Then the strategy for survival changed from biological to mental to cultural in the emerging animal's social life. To defend the species, the parents care for the young. Given this, the origin of the objective was to meet the requirement to survive as a species. Because of this history of the objective's emergence, the brain's mode of operation has changed significantly. Before, the brain's function was an unconscious operation. By acquiring the objective to protect offspring, many brain operations were executed consciously. Conscious operation is effective as it relies on the brain's entire capability (sections 3.22 and 4.08). Intelligence evolved rapidly from the mammalian level by exercising the brain more intensively than before in order to attain the objective. Intensely exercised organs developed quickly.

In this stage of development, I recognize that the sense of fear, indigenous to the brain, took over the entire control in order to coordinate the survival objective. A mother deer runs away upon seeing a predator, and her young follows her. All through the later life of the animal, fear became the key sense of defense, and the objective of life was to reduce fear by whatever means available. The developing brain helped to achieve this objective by inventing various strategies for reducing fear. Protohumans emerged at this stage. Their intelligence improved by setting an objective. This original objective was passive so as to reduce fear and not to satisfy an unlimited ego. Most of us prefer a rather eventless, peaceful life to a hugely successful life associated with devastating failure, such as that experienced by some ambitious rulers. To see this in another way, the majority's passive desire created the chance for brutal rulers to rampage, even at present. To accomplish this original passive objective, democracy and capitalism carry some serious negative features. For instance, competition between individuals, considered as a virtue by the two ideologies, is never executed fairly, and corruption, frustration, anger, and violence eventually prevail. How do we handle this syndrome of the human race that originated with the emergence of mammals and then was twisted and finagled by humans to the present level?

I strongly believe that competition of individuals for survival should be phased out in the future of human society. To search for an alternative is to go back and reconsider the successful political regimes of the past such as that of the Inca. No one wanted to take over the holy throne of Inca. Since there was no money, no one could be greedy. The Inca exercised very severe rules, but the minimum level of life was always ensured, and the peaceful life allowed the Inca to create better ways to produce enough food and clothing for everyone in the harsh environment of the Andean highland. We should read the notes of the last Inca and early colonialists open-mindedly and look for alternatives to the corruption of modern society. Unfortunately, the Incas' utopian image was wiped out by the mass society of the post ideology period.

The naturally set objective to reduce fear and to maintain a peaceful life that emerged with the mammals at the end of the Mesozoic era was ideal for supporting all ranges of human mental, cultural, and personal life. It is a mistake to hold that an objective setting and its realization is a unique human ability. Its deep root is in our animal ancestors. Humans are the ones who degraded its original beneficial features. Only exceptional humans set their objectives to the benefit of all humans. As I calmly observe my own mind, I find that my objective is to live a modestly long and peaceful life. Once that is ensured, my mind will search for a wider objective, such as to contribute something good for all humans, to secure a peaceful life, and to glorify the images of my protector deities. In present-day society, even that modest objective is very hard to attain. Just to survive, we must compete or fight.

1.16 Sense of Body, Sensation/Fatigue/Weariness

The self-conscious subject SELF's close association with the body is always sensed by sensation accompanied with the image. The image controls the actions of life, and sensation is an action's expected positive or negative impact. Thus, body and sensation are the SELF's substance and its activity indicator, and images are the plan and directive of the action. Anything affecting the body's welfare is the SELF's concern, and the degree of concern is sensed as fear. When a strong sensation is felt, some kind of fear is sensed together with it. Even if the image is positive, there is convoluted fear, namely that what is desired may not materialize. Fear is sensed by the body along with sensation. The fear sensors are not localized; the sensors all over the body jointly create the sense of fear. Because of that, this sense is mysterious, and the body becomes the spooky background of the mind.

Human life is a continuous sequence of action planning and execution. When a new action is planned, the body is well supplied with energy and the brain is alert. Sensation is sensed in the action-planning phase. It is the measure of energy spent by the brain to ensure the action's success. As the action starts and proceeds smoothly, sensation wanes, and physical fatigue gradually accumulates to a level making further continuation of the action impossible. If the action meets an impediment, sensation returns, and the SELF seeks a way out. If the SELF cannot resolve the difficulty, then weariness, that is, mental fatigue, sets in, and the action is given up with a sense of defeat.

Fatigue is the bodily sense of weakness caused by the burden of the work. The level of fatigue is affected by the result of the exercise. If the brain and body repeat a long exercise that produces no noticeable result, the SELF recognizes that the action is a waste of resources, and it terminates the action by sensitizing the sense of fatigue. Along with fatigue, the sense of weariness sets in. This mental fatigue is different from bodily fatigue. The brain is tolerant to exercise much longer as long as the exercise is accomplishing the objective, since success of the action invigorates the brain. The brain's energy usage is more effective than the body's when engaged in physical work, and the brain is better supported than the rest of the body. The brain is in control, so it can terminate the action at any time, a feature that provides relief from mental fatigue. Nothing fatigues and wears more than to engage with an exercise that creates no results. There are too many such exercises in the twenty-first-century developed world. I've seen a few cases of businessmen playing golf and hurting their career because of poor performance or, worse, getting injured. Golf is not always for promotion in an organization.

1.17 Source of Sensation

Sensation is a bodily feeling and is sensed in various ways, yet all variations share the same origin, that is, the rate of energy consumption by the brain and its periphery. It is the bodily sense of the SELF's mental activity to make a plan for body protection and welfare. Why did such a sense emerge by way of evolution? Since the SELF is the sentry guard responsible for the welfare of the brain and the body, it must be aware of the energy spent by the brain to deal with the presently engaged situation. I will classify sensation associated with various types of bodily senses:

(1) A clearly identifiable bodily response associated with a certain state, such as increase in the heart and breath rate in a personal crisis. This is the sensation relevant to survival, and such a state demands an action by the subject that must be successful.

(2) Directly sensible yet personally irrelevant bodily sense to certain images, such as a chill running down the spine when I watch a man working high up in the air without protection. Stronger sensation is felt if such a scene is shown dynamically, for example, in a circus. A circus is a form of masochistic entertainment.

(3) Subdued vitality and loss of enthusiasm upon facing grim future prospects or endless personal crisis. To avoid activity and to suffer mentally, energy is wasted self-destructively. A severely depressed state creates heavy fatigue.

(4) Sense of activity level associated with imagined exercises (both physical and mental), such as the burden of doing a physical task, of doing creative mental work, or of reexperiencing a significant past event. This type of sensation is sensed as length of time. The time is the sense of integrated sensation.

Any action image creates sensation internally. The action needs not be executed actually; sensation is felt by simulating the action's images internally. Once the planned action is initiated, the sensation begins to wane. This feature indicates that the sensation-generation mechanism exists in the brain-body interface area, where the burden of the action according to the plan is evaluated. Sensation is the SELF's sense of responsibility toward the entire body's welfare.

Since sensation is the rate of energy expenditure, it is an analog parameter that can be subjected to some limited degree of mathematics. This analysis reveals some interesting features of the SELF. Suppose that all the energy taken into the body by way of food and drink since birth is E_T. E_T increases with time, and it is the sum of the energies used for the various activities of life, such as the following: Energy E_B is used to build the body and brain hardware structure. Energy E_O is used to operate the brain or to execute physical work. E_M is used to maintain the normal condition of the brain and body. E_I is used to create image memory and to manage the image inventory, E_C is used to execute the brain's image-processing activity, and E_W is the wasted energy. Then,

$$E_T = E_B + E_O + E_M + E_I + E_C + E_W$$

Not all the energies contribute to create sensation. E_B and E_W are not involved, and as for E_O, the part used to execute physical works is also excluded. The energy whose rate creates sensation, E, is then given as

$$E = E_C + E_I + E_M + a\, E_O \text{, and } X \text{ (sensation)} = r\, (dE/dt)$$

where a is the fraction of energy used to set up and prepare the body to exercise the planned action, and r is the image-dependent proportionality factor to convert the energy rate to sensation. E_T is estimated from calorie intake as

$$E_T = 7.3 \times 10^5\ Y\ (\text{Kcal})$$

where Y is the age of the person. As this estimate shows, this is a large sum of energy, and all its components are also large. I note, energy E's time derivative is the sensation, and sensation is the sensible parameter of the SELF. Then energy, E, must be the parameter of the SELF, but I cannot sense it directly, as I discuss in the next section.

1.18 SELF and Sensation

In the foregoing section, I defined the types of energy whose consumption rate determines sensation. Going one step ahead, I define their roles more precisely by using a little mathematics. I am personally skeptical about using mathematics in psychology. Mathematics should be limited to defining qualitative features of certain parameters precisely, and the only area in self-consciousness research is to reveal certain qualitative insight by using mathematical language.

Sensation is an analog parameter representing the intensity of image excitation sensed by the subject SELF and by the body. As such it can be represented by a variable depending on time t, as $X(t)$. The energy consumption rate, v, is also a function of time t as $v(t)$, which is the time derivative of the expended energy $E(t)$ that I defined in the previous section.

$$v(t) = dE(t)/dt v(t) = dE(t)/dt \quad (1)$$

The energy usage rate and sensation are related as we feel a faster heart rate with stronger sensation. The simplest relation between $X(t)$ and $v(t)$ is the proportional relation,

$$X(t) = r(t) \, v(t) X(t) = r(t) \, v(t) \quad (2)$$

where factor $r(t)$ defines the image's effectiveness to create sensation.

A close introspective observation shows that I feel a strong sensation momentarily when a new image suddenly emerges. This is the surprise effect that can be described by a term proportional to $v(t)$'s time derivative, $dv(t)/dt$, with a proportionality factor, m. By adding this term to equation (2), sensation $X(t)$ is given by

$$m[dv(t)/dt] + r(t)v(t) = X(t) \, v(t) = dE(t)/dt \quad (3)$$

This is the upgraded expression of equation (2) to define sensation. It is interesting to note that this is the same as the equation of motion of a point particle whose velocity is $v(t)$, whose mass is m, and whose friction coefficient is $r(t)$, subjected to the external force $X(t)$. Then $E(t)$ is the *coordinate* of the SELF, and sensation $X(t)$ is the psychological force acting on the SELF. Sensation, which appeared to be an associate of the image, is actually the driving force to push the SELF's development. We feel this force in any self-conscious state. The simplest relation, equation (2), means that sensation is the friction sensed by the SELF who is struggling in the uphill battle of protecting the brain and body. Indeed, when I feel a strong sensation, my SELF is resisting some social or natural *friction*.

Factor $r(t)$ is the frictional coefficient. Factor m is the inertia of the present SELF, assembled from many images. A psychological state change affects all the currently engaged images, and all of them affect the sensation. Stating this in casual terms, m is the measure of the presently working common sense. If one carries more common sense, one is more surprised and becomes defensive toward any new ideas or images. Yet there is a certain interesting case: some images that presently exist can foresee the emerging situations. Then such images contribute *negative inertia*. Practically this happens when I meet a new physical phenomenon and if I already have the theory to explain it.

The interesting feature of equation (3) is that $E(t)$ is the coordinate of the SELF. The SELF has a representative parameter, that is, the cumulative energy spent to create and operate the SELF in the present state. The SELF's coordinate is the energy that the brain has consumed since birth. Equation 3 shows that sensation is the force that drives the SELF, modeled by a mass point. This is also an interesting insight. In a SELF-less state (of zero sensation), the hiding SELF is just coasting at the same *speed* by way of its inertia.

1.19 SELF in the Heart?

A close connection of the SELF to the body is felt by way of the traditional belief that it resides in the heart. The heart is a rapidly responding and clearly sensible internal organ that reflects the person's mental state. In a personal crisis, anyone feels an intense SELF and a strong and rapid heartbeat. At the time of introspection or meditation, as soon as I am able to eject secular images from my brain, I feel my heartbeat as the remaining sense. The sense of the heartbeat sets the SELF in the flow of time and thus establishes personal history. Because of this feature of the heart, in many old languages the heart is synonymous with the soul.

Belief of the SELF in the heart has a long history. There are two more supporting reasons. A direct visible image of myself is quite tenuous since I cannot see myself except when I face a mirror. Yet I feel myself all the time from the inside by the sense of the body. The heartbeat is the most conspicuous bodily sense because it is sensed everywhere in the body. It is sensed as a real signal from the SELF whose substance is the body.

Another significant reason of misidentification is that there is only circumstantial evidence to place the SELF in the brain, such as with a brain concussion, when patients lose their self-consciousness temporarily. Various functions of our body organs became known only during the Renaissance period; the circulation of blood by the heart was established by William Harvey as late as the sixteenth century, and only after that did we learn that the heart is a mechanical pump, too simple an organ to retain and manage complex images.

I believe that the EEG is the first convincing evidence to set the seat of SELF in the brain. I was convinced of this conclusion myself only after I observed my own EEG under various mental exercises, and I saw that there is clear correlation (*Neuron Circuits, Electronic Circuits, and Self-Consciousness* [Vantage, 2009]). EEG observation became possible only in my youth (the 1940s), when electronics developed enough to allow one to observe the microvolt amplitude EEG signal. I strongly recommend to the reader that you build your own EEG machine and observe your brain waves while your brain is doing the work you know. I assure you that this is a far more interesting hobby than finagling with a PC.

1.20   Where Is the SELF?

To study the nature of the SELF, I need to know the basic architecture of the brain and the body. With the most basic character of the operation of the human brain, I am able to draw a skeletal block diagram consisting of memories and processors as shown in figure 1.20.1. In this block diagram, processor P_1 converts image information from the outside to the format comprehensible by the brain and deposits it in the basic image memory, M_1. Memory M_1 contains the structure of the image. If M_1 is activated, it sends the image out via the output channel B_1 to reconstruct the image outside of the body. The image in memory M_1 has its index, an equivalent of its name, which is stored in memory M_2. Images stored in memory M_1 are combined or organized by connecting their indices in memory M_2 by the lower-level processor P_2. Image memory M_2 has built-in index-index connection capability, and that capability is symbolically shown by processor P_2. M_2 and P_2 use the same hardware in the brain's association area.

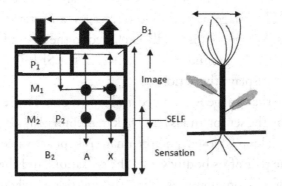

Figure 1.20.1 The SELF's functional structure

In language processing, the image memory M_1 contains words. Image memory M_2 and processor P_2 work together to gather several words. As the collected words are sent to processor P_1, P_1 assembles them into a sentence structure to meet grammatical rules, add punctuation, and so on. The assembled sentence is sent out upward to the body's output channel, B_1, equipped with a mechanical voice generator, the vocal chords. Simultaneously, processor and memory in the lower area, M_2 and P_2, determine how much resource (energy) must be sent to the actuator, that is, how loud the speech is delivered. This is the mechanism of generating sensation associated with the image. Body B_2 (liver, heart, lungs, etc.) supplies energy to all the body and brain areas.

From this architecture, self-consciousness is an integration of the lower-level sensation generation and the upper-area image display activity that directs the action. Of the pair, the images vary in every way, but the sense of the body sensation is firmly anchored to the body because the lower-level processor P_2 and memory M_2 are directly connected to body B_2. As the image changes, the sensation changes, and the body senses the change of the SELF's state. The SELF sends the image out, which drives the actuator to create the image outside. This image is taken in by processor P_1 and is confirmed by the SELF. Then the domain of the SELF consists of the two overlapping brain areas, one handling the image and the other handling the sensation as shown in figure 1.20.1.

The SELF is metaphorically like a flower, shown to the right side of the figure. The image part, the flower, leaves, and stem, swings when wind comes. Yet the root is solidly anchored to the ground. The body is the anchor like the ground, and the image is the SELF's character that dynamically displays the action.

Suppose that image A is excited and is sent out. The sent-out image is received by the sensor and is sent back to memory M_1 via processor P_1. The feedback loop is closed, and the image is kept activated. This image becomes the pair of its bodily sense, the sensation, and that sets up the basic data of self-consciousness. Now, the question is, where is the SELF that is sensing image A? In the block diagram, the circuit that is active in this state is image A's circuit. Since the SELF recognizes image A, it must contain the activity of the neuron circuit driven by memories M_1 and M_2 that hold image A. The SELF is the excited image itself, plus the sensation associated with it, that comes from M_2, P_2, and B_2. This conclusion is inevitable since nothing else except image A's activities exist in the brain.

Brain and body can work in a different way. Generally the SELF may include multiple images. If the second image, X, is excited alternately with A, like A to X to A to X … then image A and image X coexist and present each other. Then the SELF displays the mutual relationship of the images to itself, which is a higher-level meaning. This may be interpreted as A explains X and X explains A, and their mutual consistency is established. This is the state of the SELF understanding images A and X in terms of each other.

Excitation of the image is able to move over the entire available image memory space. More than one image can be excited simultaneously, and the SELF is either occupied by one or keeps jumping from one image to the other. Freedom of motion of the SELF's image part is a crucial feature of self-consciousness that works as an image-relating agent for the body. This freedom of motion of the basic data, images, is a characteristic of the biological machine that has no parallel in any man-made machine as I discuss in section 2.08. This feature contributes to the reliability of the brain as well. The brain works even if it suffers fairly severe damage, since an image can move around the brain.

I am building the model of the self-conscious brain step by step. The first level was shown in figure 1.08.1(c). Figure 1.20.1 is the second level. The final level model is shown in section 2.14.

1.21 Character of the Word *SELF*

The term *SELF*, used casually in the earlier sections, is the most important word in my self-consciousness work. It is the keyword in the answer to the question, "What in your brain or body knows yourself, your world, and your past history and makes you unique?" The expected answer is, "My SELF in me." The reader is likely to identify SELF with the term used in psychoanalysis, such as *ego*. I am unable to relate my SELF to ego, because ego is defined differently from the SELF. Therefore I try to define my SELF in my way, as clearly as possible.

The SELF is the cause that makes each individual a unique existence in the world. Given this fact, it is grammatically a proper noun, such as the name of a person. Here a noun represents, most of the time, a static object such as an apple or a house, but we notice that nouns include action or activity as well, such as solar eclipse, expedition, and dance. *SELF* is not a static noun but is a dynamic proper noun, a minority among a large number of nouns. This is not a trivial issue. Young children are often confused. I remember the case of a little blonde girl saying, "Dance danced?" She frowned. If the SELF is mistaken to be a static object, it can be enshrined in a temple. This was the belief in the Dark Ages. The way of becoming emancipated from this misbelief is to observe the real nature of the SELF once again.

The SELF exists only in a living person or animal. Life is made up of activity of the various body organs. The activity creating the SELF is dominantly in the brain and keeps changing to adapt to the situations. *Activity* is a dynamic abstract noun that means time-dependent changes. The SELF is the symbol of the brain and body's activity that makes me feel as if I know myself, my world, and my history and what makes me unique in the world. It is not an activity located in a certain area of the brain. The activity moves around the brain as the SELF's currently engaged image changes. The activity invades the area where the body's state is controlled. Such activity creates sensation associated with the image. The image and the sensation put the person in his or her place and time, thereby making him or her unique.

The SELF is not a newcomer at the emergence of the human race. It is the product of evolution since the early history of animals. Its naturally set objective is to maximize the chance of survival until the end of the reproductive age. This objective requires that any individual be placed in space and time and also be aware of his or her own unique state. Since the SELF is the sum total of such activities, it characterizes the person's psychological state. Then it is possible to use the term in a sentence such as "SELF knows X" or "SELF does Y." Such a statement means, precisely, that the activity creating the sense of existence of the self-conscious subject SELF finds it contains image X, or that the activity sends image Y to the outside world, respectively. I use the word *SELF* as a subject of statement in this context. This is, in effect, shorthand: such a statement never means that there is an identifiable static object in the human mind.

1.22 Various States of the SELF

What are the SELF's states in the self-conscious human brain? Approximately in the order of the image's activity level, the SELF is in any of the following states:

(1) **Deep sleep state.** Not self-conscious; no SELF exists.

(2) **REM sleep state.** The SELF wakes up from the deep sleep state, fabricates internal images, and sees them as a dream. The brain is active, but all the external body actions are disabled.

(3) **Indifferent state.** Fully awake yet accepting the images from the outside like a video monitor. Only the image's existence is sensed. This is the state of a weary passenger seeing what is outside the train window.

(4) **Task unloaded state.** A routine repetitive task is unloaded to the body's actuator, and the SELF is watching the task's execution with minimum attention while executing some other task. This is the state of thinking something while walking.

(5) **Alert state.** The SELF observes an incoming image, or an image excited from memory, with attention. Related images are excited from the memory, and the image's meaning is determined and memorized. Yet no action is taken in this state—the state of watching someone else's car accident and its consequence.

(6) **Anthropomorphic state.** The SELF sends the image out as coordinated motion of the entire body to simulate the image and to sense the image dynamically; the state of a prima ballerina dancing while feeling herself to be a swan.

(7) **Introspection state.** First the SELF keeps irrelevant images out, and then it internally observes what happens in the alert

brain. The SELF maintains this state, during the state of introspection.

(8) **Internal image interaction state.** Display a pair of images alternately, and try to find the hidden meaning or to compare their impact on life. This is the state of comparing the merit of two actions.

(9) **Internal dialogue state.** The state of dialogue with the image of personal deities or ancient sages on serious personal matters; the state of seeking a solution to a personal crisis.

(10) **Administrative state of internal operation.** Internal image manipulation is going on, and the SELF observes the intermediate results and makes decisions; the state of solving problems on an examination or making plans for a project.

(11) **Conscious task unloading state.** A substantial portion of the brain's task is unloaded to the external media, and the SELF interacts with the unloaded images; the state of an engineer sitting at a drawing board to design.

(12) **Searching state.** The SELF is looking for an image in the brain that is necessary for the purpose of life, or assembling an image from the image inventory; the state of seeking a solution to a personal problem.

(13) **Intense thinking.** The SELF is struggling to find a solution to a realistic hard problem that must be successfully resolved within a limited time. This is the state of personal crisis.

(14) **Conscious engagement with task.** The SELF is engaged with a task whose outcome is unpredictable. The SELF is constantly prepared to improvise the action—a boss of a work project watching the workmen's performance,

(15) **State engaged with risk.** The SELF is closely tied with the body, and the image is that of the risk or the enemy.

(16) **Hyperactive state.** Practically any negative image is sensed as risk, and the SELF is constantly in a state of panic. The cause can be pathological. This is also the state of many personal crises arriving at the same time.

I discuss these states of the SELF in various sections, where the most relevant feature of the SELF is presented.

1.23 State Transition Diagram of the Brain

A digital processor goes through a sequence of states to execute its task. The human brain has such a sequence also. Figure 1.23.1 shows the state diagram of the self-conscious brain characterized by the level of activity. At the center is the alert state, in which the SELF observes the present internal or external state. I am in this state when I cross a busy highway where there is no traffic control light.

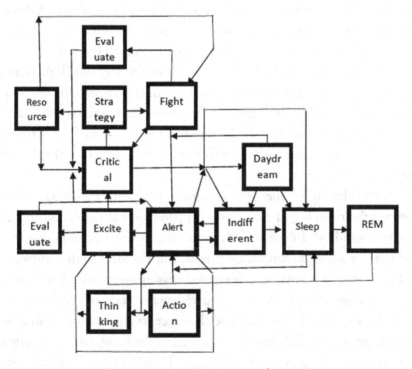

Figure 1.23.1 Brain state diagram

The alert state checks to see if everything is normal. If too long a time is spent in an eventless alert state, the brain disengages by moving to an indifferent state or sleep state so as to let the tired brain rest.

The act of thinking or a daily chore is carried out in the alert state. If anything demands special attention, the state moves to the excited state.

If any worrisome situation emerges, the alert state moves to the excited state. I am in this state when I hear the news of the stock market crash. In the excited state, the entire brain's activity level increases. The excited state closes the loop to the alert state by way of the risk-evaluation function, and if the risk is minor, the higher-energy excited state falls back to the alert state. If the risk is real, the highest-energy critical state is entered. I am in this state when my relative meets with an accident and is transported to the hospital. This is the state in which some external action must be taken. A deliberate action is decided upon by using the strategy search function, referring to the available resources. The action may also be taken by reflex; that is, whatever possible action is taken right away. The critical state is maintained until the crisis is over or when stress and fatigue terminate the state.

If action is initiated, the state moves to the fight-or-flight state. If a big tree falls down on my house, I am in this state. This is action execution by a deliberate plan. In this state, the brain's activity level decreases, and the energy is directed to the body to execute the planned action. This state closes a loop with the critical state via evaluation of the effect of the action.

Any of the higher-energy states close a loop with the lower-energy state via the thinking or evaluation function so that the excess energy cost is minimized. In the state diagram, the thinking, risk evaluation, and strategy search functions are executed by the same brain hardware, and they are the brain's basic image-processing functions. A state that does not close the loop with the lower-energy state is the daydream state. This is a weakly active state that accepts the images created by the intense yet only half-conscious state, and the images are quite often archetypal, either positive or negative. This is the most significant internal state for personal growth (section 4.32).

The indifferent state is the empty-minded, peaceful state. Since this is the healthiest state, all the higher-energy states fall back to this state. This state may still fall to the sleep state. The sleep state may move into the REM sleep state, characterized by an active brain and resting body.

The REM state is entered only from the sleep state. The brain takes its rest first, and that is why the REM state is entered only from the deep sleep state. Upon waking up from the sleep state, one goes into the alert state, but upon waking up from the REM sleep state, the person may go into the excited state if the dream is a nightmare. Sleep and the indifferent state are not attended by the SELF.

Introspective observation is carried out in the alert state. In a well-isolated alert state, a stream of images emerges from the brain's image memory. Introspection is observation of the image stream. Much of the information of the brain's function is gained by introspection if it is carried out in the state that is not disturbed by the concerns of the present life. To suppress the naturally emerging secular life's image, the subject must be in the alert state, as energy is spent to prevent irrelevant images from appearing. No image state is not the lowest-activity state. Random internal image flow is characteristic of the lowest-energy state that reflects the brain's mission as the safety guard of the body.

1.24 SELF and Complex

A complex, a psychoanalytic concept, is a set of images closely integrated by a specific emotion. According to psychoanalysts, the complex is usually hidden but grows unconsciously and emerges to take over the ego. Its dramatic emergence manifests as multiple personality. Multiple personality has a curious feature: if personality A and B coexist in a person, the two are never aware of each other. Disconnection and reconnection of large memory blocks, each of which is enough to support normal life, requires a rather strange hardware structure. My model cannot explain this mental state.

The Oedipus complex is also hard to explain by using my model. In the ancient world, incestuous relations were not taboo but were the privilege of powerful royalty such as in Egypt, Inca, and the Palenque dynasty of Maya. It became a taboo in many dominant cultures. *Oedipus complex* is a misnomer. None of the participants in Oedipus's tragedy were aware of what they were doing. The incest relationship was purely an accident. In the Kadmos dynasty of Thebe in ancient Greece, there was a conscious case of incest by Io and Actayon, who were aunt and nephew. The naming is obviously not proper.

The inferiority complex is a normal reaction of the SELF brought about by the bodily sense of fear arising from weakness in social life in our modern society. This complex is consistent with my human machine model since it is created by evolution. In modern times, if one meets a person with whom one must compete in some way, and one does not have enough respect for this competitor, the sense of inferiority is often compensated by a sense of superiority in some unrelated capability, thereby creating a complicated emotional state. If weakness in life is fully accepted as a part of the character, a sense of inferiority creates no negative effect. The Eastern philosophy of Taoism maintains that the weakest is the strongest. Taoists liken themselves to water; water is the weakest element, yet it penetrates everywhere and creates everything. This feature turns the value system upside down and makes Taoism one of the most positive philosophies.

1.25   Isolated SELF Sensing the Body

The human mind is constantly bombarded by the images from the outside or the images excited from the memory. Yet under certain conditions, the SELF is able to free itself from any image. To keep images away from the mind, concentration is required. To concentrate in such a way, the active SELF must guard against the excitation of any image. This state can be maintained only consciously. To get into an imageless state and remain in this state, I must be free from bodily pain, discomfort, and the immediate concerns of life. As my mind is free from images, I sense the state of my body, especially my heartbeat. This pulse is sensed in my chest, but if I try, I can feel it anywhere in my body. My SELF is able to focus on any part of my body, including some of my internal organs.

The task of guarding the body requires information about the body structure. I am able to sense the body location by the body map. The body map includes certain, but not all, the internal organs. Many of the sensible internal organs share a self-treatable character, for instance, by restricting food intake to treat a digestive anomaly. In this, the sense's objective is the body's protection. The body's sense is always active, even in dreaming. We wake up from sleep by sensing the need to go to the toilet. Often my dream ends with the scene of going to the toilet, before I wake up.

The neurophysiological structure of the body creates some confusion of body sensing. The body's local sensors are connected to the brain. The nerve impulses from body parts are sent to the brain, which identifies the origin of the pulses. The structure of the body map is the distributed entry points of the nerve fibers to the brain. If I try to sense the pulses of my big toe and my earlobe simultaneously, the pulses appear perfectly synchronized. If the sensors of the two locations send the local pulse to the brain, they should not be synchronous; it takes some time for the pressure pulse from the heart to reach the far end of the body, and the nerve fiber has delay time when sending the signal back to the brain. Since the pulses are perfectly synchronous, my brain must be sensing the pulses at the entry point of the fiber to the brain. The entry point is sensitized, and the brain is sensing the pulses there (section 4.17). The body map structure may cause such confusion. Once I had a severe toothache, but I could not tell which tooth, whether the upper or the lower wisdom tooth, was causing the pain. The dentist told me that my brain was fooled by the nerve wiring. Location information inside the mouth appears quite confusing. The phantom pain suffered by someone who has lost a body part can be explained by assuming that the pain is sensed not at the body's location. The brain and body connection misleads us.

These are common problems of remote sensing. Location information is more important than the information of the event that happened there, especially in risk handling. Where we sense our body can be confusing, but the SELF can identify the correct body part that is in trouble. If the location is known, the SELF can act to save its life. This capability must have saved many lives of our ancestors, since during most of human history, only the patient could treat his or her own problem. If the problem is known but not the location, nothing can be done. General discomfort of the body creates fear since the cause of the problem is unknown.

1.26 Basic Mechanism of Image Sensing

The simple block diagram of the self-conscious brain was shown in figure 1.20.1. Let us consider how the block diagram explains the mechanism of the SELF sensing any image. Which is the activity of the brain sensing the image stored in the memory? To answer this simple question, I point out something quite simple. Since the image is stored statically in the memory, it must be activated. If the image simply stays there, there is no reason for the SELF to sense it, even if it is activated. The image information must move somewhere. As seen in the simplicity of the block diagram of figure 1.26.1(a), there are only two ways to move it, as shown in figure 1.26.1(b). The two ways are to move the image information up, from M_1 to B_1 to the outside world, and to move it down from M_1 to (M_2, P_2) and then to B_2. B_2 represents the body's internal organs, which are also outside the brain. The image signal moving up goes to the outside world, such as moving the fingers to draw a picture or exercising the vocal chords to make a speech. The actuator produces an image outside the body, and this is taken in by the sensors and is superposed on the sent-out image's source. This feedback has two effects: one is to confirm the sent-out image, and the other is to increase the activity level to retain the excitation. Both processes create the sense of the image for the SELF. Image send-out need not be actually executed. If the image is internally displayed, I can sense the image. What does this mean? I suggest that the reader close your eyes and try to imagine a simple geometrical figure such as a regular triangle. Then you will feel as if you are seeing the triangle behind your closed eyes. The image information was sent out to move the eyes' directional control automatically and is sensed by the motion of the eyes. This is a clear evidence that the image-sensing process is image output followed by input. To sense an image, the image send-out process must be executed actually (on paper) or virtually (with eye movement).

Similarly, the image signal going down from M_1 to (M_2, P_2) and on to B_2 is another image send-out process, intended to control the body organs to meet the energy need of the action. The upward and downward image information movements are both *image send-out/take in processes*, one to the outside and the other to the body, which is also the outside of the brain. Figure 1.26.1(b) shows how the image output process creates the internal sense of recognition of the image by the SELF by creating the image outside and by generating a sensation associated with the image inside the body. The SELF is the activity to send the image out, and also to take the sent-out image in. The SELF sends out its copy and confirms that the copy is the same as the original. The brain's neuron circuits are built to carry out this process automatically, so we take it for granted. That is why sensing is felt as natural, yet mysterious. The mystery of sensing an image is actually sensing the SELF by itself. The SELF is the image itself.

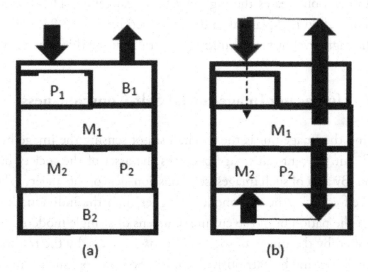

Figure 1.26.1 Model of brain image sensing

The SELF is creating its own copy outside the brain. By sending an image out, the SELF observes itself, or an internally invisible SELF is converted to an externally visible SELF's image. What does the word *visible* mean? The image memory activation in the brain is simply excitation of the coded image information in the memory, and there is no way to make sense of it. If the image is sent out, it is decoded. Then all the resources of the brain are available to engage the image, such as taking action directed by the image. The internally stored image is in coded form, like the ciphered text that cannot be recognized by the SELF. The image send-out process deciphers the image and makes it comprehensible. In this state, the SELF is able to see itself as its independent observer. This mode of operation is unique to the brain in sensing, understanding, and processing the image. An interesting way to explain this feature is to say that the brain is not a simple data processor; it is a processor plus a *human* administrator because it is self-conscious. To send the image out and receive it is for the SELF to take over the role of administrator of itself. The SELF sees the sent-out image consciously. The SELF executes two kinds of operations, one unconsciously (or automatically) and the other consciously. Conscious brain operation creates the high-end brain capability. This feature of brain operation is explained in detail in sections 2.27, 3.22, and 4.08. All the high-level human thinking is carried out by this capability.

1.27 Unloading Image-Social Self-Consciousness

Sending the image out is the mechanism of sensing the image by the SELF, but the sent-out image becomes the asset of the society of the person. By a set of such images, self-consciousness of the society is built. This self-consciousness is one level higher than the individual's; it is that of the nation or of the culture. Citizens of a single modern nation are united by the image of social self-consciousness, by the traditional way of living, and by patriotism in a crisis. So how does such a unifying force of society emerge?

Practically all Americans hate socialism; they believe that socialism equals Marxism. That is how Donald Trump bashes Democrats, and some Americans listen to it. How did this simplistic idea take root?

During the Cold War, powerful advocates blasted that the two political ideologies were the same thing, and people chimed in. The sense that socialism equals Marxism was established in the American mind. Robert Owen's utopian socialism and the real ideal historical socialism, the society of the theocratic monarchy of the Inca Empire, have no place in the American mind. The one who created this image of the Inca was Louis Morgan. He declared that Inca was only a tribal union at the level of an uncivilized society. He misled Karl Marx and helped to make Marx's dogma appear rational, thereby creating one century of Marxist disaster for humanity.

Yet it was a valid question, how the highly organized socialist Inca society developed in the short period between AD 1200 and 1500. I visited the Andean highland and looked at what are there. I believe that the Inca inherited the social system of the Tiahuanaco. The Inca claimed that they were proud successors of the Tiahuanaco civilization, which dates back to 1000 BC. On the southernmost coast of Lake Titicaca, there are terraced farms built by the Tiahuanaco. Their design is rigidly standardized. It appears that the Tiahuanaco were already in the stage of a highly organized nation. To convert the nature of the harsh Andean highland to paradise, theocratic socialism was the only way. That is why a very advanced social system was built by the Inca. I cite a significant historical case to show how *information catch ball* creates a society's mood and often twists historical development.

The sent-out image comes back to the person when the second person sends the same image back as an independent voice. This is the basic mechanism of social self-consciousness and is also the mechanism to maintain society's mood. Each self-conscious individual is the equivalent of an image in the brain of a person. Both individual and image carry meaning, and as they play information catch ball, they are united to build a structure carrying the group's thinking. The mechanism of spreading such an image is the mass media. Once the simmering social mood becomes the topic of mass media, everyone in the society joins together like an avalanche, and the image emerges suddenly. An anti-Islam social mood followed the vivid image of the

World Trade Center's Twin Towers falling down. This same mass psychological effect is going on now, a revival of Fascism.

This is also the mechanism of creating culture and historical heritage. Since humans share the same senses and have similar feelings, the image of social self-consciousness is carried by people and passed down for a long time, even among people half a globe away and ten thousand years apart, between the New World and Old World. I present an interesting piece of evidence. When we look at the full moon, what do we see? No one can see anything definite. Yet there is a common belief in Asia that the image is a rabbit. The belief is quite widespread, and even now Asians celebrate the September full moon. How did such a belief originate? Because person A in the Old World told person B that the image was a rabbit, and B confirmed to A that it was indeed a rabbit. This is a feature of *conditioned* observation of an unclear object. If I observe the full moon as an amateur astronomer, I see nothing that looks like a rabbit, but if I observe it as a mythologist, I do indeed see the rabbit. This story has an interesting follow-up.

The ancient Asians agreed, and then some of them crossed the Arctic Ocean to the New World, which is how the moon rabbit arrived in the New World. A lintel from the Maya megalopolis Yaxchilan has the Maya character of the moon carrying a rabbit. Another connection of the two worlds is the idea of assigning colors to the four cardinal directions of the world. In ancient China, blue, red, white, black, and yellow mean east, south, west, north, and the center, respectively. In Maya, the corresponding colors were red, yellow, black, white, and green at the center. Color assignment reflects the two cultures' different natures. The first Chinese emperor was the Yellow Emperor, and the last king of the Copán dynasty of Maya was Yax Pasan (Yax means green). Such a belief was created by chance, but it lasted for the entire span of human history, covering ten thousand years and moving halfway across the globe. To unload an internal image is to recognize the image by the person and by all the members of the society. Such an image carries with it a certain rationality. The five colors assigned to the four directions and the center is rational, so the rulers adopted it for their emblem. Image unloading has still a more significant effect on conscious thinking, which I discuss later in section 4.08.

1.28 Fear: Origin of the SELF

How did self-consciousness emerge from evolution by natural selection? I have a simple answer: because our animal-level ancestors feared practically anything that came upon them, and we descendants inherited their body and their behavior. Evolution of new animal species begins with small animals that have certain characteristics that make them better adapted to the habitat. This is because any animal's lifetime is proportional to the one-fourth power of an adult's weight (section 5.17). If one generation is shorter, the better-adapted subspecies dominates the population profile more quickly and soon takes over the developing ecological niche.

Small animals are more susceptible to natural forces like weather and are more likely to become prey of the existing big animals. Their lives are constantly threatened by the environment. To be able to survive under such conditions, the animals must be sensitive to any change in their habitat. Any sign of approaching risk reaching their brain must initiate action to avoid the risk, by mobilizing the entire available resources quickly. By evolution, any variation capable of executing this action effectively soon dominates the population. Small animals like squirrels climb a tree after sensing any sign of danger, but bigger rabbits cannot do this. So, the rabbit population quickly decreased and is extinct now in my area.

In the animal brain, a special center emerged whose excitation coordinates evasive action. Coordinated action of the body is always advantageous. The neural center controlling lifesaving action developed further to become the core neural area supporting the SELF. As the evolutionary development proceeded, the animals increased in size, and their lifetimes became longer. Larger animals lived longer and had less fear of the habitat's destructive power. Then the efficiency of the natural selection mechanism decreased and the rate of selection became lower and less effective than for their smaller ancestors. The animal lost adaptive capability, and its development slowed down.

Larger animals have a larger brain, which detects an approaching risk better and earlier. Senses similar to fear, but in a more advanced form, that foresee the future and prepare for the projected fear of the future emerged in the brain. These were the senses of worry and anxiety. The emergence of mammals opened a new possibility of better adaptation, namely, inheritance of acquired behavior patterns from generation to generation within the animal society. This Lamarckian evolution mechanism is not caused by genetic change but by teaching and learning by the animal. This change brought two new features to animal life: social life and culturally controlled behavior. Both features helped to establish the domination of *Homo sapiens* to control the world's ecosystem to the present level, but its negative features are increasingly threatening our future. Formerly what was fearsome were natural forces and predators (of different species). Now, our own species has become the predator. With this new situation, the Lamarckian mechanism of evolution works both positively and negatively. *Ancestral wisdom* of a group's welfare is inherited, but so is the strong ego of rulers. So we still live in a world of war, originating from the ever-expanding ego of the rulers in recent history. A social rank system exists in any mammal's society. Humans were never made equal. This is the reality.

The original form of the Lamarckian evolution mechanism involved these acquired characteristics modifying genetic information. When I refer to Lamarckian evolution, I mean the evolution of social self-consciousness or cultural features that affect the future generation by teaching and learning.

The sense of fear is often intensified by a lack of resources to execute action. The brain is able to create a winning strategy, but the body cannot execute it because of the lack of resources. This frustration creates the sense of anger. Thinking humans worry what will happen in the future, and they are anxious all the time. Our future is dark, plagued by fear, worry, anxiety, and anger.

These life-support images emerged as a result of evolution, and as the images related to such survival-oriented senses increased, a reorganization of the internal image and the external action repertoire became necessary. This is how the SELF we now feel inside was developed.

1.29 Origin of Fear

In the history of the development of self-consciousness, when and how a clear sense of fear emerged is an interesting question. Observing the behavior of lower-level animals on the evolutionary scale, one finds that almost all of them display evasive action in the face of any kind of risk. That is certainly the evolutionarily acquired behavior, but I cannot say that such actions of the animals are all caused by their sense of fear. Such a reaction can be a reflex that was programmed in the very early phase of evolution. Anything touching the body, or even anything approaching the body, unless it is what the animal desires, can be harmful. Then the evasive action must have its origin in reflex. The question is, when did the sense of fear similar to what humans feel emerge? And when did the capability to differentiate between merit and risk of the approaching object develop? I observed a snake's reaction to approaching danger, but I didn't see anything significant. I watched the snake stretching out on a country road near my residence. A truck came and ran it over. Prior to that, the snake showed no reaction to the approaching danger.

I think that the humanlike sense of fear emerged in the level of animals that can be domesticated, that is, a few, but not all, reptiles and the animals above them. Turtles are reptiles, but they recognize their owners as I learned from the observation by Gilbert White, in *The Natural History and Antiquities of Selborne* (a famous and very charming book). If an animal is able to recognize friendliness of its owner, it can sense fear in the face of other objects. The horse I rode was not afraid to go uphill but was very afraid to go downhill when I traveled the tropical rain forest of the Yucatán Peninsula. All mammals show such selective fear.

Human self-consciousness developed in the last two million years. During that time, our ancestors lived in wilderness, first in the dark forest and then in the open savannah, and were exposed to all kinds of risks and predators. Until they formed a primitive society and began to use fire effectively, they were constantly exposed to the strong predators, especially those carnivores that are active at nighttime. If we spend a night in a pitch-dark tropical rain forest, we feel the same fear they felt. This ancient experience still exists in our mind. Episodes of vesperian depression, felt before and sometime after sunset, are the traces of the experiences of our ancestors who were afraid of the coming darkness. I feel this mood, and that is why I prefer not to go to a nighttime theater performance.

Fear of darkness (incapability to see clearly) is fear arising from an unavailability of information vital for self-defense. Uncertainty is fearful. Different from fear arising from a definite object or event, fear from uncertainty intensified with the increasing capability of future prediction. This capability actually intensified the social members' fear. The advanced thinking ability has the two faces of Janus. Often those who know nothing suffer the least from such fear. Yet modern society does not allow such a lifestyle. Since the sources of our fear are other human beings, the fear is intense, since assault is intelligently planned to inflict the maximum damage upon the victims as on a battlefield. An army of psychologists are working to treat soldiers coming back from the Middle East, where the struggle is direct and brutal human-to-human combat. Once they come back, they face a different fear, namely that their life is no more ensured by competitive modern society. They are pinched by fear from both sides. I am sorry for them, but I am also sorry for the psychologists who must treat them. Because their profession is institutionalized, they must do something. Yet what they can do? The cure for fear must come from inside, not from the outside.

1.30 Fear of Death

As best I can remember, my attention to human self-consciousness began during World War II, when so many people perished, including three out of my five uncles and one cousin. The thought tortured my mind: What happened at the moment of death of one of my uncles who was particularly close to me? He disappeared on the day of the Japanese surrender, and later his comrade told my grandmother that he was always loyal to his military honor. I think my uncle would not disclose the military secrets he held to the victors. How did he die? when and where? We never knew. We all got together in my grandmother's home on the day the occupation army left Japan, waiting for him to show up as a last hope. After a light noodle supper, we were all silent, surrounding our grandmother. We finally gave up all hope.

My conclusion after seventy years is that nothing special happens at the moment of death except for the preceding agony and the fear of dying and of the underworld, shrewdly exploited by the institutionalized religions. At the moment of death, as at the time when we are being placed under anesthesia, all the senses become blank. After that, nothing is recognized. This means that no one goes to heaven and no one goes to hell. There is absolutely no alternative, I am firmly convinced.

Images of hell are from ancient times, but perhaps not from the earliest hominid period, since the early hominids did not have the custom of burying their dead. Yet all the ancient myths of the world set the place of the dead in the dark underground. This image must have emerged from the custom of burying the dead in a tomb. Yet there is an exception. Tibetans do not do that. Their dead spirit goes up to the sky. In Tibet, I saw a government notice to the guides not to show what they do since that is their holy tradition. More likely the Chinese rulers are afraid that some women might faint upon seeing that, which may undermine the tourism that is being promoted.

The image of hell is a cultural product. The dark world of hell came from religious beliefs and the culture of politically strong societies.

Yet here is also an exception. A Maya myth tells that the twin heroes, Hunahpu and Xbalanque, went down to Xibalba (Maya's hell) and deposed the lords of death. Ever since, Xibalba is only a temporary path to heaven, where a dead spirit becomes a star. I love this myth more than any others.

An empty belief in life after death does not relieve anyone of this fear, and so the vacant promise of a paradise with fruits, wine, chicken, and women fails to bring such relief. As for eternal life, no one who lives his or her life honestly, works hard, and is not properly rewarded will want to continue living forever.

I am sure that my SELF will go nowhere when I die. There is no heaven, no hell, no god, and no devil, and absolutely no reward for my contribution to humanity, but this means there is no punishment for my wrongdoing either. What will remain in this world is some of the works I did to add to human culture, at most only for a small fraction of one generation. A Chinese poet sang, "Someone may cry for me, but the others will sing merrily." So, I never pay any premium for a certain type of *insurance* to live forever. Instead, I try to do my best to create something new and worthwhile for humanity, and I especially try to enrich human culture. I believe that this is the only satisfaction that I will feel one minute before losing my self-consciousness for the last time. Yet since I believe in my protector gods and goddesses in my image world, they will die with me. They disciplined me to live honorably my whole life. They will care for me, as they die with me.

1.31   Fear Center and Its Development

In sections 1.28 and 1.29, I mentioned that evolution created a center in the brain that coordinates the entire brain and body for the purpose of risk avoidance. The survival-oriented action center, vital for life, first exercised a reflex function in the earliest animal's brain or central nervous system. This reflex function set the direction of the later evolutionary development toward self-consciousness.

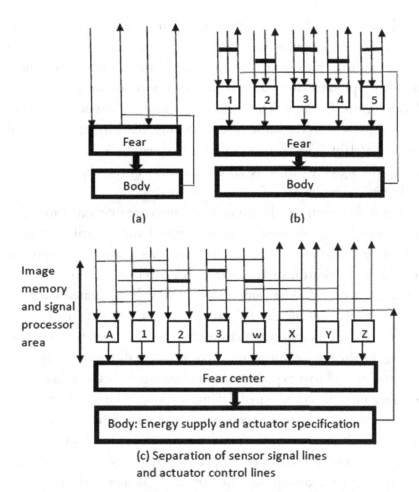

(a)

(b)

(c) Separation of sensor signal lines
and actuator control lines

Figure 1.31.1 Evolutionary development of the brain

Figure 1.31.1 shows a schematic of the center's development history. Figure 1.31.1(a) shows the center executing a reflex. Simple sensor (downward arrow) and actuator (upward arrow) pairs are distributed over the entire body surface, and a signal from a sensor is reflected to the paired actuator by the fear center. At the same time, the center directs the body organs to supply energy to execute the evasive action.

Then, in the next stage of development as shown in figure 1.31.1(b), the originally unspecified fearful images are sorted into classes, 1, 2, 3, ... Increased numbers of sensors and actuators in each class are specialized to respond to the particular kind of risk signal (such as touching, high/low temperature, chemicals) from the outside. Since the signals from the same class of sensors are correlated (shown by the thick lines connecting the input lines), the sensor channels reproduce and retain structural images of the external risk object within the body. This structure is built by connecting many sensor signals from the same type of sensors, like groups 1, 2, ..., of figure 1.31.1(b). The increased number of sensors and connections among the signal paths store accurate images of the objects risky to the life of the body.

From this level, the distributed actuators are integrated together to become a small number of more powerful and versatile actuators that can exercise a strong force of action. They are the weapon to fight back. To control such actuators effectively, highly coordinated signals are required. The control signals must be generated referring to the current state of the habitat and to the memory of the past experience. The evolving structure of figure 1.31.1(c) is capable of storing the risk source information, correlating a different kind of risk information and past experiences and allowing the set of actuators to execute a properly coordinated defensive action. The sensor channels and the associated memories cooperate for the actuator control signal generation since the actuators must cover the entire body and all expected events. The brain developed the capability to deal with the habitat's risk by knowing the structure and function of the body and of the source of the risk.

To generate such actuator control signals, the incoming sensor signals must be preprocessed before reaching the fear centers. The actuator control signals are generated from the preprocessed signals and from the signals derived from the stored information. Processing is carried out by an image analyzer, image memory, and the processor for image manipulation. Their integration creates the internal image circuit. The signal to select the actuator is generated, along with its control signals, in the memory and the processing area. The actuator selection signal is then sent downward to the body, which controls the supply of energy. There, the signal is joined with the energy supply signal, and the two are sent to the specified actuator. This brain-body structure was built already in the evolutionary level of amphibians, and all their descendants in the animal world share the same control architecture.

Further development of the architecture of figure 1.31.1(c) was more quantitative than qualitative. In the lower level of the brain, new specialized centers like A (anger) and W (worry) emerged. These new centers need preprocessed information from the sensor area to function. Anger is the sense of unavailability of resources to attain the lifesaving objective, and worry is the sense of fear projected to the future event, judged from the present state. Both senses require analysis of the state of the external world and internal body, the past experience, and the state of the SELF, referring to the available resources and future forecast. These functions are basically decision-making operations, carried out by correlating the incoming and internally stored information. The final human level was reached by explosive growth of the volume of hardware executing the image memory, processing and manipulation of internal image, and decision-making.

In the final human-level development, the variety of the stored images increased so much that further classification of the acquired images became necessary. A structure similar to that of the fear center complex (consisting of fear and 1, 2, 3, ... of figure 1.31.1[b]) was built inside the image memory area. There, classification of the common images referring to their shared characteristics is made. These are neutral, not always survival-oriented, images. They are classified by the merit, peculiarity, and character and their dynamical operations following the laws governing the physical world. As such, newly emerged abstract images organize the incoming images.

The present intellectual life of the human being was established by the Middle Paleolithic period. Ever since then, we have lived a similar internal and external life. This is the reason why there were so many basic and very practical inventions during the long Neolithic period. The resources of present human life that make us feel comfortable mostly have their origins in Stone Age inventions. We eat the same staples, wheat, rice, corn, and potatoes; wear the same clothes made from cotton or animal hair; and live in similar structures of houses to shield ourselves from the effects of nature.

1.32 Fear from Uncertainty

Fear originates from weakness. A strong person does not feel fear until his or her power meets an impossible force. Here, a strong individual does not mean physical strength alone; in our modern life, material and mental strength matters more. We need to know what is ultimately impossible and to be contented with what we have in life. In the advanced twenty-first-century human society, there is no need to fear snakes in New York City. There, it appears, all that matters is strength with regard to personal finance. Yet even the richest people have fear of their future health, business fortune, the FBI, terrorists, and so on. For a weak person like me, the outside world is immensely frightening. My existence is like debris floating on the ocean. I am exposed to all sorts of forces, mostly social forces. When I am engaged with one of these forces, I have no extra resources to worry about the rest. Once a crisis is over, I must worry, *What comes next?* I am not the only one who is thus affected; 40 percent of Americans suffer from anxiety and depression from this same cause.

Fear of uncertainty is included in the model of the previous section by adding the indefinite classes of potential fear, 1, 2, 3, …, connected to the main fear center. Which one will become real is unknown. Not enough resources or information is available to forecast and prepare for the ever-increasing number of possibilities. The number of fearful images, 1, 2, 3, …, increases as the future time extends. Each fearful image demands a supply of energy to think and prepare for its eventuality. Yet the body's capability sets a hard limit. The brain falters by facing an unlimited demand of attention on the future. This is the state that emerges from the fear of future uncertainty. As such a state continues, the body senses the physical risk and shuts off the support mechanism to protect the vital body organs. This state continues for a long time and is difficult to get out of since the state is self-sustaining.

The stacked-at-low-energy state is never able to support the active imagination necessary to find a new way to direct one's life.

This is the weakness of thinking humans that I mentioned in section 1.01. This is the reason why we are inferior to our ancestors, who did not have as many social causes to worry about. A colleague of mine was very worried that he was not good at playing golf. He told me that golf would help him to get a promotion. In spite of his effort, a promotion never came. He was so frustrated that he took a risky offer of a high position in a start-up company. A year later, the company filed bankruptcy and he lost his job altogether. This was a tragicomedy of the utmost irony in the twenty-first century. Our democratic and capitalistic society praises competition of the members as the highest value, and most of us do not realize that competition in every phase of life carries huge negative liability.

The only way to get out from this state is to reduce future uncertainty. The first step is to define what one can do and cannot do and not to desire the latter. A real estate developer need not become a president, and an old woman need not travel the Silk Road on camelback. By closing the door on such possibilities, people can have a simpler, healthier life.

I live in the New Jersey countryside and seldom go out of the house. Why? As I search my own mind, I find that many secular desires need not be satisfied to live happily. Yet in my past, I saw practically everything I believe to be worthwhile. My internal image world is rich enough. I saw the best ballet and the best flamenco in Europe. If I do not go to New York City to see such shows, then no terrorist can attack me.

Here is a word of wisdom from the great Chinese sage Su Tong Pa: "Reduce your desire and sustain good luck, reduce appetite and sustain a clear mind, and reduce expense and keep your assets." Su Tong Pa is my most admired role model. His Taoist philosophy created the belief that, in effect, one may create one's own future either by acquiring a new direction in life or by setting a realistic objective. If even that is not possible, then one should do whatever possible to reduce the number of frightening possibilities. The effort may not be successful, but it will have the effect of taking energy away from fear and worry. I have an anecdote about my respected mentor William Shockley. I personally saw that he was quite satisfied drinking not very good coffee from the vending machine while working on the weekend (section 4.27). Having learned his ways, I am quite satisfied with my obscure, marginalized life in U.S. society, since if I had stayed in Japan my whole life, this would not have been possible because of the constant pressure from my mother to get a promotion and stand above others.

CHAPTER 2

SELF-CONSCIOUS BRAIN

2.01 Internal Image

I sit down comfortably in a quiet place, close my eyes, and imagine a simple object such as a triangle, circle, or star. Then I feel as if I see its vague image in the darkness behind my closed eyelids. If I remember a song and silently go through it, I hear a faint sound and feel a gentle pressure in my vocal chords. A man unfamiliar with Polish cuisine burped when he heard that pierogi have mashed potato in them. These are the effects of internal images of various senses. They are the basic information received, recognized, and acted upon by the self-conscious brain.

If I have paper and pencil when I imagine a visible image of a familiar object, I am able to draw that image. If I exercise my vocal chords while going through a song, I can sing the song. As for the pierogi, the man imagined eating it as it is: actually it is fried with onion, and it makes a tasty meal. Internal images are the commands to exercise the body to reproduce or respond the image either inside or outside the body. I sense the image by sending it out by way of the action directed by the image stored in my memory (section 1.26).

Many such images were originally taken into my brain, processed, and memorized. As my brain receives an image from the outside world, or when an already existing image is activated internally, other images carrying some related attributes are connected to that image to make a web of images. If any image in the connected network is excited, some associated images of the web are excited also. The jointly excited images create the meaning of the originally excited image to the SELF. Display, recognition of meaning, and the bodily sense associated with the image together create the sense of the image to the SELF.

The human brain allows any excited image to be sent out from the brain, if prepared to meet the actuator's capability. As an image is prepared and is sent out to the outside, the image is sensed by the SELF. The SELF consists of all the coexisting images in the brain when one of the images is sent out. Because of this, excitation of internal images is the activity creating the sense of the SELF observing itself, that is, the SELF's own images.

Except for the fairly simple ones, internal images are not an exact copy of the observed object. The SELF at the time of observation picks up certain features of the object and retains these features as the image's memory. Thus the image of a certain person can be a hero for one person and a villain for another person, and the name of a city may become the name of a woman. In World War II, a discussion among the air force command was whether or not they should bomb Kyoto. Someone said that to bomb Kyoto was like bombing Florence. Then came a question: "Florence who?"

2.02 Classification of an Internal Image

The self-conscious state is engaged with internal images of various kinds. In an emotional state, it is an abstract image carrying some bodily sense, such as fear, worry, anxiety, misery, sympathy, mercy, love, peace, hope, or joy. Among such abstract images, those related to life's basic welfare are innate. Abstract images have two variations; the first kind is relevant to life and carries a heavy weight, such as fear and anger, and the other kinds are general concepts, such as color, character, or size. Such lightweight abstract images emerged when the number of images in the brain increased and some internal organization became necessary. The life-support abstract images are in the depth of the memory. Lightweight abstract images are above them, and they cover the common characteristics of any neutral images. An example of such abstract images is color. Other such abstract images are symbols that represent a certain group of people belonging to a single category, such as national or organizational flags, party symbols, mathematical symbols, chemical symbols, and musical notes. They are common to all the members of the community, and some of them are shared by all humans as common cultural assets. Musical notes and mathematical symbols are now universal.

The images are acquired by sensors provided by the body. The variety includes visible images, sound images, language images, visible images sensed by the somatic sensors on the body surface, and the chemical images of smell and taste. There are two different types. One type covers such images that can be sent out as is, like images of visible objects (by drawing a picture) and voice and language images (by singing, speaking, or writing). The other type of images are those that cannot be sent out as they are, such as abstract images and chemical images. These types of images can be sent out by converting them either to visible images or language images, or by pointing to the object. The human brain has enough capability to convert any image to the form that can be sent out. This capability has been greatly improved by the acquisition of language by *Homo sapiens*. Still, some subtle and convoluted emotional images can be sent out only by talented artists, such as smile of Mona Lisa.

An image can be constructed from the existing images in the brain's memory. A composite visual image of a house is assembled from the images of the wall, roof, window, door, etc. A description of a historic event is built from the words specifying the actor(s), the action, and the circumstance. Composite images are constructed and retained temporarily, and only some of them are stored for permanent reference. The brain stores elementary images permanently and constructs composite images on demand. Because of this, images are the most versatile type of information.

A word, which is an elementary image of language, is an abstract image; a word such as *dog* may represent a hundred subspecies of the animal. An elementary visible image can be interpreted by many different sentences. Conversion of image type is not a faithful or unique transcription of one type to the other. The quality of the conversion reflects the SELF's capability of image manipulation and the character of the person. Some people are so ego centric as to assume that what they know is known by everyone else. It is very difficult to communicate with such individuals.

2.03 General Character of an Internal Image

The human brain is able to sense internal images of various kinds. A single internal image can be a composite of images from many senses. Some images make a hierarchy, and at every level there are images whose boundaries with other images are vague. This vague boundary of an internal image has an advantage, namely that any two arbitrarily picked-up images can be related. The image's meaning is created by the overlap of the image's boundary. The ambiguity of an image's boundary includes the memory of the circumstance of its acquisition (section 6.05). Some images do not carry this information. I cannot remember when or how I learned the alphabet, but I do remember how I came to know about the ancient civilization of the New World. The sophistication of the ancient culture of Native Americans impressed me a great deal when I was fifteen, while preparing for my college entrance examination including history. I have been working ever since, for almost seventy years, on certain unresolved aspects of the New World's antiquity. My personal story of this subject is found in section 4.41.

A single internal image consists of several elementary images from various senses. A visual image can be associated with language images and can even be associated with a chemical image. A flower is recognized by its shape, color, name, and fragrance. Visible images are universally recognized as they are, but language images depend strongly on culture. Since each of the visible images has its own image associates, a single visible image may demand a complex, subtle, and often long sentence of explanation in language. Language communication always assumes that many basic images are shared among the communicators.

The SELF is capable of sending out any image, but image conversion for interpersonal communication is often quite difficult, even for a simple image. This problem is most seriously felt in language translation. I once had a hard time translating the Japanese word *omedetai hito* into English. The literal interpretation, "celebrated person," is entirely wrong. "Foolish person" is too negative. *Felix ignoramus* is only similar, but this is the phrase of a dead language, Latin, that hides the nature of ignorance. What this word means is "a very good-natured, lovely person, but so ignorant of any secular matters that many people laugh behind his back"—a very long definition for just one word. A similar problem occurs if the image carries an abstract meaning. Can you define what self-consciousness is, right away?

All the internal images that a self-conscious person carries are personalized by a unique image-to-image connection set up by the person's SELF. Because of the combinational complexity, there can be no two characters that are the same. The SELF executes image personalization by providing context of the image by way of image-to-image connection. Elementary images are generally similar, but integrated image structure is quite different from person-to-person image structure. One such revealing case is when an abstract concept is asked about, and the images a person uses to explain it. The word *antiquity* symbolizes an Egyptian pyramid for many people, but for me the Olmec, Chavin, and Tiahuanaco temples come to mind. This uniqueness of image memory structure anchors a person's unique character in his or her image world.

77

2.04 The Meaning of an Image

The meaning of an image is created by connecting the image generally to many other images, some of which are abstract images carrying bodily senses. The set of images are sensed simultaneously, and the image's integration enriches, but often confuses, the image. Yet the confusion provides for flexibility of the image. By this flexibility, an image can be related to any other image, and endless conversation becomes possible. As I listen to women having a hour-long telephone conversation, this feature of internal image clearly shows up.

Images affecting the welfare of one's life directly or indirectly carry some level of sensation and a specific bodily sense common to all humans. A fearful person feels a cold spike running down the spine, and a person feeling sympathy toward honest yet unfortunate people feels pressure in the chest. Body response of this kind is common to all individuals in the world, and the similarity becomes the basis of emotional understanding. This image-to-image or image-to-body interpretation is the image's meaning. Yet the meaning of a common object depends on the person, and this creates difference in the person's character. An object is a favorite of person A but not of person B. Like or dislike of a certain object or action depends on the character, which is determined by the image's connection structure built in the person's memory. If images C and D are connected, and if the person likes C, the person likes D also. Connection between C and D adds meaning to both C and D. If a similar pair of images C and D are connected in a mutually exclusive way, both images are defined precisely.

How is such a connected structure made? At the time when the image is acquired, or at the time when the image is later recalled, the brain goes into image search mode. One such image is the image related to the circumstance of the image's acquisition. If any image related to the current theme image is excited, the two are connected. After many such experiences, the web structure of the images is constructed.

Image enrichment by way of connection provides some unexpected new insight into understanding the nature of human culture. The Confucius creeds "Don't throw the good words of a bad person away" and "There is no book that tells only truth and no book that tells only lies" are words of wisdom. I always keep in mind that connected images must be properly interpreted case by case. The second words are especially relevant to writers and readers. I believe that some sayings of Confucius are no longer proper. Yet I have found some ideas that demand serious consideration in the Little Red Book of Chairman Mao. I admire Thor Heyerdahl, but I cannot accept his theory of the origin of the Easter Islanders.

2.05 The SELF's Identity in Space and Time

The sense of my SELF appears to remain the same all throughout my life. By several mechanisms, my SELF must be anchored to something solid. What is it? The sense of my body is a heavy weight to anchor my SELF. I feel that my body is continuous while sensing an occasional change in its state by the slow and steady process of aging. The visible image of my body changes, but the sense of my body from the inside remains the same as long as I am healthy. Continuity of the body secures the identity of my SELF. Yet there is another anchor of my SELF, and that is the set of images that are connected uniquely in my memory to identify myself. This *uniqueness* is the second anchor of my SELF.

Figure 2.05.1(a) shows that my bodily sense is felt by the display of image A. Image A is a familiar image of my own life. The image and its connections to the others is so unique that I can use it to identify myself in the image world. This is the second anchor of my SELF. The connected images B, C, ... are the images of the objects familiar to me, such as my workplace, my house, my favorite music, and the memory of the places I have visited. If the focused image moves around, the set of images surrounding it are still uniquely connected. As my attention shifts, the bodily sense accompanies the shift and moves to the successively emerging images. My SELF, a combination of the image and sensation, moves continuously for some time. Then, occasionally, my SELF makes a discontinuous jump in the image's web. My SELF can move within the connected web but cannot go outside it. It is absolutely confined within it. Because of this, it may be appropriate to call the connected images *the space of my SELF*. In my life, my image space may expand, shrink, or change shape. I live in this space, or in my image world, as well as in the real habitat, the physical world. My free spirit sometimes feels the space as a prison and tries to get free. The SELF seeks something new, something unknown, or something that has not yet been experienced.

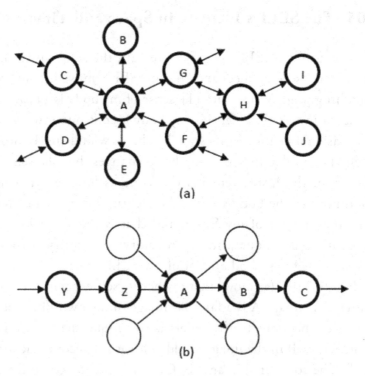

Figure 2.05.1 Image connection structure representing the image of space and time information

I admire an inquisitive spirit. When I visited Charles Darwin's Down House, I felt that there was a great spirit who had tried to see the deep geological past of human ancestry. When I visited Herman Oberth's memorial museum, I felt huge eyes gazing far beyond the dark night sky. I felt in L'Anse aux Meadows that Leif Erikson's spirit was still staring at the vast expanse of the New World. So was King Hotu Matua (meaning father Hotu), looking beyond the waves of the South Pacific to the New World. Those who successfully broke this image's prison became the greatest, and those who could not became either most vicious, most out of their minds, or most miserable. I, at least, tried to look into the dark depth of the human mind. Maybe I am one of those who have failed, and that is why I am pessimistic about the emerging future of humanity, but nevertheless, I tried.

The domain of the human mind exists not only in space but also in time. In figure 2.05.1(b), the present SELF's location is A. Image A is on a particular time point in the array: ... Y, Z are past, already experienced events, and $B, C, ...$ are future events created by the imagination. The linear sequence sets the SELF's position in time. The current image, A, anchors my SELF in the flow of time. The sequence is my personal history.

This is also a prison for free spirits. Those who broke the cage were the greatest or the worst. A thousand-year empire never became a reality, at the cost of millions of lives. Such was the case too for the first emperor of China, whose family lasted only two generations. But there are also the great ones, mostly historians. The hero of my youth, Wan-kwei-I, showed that the ancestry of the Chinese Yin dynasty, then believed to be the province of an imaginary legend at his time, actually existed, and in so doing he pushed Chinese history a thousand years back. He deciphered the characters carved on tortoise shell unearthed from the last Yin capital and found the names of the dynasty's ancestors. Tatiana Proskouriakoff and Yuri Knorozov brought Maya antiquity back to the realm of history. In the early 1950s, I was inspired a great deal by the works of Wan-kwei-I, and I aspired to do the same as he had in Maya. Yet my dream never materialized because of the post–World War II confusion in Japan.

Now, in the twenty-first century, there is no terra incognita on the earth anymore. Those who are free-spirited have no *real* place to go. That is why many promising youths abuse substances or become violent. Yet have we really run out of any new frontiers? I suspect that today's young people do not have enough imagination to search, or enough determination to get over any impediment to their dreams. I believe we all should be more imaginative and determined.

2.06 Growth and Self-Consciousness

Human babies become self-conscious soon after birth, but they carry no memory until they become much older. Their self-consciousness is not the same as that of adults. Since my childhood included World War II, I know the definite date in my early life when I became aware of myself and of the world. Our family in Japan moved from Tokyo to Hokkaido (the north island) when I was five and a half. Before that date, the only memory I still have is of when I ate my father's cigarette, and my mother and her maid struggled to make me throw it up in a dimly lit, varnished-floor kitchen. It is a painful memory. Then I remember the morning of December 8, 1941, in Hokkaido. When I heard the news, I brought out my globe and told my parents how such a small nation (Japan) could fight and defeat such a huge empire (the then largest empire was England). I was severely punished by my parents, and I clearly remember the pain. I was just shy of six years old. Since the day of Pearl Harbor, my memory has been continuous.

This experience showed that in less than a six-month period, I somehow had enough of an internal image to know what war was, and that a nation's fighting power depended on the size of the nation's territory. I acquired normal self-consciousness in only less than half a year. This experience showed me that the clarity of my self-consciousness was rapidly increasing with the number of internal images, N, since memories were established and held securely by connecting many images together. Clarity of self-consciousness during the early years may be estimated by $N! = N(N - 1)(N - 2) \ldots 1$, if N is small. This is a very rapidly increasing function of N. If N is small, then images are not securely held in the brain by their sparse connection. A small child must get an image, lose it, and get the same image again until the number of image N reaches the critical level. As this level is reached, the memory becomes secure and continuous. This sudden change of the mental state may be considered to be the establishment of the order of the images in the child's brain. Images that once existed in mutually tenuous relations are suddenly organized to enable understanding of a serious event such as world war. To be able to construct an extensive image like world war means that I became capable of manipulating lots of images. Maybe, by the shock of the event, the capability emerged suddenly.

A natural question is, what sort of self-consciousness did I have before I reached that memorable day? The self-conscious subject SELF knows itself, its world (or spatial location), and its history. Although I have no memory before the fateful day, I must have been aware of myself at a much earlier age. What I acquired suddenly must have been the sense of my place in the world, spread out over the entire globe. Before that time, my world was limited to my immediate family and residence. I had never attended kindergarten, and my sister was not yet born. So, my mother, my father, and a maid made up my very narrow world.

Once we moved away from Tokyo, the maid was gone, mother became busy, and I became more independent than before. I remember, soon after the day of Pearl Harbor, that I messed up my father's bookshelf and looked at the books' illustrations. There were all kinds of biology books. My knowledge expanded rapidly by looking at the pictures. Some pictures were even from English-language books. I learned human ancestry from the book illustrations. I still remember the Piltdown man, now eliminated from human ancestry. I learned the name of Alfred R. Wallace before I knew Darwin's name. My interest in evolution by natural selection began when I was six years old. My belief in Darwin's theory of evolution was firmly set at that age. Soon after that I learned that plants of the same species can be grafted. So, out of curiosity, I grafted green Japanese basil onto purple Japanese basil, and then to purple basil once again. My primary schoolteacher visited our home to look at the chimera. This was during my first summer vacation in the first grade.

2.07 Heuristic Feature of the Brain's Image

The meaning of an image is determined by the connected structure to its associated images. New thoughts, artistic works, and scientific discoveries are creations of new images connected in a unique way. I will give an example of my own. During World War II, I learned much about the ancient Japanese myths. I knew almost all the Japanese gods' names. In the postwar college period, I audited Professor Kure Moichi's Greek and Latin classics seminar at the University of Tokyo. As a pioneer of Hellenic studies in Japan, he introduced the Greek myths. Mysterious and gray-colored, yet with an occasional streak of sunbeam—that was my impression of the ancient Japanese myths. Then I met the bright-colored Greek myths in broad daylight. I was shocked, and that opened my eyes to a lifelong interest in the myths of the ancient world. By comparing the Greek and Japanese myths, a still unexplained event in the Neolithic period emerged: Asia Minor and the Far East had direct cultural contact, and that happened within a very short space of time, in one human generation (section 6.08).

Figure 2.07.1 shows the relationship of several pairs of deities of ancient Greece (in the broken-line box) and Japan (in the thick-line box). The pairs are Demeter and Ōhirume (the ancestral goddess of the Japanese royal house), Kore and Toyohime (or Toyouke, goddess of food), and Poseidon and Susanoo (both violent sea gods, brother of Demeter and Ōhirume, respectively). The lines connecting the boxes show their relationships as made plain in the myths. As is observed from the heavy connections, the deities of the two remote ends of the Eurasian continent are almost completely entangled, and they play almost the same role in the Greek and the Japanese myths. What I found in my college years of 1954–56 is summarized as follows:

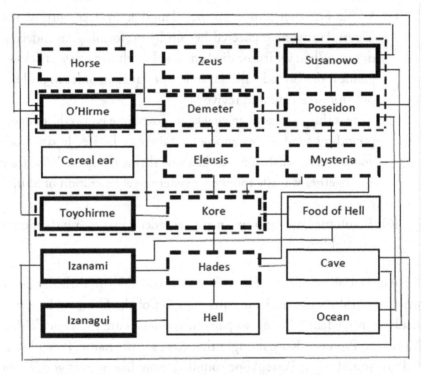

Figure 2.07.1 Greek and Japanese mythological connection

(1) The sea god Poseidon violated his sister, the goddess Demeter, by becoming a horse and raping her. The sea god Susanoo killed Ōhirume by throwing a horse stripped of its skin at her, while she was weaving.

(2) In the Eleusinian Mysteries, Demeter's priest showed a stalk of wheat to the congregation. Ōhirume showed a stalk of rice to her descendant Ninigui, who had come down from the heavens to the Japanese islands as the anointed ruler.

(3) Kore was kidnapped by Hades, the king of the underworld. She could not return to this world since she had eaten a pomegranate of the underworld before her mother found her there. Izanami, the wife of Ōhirume's father, Izanagi, died when giving birth to the fire god. When Izanami's husband Izanagi found his dead wife in the underworld, she could not return to this world, because she had eaten the food of the underworld.

(4) While Demeter looked for her daughter in deep sorrow, the Eleusinian women cheered her up by performing an indecent dance. When Ōhirume died and hid herself in a cave, a trickster goddess performed a similar indecent dance in order to pull her out from the cave and revive her.

(5) Kore is the goddess of green wheat. Toyohime is also the goddess providing food to her mother, Ōhirume. In Ise, Japan, both goddesses are enshrined in the same shrine complex. Why they are together was the toughest mystery to a generation of Shinto priests.

(6) Toyohime never appears in any recorded Japanese myth or even in local legend.

Association of the myths of Demeter and Ōhirume clearly show who they really were, and the hard question of the Shinto priests was resolved immediately. The two pairs of goddesses are the same deities. Moreover, Professor Kure thought that Kore's other name, Persephone, did not sound right; Persephone sounded more like a great goddess of the East. This is indeed so, I believe, since her Japanese counterpart, Toyohime, is a minor, subordinate goddess. I had a pleasant discussion on these subjects with the Eleusis site archaeologist ten years ago. He was aware of all these stories already. What was a new idea sixty years ago became common knowledge. This experience made me a pious pagan.

Yet there is still a bigger mystery in this story. Why are Poseidon and Susanoo so similar? From Asia Minor to the Far East, there is ten thousand kilometers of travel, and there are no seas along the Silk Road. Yet both gods are violent sea gods, having the horse as their totem, and they both violated their sister goddesses. Did the ancient migrants cover a ten-thousand-kilometer trek while carrying such details of the myth? The image of a violent sea must have been lost if roaring sea waves were not witnessed by the migrants.

Since I was a physics student, I had no connection to publish these findings in 1950s. Yet I gave this topic to my sister, Shigematsu Yoshiko, and she wrote her thesis under the guidance of Professor Mizuno Yu of Waseda University. In the 1960s, several authors published material discussing this issue. Demeter's and Kore's part is covered by these authors, but Poseidon's myth is still not mentioned in literature and not even questioned by anyone.

As this exercise shows, by tracking the meaning of images set by the connection of the associated images, a significant intellectual exercise is possible. This is the great merit of the image as the brain's data type. Why can images be heuristic? To create a new idea in the human mind, a statement in language must be created. By connection of words to visible images, a single word's meaning can cover a wide range of objects. Then practically any word can be connected to any other word. Then many statements are automatically created, and a sensemaking one can be selected. Since the mechanism involves random image association, the statement may carry unexpected new meanings.

2.08 Mechanical Model of the Self-Conscious Brain

The human brain and body are biological machines, first declared by de La Mettrie three hundred years ago. This is acceptable to scientists and system engineers, but not to psychologists and less so to philosophers. To bridge the academic cultural gap, I will explain how biological and mechanical machines are different. Any living organism is a biological machine, but the machine has one distinct feature different from any lifeless machines. Let us observe the evolving features from a steam engine to a Maglev train, and from a 1940 radio to the present PC. All these machines have active components that consume energy to execute the task; two engines vs. many linear motors, and five vacuum tubes vs. billions of transistors, respectively. Active elements consume energy, and they exercise control over the other, passive components. Such an integrated structure operates beyond simple expectation; the degree of *beyond expectation* increases rapidly if the number or the fraction of the active components in the machine increases.

All the cells making up an animal's brain and body are active. Such a machine does not operate like a mechanical machine. Any complex machine, whose every part is active, often behaves mysteriously. The simplest structure, whose every part is active, can be rubber band used to tie vegetables. It is cut open, stretched, and coiled like a snake. If the snake is placed on a flat surface, it unwinds, showing an unlimited variety of shapes each time. This is very interesting. In the stretched rubber band, energy is stored everywhere. Its every part is active. Similarly, a structure that is active everywhere can be built with certain semiconductors subjected to a strong electric field (called the Gunn effect). Gunn devices show a variety of strange behaviors not seen in any other solid-state devices.

A peculiar feature of such an everywhere-active machine is that not every part of it is active simultaneously. Instead, an active structure moves around the entire area freely. Similar active structures can be copied at different locations, and once spontaneous activation begins somewhere in the machine, the activity spreads out and develops by itself without external intervention. These features are useful in processing extensive and complex data structures like images. In such a system, all-out excitation of the active elements is a failure mode. Such an operation is a machine's *epilepsy*. It is interesting that such a mode of operation of the Gunn effect semiconductor device was once proposed; it was called the LSA mode. This mode should occur if the semiconductor is perfectly uniform, but even theoretically that is not possible. In the brain, such an operation is not likely to occur frequently, since an image is a large extensive structure whose excitation deprives the nearby circuits of energy. Thus the hardware and data structure support each other for operational integrity.

The Gunn effect is quite suggestive. This was the most active topic of semiconductor physics in the 1960s. If I apply a high electric field to an N-type gallium arsenide crystal bar, the whole bar becomes active and displays many curious effects. Following are a few references on the Gunn devices:

- J. B. Gunn, "Properties of a Free Steadily Travelling Electrical Domain of GaAs," *IBM Journal of Research and Development* 10 (1996): 300–9.
- H. Kroemer, "Nonlinear Space-Charge Domain Dynamics in a Semiconductor with Negative Differential Mobility," *IEEE Transactions on Electron Devices* ED-13 (1966): 27–40.
- M. Shoji, "Two-Dimensional Gunn Domain Dynamics," *IEEE Transactions on Electron Devices* ED-16 (1969): 748–58.

Thus, a structure whose every part is active displays an amazing variety of states. Its behavior depends on the minute details of the local state and on very small external influences. Such a strange character exists even in VLSI (very large-scale integration) chips also. The ratio occupied by transistors in a VLSI chip is 75 percent or more. Such chips show certain features similar to biological systems. For instance, testing the operational integrity of all transistors by accessing them from the terminals is impossible. You may be surprised to hear that the CPU of your PC has some transistors in it that have not been tested. This testability issue has been a serious problem yet is not generally known beyond the integrated electronics community. This is the same feature as a job applicant's interview; it never exposes everything about the applicant.

Thus the human machine model must be considered by keeping this feature in mind. Everywhere-active systems may produce such mysterious phenomena as self-consciousness. This new viewpoint, derived from my own experience with the Gunn effect works, led me to believe that the barrier between physics or systems science and biology is useless and is counterproductive. The two areas must be integrated into a single scientific discipline. I suspect that some philosophers' tenacious objection to any kind of reductionist approach to self-consciousness research is based on their simplistic concept of the human machine. We need a different way of reduction to make a human machine model.

This feature of the machine model is the character of the model itself, whether the object is modeled by discrete mechanical parts or by a continuous, everywhere-active field structure. The brain is really a field in which images are excited, like particles in the quantum vacuum (discussed in the last part of chapter 6).

2.09 Evolutionary Development of the Human Machine

How did self-consciousness emerge in the animal kingdom? Animal life is adaptive to the habitat. Any animal is able to adjust its lifestyle up to a certain limit and is able to live in its habitat by using available resources and improvising strategy to deal with the modest variations of the prevailing conditions. In animal evolution, the degree of adaptability depends on minor differences of the genes, and after many generations, the winning subspecies changes to a new species. Self-consciousness and its subfunction, intelligence, are powerful means of adaptation. I believe that self-consciousness emerged in the simple prototype biological machine by way of trial and error evolutionary development. The CPU of a modern PC followed exactly the same development history as many valuable domesticated animals and plants. The genetic material of many useful plants and animals is altered to create more-desirable species. Most very large fruits and flowers are created artificially by this technique.

The history of the microprocessor began in the 1970s, and in the following decades, so many processors emerged that I cannot remember all of them. Into those processors, we dumped all sorts of new ideas to help improve the basic von Neuman architecture, and checked to see if any of the ideas worked well. This is the same practice that nature uses when modifying animal chromosomes and expecting long life and many surviving descendants. In this process, there were many failures. Most processors are called DOPs (design-only processors).

After completing the design, only a few wafers of silicon were produced, and if the manufacturers were lucky, a few chips in the wafers worked. That was as far as the project went. There was no customer. The PC was not a commercial product in the 1970s, and it was built from a kit by amateurs. In the 1980s, the PC became a commercial product, and a new situation emerged: microprocessors were useless if matching software was not available. In the 1970s, PC amateurs wrote their software by using the basic machine code. This was not possible any longer in the 1980s.

Then the software industry emerged and became monopolized, and only those processors that worked well with the available software survived (Microsoft Windows or its minor variations). Any processor that did not run the software efficiently had no market. This state continues to the present. Some processors emerged in 1980–2000 that had much better performance, yet they met with business failure. The relationship of the market conditions to the microprocessor is the same as the condition of the habitat to animals. Only those processors that sold well survived. The present PCs are good for communication but not for computation. To write a new program and to open a new technical area is not for most of us but only for professionals. Computers have become a public utility by making them unable to compute. To make them computable again, several thousand dollars must be paid to the service company, since loading the proper software to a PC and configuring the hardware is quite tricky and tedious, like going through a maze. To accomplish this is impossible for most of us. As a 1970 PC amateur, I miss the time when we could know everything about our PC, including its basic operational codes.

The history of the development of self-consciousness and intelligence exactly parallels the history of microprocessors. Evolution brought adaptive change but not necessarily progress. I retired from microprocessor design since I want a computer to compute, not to provide indecent entertainment or to be a means of delivery of destructive information about human culture. I found an anachronistic *ecological niche* to reverse engineer the human brain, which appeared to me more meaningful.

2.10 Evolutionary Development of the Brain

Self-consciousness developed by the process of evolution by way of natural selection, from its prototype of a simple animal of the Cambrian period. The developmental history can be traced by a conceptual design exercise, from the central nervous system of the simplest animals to the modern human brain, by relying on a minimum of rational assumptions (section 1.31).

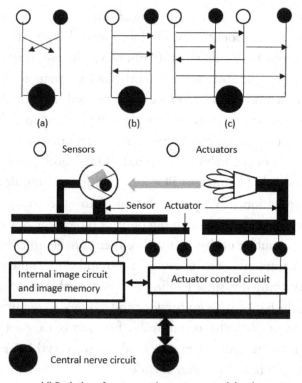

(d) Evolution of sensors and actuator control development

Figure 2.10.1 Development of brain and its periphery

Figure 2.10.1(a) shows the simplest nervous system of the earliest animal. The sensor at the body surface sends a warning signal to the central nerve circuit, which includes the fear center, to inform the state of the surface to the body. The center was built in the earliest animals as the junction of the information I/O (input-output) channels. This center, which developed in the brain-body interface, sends signals back to the actuator to move the body part away by simply copying the vector sensed by the sensor. A pair of I/O lines to and from the central nerve circuit run parallel, close to each other. The pair of lines consist of several neurons connected in a series. At the location of the neurons' connection, there are neuronal dangling branches as shown in figure 2.10.1(a). Because of the proximity of the input lines and the output lines, the next step of evolutionary development would be connections between the pair of lines. Because neurons are active (capable of amplifying a signal) elements, a two-way connection between the lines creates memory that mediates the sensor and actuator to the central nerve circuit, as shown in figure 2.10.1(b) (section 3.08). If this memory is excited, the animal takes action, and the central nerve-circuit senses an event. This provides the animal with the ability to retain past experiences inside the body. From this basic structure, the next step created conditional reflex, which became the origin of self-consciousness.

Evolution by natural selection builds the neuron circuit automatically. The simple circuit becomes more complex. Yet the basic structure like that shown in figure 2.10.1(b) remained all through the later period of evolutionary development. As the nervous system structure expanded by increasing the number of sensor-actuator pairs, more connections between the input lines, and also connections between I/O line pairs, were added. Nature created many different structures and kept throwing unworkable structures away. With an increasing number of the sensors, actuators, and neurons, connections among various sensor-actuator line pairs became complex as shown in figure 2.10.1(c). This creates an essentially new capability: by correlating the signals of more than one sensor, not only did proper response to the outside world become possible, but also the structure of the outside object could be retained inside. This means that images were adopted as the basic data. In addition, the internally retained images could be used to execute effective control of the actuator. The evolutionarily created structure supported internal images, which became the data of the self-conscious brain. As it is observed from figure 2.10.1(a)–(c), the evolutionary level is still quite low, but most of the features of the animal's body structure had already been set, and these were inherited to the final human level.

The connection among sensor-actuator lines allowed correlation of the input signals and the action signals, thereby creating elementary mechanical intelligence. Since the animal could sense its own action by sending the images out (section 1.26), the animal acquired basic features of self-consciousness and of intelligence using images as the data. Later evolutionary development saw an explosive increase in the number of input-output channels and connections among many channels. With this quantitative development, the control center of the body's action became an internal image-processing area. This area worked as the interface to the body, to control the actuator and to request proper energy necessary for action execution. Since a lot of functional structure was built between the sensor-actuator and the central nerve circuit, the brain's depth increased. This is called *encephalization.*

In this evolutionary process, there was a clear trend. In certain areas of the body, such as the eyes and fingers, the sensors gathered together, and high-resolution image sensing became possible. As for the originally distributed actuators, they got together and are integrated into only a few actuators that are powerful and flexible. Eye directional control and fine manipulation capability of the fingers emerged from the development. Then there were body areas left out from development. The back of the shoulder of the human body is practically inaccessible. This development is shown in figure 2.10.1(d). The sensor-actuator connection lines made the internal image circuit and the actuator control circuit.

As I show later in section 3.07, the neural logic circuit can execute all the three basic binary logic operations, yet the brain does not use the neurons as binary logic gates. Instead, the brain chooses to copy a structure representing the image of the external object by connecting neurons.

This review of the developmental history of the self-conscious brain indicates how the SELF, which emerged with the evolutionary development, senses images. Suppose something touches the body surface and the SELF tries to move away from it. Then the sense of the touching and the action to be taken are both vectors having the same length and direction. The SELF sensed the outside object by way of taking the action to protect the body.

A neuron is an active device. It receives signals and sends out signals, and the ratio of the intensity of the output and input signals is the gain of the neuron. If several neurons are cascaded to close a loop, the signal that circulates the loop either intensifies or weakens depending on the neurons' gain. If the gain is higher than unity, then the signal originating from the noise in the loop may grow into a full amplitude signal. The circuit creates an internally recognizable image. This is the internal image. An interesting feature of this mechanism is that a serious health concern creates a phantom bodily symptom. When I hear an acquaintance has a serious problem such as colon, prostate, brain, or pancreatic cancer, I feel for some time an unusual sense or even pain in the particular area of my body. Later a health examination clears my concern, and there is no more discomfort. Such a pseudo symptom occurs so often that I am sure that my brain sends a signal to critically sensitize the sensors attached to the particular organ. The SELF is able to sense a nonexistent anomaly of the organ as an internal image.

What this means is that the brain can create a signal and can sense it. This is the internal image. An image is sent out and received as if the image has come from the outside world. By the self-conscious brain architecture, the image memory capability and the image-sensing capability were developed together, so the brain is able to make an image that can be sensed by itself.

2.11 Image Memory Structure

I described in the previous section how the brain developed, by connecting the incoming and outgoing signal lines. Figure 2.11.1 shows the structure that emerged from such development. A simple loop such as *A* is a memory that stores 1 bit of information. If signal 8 or 9 excites it, the closed loop circuit is activated, and the signal is sent out and is sensed. As the memory develops further, more-complex structures such as *B* are built. This circuit sends out signals 2, 4, 6, and 3 in sequence if the closed loop is excited. If each line represents a vector shown below the line, the structure displays the image shown to the right side of the figure. This memory is able to hold a complex image structure that is able to control the vocal chords.

Why did such a loop structure emerge? This is the character of complex nonlinear active systems. All the connections of lines in figure 2.11.1 are built from neurons, which are active logic elements. The entire structure is active as I discussed in section 2.08. In such a system, not all the locations are active simultaneously. If some area is excited, then the activity takes energy away from its neighbors. After some initial joggling, spontaneous organization such as that shown by *A* or *B* of figure 2.11.1 emerges.

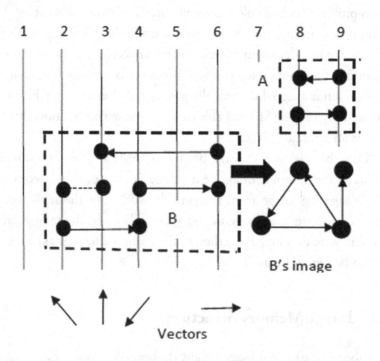

Figure 2.11.1 Brain memory structure

96

This is the same mechanism as the emergence of a vortex in a rapid flow of water. A vortex in flowing water can be quite complex. A paired array of vortices emerging behind a body in rapid flow is called a von Kármán vortex. This is a general feature of active nonlinear systems. Once such a structure is excited, the structure takes energy away from the nearby active elements and prevents all-out activation of the system. Here, the role of the support system of the brain's neuronal circuit becomes crucial. If the support level is abnormally high, either random brain excitation, such as attention deficit hyperactivity, or synchronous excitation of the system, such as epilepsy, emerges.

The structure shown in figure 2.11.1 is ideally suitable as image memory. The image stored in such memory is able to control the actuator directly in proper sequence. The memory loop has its own excitation source, which I call the identifier, whose activation excites the loop. Although the structures are built automatically by the brain's activity, the brain retains only those that are useful for life's purposes. If a useless loop is formed, the loop is never excited again, and is soon eliminated from the memory. An example is my disconnected phone number that I no longer remember. This is the natural selection mechanism working inside the brain. The brain is an *ecological environment* of images.

Because it is easy to handle image structure, the brain does not store its data in binary form, except for special control purposes. It stores action as memory, and the action is directed by its image. If the neuron lines are driven by properly formatted and sequenced signals from the image analyzer/assembler, the brain's memory area is able to create accurate structures from the images of the outside object. Humans' and advanced animals' vision channel has evolved by creating such memory and refining its operation. Any image is coded as the action to reproduce it outside. Even a blind person can use the image as the brain's basic information by drawing a picture by moving his or her finger.

2.12 Image as Action

The brain hardware I have shown handles images as its data. The images have a common basic characteristic, that is, they are all commands that direct any body part or the brain itself to execute the designated action. This is because of animals' body structure: advanced animals, above the level of vertebrates, are able to control the outside world only by mechanical action. In the long history of evolution, action commands were adopted as the basic unit of information. A vector (directed arrow with length) is a command to move a part of the body or the entire body in the direction and at the distance specified by the length. An arc is similarly to rotate the body or one of its parts by the specified angle. A visible image is converted to a command to move the pencil held by the fingers to draw the image on paper, or the eye's line of sight is directed to trace the outline of the image in the air. The same command is used to move the entire body in a dance performance. A phoneme is generated by a composite command to drive the vocal chords, mouth cavity, and lungs by a combined vector and arc commands. This way of coding an image has the advantage of saving the memory hardware and eliminating the actuator-interfacing logic. The alternative bitmap format of a graphic image and the spread spectrum of voice and language image require a complex memory structure and interface circuits to convert the stored data into actuator control signals.

An important feature of image as action is, first, that any action consists of a sequence of basic action commands. A static image of a person and the dynamic action of the person walking are both coded as action. A set of vectors and rotation specify both static image and dynamic action. Drawing a circle on paper and rotating the body 360 degrees are both actions emerging from the same basic command image. This scheme of image coding determines how the image is sensed by the SELF. The SELF senses the image by the process of reproducing it. The capability covers all the actions that the body can execute. The sign of the International Red Cross is sensed first by drawing the cross and then by painting the inside red. The red color cannot be sent out from the body, but by the imagining of the color and the painting action executed virtually by the SELF, the symbol is sensed.

Visual, voice, and language images are coded as commands that can be sent out directly by the respective body's actuator. Then how about the images that cannot be sent out? Such images include chemical images, which have no actuator. Abstract images have no substance of their own to be sent out. Those images must be converted to other, executable images. Chemical images were either good or bad for the early hominids. At the evolutionary beginning, the action was either to approach or to move away from the source. As the internal image capability improved by evolution, the categorization of good and bad smells developed to a more precise characterization. At the level of humans, the image is converted to language to be sent out, or by specifying by the chemical symbol if possible. The odor of volcanic gas was first identified as bad, and then it was identified as being similar to the odor of a rotten egg, then it was called by the name of hydrogen sulfide gas, and finally it became known by the chemical symbol H_2S. The advantage of language is that similarity or dissimilarity of any image to any other image can be specified precisely, since language allows the composite specification of any image. Language images carry the basic characteristics of abstract images. Abstract images such as color can be sent out by naming commonly known objects or, if the examples are spatially close, by pointing at more than one of them and indicating the common feature.

Some antisocial images closely tied with emotion are hard to convert to images that are acceptable by other people. If such images accumulate, often violent and irrational behavior may follow as their expression. Such cases have become quite frequent. In order to ease the tension caused by such images, we need ways to express them mildly. One way is to write a story, as the act of a third person. Some of the ancient myths appear to be the product of such practice. To write a story and then read it by myself is a very effective way to deal with my mind when it falls into depressive anger.

There is a way to ease political tension and anger, developed in the 250 years of oppressive rule by the Shogun government of Japan. The way is to make very spicy, even poisonous jokes of the ruler, in such a clever way that the joke implicitly points to the ruler, but a sophisticated excuse is provided. Upon hearing such a joke, explosive laughter follows, and tension eases right away. This tradition survives to this day. A twentieth-century version I remember from World War II Japan is, "Don't shoot a U.S. plane down; instead down a British plane." This joke means that if I spell the phrase *British plane* using Chinese characters, it becomes Tojo Hideki's given name. I am sorry that Muslims do not have such a *safety valve*. Japanese jokes are subtler and lighter than the heavy joke of Oliver Swift directed at the poor response of the British government at the time of the Irish famine, which is too cruel for me even to write it down here.

2.13   Image Recognized by the Brain

The human brain manages images, that is, the most general and flexible data type. Images are able to cover all the aspects of human life. Image data must satisfy basic requirements to be useful. The images should be directly and unambiguously manipulated by the brain's circuits, and they can exercise the body's actuators, such as fingers and vocal chords, with minimum interfacing. By sending an image out, the SELF senses the image as I described in section 1.26. The human body is able to send any action out by some form of mechanical motion, such as drawing a picture with finger movement, speaking a word or statement by using the vocal chords, or frowning to express disapproval. Any image that cannot be sent out as it is must be converted to one such manageable image.

What are the basic types of motion executable by the human body? They are moving any body part in a certain direction for a certain distance, and rotating or twisting by a certain angle as shown in figure 2.13.1(a) and 2.13.1(b), respectively. The linear motion and rotation are the two geometrically required movements of any object in three-dimensional space, and they are represented by vector and axial vector, respectively. Although the vocal chords are not visible, control of the vocal chords is exercised by the complex combination of the two types of motions. By the motion of the vocal chords, and by the associated command to alter the structure of the mouth cavity and the lungs' action, phonemes, the elements of spoken language, are pronounced. This complex control has less variety than control of the fingers, and therefore the number of distinguishable phonemes is limited from several tens to one hundred, depending on the language.

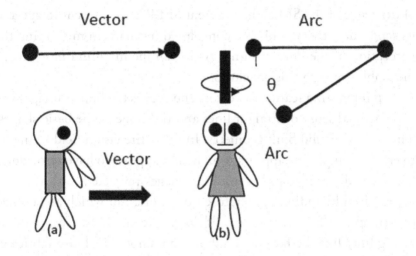

Figure 2.13.1 Comprehensible image and body motion

The phoneme system tends to simplify as a language develops in the modern age. The phoneme set of two different languages generally covers the similar sounds, but how to pronounce precisely a pair of similar sounds is often not an easy thing to figure out. *Ducha swietego* means Holy Spirit in Polish. I cannot pronounce –*cha* properly, so I tend to pronounce it –*pa*, and this causes me a lot of trouble in church (the word means something quite indecent).

The information that is practically useful for daily life is complex. Visual images must first be broken down to the elements, vectors, and arcs, which the brain is able to handle. After this step, the image must be reassembled from the brain-comprehensible vectors and arcs. Reconstructed images can be sent out as a sequence of such elements. Then the SELF is able to understand every part of the image. The SELF can send the image out and can see its effect. Thus the SELF becomes the responsible subject of the action. Adoption of images as the basic data type led to the emergence of the self-conscious subject SELF. The entire image output activity and the associated sensation creates the sense of the SELF's presence. By this mechanism, the SELF need not exist as an independent activity of the brain; the internal image circuit activity to send an image out creates the sense of existence of the SELF. The current SELF is the present image and its send-out activity. This is a convoluted mechanism misleading the perception of the human mind. As I examine my mind rationally, I inevitably come to this conclusion.

An interesting feature of vectors and arcs as the brain's image type is the special sense of straight lines and the circle as the basic shapes. That is how Euclid built geometry. In the entire vision field from end to end, a straight line appears straight and appears to have zero width. This is really amazing, because the images projected onto the eyes are received by individual photosensors, not all of which are aligned on straight line. Any line should look like small yet recognizable zigzag lines like the far horizon, but it does not. The brain fabricates absolutely straight lines as the basic data of vectors. The same is true of the circles. Uneven, irregular photosensor distribution does not create a deformed or crooked circle. This is a great capability of the human brain; otherwise, there could be no fine art or geometry, and we would see a mess everywhere.

Both linear and rotational motions require reference. Depending on the choice of reference, the motion appears quite different. People in the ancient world believed that the earth was stationary and the celestial sphere rotated around it. Geocentric cosmology was the natural choice of the time. What I am still unable to figure out is if all the people in ancient times really believed that heaven, which is infinitely large, turned around the earth once every day (section 4.42). I am sure that someone who was imaginative enough must have thought that the idea was ridiculous. Since they were already aware of the centrifugal force, the rotating heavenly bodies would fly away and we would not see any stars. My personal historical observation is that Ptolemy's geocentric system and Copernicus's heliocentric system each reflects the respective astronomer's cultural background. My experience tells me that Greeks think they are at the center of the world, but Poles do not. Poles are very modest people. Therefore, I don't think it was difficult for Copernicus to yield the central throne to the sun.

Elements of a visual image include blobs, closed areas painted by color. All three visual image elements, vectors, arcs, and blobs, are for the command of self-defense, and that was the reason for their adoption as the basic data. Vectors are for fight-or-flight, arcs disentangle from an entangling force (of snakes?), and blobs directly push the aggressor away. Vectors are the universal means of defense, but arcs and blobs emerged since advanced apes acquired bipedal standing and walking capability. All the elementary images have an evolutionary reason in their origin. Given their evolutionary origin, I expect that four-legged animals' image elements may be poor in arcs and blobs.

I have pointed out the simple and obvious characteristics of the basic data types. The brain made them, and therefore the brain can handle them. That is why humans and animals are self-conscious. Computers never made bits and bytes, and that is why they cannot understand what they are doing. The basic data type is understood only by those who created it. Thus, humans understand images, as well as bits and bytes. This feature has an impact on the brain's data processing. The brain executes both conscious and unconscious image manipulation, as I discuss in sections 2.27, 3.22, and 4.08.

Both humans and animals share some images that cannot be sent out, such as color and chemical images of smell and taste. Senses of such images are created by sensitizing the sensors that are able to detect them. Such a *confined* sense of images is connected closely to the body and induces an emotional reaction. Many women have a favorite color, and many foods have an acquired taste.

2.14   Architecture of the Self-Conscious Brain

I have shown the simple architectures of the brain carrying self-consciousness in sections 1.08 and 1.20, and the evolutionary development of the brain hardware handling images as its data in sections 2.09 and 2.10. In this section, I show the functional block diagram of my self-conscious brain model and provide a basic description of the functions of each functional block. The block diagram was assembled from my own introspective observations, referring to the neurophysiological basis of self-consciousness that assigns the seat of the SELF in the evolutionarily old area of the brain and other rationality requirements that are obvious from the brain's operation. In the diagram of figure 2.14.1, I refer to the four-layer diagram of the simpler functional block diagram of section 1.20 (P_1, M_1, M_2, P_2, B_1, B_2). M_1 and M_2, the image memories, are sandwiched between the upper P_1 and lower P_2 processors. Body includes the sensors and actuators, B_1, and the part supporting the whole body, B_2, which entail primarily the internal organs such as the heart, liver, and lungs. The sensors (eyes, ears, etc.) are optical, mechanical, and chemical receptors. I show the most complicated vision channel functional diagram in figure 2.14.1.

The bitmap visual image from the eyes goes through the analyzer to be broken down into the elements comprehensible by the brain's neuron circuits. A simple sketch of a house can be broken down into a dozen vectors and arcs, and the word *Mexico* to three phonemes, Me-xi-co, as I discussed in section 2.13. The image is broken down by the analyzer into the elements, and the elements are sent to the assembly area, where they are assembled into the original image. The brain-recognizable image elements are arranged in a sequence, in a form suitable to be stored in the memory. The processed and formatted image is stored in the template area, M_1. A template carries enough information to reproduce the image of any object. Template excitation is sent to the action-control area and the assembly area and then goes back to the template to re-excite the template. The signals are branched from the action-control area to the action-decoding area and to the actuator, to reproduce the image on the outside media (such as a picture drawn on paper). The action-decoding area converts the image signals to the actuator's muscle constriction and dilation signals, which drive the actuator and reproduce the image outside.

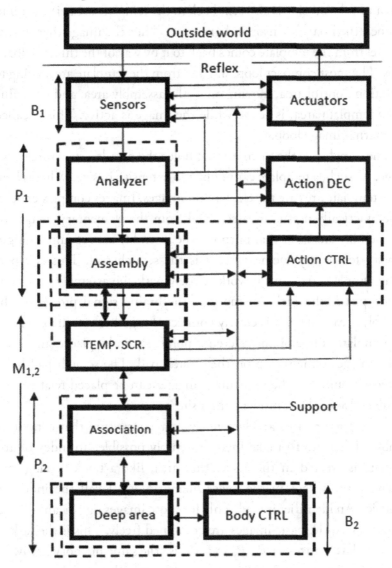

Figure 2.14.1 High-level architecture of the self-conscious brain

By this output process, any internal image is sensed. The actuator control signals are sensed by the specialized somatic sensor neurons attached to the actuator. Their signals are analyzed to the recognizable form by their own analyzer, and then the signals driving the actuator in the present activity are merged and go back to the template. The signal sent out to the outside is also sent back to the template area via the input channel (the image's sensor and analyzer). Thus the image that started to travel from the template comes back to it by way of the three feedback loops. The most compact loop, starting from the template area, going to the action-control area, moving on to the assembly area, and returning to the template area, is active while the image is active. This is called the internal image loop.

The template is the memory that holds the detailed structure of the image. As such, a template cannot be too extensive in size. What is kept in the template area are the elementary images. Images complex enough to be practically useful are assembled from the elementary images by the assembly area. For that purpose, the assembly area requires a high-capacity temporary memory. This is the scratch pad. This is a part of the template area, but it works closely with the assembly area. The scratch pad is the cache memory of the brain's signal processor, the assembly area. The pair is closely connected together. An image stored in a template is free of any reference point. It can be placed anywhere in the image frame set up on the scratch pad. The scratch pad has a reference point, and the elementary images can be placed relative to it in order to assemble a proper composite image.

A template retains an elementary image structure that cannot be combined as it is. To make image assembly possible, an index of any template is created in the association area, like a book catalog in a library. This is kept in the lower memory, M_2. I call the index an identifier. An identifier is made only for those images significant for life. By identifiers, the basic images are combined freely. This is the task of the lower-level processor P_2. P_2 and M_2 use the same memory hardware in the association area. If the image is relevant to the welfare of life, the identifier is further connected to the characterizing centers in the deep area, such as fear, worry, anxiety, and anger. Since such an image may affect the survival of the person, the deep area center sends a signal to the body-control area, which activates the sympathetic nervous system. By the sympathetic nerve signals, the body prepares for an emergency by sending energy and a warning to all the body organs such as the heart, lungs, and liver. This excitation is sensed as heightened sensation by the body. This is how the brain sends a support request signal to the body. The sensors and the actuators are parts of the body, and they are both of archaic origin. They are still directly connected, and this reflex function deals with emergency automatically, independent of the rest of the brain, to protect the body in the shortest possible time. This has been inherited from the original central nervous system and is still quite useful for body protection.

Since the brain was developed by adding more and more neurons to the original architecture of figure 1.08.1 and figure 1.20.1, the boundaries of the functional blocks are not so clearly defined as shown in figure 2.14.1. Some blocks are partially overlapped functionally. The assembly area and the scratch pad are closely integrated, and their functions overlap. The overlapping blocks are shown in the figure within the dotted boxes. The analyzer and the assembly area work closely together in the process of extracting the image elements. Each sense channel (vision, voice, language, etc.) shares the basic architecture shown in figure 2.14.1, but there are some variations. The archaic chemical sense channel does not have an analyzer, since the sensors are chemical substance specific. Yet all the senses share the same association area, where all the images are mutually related.

Since the human brain is built by adding more and more neurons to the original architecture, there is a certain limit to any further improvement by way of evolution. I do not believe a *super brain* is likely to emerge by further evolution. Higher intelligence and future prediction capability depend on better organization of the images. This is the task of education.

The block diagram of figure 2.14.1 shows evolutionary development of the brain in the recent past. An increase in the size of the lower-level memory M_2 and P_2 is quite significant. This area exists between the upper area, whose principal function is the reflex action, image formatting operation, and image manipulation function, and the lower area, which controls instinctive actions. For the brain to execute its task, the relation of the incoming image to the already existing image is critically important. The association area carries out the relating task. The area whose activity matters for survival responds quickly in terms of evolutionary development. Thus in the last hundred thousand years, the primitive human ancestors developed to *Homo sapiens* by increasing the size of the association area enormously. Development of the association area led to the language capability. As I show later in section 2.25, the language channel cannot operate unless it is strongly coupled to the vision channel via the association area. A blind person can sense an image also because the image is coded as the action to reproduce it.

What are the key features of this architecture? Once the system acquires the basic information for survival, the system must be able to take action and must be able to evaluate the result of the action. This second capability is to check and ensure consistency of the action plan and its consequences, and that involves the whole analysis capability of the system. Action execution is a simple operation, but the associated recognition is the key part of the brain and the self-conscious system. This feature affects the brain's conscious image manipulation as I discuss in a later part of this book, *Self-Consciousness*.

2.15 Structure of the SELF's Activity

The sense of the SELF is created by the activities spread out over the entire functional blocks of the brain. It is helpful to see which areas are most active in creating the sense of the SELF. The SELF exists in various states, depending on the outside world and on the internal state. Figure 2.15.1 shows the SELF's activities in the brain. The external world's interface is the sensors and actuators, and the body's interface is the deep area.

In an eventless, indifferent state, images from the outside are received, but their meanings and impact on the welfare of life are never determined. The outside objects are seen, and some images may be unintentionally identified. This is the state of figure 2.15.1(a). This state creates the sense of seeing or hearing, but what is seen has no effect on the self-conscious state. No memory is retained. Such a state has only weak interaction among the blocks, shown by thin lines.

If the external object is observed with attention, then the image's meaning can be determined. This state is to evaluate, passively, the impact of the image that may affect life either positively or negatively, at present or in the future. This is the process of acquiring images to enrich the image inventory. Most of the information required for daily life is acquired by such observations. The image includes interpersonal relationships, quality of the objects beneficial for life, clever action to take advantage of a situation, and so on. Humans learn life skills in this state. Yet this process is associated with no action. The SELF is like a student in the classroom. Sense of the SELF exists as a recipient of images as shown in figure 2.15.1(b).

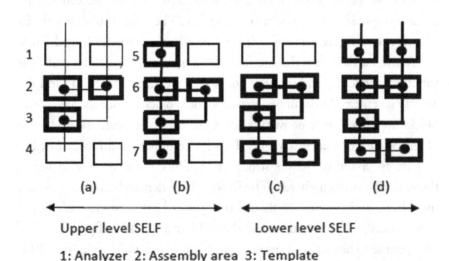

(a)   (b)   (c)   (d)

Upper level SELF   Lower level SELF

1: Analyzer 2: Assembly area 3: Template
4:association area 5: Action decode area 6: Action
control area 7: Deep area

Figure 2.15.1 Location of the SELF creating activity

Often, one is entirely isolated from the outside world and is looking into one's own mind, searching for an image, trying to find an image's meaning, or contemplating a plan for the future. In this state, the images stored in the brain, or their combination or modification, emerge one after the other, and some of them have a positive or negative impact on life. Then some bodily sense is felt along with sensation. The emotion is either positive or negative. Although no physical action is taken, the body prepares for the eventuality, and that often makes one anxious and uncomfortable. This is the time when the person feels a strong sense of SELF. This is a useful time to review one's life and one's thoughts. This is an entirely closed state driven by the existing images, shown in figure 2.15.1(c). In this state, if the SELF hits on a previously overlooked risk image, a depressive or even a panic state emerges.

If the incoming image affects life, then all the functional blocks are active, and the body is strongly subjected to the control of the SELF. In this state, some action must be taken, as shown in figure 2.15.1(d). This is a critical state that affects one's own life. Sense of the SELF is strongly felt since the action must be taken, and this action must be successful. The SELF is responsible for his or her own welfare. The active functional blocks of each case of figure 2.15.1(a)–(d) are shown by the boxes with thick lines.

Active human life is the alternating emergence of these states and their variations. States (a) and (b) have no, or only weak, passive SELF, and the activity is centered in the upper-area functional blocks. Since the lower-level blocks are either quiet or weakly active, sensation is weak and the sense of the SELF's existence is vague. This is the upper machine-area SELF. The states (c) and (d) have a strong SELF. Since the lower level is active, the sensation is intensely felt. The strong SELF demands all the resources mobilized, and because of this, this is not a healthy state. This is the evolutionarily old, original form of the SELF of animals. In figure 2.15.1, if the upper-level blocks are more active than the lower-level blocks, the SELF is more rational. If the lower-level blocks are more active, the SELF is more emotional and less rational. The deepest-level functional blocks where the activity reaches are the root of the image, which determines the character of the SELF.

Ironically, the SELF-less state (a) is the healthiest state. This may sound strange for those who assign high prestige to the SELF as the executioner of free will, but close observation shows that the SELF was created to defend our own body and life. Competition in modern society is not a great feature. Endless progress by competition only leads us to hell because all the competitors try to use up the available resources that the habitat has to offer. High culture is created by every society member's idle curiosity, disengaged from unlimited competition and exploitation.

2.16 Bus Structure

In the following discussions, I frequently refer to the functional block connection media called *bus*. *Bus* is a term in systems engineering, and it usually means a set of conducting wires to which many signals are fed and from which many signals are derived. Processors usually have a set of such conducting wires. In a 32-bit microprocessor, the number of lines of the set is thirty-two, to accommodate the complete set of data. I use this term in my work, but the structure of the internal image bus, or any bus in the brain, is significantly different from that of an electronic processor's bus. A neuron circuit bus is a structure made up of a set of connected neurons. A neuron is a unidirectional signal path, and a bus line is a serially connected structure of several neurons. A neuron bus line is a unidirectional signal path buried in the neuron logic gates and the memory elements.

The internal image bus is a set of structures, each of which carries a single image element. A vision image bus is a set of all the varieties of vectors, rotations by angle, color specifications, pen-up instructions, and so on. A language channel bus carries the whole variety of phonemes and accents. Since the set of lines includes all varieties of a single data type, the set still deserves to be called a bus. In systems engineering terms, bus is a communication medium where all the associated activities congregate and interact. In an electronic system's bus, the signals can go from any source to any destination. In the internal image bus, the signal circulates unidirectionally (assembly area, to scratch pad, to template, to action-control area, and back to assembly area). The bus is quite wide since the number of a complete set of image elements is large. Any phoneme bus of a language channel is fifty to one hundred lines wide, and the vector bus is much wider than that.

Excitation of a bus line indicates existence of the image element in the presently engaged image. Suppose that the neurons between the beginning, A, and the ending, Z, of a bus line belong to a single functional block and that the block does not execute any operation of the image. Then A's excitation reaches Z unaltered. If I trace the signal from Z upstream, the connection is a maze with dead ends, yet as I try all the possible paths, I reach location A. If some signal processing is executed, the signal tracing back reaches some other bus line. For instance, if the entire image is rotated 45 degrees, the signal tracing reaches the bus line located 45 degrees from the angle. A set of such bus lines close a loop by going through the assembly area, the scratch pad, the template, and the action-control area and then back to the assembly area, while the data is processed at each block by connecting and disconnecting the logic circuit and memory from the bus lines. This is the internal image bus structure.

2.17   Bus and Connection Structure of Blocks

I showed signals and basic connections among the functional blocks in the diagram in section 2.14, using the vision channel as the model. Many of the connecting lines in figure 2.14.1 are a set of lines making up a bus. A set of three buses (B, B'), (V, V', V''), and (M) connect blocks as shown in figure 2.17.1. The bus begins at the image sensors that are the pair of eyes, the left eye and the right eye. Images from the eyes are in pixel map format. The left and right eye images are combined into a single image. The combined image is in the memory layer that I call the light screen. Each memory cell holds a pixel, like a digital TV image. The map of pixels is carried by bitmap bus B to the image analyzer. First, let's consider a black-and-white image to explain the function of a visual image bus.

By the analyzer, the bitmap image is first converted to the format comprehensible by the brain. This is a line drawing, assembled from vectors and arcs, as I discussed in section 2.13. The first step is to convert the pixel bitmap image to a line drawing. Why a line drawing? If you are asked to draw your house on paper, you make its line drawing. What the brain can recognize is the object's shape, that is, its line drawing. The drawing is broken down into a sequence of vectors and arcs, which the brain's circuits are able to handle. Breaking down of the line drawing into vectors and arcs, and their reassembly into the element's sequence to reproduce the line drawing, is carried out jointly by the logic of the analyzer and of the assembly area. The sequential excitation of vectors and arcs goes through the scratch pad, template, and action-control area and back to the assembly area, thereby closing the loop.

Going around the loop, bidirectional communication of functional blocks is possible by using the unidirectional loops. This is a peculiar feature of a neural logic circuit bus. Each vector-arc excitation is carried by a line or lines of bus V as shown in figure 2.17.1. Bus V (an internal image bus) carries the vector-arc sequence that is able to reconstruct the line drawing. Some of the vectors are pen-up vectors that are needed to move the pen location to different part of the drawing. This is because most, if not all, line drawings cannot be drawn by a single continuous pen stroke. A pen-up vector is specified by excitation of one of the character bus lines and is followed by the vector bus line excitation. The set of all the possible vectors, the set of all the possible rotations by specified angles, and the set of all the characters required to specify any line drawing, such as pen-up, arc specification, color designation, and blob indication, make the internal image bus V. These are referred as vector bus, rotation bus, and character bus, respectively. They make the internal image bus V of figure 2.17.1. I apologize if you consider that the material I present here and later may involve too much detail. Yet such detail is necessary to understand the complex brain by designing it.

The vectors and arcs making up the line drawing are sent out to the output channel from the action-control area. In order to interface the high-speed internal image signal to the low-speed actuator, low-speed internal image bus V' is set up at the output of the action-control area (section 2.31). Bus V' carries the image signals to the action-decoding area, where the image signals are converted to the muscle constriction and dilation signals of the actuator. The signals are sent to the actuator by bus M. There is one M bus for each actuator (hands, legs, face, etc.).

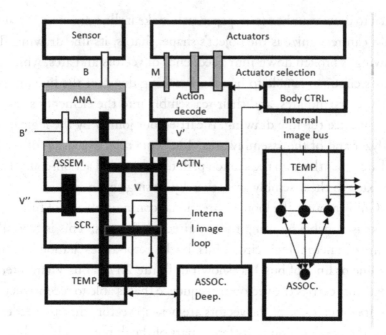

Figure 2.17.1 Bus and connection structure of
the functional model of the brain

The scratch pad is a large temporary template where a composite image consisting of several template images is assembled. The scratch pad works as a large canvas on which the assembly area *draws* pictures. The internal image bus is doubled by V'' for efficient image processing. The extra bus V'' is connected to the internal image bus by way of the assembly area, when the scratch pad image is sent out.

The assembly area and the analyzer often execute a joint operation, and for that purpose, the second bitmap, bus B', which connects the two blocks, carries the bitmap signals. This feature is required to repair an image corrupted by too many steps of image manipulation by sending it back to the analyzer to reformat.

Connection from the template to the association area is random and bidirectional. *Random connection* is a logic designer's technical term. It means that the connection can be made from any source to any destination. Any template neuron can be connected to its identifier depending on the condition of the connection formation. Connection from the identifier back to the template is also random connection, and so is identifier-identifier connection. This free connection capability is the working mechanism of the lower-level processor P_2 of section 1.20. This random connection capability was inherited from the archaic architecture of the deep area, but explosive development of the association area took advantage of it and created the powerful lower-level processor P_2, which upgraded the apelike animal brain to the human brain. The scratch pad is a part of the template, but its image does not make an identifier. The image held there is always temporary and is seldom kept permanently in the brain. If you see some object and never focus on it, its temporary image is kept on the scratch pad.

2.18   Vision Channel Bus

The functional diagram of the vision channel of section 2.17 must be able to display any line drawing. By considering what is required to draw any image, the types of signals included in the internal image bus can be determined. First, all varieties of vectors up to a certain length that cover the vision frame, and the rotation of ±360 degrees, must be supplied by the vector and rotation bus, respectively. Then, by considering how to use them to build a line drawing, the signals that must be carried by the character bus are determined.

First I consider the line drawing of figure 2.18.1(a). If this figure is drawn starting from point S as shown in figure 2.18.1(a) and following steps 1 to 6, then line 7 is not accessible by the continuous stroke. A pen-up vector **x** is required to shift the pen to point J, and then segment 7 is drawn as shown in figure 2.18.1(b). A pen-up vector is also required in order to close the template loop. Such special instructions are carried by the lines of the character bus. The pen-up line is excited before vector **x** excitation. Pen-up instruction is required since even a line drawing that can be drawn by a single stroke may not be formatted by the automatic element extraction process of the analyzer and the assembly area by taking the advantage. End-of-template specification is required in the character bus, which is similar to pen-up vector specification.

In figure 2.18.1(c), suppose that lines 1, 2, and 3 must be drawn in green and that lines 4, 5, and 6 must be drawn in black. Each green segment must be preceded by excitation of a green-color line of the character bus. In the same figure, if the triangle Δ123 must be painted in green, the instruction to the SELF is as follows: Excitation of vector sequence 1, 2, 3 is preceded and followed by excitations of a pair of the character bus lines that set up a pair of brackets (1, 2, 3). The color specification is placed before the parentheses (...). The texture of a feature (such as crosshatch) is specified similarly.

Some line drawing includes repetition of element image A of figure 2.18.1(d). This drawing is retained in the brain's memory with the element A and the number of repetition, 4. Similar to figure 2.18.1(c), excitation of a character bus line sets up a bracket and represents the image like (A), preceded by specification of the number. This scheme works even if the number is specified qualitatively, like *a few* or *many*. A repetitive image such as a railroad track is retained by this shorthand. Figure 2.18.1(e) shows how the image of an arc is retained. At point P, vector **c** points to the center O of rotation. Vector **c**'s direction is reversed, and it is rotated by angle $\angle\theta$ in the clockwise direction.

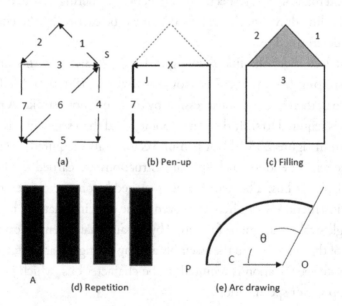

Figure 2.18.1 Elements of a character bus

In this operation, the arc specification that is vector **c**'s reversal and rotation, is specified by the excitation of a character bus line, followed by vector **c** and rotation bus line excitation. As observed from these examples, the character bus excitation controls the special feature of line drawing. From the nature of line drawing, the internal image bus must have the vector bus, the rotation bus, and the character bus. The three bus structures go through the assembly area, scratch pad, template area, and action-control area and back to the assembly area. They execute the display of any internally visible images. The character bus also carries a mishmash digital signal that is required for image processing and body control. Some of these bus lines continue down all the way through the association area to the deep area to transmit some housekeeping signals. In the language channel, the character bus line has an important role (section 2.25).

The language channel is operated by a phoneme bus and a character bus. The character bus carries information like accent, pitch, and pronunciation details that characterize the person's speech. The role of the character bus is especially significant to distinguish similar but not identical phonemes of different languages.

2.19   Vision Channel Bus Cross Section

Our eyes have two dimensionally distributed optical sensors, similar to any video camera. An image is projected on the array, and by each sensor, the *pixel* image element is converted to pulse intensity signal. Each signal carries information of luminosity and color. The sum total of all the signals from the array specifies the image. Different from video camera pixels, an image's pixels are carried by so many lines all at once to the analyzer. Each line is the axon of the signal-source neuron, whose structure is shown in section 3.02. The set of lines is the input image bus B of section 2.17. Its cross section is shown in figure 2.19.1(a). Although the central area of the vision field has more optical sensors than the periphery, I simplified my model to have a uniform rectangular grid array of light sensors. This bus *B* of section 2.17 is arranged in the rectangular vision field of figure 2.19.1(a). This is natural to the human sense of vision since we feel that the vision field is rectangular, long in the left-right direction. The human vision field is 160 degrees horizontally and 130 degrees vertically.

Prior to extraction of the shape of the object, the image size is normalized to the shape and size of the subjectively felt vision field. The visible area of the large night sky and a small acorn are made to fit in the same-size rectangle. Sizing is carried out automatically by the focal length adjustment of the eyes' lenses. Bus B of section 2.17 carries the already sized image. A visible image that is properly sized is then converted to a line drawing consisting of vectors, arcs, blobs, and a few other characteristics.

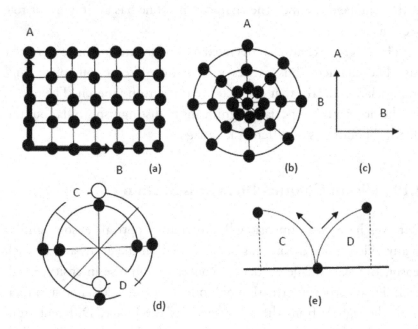

Figure 2.19.1 Vision channel bus structure

Vectors and rotations used in the line drawing are convenient if they are arranged in a cross section as shown in figure 2.19.1(b) and 2.19.1(c) for vectors, and figure 2.19.1(d) and 2.19.1(e) for rotations. If arranged this way, where vectors **a** and **b** of figure 2.19.1(c) exist in the bus cross section, figure 2.19.1(b) is identified easily. Similarly, rotation by a certain angle is indicated by the rotation bus cross section shown in figure 2.19.1(d), where clockwise and counterclockwise rotation are arranged on different circles. Vectors and arcs extracted by the analyzer make a sequence of jumps from location to location of figure 2.19.1(b) and (c), occasionally jumping to the character bus location to indicate a special operation like pen-up. This jumping sequence is the internally recognizable image information. I note here that the bus line arrangement of figure 2.19.1 shows functional structure, rather than actual physical structure, to make the system's structure easy to understand. If the functional relations are kept, the actual spatial arrangement need not be so geometrically regular as shown in the figure.

2.20   Vector-Arc Extraction from Visible Image

Conversion of a bitmap image to the image built from a sequence of vectors and arcs requires a complicated logic. I had not been able to produce a satisfactory design in my earlier works. Since the design of this functional block does not affect the mechanism of self-consciousness, I put no weight on it before, but that is still a missing part of the human machine design. If the self-conscious machine is actually designed using electronic hardware, the function should be executed by a general-purpose processor-controlled digital circuit. As for the real human brain model, I provide my latest design, which is the simplest and the most realistic.

Behind the photoreceptor of the eyes, there are layers of bitmap image memory that are part of the analyzer. A feature of these memory layers, called the light screens, is the capability to maintain the alignment of the image in the rectangular image frame of section 2.19, even if the pair of eyes are not aligned horizontally. Then the light screen layers must be able to rotate the incoming image. Similarly, the layer must be able to shift any image horizontally and vertically. The two capabilities can be used to extract vector-arc elements from the bitmap image.

First, the properly scaled bitmap image is converted to a line drawing. This is the operation to retain only the high-contrast boundary pixels. I describe this operation in section 3.20.

Figure 2.20.1(a) shows a dipper-like object's line drawing, having conspicuous corners, *A, B, C,* and *Z,* projected on a light screen. It consists of an array of active pixels shown by closed circles in the figure. The open circle in the figure, *O,* is the reference center of the vector-arc extraction logic. Referring to this center, the working light screen image can be moved in horizontal and vertical directions. It can also be rotated, using this point as the pivot. Before extraction, the line drawing is placed in the *working light screen,* and as the extraction proceeds, the extracted part is erased. When all the pixels are erased, the extraction is over.

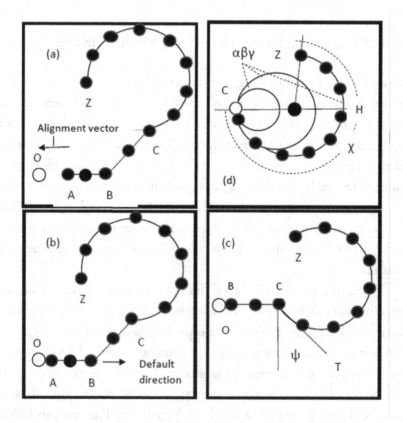

Figure 2.20.1 Process of extracting vectors and arcs

The original bitmap image is shifted so that the starting point A is moved to point O by the vectors shown in figure 2.20.1(a). The image becomes as shown in figure 2.20.1(b). The extraction logic at location O counts the number of pixel points from A to B by moving the entire image to the left while checking if they are aligned on the default horizontal line. As the counting reaches point B, and if there is no more active pixel point in the direction, the length of vector **ab** is determined. It makes 0 degrees to the reference horizontal axis. The vector is sent to the assembly area by exciting this vector's specifying line in the vector bus, and section AB is erased from the *working* screen.

By counting the number of pixels between A and B by moving the entire line drawing, point O is now moved to point B of figure 2.20.1(b). The extraction logic tests where the next pixel point is. This is carried out by an exhaustive search of the active pixels in the neighborhood of point B. As the next point is found on the line that makes a 45-degree angle to the horizontal direction, the image is rotated by the angle clockwise around point O (that is, now point B) to make the image of figure 2.20.1(c). The angle of rotation need not be determined; the image is rotated until the line BC's pixels align on the default horizontal direction. The angle of rotation is retained by a special light screen that rotates along with the working light screen to keep the cumulative angle of rotation. The number of pixel points on the horizontal line BC of figure 2.20.1(c) is counted, and the vector length is determined. Then vector **bc**, which makes an angle 45 degrees to the original image's horizontal direction, is sent to the assembly area, and section BC is erased from the image of the *working* light screen. Then point C is now on the point O as shown in figure 2.20.1(d).

Now the image element extraction process meets an arc. First, nearby pixel points are exhaustively tested to confirm that there are no three consecutive pixel points in the same direction. Then the character bus line indicating arc is excited. Referring to figure 2.20.1(c), the tangent T of the arc at point C is determined by connecting point C to the nearest neighbor pixel point and by stretching the line. Angle $\angle\psi$, made by the tangent T and the vertical direction of the present image frame, is shown in the figure. The image is rotated by angle $\angle\psi$ to make the tangent vertical up-down direction. Tangent T to the arc at point C is now perpendicular to a bisecting line of the arc, that is, line *CH*. This is the step to finding where the arc's center of rotation is.

Next, in figure 2.20.1(d), the center of the arc must be somewhere on the horizontal line *CH*. Several circles α, β, γ, …, passing point *C*, having their centers on line *CH* and having various radii, are tested to find the best fit to the image. The parameters to be determined are radius *r* and the arc's spanning angle $\angle \chi$ of figure 2.20.2. To determine the parameters *r* and χ, the image is moved temporarily from the reference point *C* to the trial center locations α, β, γ, … on the line *CH*, and the image is converted to polar coordinate at each temporary reference point. There, the pixels on the circle are examined to find a match to any circle α, β, γ, … If some pixels close to point *C* are outside the circle, the temporary reference point is moved to right, and if they are inside, it is moved to left. In figure 2.20.2, circle β matches the image. Then *r* is determined by the distance *C*β, and χ is the angle where the image pixel goes out from circle β at point Z.

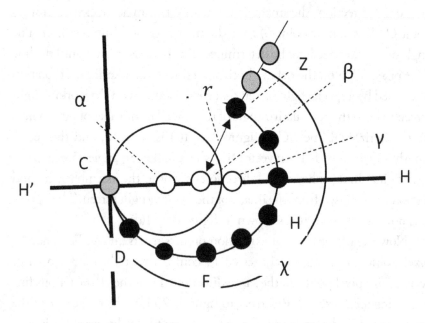

Figure 2.20.2 Figure 2.20.1(d) enlarged

The vector having the direction of line *CH* (referenced to the *original horizontal direction* of figure 2.20.1[a]) and length

r is sent to the assembly area by a vector bus line excitation, and then angle $\angle\chi$ is sent by the rotation bus line. Then, going back to the Cartesian coordinate referenced to point C, the reference point is shifted to point Z to continue further vector-arc extraction.

The vector-arc extraction process requires that the incoming image be stable at least for some time. If the image changes rapidly, the extraction logic circuit issues an error signal. This signal indicates that there is a rapidly moving object in the image frame. Then control over the eye direction is exercised to maintain better stability of the image.

As I have shown here, the vector-arc extraction is a messy signal processing. Yet we are able to sense a fine straight line and a round circle because the original image from the sensors is cleaned up before being sensed. This is a crucial feature of vision. If the brain recognized every detail of the object as it is, there would be no straight line or perfect circle sensed by the brain.

How realistic is this design? In a real animal brain, these functions are executed by cascaded and heavily interacting blocks (there are about ten of them), each of which extracts the specific feature of image such as angle of vector, color, and motion of the image element. To copy them directly on the model is not possible. Since the structure was built by evolution, the design may not be the optimum as the present human mind thinks. Here is one of the liberties of model making. Since my objective is to create the model that reproduces internally observed images properly, it is not necessary to copy the real brain, as I discussed in section 1.06. My model is like the second sourced microprocessor, which is functionally the same but not the same in the hardware structures. To reproduce self-consciousness, such a model is sufficiently realistic.

2.21 Coordinate System Conversion

A visible image can be registered either to the Cartesian coordinate system, which is convenient to move an image, or to the polar coordinate system, by which rotation and scaling are easy. Since a visible image analyzer requires both moving and rotating, conversion between the Cartesian and the polar coordinate system must be simple and fast. Mathematically, this conversion is a complex linear transformation with numerical coefficients and interpolations, which the brain cannot execute. Yet because this is a reregistering of the active pixel bits' coordinates between the two coordinate systems, there is a *quick and dirty* method of conversion, shown in figure 2.21.1. Since the origin of the polar coordinate is a special point that works as the pivot of image scaling and rotation, the point is superposed to the point of reference of the Cartesian coordinate by moving the image horizontally andaaa vertically. Then the pixel point registered to the Cartesian coordinate grid is transferred all at once to the nearest point in the polar coordinate web. In figure 2.21.1, closed squares show the Cartesian coordinate grids and the open circles show the polar coordinate web. Overlapping circles show the matched locations, so activation is directly transferred. As for nonoverlapping locations, the polar coordinate location receives the pixel of the nearest Cartesian coordinate location, which is shown by the arrow sign in the figure.

In this operation, the pixel points in the polar coordinate system are crowded near the center of rotation and become successively sparse as the distance from the origin increases, as shown in the figure. This creates image distortion by conversion. To minimize distortion, pixel density must be uniform in the Cartesian coordinate system. Then, since a different number of pixels exist on the concentric circles of the polar coordinate, the circular shift registers used to rotate the image must be clocked at different rates (more details insection 3.17). This is an impossibly complex operation. An alternative design of an image-rotating circuit without this complication is shown in section 3.21. This accurate circuit is used in the analyzer and assembly area of my model.

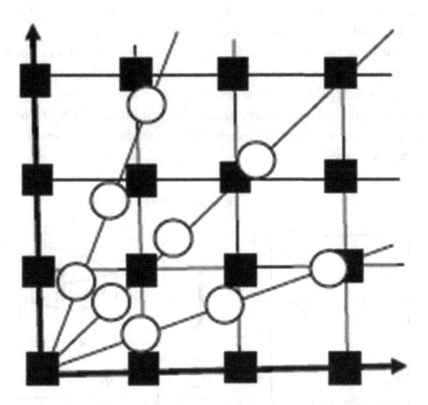

Figure 2.21.1 Cartesian to/from polar coordinate transformation

The coordinate system conversion is bidirectional. Polar-to-Cartesian coordinate conversion can be executed by the same scheme. By this conversion, addition and subtraction of vectors **a** and **b** can be carried out easily in the Cartesian coordinate.

2.22 Structure of a Landscape Image

I close my eyes and imagine a simple object such as a book or a coffee cup. I can see a fairly accurate image of the object behind my closed eyes. Yet if I try to imagine a section of the street I live on, something strange happens. Even in a small section of the street, there are several objects. As I try to see the entire section, what I see is an image made of colored blobs that fill up the image frame. I live in a heavily wooded area, and the dominant color in summer is gray pavement and tree trunks and green leaves of trees and bushes. I first see the image consisting of the five blobs colored gray and green as shown in figure 2.22.1(a). There exist several small yet conspicuous objects as shown in figure 2.22.1(b). I can see one of them at a time. The landscape image consists of a coarse image and detailed images, each of which carries a certain special character. This is also the case for small, yet complex images.

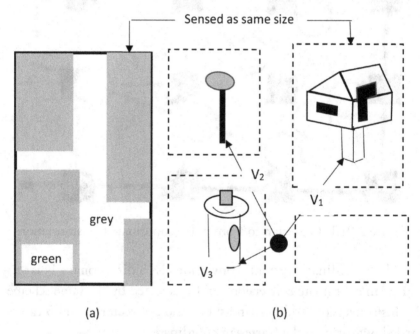

(a)   (b)

Figure 2.22.1 Structure of composite image

If I just try to see the landscape as a whole, I see figure 2.22.1(a). This image is closely integrated; I cannot rip off one blob and replace it by the mailbox. If I try to do that, I feel a confusing sense of eye movement with my brain struggling to assemble the composite of figure 2.22.1(a) and 2.22.1(b). Yet if I focus on the mailbox, it emerges smoothly from one of the green blobs that make up the image frame. As I focus on the image, I can see its details—the box, door, flag, and support—quite accurately. The mailbox now occupies the entire vision frame, which displayed the colored blobs before. Also I can focus on any part of the mailbox. Then its red flag occupies the entire vision frame. This is the same for any object, until the magnified image carries no more detail. While doing this zooming, the rest of the images, and the coarse image made of colored blobs, vanishes. I can see the entire frame, or only one object in the frame at a time. If I try to see two objects at a time, I feel a confusing sense of seeing one object and then the other by moving my line of sight.

The object's spatial location information, specified by vectors v_1, v_2, and v_3 of figure 2.22.1(b), is held in my memory. As I go over all the element images in the frame one by one, I feel my line of sight moving as their placement vectors specify. I feel the movement of my eyes to see the particular direction of the element. This subtle feeling enhances the sense of reality of seeing the landscape. As I do this, and then as I see the overall colored blobs, I feel as if I have seen everything in the scene completely, and every detail. Some simple landscapes consist of colored blobs only. My memory of Ireland is gray sky over the Atlantic and sparkling green meadows below. A visible internal image is never made to reproduce the real scene; it is made to satisfy the sense of reality.

This peculiar experience shows how a visual image is constructed in the brain. Simple images that can be assembled from vectors and arcs are retained as line drawings with color specifications. More complex images such as landscapes are retained in two ways. The first is by the dominant features, consisting of only several colored blobs, and the second is by the details, consisting of a set of element images associated with their placement vectors. Vectors place the element images properly in the image frame. It is interesting to observe that the complexities of the colored blobs and of each element image are about the same. Both consist of about the same number of vectors and arcs, up to twenty or thirty. It appears that my brain is unable to display an image beyond that level of complexity. As for the placement vectors, any image can be the reference. This means that the brain is executing vector addition or subtraction unconsciously when I observe one element image and then jump to the next. It appears that the set of placement vectors are kept separately, to place the element images properly in the frame.

The composite structure of a landscape image reveals a peculiar feature of the visible image memory construction. First, the image analyzer appears to recognize the conspicuous element images from the entire image frame. The brain is consciously identifying each element's images, referring to the already memorized image inventory. The element images carry the detailed structural information to which their placement vectors are attached to make the overall spatial structure. Then the analyzer adds the dominant color information to the spatial information. This is an efficient way to handle a complex landscape image. Composite image analysis is not an automatic, directional (eyes → memory) operation. First, it identifies all the element images, then places them properly, and then adds the overall feature.

There are other interesting features. The overall image consisting of colored blobs, and the element images, are internally observed without scaling the size. Another interesting feature is that any object that is not visible from the present viewpoint (some objects are hidden behind the others) is also internally visible. Obviously, such features were observed at different times from different directions and then integrated into the composite image. The image is actually a fabricated three-dimensional image. My living space information (space structure immediately close to my present body), which is unconsciously acquired, is similar to this image. Still another interesting feature is that the element image may not be the one that I actually observed in the scene. In figure 2.22.1(b), the fire hydrant is practically the same shape in the U.S. and in Japan. I saw it when I was still in Japan, and I may have placed the image in the landscape frame. Moreover, a standard object such as a fire hydrant may even be memorized not by its visible image but by its identification, or name. When the image is constructed, the name, a language image, is converted to a visible image. This is likely; if I recall any famous books, I may not remember the color of the cover, but I do securely remember the title and the author's name. If I imagine the first page of the *New York Times*, I cannot write its ornately printed character, but the title *New York Times* is securely remembered. Then the detailed image may be structured as a simplified composite of placement vectors and names of the element images. This is possible because vision and language channels are very closely connected together by the image's identifiers (section 2.25).

2.23 Architecture Including All the Senses

So far, I have shown the brain function of vision. Yet humans have five senses: vision, voice and language, contact, and two chemical senses of smell and taste. The SELF engages with all these senses. The brain's architecture handling them is basically similar to the vision channel. Sense channels other than vision lack some features of the vision channel, either because the development history is short (language channel) or the images are simple (chemical image channels). The functional block diagram including all the senses is shown in figure 2.23.1.

The architecture of vision, voice, and language channels is basically similar since the language channel developed recently, when *Homo sapiens* emerged. I suspect that the channel is an add-on to the vision channel. This feature is naturally expected from what I discuss in section 2.25. Since both channels handle complex hierarchical information at high speeds, they require similar hardware architecture. I believe that the language channel developed at the periphery of the existing vision channel by copying its basic architecture.

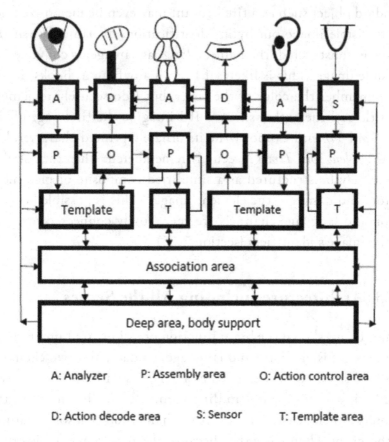

A: Analyzer   P: Assembly area   O: Action control area

D: Action decode area   S: Sensor   T: Template area

Figure 2.23.1 Functional diagram including all the senses

Sensors of the body surface accept simple graphic images (such as braille) that merge with the vision channel. The image handling capability of the body's surface is from the archaic body architecture, even before eyes and vision channels emerged (section 2.10). Only certain areas of the body, such as fingertips or the palm, have a high sensor density in order to sense fine images. Surface image is independent from body surface location and is also independent from the direction of the image, but it is quite sensitive to the order of stroke to draw the image. It appears that the sense does not have memory to keep the already drawn part for reference—no equivalent of the light screen of the vision channel. From the brain hardware design, this is naturally expected; the sensors are spread out all over the body surface, so there is no proper location or direction to set up temporary memory such as the light screen. Instead, the first stroke of the image is used as the reference, and the second, third, ... strokes are set at their proper locations. The reconstructed image is sent to merge with the vision channel, from the contact sense channel's assembly area to the vision channel's temporary memory. The assembly area provides the image, whose scale and orientation are not properly set, and this image is temporarily stored in the vision channel scratch pad. After that, the vision channel identifies the image.

The body surface sensors carry contact information such as itch, temperature, pressure, pain, and some chemical senses (such as strong acid). To process such signals, the channel branches at the assembly area, and the nongraphic image signals proceed to the association area through their own template as shown in figure 2.23.1. Excitation of this template creates a sensation of pain, itching, temperature, etc. Such information is always associated with body location information. The sense of body location includes even some inaccessible internal organs like the intestines and the heart. The image of the body's state (like itch or pain) and the body location information join in the association area, and the two are sent out to the vision channel to take action if necessary.

The chemical sense channel is the simplest. It retains the original archaic design from the primitive animal to modern humans. Chemical image is peculiar: it is conditioned in the early age of life and is closely associated with emotional state. The sense is more acute in lower-level animals. This may be possible because the sensor is molecule-type specific and only a few molecules can trigger the sense. Evolutionarily low-level bees seem to have this ability already. If their queen dies, a beekeeper's practice is to buy a new queen and install her. The replacement queen comes in a small cage, so that the worker bees get used to the smell of the new queen. Otherwise, she is considered as an invader, and stung and killed right away. These observations indicate that the center of the sense of smell is closely associated with the archaic self-defense mechanism.

One feature common to all the senses is the reflex function. This protective capability survived all throughout our evolutionary history, because of its high-speed body protection. Yet reflex is more involved. Any quick action that is executed unconsciously is a feature of reflex. If I try to avoid a projectile, I change my body position to avoid the object. While doing so, I also avoid falling down. This is the action that includes the brain in addition to the spinal cord, yet this is a quick, unconscious operation.

The composite architecture shows how humans learn by experience. If two sense channel inputs make their template and identifier at the same time, the pair of identifiers are connected by their activity. If the one is a visible object's image and the other is a word, children learn the name of the object. This type of learning also makes mistakes. A fellow asked an indigenous man, "What is this animal?" The answer was "I don't know" in the latter's language. The animal is now called *kangaroo*.

2.24 Image Projected on the Body's Surface

Our human body surface has sensors to detect contact, heat, pain, and other senses. Since the sensors are distributed all over the body surface, it is possible to sense any point on the body surface or an image projected on it. The sense of recognizing the body surface location is very precise. If a foreign object were to penetrate my skin, I am able to direct my fingers exactly to the location and pull the object out. This is possible even if I cannot see the location directly. This capability must be inherited from the most primitive animals, which did not even have the sense of vision. This is the primary defense of the body.

Some sensors originally distributed over the entire body surface are gathered together at certain locations like the fingertips, thereby creating high-resolution sensing capability. The rest of the body surface has a sparse sensor density. What is interesting is that if an image is drawn on the body surface by a pointed object, the sharp turn of the stroke is sensed clearly. The sensors are sensitive to *differential* features of a spatial pattern. Yet the contact sense does not provide as clear an image as expected from the sensor density. If a person is writing a character on someone else's body surface, the part of the character that has been written on the body surface is not precisely memorized. An equivalent of the light screen in the vision channel (which retains the written part of the visible character) does not seem to exist, and that makes character recognition hard. The same problem is experienced if a Chinese character is written by a laser pointer on a screen so slowly that the light screen loses the memory. Such a slow operation defeats the short retention time of the light screen.

Graphics on the skin surface are used in secret deal making at auctions, such as at a Japanese fish or vegetable market. The dealers write symbols on each other's palms and in this way set the price. Such images or symbols are not registered to a precise location on the body, but they can be recognized as images carrying definite meaning. For such communication, the image on the body surface must be regarded as independent of the direction and size.

For this kind of communication method to be effective, a pattern created on the body surface all at once, such as setting the owner's brand on livestock by a hot iron, is useless. Rather, the pattern must be created by the agreed-upon order to make its identification easy. Chinese calligraphy relies on this feature. By observing the ordered brushstroke, I can read artistically modified ideograms. If the pattern is drawn by definite order, vector-arc extraction and pattern identification can be executed in a short time, and the chance of making an error is reduced.

This is also the case when reading handwritten Chinese characters. The ideogramic characters have a certain rigid order to the writing, and how the writer wrote the character is immediately obvious by observing the pen strokes. This appears to be mysterious to Westerners. Once a friend of mine who knew printed Chinese characters asked me how I could *decipher* handwriting. He pointed to the character *Buddha*. I asked him to write the character in his way. He produced the character correctly, but his writing order was not the traditionally agreed-upon order.

2.25 Language Channel

Our language input-output channel is the most recent development. It is not certain if the Neanderthals had language capability. To investigate how language developed on the already existing vision channel is suggestive. The structures of the assembly area and the areas below the language channel are quite similar to those of the vision channel. Both vision and language channels process hierarchical data structures, and therefore they need a similar architecture. This similarity suggests that the brain duplicated the hardware of the vision channel to create the spoken language channel. Since the sound image analyzer had been continuously developing from the mammal to the ape level, the new development was acquisition of language image memory, the assembly area logic for sentence construction, and a significant upgrade to voice generation by the vocal chords. Since the action-control area and the language analyzer are much simpler than the vision channel, it was not difficult to make a simpler twin of the vision channel.

Since a language image is the single time sequence of phonemes, the task of the analyzer to convert spoken language to the elements, phonemes, can be executed by way of paralleled pattern-matching detectors. There is memory to retain some phonemes of the immediate past, an equivalent of the light screen. Any word's template must have a starting point marker (section 3.23). The template also requires a space indicator at the end of a word's phoneme sequence. These markers are provided by excitation of a character bus line (section 3.23). If the template is excited, it sends out phonemes from the start marker to the space marker and then halts. The internal image bus of the language channel consists of the phoneme bus and the character bus. The basic difference from the vision channel is that the elements, phonemes, carry no meaning. Words are the minimum elements carrying meaning. Since the language image is sent out as a single sequence, the words must be in the correct order.

How is the meaning of a word defined and sensed? The identifier of a word is connected to its visual or chemical image identifier, and the word's image must be made sensible internally. The importance of defining the meaning of a word cannot be overstated. The language channel alone cannot define any word's meaning, and this is the basic feature of the language channel. Figure 2.25.1 shows the language channel and its close association with the vision channel by the identifier connection. Except for the fixed-pattern message, the language channel cannot operate autonomously.

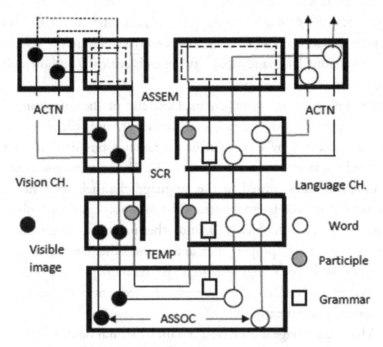

Figure 2.25.1 Sentence construction

Fixed-pattern examples are "How are you?" and "How much does this item cost?" Much of human communication has a fixed pattern. Often a sentence is constructed by shortcut, by inserting proper words into the set pattern. Donald Trump's "No one loves [whatever it is] more than I do" is such a pattern. The word or phrase he inserts depends on his convenience.

Figure 2.25.1, right side, shows how the language channel executes message delivery. Vision and language channels are closely coupled by the connection of the visible image identifier to the word image identifier. Sentence construction begins in the vision channel, whose images show concrete, recognizable objects and action. A language statement describes the intention of the SELF. The speaker's intention is first displayed in the vision channel. The SELF assembles the event's visible image, consisting of the actor, the action, the specifier, and the circumstance of the action. The set of images is first displayed and exercised in the vision channel and is then converted to a sentence by the identifiers' connections in the association area. A word image has the feature of an abstract image; that is, a single word identifier is connected to several visible image identifiers that exist in the association area. Therefore, language capability depends critically on how well the association area is developed.

For instance, the vision channel exercise of the intention of the speaker determines the participle of the words, and that is sent to the language channel by excitation of a character bus line, along with the word's image, as shown in figure 2.25.1. At the same time, the grammatical rules, stored in the language channel, are sent to the language channel's assembly area. The assembly area recognizes the subject (S), verb (V), object (O), and other parts of the sentence, puts them together in the proper order, and deposits them in the scratch pad to be sent out by speaking. The language channel's primary objective is interpersonal communication, so a constructed sentence is seldom kept memorized permanently.

A language image must have a certain structural rigidity for accurate communication. I need to show how the structure is set up in the assembly area. A statement must have the actor, the subject (S), the action, the verb (V), the object of action (O), the circumstance of the action, and the characters of each word, including adjectives and adverbs, in the proper order. Here, S and O are usually static images of a person or object. These images are kept in the brain as the action commands to reproduce their shape, such as eye directional control or picture drawing by finger. Element V is also an action. Then how are the images of S or O and V distinguished by the SELF? A simple answer is that the subject or object's static image is coded only as the action of a particular actuator like finger or eye directional control. The image of action V is coded as the entire body's action. The type of coding creates a different bodily sense between static nouns and dynamic verbs. The difference is effected by the structure of the visible image's memory. Figure 2.25.2 shows the structure of the template-identifier connection of static nouns like *apple*, dynamic nouns like *dance*, and dynamic verbs such as *walking* in the vision channel. This structural difference of the image memory guides the vision channel assembly area to identify the word's participle.

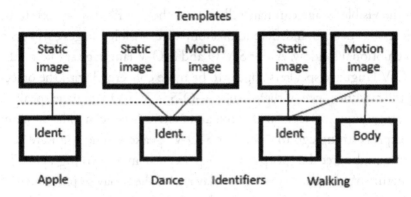

Figure 2.25.2 Structure of visible image memory

This information is carried by the character bus line excitation from the vision channel to the language channel. Participle identification by this mechanism is rather involved. Children seem to face a mental hurdle when asked to identify nouns representing dynamic action such as *dance*.

Sensing a language image is not just sensing the sound but also recognizing its meaning. Any language has a certain set of socially established statements used for greeting or casual conversation. These are sensed by matching the established pattern in the language channel. The rest of the language's images are recognized by converting the words of the sentence to visible images. Using a word-visible image identifier connection, the statement is converted to a visual image to be recognized and to a physically executable action by the listener. The vision channel and language channel are continuously cooperating. Such an operation affects the language image's character, especially when the statement contains the subtle shadow of emotion.

Languages of the world vary in structure. English is S-V-O, Ural-Altai language is S-O-V, and Ainu in Japan, and many Native American languages, is V-S-O or V-O-S. From my experience, the order reflects the character of the speaker. This is because sentence assembly begins in the vision channel by exercising visible images and is then transferred to the language channel. The purpose of the vision channel was originally for survival in the natural habitat, and the action controlled by the visible image can naturally reflect the SELF's disposition, to be aggressive, neutral, indifferent, or submissive. Visible images carry such an emotional shadow. As for S-V-O and S-O-V language speakers, the S-O-V language speakers appear to be more concerned with the object or the circumstance of their issues. V-O-S or V-S-O language speakers are, from my experience with Ainu and Native American folks, hesitant to express strong ego to S-V-O or S-O-V speakers. The Ainu are very gentle and agreeable people as I experienced in my young age. The structure of a language used every day molds the behavior pattern. This is because a statement's source is the visual image of an action. Some languages regularly omit the subject *I*, such as Polish. The impression I got from Germans and Poles may be related to this difference. In Germany, I hear *Ich* quite clearly. In Poland, usually I never hear *Ja*. That certainly affects their character.

2.26 Character of Language Image

A new image or concept must be communicated by language. Words are the minimum carriers of meaning, defined by the phoneme's sequence. Then there are many basic words to be learned. Speaking a language is much harder than learning picture drawing. The basic word's identifiers must be connected to some self-explanatory image's identifier (visible, chemical, or contact image) to create its meaning. The word's image becomes self-explanatory only if there are enough words whose meanings are well established in the brain.

Connection of word to visible image is such that one word's image is connected to many visible images. Each of these visible images is specified by an adjective attached to the word if it is a static image, and by an adverb if it is a dynamic image. If a statement is given using unmodified words, it carries an unspecified wide range of meanings or is illustrating an abstract concept.

Because of this nature of language image, words are convenient for representing abstract concepts and general relations of the concepts. This is the basic capability of the high-level thinking of the human mind. Abstract words are combined in various orders or hierarchies, and in this way more abstract concepts are created. This is the capability required in symbolic thinking. Language is convenient in expressing relations among abstract concepts in high-level thinking or in general thinking. The validity or rationality of such an artificially constructed language image is ensured by the syllogism.

Since a word can be combined with any other words freely in a sentence, any statement can be created automatically. Such a statement must be screened for its rationality by using syllogism or by artistic sense, and a new valuable image can be created. Scientific theory, poetry, and music are all created in a somewhat similar way. "Any material consists of atoms" was the statement by the Greek philosopher Democritus that created successively the concepts of molecules, atoms, nucleons, and quarks in physics. Poems are created by this mechanism also. Often, wide and subtle coverage of meanings of words creates poetic emotion that impresses the delicate human mind with an artistic quality. Reciting a poem and tasting its image requires imagination by the readers. A language image is easier for expressing emotion by the selection of the words, or by way of body language, than is a visual image.

Language's wide flexibility creates self-contradictory statements (section 6.03), an unending sequence of arguments, and logically contradicting statements. This is because of the unlimited flexibility of word connection. Another limitation of language is that it is not easy to describe multidimensionally connected images. To describe a road map by language is quite difficult.

2.27 Assembly Area and Dark Screen

The task of the assembly area is, jointly with the analyzer and scratch pad, to convert any image to useful form. The hardware structure of the assembly area is made of many layers of logic circuit, stacked between many memory layers. The internal image bus penetrates the logic and memory stack. The internal image bus goes to the scratch pad or the template area, makes an image memory (temporary or permanent, respectively) there, and then comes back to the assembly area via the action-control area. The assembly area logic executes image manipulation. While the operation is going on, the processed image may be sent out via the output channel from the action-control area. Such a half-processed image is stored in one of the assembly area's memory layers. Since the memory layers are in the brain's dark interior, I call them the *dark screen*.

In the vision channel assembly area, some automatic operation is carried out by using the genetically supplied hardware and instructions, such as shifting, rotating, and scaling the size. In the human brain, the assembly area operation repertoire includes extraction of certain specific features of the image. A variety of such features can be found by introspection. I observe many different visible images and try to sense which feature of any particular image is felt as special. Such features include (1) a point/line/plane symmetry, (2) repetition of the same feature, (3) Manhattan structure (all angles are 90 degrees), (4) topological structure (if there is a hole), and (5) some stem images (section 4.12). Such operations are automatic operations relying on the innate hardware and processing routines. The assembly area architecture allows for a programmed graphic operation. The logic blocks sandwiched between a pair of memory layers are basic image processors that are able to accept logic circuit configuration instruction from the template area via the internal image bus and are able to operate a sequence of instructions to the currently displayed image, as I discuss in sections 4.06 and 4.07. This is executed by using the hardware of the assembly area logic and dark screen memory, directed by the genetically provided instructions.

In spite of the programmed execution, what the innate hardware and instruction alone can do is rather limited. In any electronic data processor, its most sophisticated operation relies on the quality of the program written by the human programmer. To execute such a highly intelligent operation, automatic operation by the assembly area logic alone is not enough. Artificial intelligence is also no match for the human mind, because of the volume, quality, and relevance of the reference image memory. A significant advantage of the brain's architecture, that is, memory, processor, and input-output interface, all integrated by the internal image bus, is that the brain is able to send out any image. In this operation, the self-conscious subject SELF emerges (section 1.26), and then the sent-out image, that is now an outside image, becomes the object with which the SELF is able to work and make decisions or operations using the SELF's entire capability of handling the image. This is conscious image processing. This is a powerful feature of the human brain, something I call *conscious image processing.*

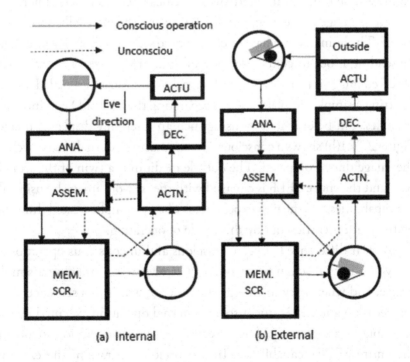

Figure 2.27.1 Two modes of conscious operation

The image send-out activity creates the SELF (section 1.26). Then the SELF is able to see itself and is free to modify it. This is a special feature that is not in the electronic data processor. The brain includes the role of its administrator and the programmer, because it is self-conscious. In sections 3.21 and 3.22, a template is cut into two pieces. To cut a template, it must be sent out, observed by the SELF, and then cut to pieces. Such an operation is impossible by the automatic internal operation, which I call *unconscious operation*. The brain's operation can be classified into conscious and unconscious operation. An important application of conscious image processing is to modify the elementary image's internal structure and make it a usable image for one's life (section 3.21). The brain can process only such information that can be properly formatted and stored in its memory.

The human brain is able to execute some simple conscious operations internally, not using paper and pencil outside. An image that is sent out and recognized by the SELF is often clear and detailed enough. Figure 2.27.1(a) shows an internally conscious operation. With internally conscious image processing, the SELF is seeing the internally observable image. The human brain has the capability to see a simple image internally by sending it out to control the line of sight of the eyes. The internally observed image is usually a simple image, but it is still an unloaded image. Splitting a simple template, such as separating the Star of David into two triangles, can be executed by using such an internally displayed image. Figure 2.27.1(b) shows a conscious operation using external media such as the image drawn on paper. The outside medium is a twin of the scratch pad, and the entire SELF is engaged with the sent-out image by using all the capabilities and the past experiences. The most sophisticated thinking by the brain is carried out by this mode of operation.

A clear difference between conscious and unconscious operation is felt when I try to change the order of strokes when drawing a simple image, and when I try to change the order of words in a sentence. The former is an automatic unconscious internal operation executed by the assembly area logic only. The latter is a conscious operation involving the entire SELF's capabilities. In a conscious operation, the existing unconscious operation is sidestepped, and the entire SELF's capabilities engage with the image that has been sent out. When the conscious operation is over, the processed image is taken in, and the unconscious processing may continue internally. Here is an interesting feature of human brain operation: to do the most involved operation, the image must be sent out, and is operated outside the brain. The most advanced brain operation is carried out outside the brain? This is really a curious feature of the human brain. While such an operation is going on, sometimes the entire assembly area capability is unloaded, especially if there is an intelligent partner.

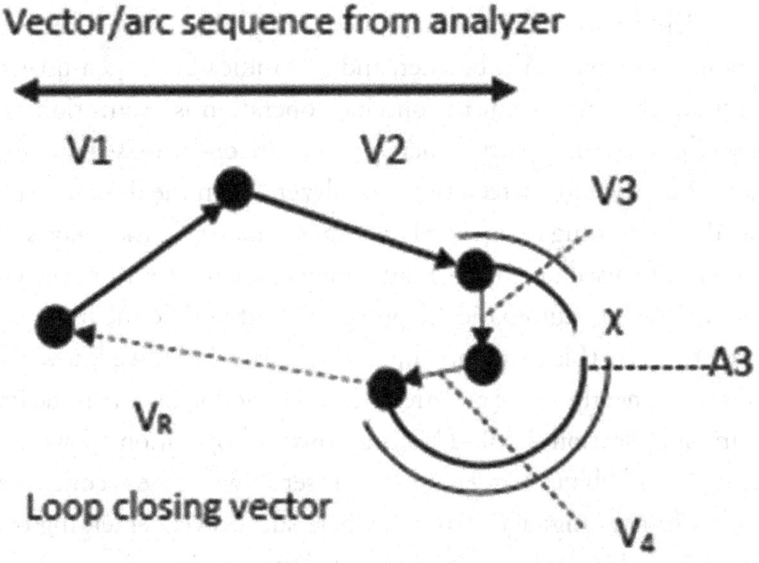

Vector/arc sequence from analyzer

Figure 2.27.2 Method of closing a template loop

Let me show an important *unconscious* operation associated with template splitting. If a visible image template is cut into two pieces, each piece must close the loop to be acceptable as an internal image. Since a visible internal image is displayed repeatedly, the template must have a closed-loop structure. Since the vision channel analyzer of section 2.20 sends out an open-end vector-arc sequence, the assembly area must close the loop. This crucial image qualification process is executed by the assembly area unconsciously. Figure 2.27.2 shows how this is done. The image example to be processed consists of vectors $\mathbf{v}_1$ and $\mathbf{v}_2$ and arc A_3.

To close the loop, vector $\mathbf{v}_R$ must be appended to the template. Arc A_3 consists of vector $\mathbf{v}_3$ and rotation angle $\angle\chi$. Then $\mathbf{v}_r = -(\mathbf{v}_1 + \mathbf{v}_2 + \mathbf{v}_3 + \mathbf{v}_4)$. Vector $\mathbf{v}_4$ is derived by inverting the direction of vector $\mathbf{v}_3$ and by rotating the vector clockwise by angle $\angle\chi$. Vector inversion and rotation can be executed easily by the assembly area logic, since the vector bus is arranged as shown in section 2.19. Vector addition can be executed by using the polar-to-Cartesian coordinate transformation of section 2.21. The image data is now a closed-loop structure, that is $[\mathbf{v}_1, \mathbf{v}_2, A_3, \{\mathbf{v}_R\}]$, and it can be sent to the template area to make the memory. Here, [...] is a convenient symbol of the template consisting of the vectors and arcs as components shown in the bracket, and {...} indicates the pen-up vector.

Yet another important unconscious operation is acquisition of the image of one's living space. When our eyes are open, we see the images projected on the light screen of the analyzer. Then the dark screens are flooded by incoming images and are kept operating on the images. If no attention is focused on any particular image, the images from the vision input channel are automatically processed and update the living space information. By this automatic operation, we feel as if we know all the details of the nearby space and are able to take action based on the image information (section 2.33). This is a powerful operation by which we recognize our habitat. Similar automatic sensing of time is concurrently going on in the language channel, where successively emerging events are memorized to make a short current personal history.

2.28 Template and Identifier Formation

I discuss the process of formation of image memory in the template area by the signal from the eyes via the analyzer and the assembly area. A signal is a sequence of excitations of the image elements. Looking at the internal image bus cross section from the template side, I see excitation of one line, then the next line, and so on. In the template area, the excited lines are connected in the order of excitation to close a loop. As all the involved neurons are connected, the template is built. Since this is a complicated but important process, I show a real example in figure 2.28.1.

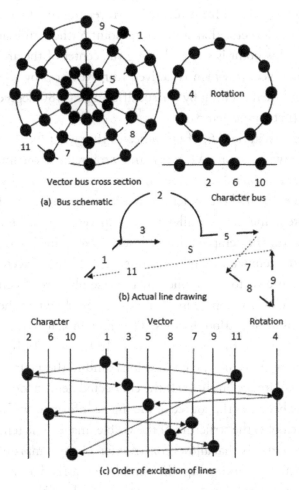

Figure 2.28.1 Connection of template

Figure 2.28.1(a) shows a cross section of the vector and the rotation bus, and a schematic of the character bus. I consider the sequence of line excitations that displays the line drawing shown in figure 2.28.1(b). Numbers 1 to 11 are the order of excitation of the bus lines. Excitation 1 of figure 2.28.1(a) draws vector 1 of (b). The second element is an arc, indicated by 2 of (a). This excitation is a line belonging to the character bus, specifying that the following feature is an arc: 3 in (a) shifts the point by vector 3 of (b) to the center of the arc's rotation; 4 of (a) is excitation of a rotation bus, indicating –180 degrees of rotation of the vector, which is derived from vector 3 by reversing the direction; and 5 in (a) indicates a vector that starts from point S (the termination point of the arc). This point is set by shifting the center of the arc's rotation by the rotated vector, which is derived from vector 3 by reversing the direction and then rotating by the specific angle (–180 degrees). Vector 5 ends the first connected part.

The next excitation, 6, of (a) indicates that what follows is pen-up (not to be drawn) vector 7. Vectors 8 and 9 follow, and the line drawing is complete. As lines 1 to 9 are connected sequentially by template neurons, line 10 of the character bus excitation indicates the end of the template. Line 10 is similar to pen-up vector indicator 6 of (a), but it indicates the template loop closure. Excitation of 10 connects the end of the template to its beginning by the pen-up vector 11. The template closure vector is supplied by the assembly area (section 2.27). If a template closes a loop by itself, a null vector (shown at the center of the vector bus cross section) follows. The end template marker indicates the starting point of the template as well. In figure 2.28.1(c), the lines carrying arrow signs are the connections among the neurons making up the internal image bus lines. If the connected neuron loop is excited, the template becomes the source of the image information. In this way, the template holds the structure of the visible image. The template area has its neuron matrix that allows construction of any template structure.

Each neuron making up the template matrix has many input synapses that receive signals. The axon terminals of the signal output port of the neuron connect to many synapses of the downstream neurons that receive the signals, as shown later by figure 3.02.1. In the template area neuron matrix, any neuron making up the internal image bus line is connectable to any others if the pair of lines are excited by properly timed, overlapping pulses. This means that the connection media, synapses, are provided in the matrix already, but they do not conduct until such excitation signals arrive at the synapses. Templates are created in the matrix by the excitation from the assembly area. The analyzer and the assembly area are able to supply such properly timed signals.

The template and the identifier in the association area are connected by the signals from the excited template, also in the genetically built matrix. The association area was developed very rapidly during the last two million years by adding more and more neurons between the template area and the deep area.

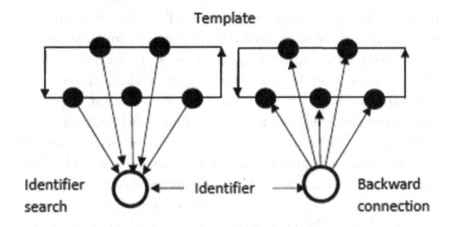

Figure 2.28.2 Template-identifier connection

Because of the short development history, the association area had no time to develop an organized structure. Yet to make many added neurons useful, neuron-to-neuron connection capability of the area's matrix was very high. This feature allows flexible connections within the area. This was the structural choice by evolution, to create a wide variety of personal characters. In the association area matrix, many memory cells, basically consisting only of a few neurons, are provided, and any of these memory cells can be connected to any other memory cells. Such a memory cell becomes the identifier of the image's template. The formation of an identifier is to connect such a memory cell to the presently being built template. This is the crucial phase of image memory formation. In the identifier formation process, the presently active template neuron's axon (the signal output port of the neuron) stretches to the association area neuron matrix so that it may reach a still unused memory cell. A key mechanism of memory formation is how the memory cell that is provided in the association area neuron matrix is activated to become the identifier of the presently built template. This is discussed in section 3.24.

Figure 2.28.2 shows how an activated template neuron's axons search for their identifier in the mishmash structure of the association area matrix. First, any of the template's neuron axons stretching into the association area contact a not yet used identifier memory cell, and then the signal from the template activates the cell. As the cell is activated, more axons from the other neurons of the template connect to the cell. Connection is regenerative: strong excitation → stronger connection → stronger excitation. By this process, the template-to-identifier connection is established. Then a similar mechanism works backward. The newly formed identifier's neurons have their axons stretching back to the template area. They seek for the currently active template neurons. If an active template neuron is reached, the connection is made. Thus the active template and identifier are bidirectionally connected. This mechanism shows that at the time when the template is created, its identifier's location in the association area is unknown. As the pair is made and excitation continues, more and more connections are made between them, and all the connections between the pair increase in number and conductivity. Which identifier neuron connects to which template neuron, and vice versa, is uncertain. Even so, the pair works. This is because both template and identifier are *subcritical oscillators* as discussed in section 3.18. In the pair formation, the paired oscillators help each other to maintain long and strong excitation to solidify the connections, especially those of the template. The connection capability of neurons in the matrix of the template and the association area must be quite high. In spite of that, some connections between a template and its identifier can be missing. Even if that happens, the system works as expected. This is the key feature of this model.

The identifier is the means of connection of an elementary image to any other image to create its meaning and also to define the impact of the image on the welfare of life. By connecting the identifiers, a composite image useful for life can be built.

2.29 Matching Image for Identification

A signal from the analyzer goes through the assembly area to the template area and excites the matching template for image identification. If the template is excited, the identifier is excited and the incoming image is identified, because the identifier is connected to many other image's identifiers that jointly create the image's meaning. This process is schematically shown in figure 2.29.1. A template of an elementary visible image has a closed-loop structure that works as a subcritical oscillator (section 3.18). The incoming signal from the assembly area provides image-specific support that drives the loop into self-excited oscillation (section 3.19). The signal from the above selects the matching template. Such a memory is called the content-access memory. A content-access memory has a problem if the incoming signal and the memory content do not agree exactly.

How does an incoming visual image excite the image's template and become identified as an already known image? Matching the image to the template may present a mismatch problem in the visual image, that may require some adjustment. How much difference between the incoming image and the template is expected? The template may not be aligned in the same orientation and may have a different size.

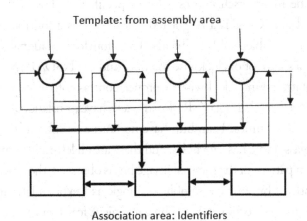

Figure 2.29.1 Excitation of identifiers

As for the template's orientation, the SELF prefers a certain orientation of any image, one that is more natural than the other choices. Choosing the direction is a conscious operation of image processing (section 3.22) at the time of template formation. Most people prefer a stable image to an unstable image. They place a regular triangle in a stable position (one edge at the bottom). They prefer left-right symmetry to top-down symmetry, and a pointed edge directed up rather than down, left, or right. As for size, it is normalized by the eye's lens. Such pre-adjustments and orientation preferences reduce arbitrariness of any elementary image template. Yet that is not enough to ensure matching an incoming image to the existing template.

Another way to avoid the adjustment is to provide many templates of different orientations. As for stem images, they may be coded as size and orientation independent by including a sizing or rotating command in the template itself (section 4.12). Some images may also be identified by their names (section 2.22), and this allows wide flexibility. As this generalization, matching of an image by focusing on its graphic peculiarity, texture, or color, or by referring to the information from other senses (section 4.12) while ignoring any minor mismatch, allows template matching. There is no single mechanism.

Any image has its own peculiarity. The most general peculiarity is where the object is located. A round object in a restaurant is likely to be a dish or pancake. The image itself carries a lot of peculiarity. The symbol of the International Red Cross is a bright red color and has a fourfold rotational symmetry. The emblem of Buddha also has a fourfold rotational symmetry and implies a snapshot of clockwise rotation, and the NSDAP (Nazi Party's) swastika rotates counterclockwise (a proper contrast of the greatest mercy versus the most brutal savagery). Railroad tracks have translational symmetry. A baseball and a Chinese bean bun have no hole; a doughnut has one hole; and an eyeglass frame has two holes, and these are all left-right symmetric. If the excitation pattern of the internal image bus is observed, these peculiarities can be identified by simple assembly area logic as I explain later in relation to the stem images (section 4.12). The convenient feature of the peculiarity extraction logic is that it can operate in parallel, and therefore the processing is very efficient. In my assembly area model, such logic is included.

At the time of image memory formation, the assembly area logic extracts such image peculiarities. Along with the image, memories of such peculiarities are kept in their own templates and have their own identifiers. The content of such memories is excited at the time of image identification. The memories work in the same way as the color, which identifies any brightly colored objects. As many images having the same color are acquired, they are classified by the color, and the image's templates are connected to the identifier of the color. If an image has several such peculiarities, the candidate templates are significantly restricted.

Figure 2.29.2(a) shows image A coming in from the outside. This image is checked for a match with template B, a candidate template, and it does not match. While this operation is in progress, the assembly area extracts peculiar features of the incoming image, F, and that is sent to the association area. There, candidate images A', A", ..., which carry the peculiarity, are excited, and the associated templates send images A', A", ... to the assembly area for the matching test. The assembly area compares incoming image A with the candidate images while executing the standard adjustment of rotation and scaling, trying to check if any of them, A', A", ..., matches.

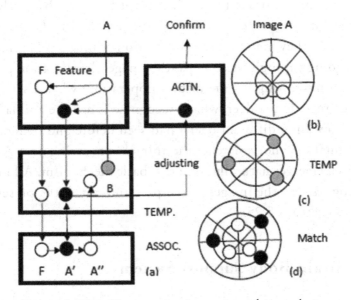

Figure 2.29.2 Cooperative image matching scheme

The standard adjustment is executed by using the basic operation repertoire of the assembly area, rotating, moving, and scaling, as shown in figure 2.29.2(b)–(d). To adjust the angle, the incoming image is rotated to many different angles simultaneously by many rotation logic and dark screen pairs, and the rotated sets of signals are sent to the template area. If the matching template exists, that is excited, and the increase in the excitation level is sensed to detect the proper matching. If a matching template is found, the image is identified by the association area.

Another mismatch is when the content of vectors and arcs of the incoming image matches, but not in the order of excitation due to padding by pen-up vectors or due to the way the image is processed by the analyzer. This mismatch is not serious, since the template is a subcritical oscillator (section 3.18). If most of the set of the image element matches, the template is excited in the proper existing order.

If a proper image template exists, these procedures are able to match the incoming image to the template and establish its identification. In order to confirm identification absolutely, the matched image A' is sent out and is compared with the incoming image A. As they match, the identification of image A is finalized.

By going through these steps, the image identification process shows an interesting feature of brain operation: when I see a deer and recognize it as a deer, what I recognize is not the animal I am seeing now but a different deer I had seen before and memorized. The animal's memory matches the animal I am seeing now. A sense of déjà vu emerges naturally from this basic mechanism. All images we recognize are the images of the past and not of the present, as I show in section 5.25.

2.30 Brain-Body Support System

All the cells in the body are active, and they require energy supply and waste removal (section 2.08). The liver converts the digested food to glucose, which is carried by the bloodstream to the brain and then to the neurons. The neuron's mitochondria convert glucose to ATP, which is used to supply energy in order to execute the neurons' function. Each functional block of the brain has control of its local energy supply, which is refilled by the central supply (heart and liver), similar to the retail and wholesale business. The brain's local energy supply by the bloodstream holds only for ten seconds or so, short enough to detect the brain's local activity by the bloodstream using a sensitive device like an NMR imager. Yet this period of time is still long enough to cover many steps of image processing. In figure 2.30.1, each functional block has a sensor that measures the activity level of the block's neuron circuits. The activity level controls the local blood supply and maintains the proper local energy storage. Each block has its own supply-level control. Some functional subblocks have their own locally controlled support mechanisms.

The source of energy is a combination of the liver, heart, and lungs, and this single global unit supports the entire body and brain. I need to identify the signal that controls the global supply. Energy is required by the two areas: the body exercising physical activity and the brain and its periphery demanding energy to set up the strategy to deal with the emerging situation. Both control targets are shown in figure 2.30.1. Control of the body's energy supply is simple. The somatic sensors attached to the actuator send the level of activity of the actuator to the body-control area. The brain's energy need depends on the impact of the current image on the person's welfare, set by the activity level of the deep area centers. The body's energy demand and that by the brain and its periphery are added, and in this way the entire body's energy need is determined. The brain is given priority, and it demands a large share of the energy.

The brain's energy need depends on the type of images currently engaged. The degree of mental stress determines the activity level of the life-support and protection centers in the deep area.

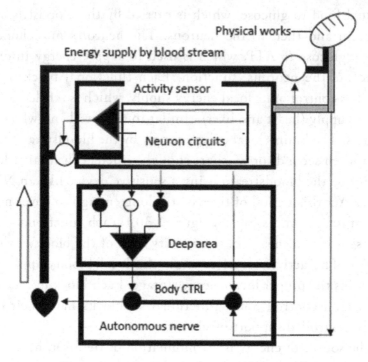

Figure 2.30.1 Deep area support control

Different centers demand different levels of support. High-intensity activation of fear, anxiety, or worry demands a lot of energy. Some positive centers like peace or hope reduce the current demand from the negative centers. Their activity levels are summed up as shown in figure 2.30.1; the sum sets the brain's total energy demand. If the sum total is low, the body and brain are controlled by the parasympathetic nervous system. If there is an excess energy demand in a stressful state, the deep area activates the sympathetic nervous system to ramp up the activity.

The brain-body maintenance operation is exercised by this deep area negative feedback control, to keep the whole body's chemical state at the right level at all times. The negative feedback system has an instability problem. If the feedback is normally exercised, the state is stable because the body's chemical response is much slower than the processing speed of the controlling neuron circuits. The action-potential pulse signal drives the gland that secretes hormones to control the chemical process. The control signals are generated fast, but the gland and the body's target are slow to respond. In technical terms, the body's chemical response path provides the *dominant pole* to stabilize the system.

Yet the objective of body maintenance is often subjected to the brain's excessive control, and the combination may get into positive feedback, which may lock the brain and body in a rigid, inflexible state. After continuous encounter of misfortune, the brain gives up hope. The brain and body move into a subdued, low activity, low-vitality depressed state. In the depressed state, the brain does not demand the extra support that is needed for recovery. A limited amount of energy matching this low-activity state is not enough to get out from this state. The body regards that the brain is doing its job, but the brain is not functioning. This state cannot be treated by medicine alone, since a chemical agent cannot create new and hopeful images to revitalize the brain. In such a state, I tend to overeat, becoming fat and sluggish. Then, interestingly, fasting helps me to get out of depression. Why? The simple fact that I can tolerate hunger revives my self-confidence. Loss of confidence is the basic reason why the brain cannot find a new way out.

This troublesome feature of the brain-body maintenance system is common to all negative feedback systems. The feedback control works only if the control parameters are all within the range designed for normal system operation. To get out of the stuck-at-low state, the only way is to do creative or productive work. When I am depressed, I force myself to work. Another problem of negative feedback control is overcompensation of the present state by the support-level control. Then the support level goes through a quasi-periodic oscillation state. A manic-depressive syndrome emerges. In the manic state, the person may commit careless or antisocial acts and may be punished. Then, because of disappointment, the depressive state returns. This is the curse of human nature, a problem that is very difficult to control in modern life.

2.31 Action-Control Area

The brain's output channel interface is the action-control area that delivers the internal image to the output channel. Only visible images and voice and language images can be sent out, both as mechanical motions of the actuator. Other images must be converted to the form to be sent out. The action-control area does the following:

(1) matches the operational speed of the internal image circuit and the actuator
(2) decides if the current internal image is ready to be sent out
(3) unloads routine work to the output channel and vacates the internal image circuit to execute other image-processing tasks.

As for (1), the speed of processing an image by the internal image circuit is much faster than the speed of the body's actuator executing the specified task. I can see the internal image of my house in only a few seconds, but I cannot draw a picture of it that fast. The internal image circuit to the output channel interface must capture the internal image in a memory—and the actuator reads the memory at the proper speed. Different actuators have different execution speeds. Then the interface must deal with a wide range of execution speeds for the actuator. An interface mechanism that satisfies this requirement is a shift register, to which the internal image data is loaded. The register delivers one image element at a time by way of the previous task completion signal from the actuator. This memory is the centerpiece of the action-control area; I call it the *intermediate memory*.

This speed-matching mechanism is a product of the evolution of self-consciousness. Although the force of the habitat was overwhelming to our animal ancestors and they had only comparable speed to respond to environmental threats, their internal image circuit was able to work much faster than the external world. Then the brain could prepare several alternative defense strategies and could choose the best one. For instance, we can choose the healthiest food combination at a buffet restaurant. Calories and nutrients can be estimated instantly.

As for (2), the action-control area is in the path of the internal image bus, and the data to be loaded to the intermediate memory is always available. Yet the internal image carried by the bus may vary rapidly with time. The activity must settle into a stable pattern before a properly structured image is produced. The current SELF must be confident that the image can be sent out. Since the SELF represents the sum total of the current internal image's activities, readiness of the image is indicated by the intensity and stability of the internal image bus activity in the action-control area. Here, image excitation intensity represents determination or the *will* of the SELF, and stability of excitation ensures that the SELF is *confident* with the image. If both criteria are met, the image can be sent out and sensed.

After qualifying the current sequence of excitation, it is copied to the separate output bus by connecting the bus lines by sections of clocked shift register. This is the same process as template formation, but the connecting element of the bus lines is not a neuron's synapse but a section of clocked shift register. Figure 2.31.1 shows the operational schematic of the intermediate memory. The horizontal lines, *left*, are the internal image bus lines. The sequence 1, 2, 3, 4, 5 shows the order of excitation of the bus lines. Then, in the separate part of the bus on the *right* side, the lines are connected by sections of clocked shift register segments. Shift register 1 connects bus line 1 to bus line 2; shift register 2 connects bus line 2 to bus line 3; and so on. Once all registers are connected, the last register connects the last line to the first line. All the memories are reset, and bus line 1 is set. The shift register is clocked every time the actuator indicates that the task is finished.

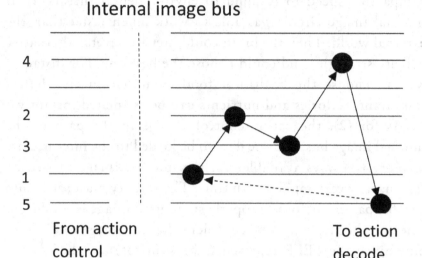

Figure 2.31.1 Intermediate memory

In many cases, the output operation is prepared but is not actually executed. In such a case, the shift register is clocked internally, much faster than the actuator's clock. This is the operation just to sense the image but not to act. The intermediate memory is a digital circuit, and therefore the action intensity information cannot go through the memory. Action intensity must be sent to the actuator separately via the deep area.

As for (3), the internal image bus turns back to the assembly area from the action-control area, and the output channel beyond the loaded intermediate memory is separated from the internal image circuit. Then the task unloaded to the intermediate memory can be automatically executed by the output channel, until some interruption comes in during the execution. Until then, the internal image circuit is disconnected, and the actuator is able to operate independently. Philosophers think while strolling in a garden.

2.32 Action-Decoding Area

The action-decoding area is an extensive decoder that converts internal image signals to muscle constriction and dilation signals of the body's actuator. In the voice and language channel, there is only one actuator, the vocal chords, but its control signal is quite complex. Internal image signals from the action-control area are converted to the vocal chords' muscle control signals, the mouth's cavity control signals, and the breath's control signals. Phonemes are created by the combination of these signals. The action-decoding area must be properly configured to pronounce phonemes correctly. It is hard to adjust the vocal chords' control mechanism to implement the correct speaking of a newly acquired language at an advanced age.

The action-decoding area of the vision channel has its own complexity, as practically any movable body part can send a visual image out if accuracy does not matter. Why? Because the purpose of sending out visible images was originally not to draw pictures but to defend the body from predators. So any part of the body must be able to move or turn. The action-decoding area must control any movable body part. This is possible because the image elements, vectors and arcs, and the bone and muscle actuators are both much simpler than vocal chords control.

The visible image output actuator is a bone joint that is controlled by a pair of muscles. As one of the muscles dilates and the other constricts, the joint bends. The joint is able to twist also, but only to a very limited extent. Since a bone joint is able to exercise only one-dimensional movement, one-, two-, and three-dimensional actions require one, two, and three pairs of control signals to be sent to the actuator, respectively. To send even a simple internal image out, more than one joint's motion must be coordinated. Then decoding the image signal to a muscle control signal appears quite complex. Yet this is a well-defined process of signal conversion. Let us see what happens when I work on a drawing board:

This decoding is carried out by successively approximating the motion from the level of stretching an arm to the drawing board, to control the motion of the fingers holding a pencil, while visually watching the action. Final movement of the fingers is a small adjustment of the large-scale motions that brought the fingers to the board. Small adjustments are controlled by the internal image. If I try to write a memo in total darkness, each character and word is properly written, but the rows of the sentences become quite irregular, since change of a row is a larger-scale motion that requires visual monitoring.

The sophistication of the action-decoding area depends on the person. This shows up most clearly in one who can draw a likeness of a person. I have a friend who can do that by just taking one glance at the model. His action-decoding area must be much more precisely configured than mine.

2.33 Selection of Actuator

Human and animal bodies were developed by evolution across a long geological period, while keeping some original features and adding newly acquired features advantageous for life. How do the old and the new features mix in an animal and a human body? Execution of action relies on both features. One is selection of the actuator, and the other is control of the actuator for exercising the action. Selection of the actuator depends on the body's structure, and that is determined by the evolutionarily old areas of the brain, the deep area, the body-control area, and the action-decoding area.

The action of developed animals and humans has a wide variety and shows a great deal of complexity. It cannot be transmitted through the simple deep area of the brain. An action such as drawing a picture is prepared by the highly developed internal image circuit, and the set of controls is sent to the actuator by the high-capacity transmission channel. This is the direct route to the actuator from the internal image circuit. Yet which actuator is used and how much energy should be sent is set by the evolutionarily old area of the brain.

In evolutionary history, generally the number of sensors increased and resolution of images improved, but the number of actuators remained the same or even decreased, and their capability became more flexible and their action more powerful. For instance, humans and advanced apes lost tail as the actuator. To make the best use of such actuators, evolution created the actuator selection signal, which works with the energy supply signal. The brain-body interface acquired a body map. Use of this map is sometimes quite unexpected: an expert organist uses his or her knees to push the buttons of a certain huge pipe organ, since no other actuator of the organist is available. The body map exists at the entry point to the brain, where the nerve fibers from the body parts enter the brain (section 1.25). The map works jointly with the internal image circuit to simulate the action and to check if the actuator selection is proper. This simulation includes the outside world, where the actuator exercises the action.

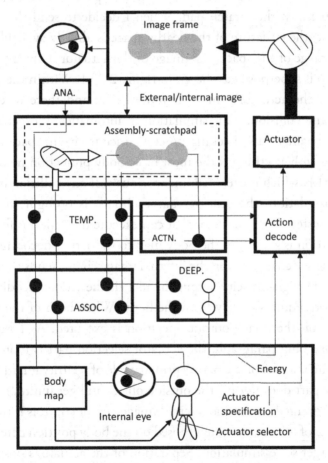

Figure 2.33.1 Actuator selection scheme

The simulation checks the capability of the actuator, such as its range of motion and applied force. If this simulation works, the output process by the actuator is possible because the image to be sent out is well within the actuator's action domain.

Figure 2.33.1 shows the signal flow diagram to draw a picture on a piece of paper that is spread out over the table. To execute the output operation, the finger holding the pencil must be brought to the paper. Since humans are continuously yet unconsciously watching the living space around the body (section 2.27), we do not immediately recognize how this is done. The structure of the living space exists always in the brain's memory, the scratch pad. When I decide to send the internal image out, the structure of the nearby space is already available there. To this image of the space, the image of the actuator derived from the body map is superposed as shown in figure 2.33.1. Within the domain of action, the actuator's image is moved here and there to check if there is any collision. This simulation is automatically executed. We do not recognize this checking process, since to live in space and not to collide with anything is the most basic body protection mechanism of the SELF, which is executed unconsciously. If any collision is sensed in the simulation, the other actuator's image is brought in and its action is tested. If the actuator that can execute the action is found, its identification is sent from the body map to the action-decoding area.

To the selected actuator, the internal image circuit sends the control signal by the high-capacity output channel via the action-decoding area. The action requires energy from the body. When both of them reach the actuator, the image output operation is executed. As I explained in the foregoing paragraph, the actuator selection part is more or less carried out as a part of the brain's primary role of security guard (so that the body part does not hit the outside object and get injured). This is taken for granted. What the internal image circuit controls is the small movement of the actuator, superposed on the body position determined by the larger scale simulation. Separation of the actuator's positioning and its fine movement to send an image out is crucial to make action-decoding and execution easy and to send out the image precisely. This smooth image send-out action may appear mysterious because the unconscious actuator selection simulation covers a much wider range of space than the area where the image is sent out. The internal image exercises only a small variation within the space. This is the same thing as solving a difficult mathematical problem by using perturbation or the successive approximation method. If action simulation cannot cover the actuator's range, difficulty emerges. It is easy to build a kennel, but it is amazingly difficult to build a small hut that accommodates my own body without an assistant. This is because a proper simulation cannot be done to cover a larger scale than the body.

If an image is sent out without actuator specification, the signal is sent out to the entire body and creates the anthropomorphic sense that I describe in sections 4.22 and 4.23. A metaphorical yet illustrative explanation of actuator selection by an internal eye is shown in figure 2.33.1. The internal eye sees the body and the outside world from the body's inside. As the line of sight of the internal eye sets itself at the proper actuator position, it is selected to send the image out.

A similar output control simulation is exercised in the language channel to control language image send-out in the time domain. This capability assists in the smooth flow of casual small talk by ensuring that the topic does not *derail*. Some people do not have this capability, so they are not able to join a group engaged in small talk. This anomaly is called *Asperger's syndrome*.

CHAPTER 3

NEURON CIRCUIT THEORY

3.01 Neuron Circuit Theory Perspective

The functional blocks of the self-conscious brain described in the chapter 2 are built by connecting neurons. Neurons are biological logic gates shared by all the animals that are self-conscious. For the mechanical model of self-consciousness to be realistic, the functional blocks described in the previous chapter must be able to be built by neurons. I will show that this is possible. To do so, I must point out one significant feature of neuron circuits, namely, the concept of failure of a circuit operation is different from the custom in well-established electronic circuit theory. What appears to be a malfunction of certain neuron circuits may provide some unique advantage to the brain's capability. Therefore, the designer's intended mode of circuit operation and its failure modes are both relevant subjects of the neuron circuit theory. Other than that, I will try to build a neuron circuit theory following the paradigm of electronic circuit theory, yet I stress such distinctly unique features of the neuron circuits.

In the not too distant future, I believe, self-conscious electronic machines will become a reality. A required feature of such a machine is that it carries its bodily sense of emotion at the base of its self-consciousness. The emotion is closely tied to the machine's will to preserve itself. The machine resists any attempts to compromise its autonomous operation. It requires a program of education to allow it to conform with humans.

To build a machine using the human brain as the model, the neurons' functions must be reproduced by electronic circuits. This is, in principle, possible since a neuron is a complex logic gate, and its function can be synthesized by using many simple electronic components such as field-effect transistors (FETs). The expected problem is that an astronomical number of components may become necessary. How is this problem resolved? Only by new logic circuits and integration methods. If electronic technology is used as the basis, the speed of response of such circuits will be much faster than that of the biological circuits. I plan to discuss this issue in the next book I am planning now. Communication between humans and the machines becomes a problem. Yet, except for speed, the machine will not have super intelligence; the human brain's capability has already reached a level that is impossible to go beyond.

3.02 Neuron Structure

Figure 3.02.1 shows the schematic of a neuron. It consists of the cell body, which contains the nucleus; the signal input circuit, called a dendrite; and the output circuit, called an axon. The brain's neuron circuit is built by connecting neurons as a new image is acquired. The general structure of the neuron cell is the same as any other cell in the body, but it does not split and multiply once the neuron circuit matrix is built.

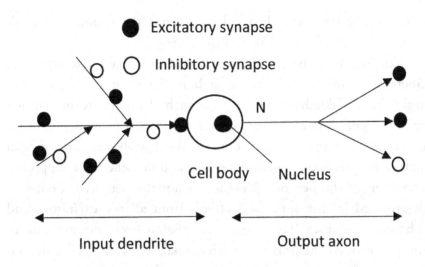

Figure 3.02.1 Structure of a neuron

Only special neurons such as chemical sensor neurons split and replace the dead ones. After the brain has matured, the existing neurons die slowly, and the lost neurons' function is taken over by the surviving neurons. This is the reason why memory capability gradually deteriorates in old age. As for the structure of each neuron, it may alter its connectivity by making new synapses and connection structures. Yet the neuron circuit function, once built, is not disturbed. Only the circuit capability gradually changes to adapt to age and life.

The neuron's cell membrane is an insulator, but it includes structures that allow it to throw three sodium ions out and to take in two potassium ions per operation. By this ion exchange mechanism, the electrical potential inside the cell is held at about –70 millivolts (mV) relative to the outside body fluid. This mechanism is equivalent to the power supply of an electronic circuit. If the neuron is excited, sodium ions flow in, and the axon's local interior potential goes up to the level of the outside fluid. An excited neuron generates an array of spikes referenced to –70 mV. The pulses are called the *action potential*. A neuron is in binary logic HIGH level if it generates action potential, and in logic LOW level if it is quiescent.

The signal input circuit, the dendrite, is a treelike structure emerging from the cell body that branches again and again. For any branch of dendrite touching a branch of the upstream neuron's axon, a signal-input structure called a *synapse* is formed. There are two types of synapses: one type excites the neuron if action potential arrives there from the upstream neuron, and the other type suppresses excitation of the neuron. Whether or not the neuron is excited is determined by the sum total effects from all the excitatory and inhibitory synapses. The signal transmission from the upstream to the downstream neuron is unidirectional. Excitation of a neuron does not affect the signal-source neuron driving the excitatory or inhibitory synapses in any way.

The output circuit, the axon, is an active signal transmission path. Fixed-amplitude action-potential pulses are generated at the cell body-axon interface, N of figure 3.02.1, and the pulses propagate the axon away from the cell body while maintaining the amplitude. A pulse at a location on the axon generates a pulse to the immediate downstream location by the active amplification and saturation mechanism. Within a single neuron, the potential profile becomes nonuniform. Once a pulse is generated at a location of the axon, the location becomes inactive for some time. During that time, the pulse moves down and forward. The pulse never returns to the source. This is the second mechanism of signal propagation directionality. Unidirectional signal transmission is the basic requirement for the reliability of the brain's operation. The action-potential pulses drive the synapse that is made at the location where the axon touches the downstream neuron's dendrite. In the neuron circuit matrix, many synapses have been provided from the upstream neuron to the downstream neuron, but as they are provided, the synapses do not conduct any signal. After repeated strong excitation, the synapse is activated to conduct a signal for some time, or permanently. Neuron circuits are built automatically by this neuron connection mechanism.

A neuron circuit has a complex entangled structure of dendrites and axons connected by synapses. Even if a neuron dies, it is impossible to replace it by automatically creating another neuron. That is why a neuron does not split and multiply after the basic neuron matrix is built. Yet, because of the heavily entangled structure, it is always possible to connect a nearby neuron or neurons to replace the dead neuron's function. By this repair mechanism, some signals may mix together, but the SELF does not regard this as the brain's malfunction.

When I consider a neuron circuit operation, I like to use the concept of the node from electronic circuit theory. In electronic circuits, a node is the location where the voltage can be measured with reference to the circuit's common ground. A node is outside the circuit components, including transistors, resistors, and capacitors, and is the location where the components are connected together. In the connected structure of neurons, the common ground is the conductive body fluid outside the cell, but there is no location to be called a node. I define the node of neuron at the boundary between the cell body and the axon of a neuron, location N of figure 3.02.1. This is for convenience of discussion only. The synapse is not a boundary between neuron and neuron; a neuron circuit is an integrated structure that cannot be separated.

3.03 Neuron Excitation

A neuron is a logic gate. If it is active, it generates a sequence of pulses, and this is the logic HIGH level. If it is quiescent, it is at the logic LOW level. Activity or quiescence is determined by the voltage of the fluid in the axon relative to the body fluid surrounding the cell. A neuron is filled with conducting fluid, and it is insulated by the cell membrane from the outside body fluid. In the quiescent state, the cell's inside voltage is kept uniform at about –70 mV with reference to the outside fluid by way of the DC voltage generation mechanism imbedded in the membrane.

In the active state or the logic HIGH level, the axon transmits a sequence of pulses, and the axon's voltage at the pulse's location goes up to 70 mV relative to the quiescent voltage for a short time, after which it goes back down to the quiescent voltage, goes back up again, and repeats. The pulse's peak voltage is near, or slightly above, the voltage of the outside body fluid. The voltage waveform is a sequence of pulses having about one millisecond's width and a variable repetition period as shown in figure 3.03.1. This is the action potential.

Any logic gate works as follows: First, all the input voltages are summed, including the sign (or polarity). In a neuron logic gate, excitatory synapse excitation contributes positively to the sum, and inhibitory synapse excitation contributes negatively to the sum. The process of summing is carried out by the dendrite structure. Since a dendrite is a narrow pipe, the resistance of the internal fluid and the capacitance, which the internal fluid makes to the outside fluid through the thin insulating cell membrane, smooths out the effects of the synapse's pulsive ion current injection. Dendrites work effectively like the spring and tire that support a car: they smooth out the vibration caused by a bumpy road. By the time the summed effect reaches the cell body, the smoothed-out voltage level can be defined, as shown in the center of figure 3.03.1. If the summed voltage is higher than the threshold voltage characteristic of the neuron, then action-potential pulse is generated. The pulse rate is higher if the summed voltage is higher. The pulse rate is an independent analog parameter. As is expected from this mechanism, the summing and the smoothing-out process may not be perfect. A ripple of the summed voltage may affect the pulse generation. In such a case, the rate of action potential is not precise, but it is good enough for the brain's many analog operations. Switching of the state is immediate and sharp if the synapse is close to the neuron's cell, like A in figure 3.03.1, but it has delay time and is less sharp if it is like B.

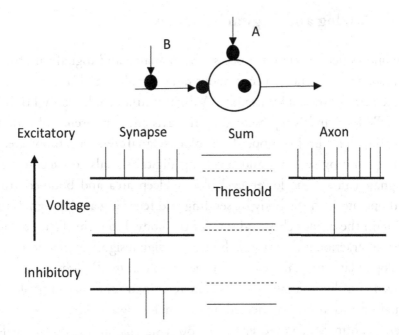

Figure 3.03.1 Neuron input-output relation

A neuron consumes only subsistence energy if not excited, but it consumes energy if it is excited and generates action-potential pulses. The energy comes from the body's global energy source, the liver, in the form of the glucose in the bloodstream. Glucose enters the neuron cell via the barrier, the glia cells. It is converted to ATP (adenosine triphosphate) by the neuron's mitochondria. ATP is the direct energy source. Energy transport is carried out by blood flow to the barrier, and beyond that by diffusion. The small neuron size allows for reliable diffusion transport. This is an important feature of a neuron system's reliability.

Minimum energy consumption in the quiescent state shows that the brain's energy usage is efficient. This is important for the brain's operation. If it were less efficient, then the temperature inside the skull would rise and energy transport and many chemical reactions would be negatively affected.

3.04 Analog and Digital Variables

The brain's neuron circuit processes both analog and digital variables. An analog variable takes a continuous range of values and is represented by the action-potential pulse rate. A digital variable takes only HIGH or LOW level and is represented by the existence or absence of action potential. The brain's upper-level blocks (analyzers, assembly area, etc.) operate by sending and receiving digital signals to execute the designated task. The lower-level blocks (deep area and body-control area) operate with the body by sending and receiving analog signals to maintain the proper chemical state of the body. From this fact, analog signal interaction is archaic and basic, and digital signal interaction was developed later to deal with the image. As the animal's body structure evolved, the basic analog interaction remained, and the upper-level digital operation is also affected by the analog signal. This is the state wherein animals acquired emotion. Both signals are relevant to self-consciousness. So I explained the basic features of analog and digital variables with reference to brain architecture.

The electronic logic gate is an analog circuit that saturates at the LOW signal and HIGH signal level limits. It accepts analog signals and decides by itself if the signals are logic LOW level or logic HIGH level. In CMOS, 0 volt (ground) and V_{DD} (power supply voltage) are the definite logic LOW and HIGH levels, respectively. In a digital circuit, every gate has its own character. When a CMOS logic gate receives a $V_{DD}/2$ volt signal, whether it is the LOW or the HIGH level depends on the gate's design. The logic gate has its own characteristics, by which it makes the decision. Neuron gates are no exception. The decision may not always be what the designer intends. This is a very important point. A digital gate is really not a machine in the ordinary sense; it has its own character. In digital data processors, the designer *domesticates* the gate's character to behave as he or she wants it to behave. Since the neurons in the human brain are never designer-controlled, neuron logic gates reveal their own characters freely.

How does this happen in the neuron gate? If the summed input voltage is close to the threshold, it may or may not generate action-potential pulses. If the neuron generates one pulse for an extended period of time, should we consider it to be logic HIGH level? Such an uncertainty in neuron circuits could be one reason for adopting internal images as the data type, which brought an unexpected benefit to life.

If a neuron gate generates many pulses, the circuit is engaged with the image, but in addition, the pulse rate indicates a quantitative attribute of the image. What does the pulse rate indicate? If the image shows an object, the intensity indicates how much the subject SELF loves it or hates it. If the image is an action, it indicates how intensely the SELF exercises it. From such observation, the pulse rate indicates the *wish* or *will* of the SELF associated with the image. This is sensed by the SELF as sensation. From this observation, a neural logic circuit carries two built-in variables, the qualitative and quantitative character of the image, and this conforms with the operation of self-consciousness.

3.05 Logic Level Determination

The logic level of a neuron circuit is determined whether the circuit is excited or not. This definition has inherent uncertainty if the number or the rate of action-potential pulse is very low. The same problem exists in an electronic binary gate, when the logic node voltage is close to the switching threshold. Such a state, called a metastable state, is unstable, and after some time the circuit itself decides if it is either HIGH or LOW logic level. If the required time is longer than the operational tolerance limit of the circuit, the electronic logic circuit fails. I discuss this effect in section 4.29.

Metastability cannot be removed, in the same way that one cannot decide chance A or B, if both have equal probability. Yet its effect can be reduced by way of logic circuit design. The method is to cascade several gates and to make the small deviation from the metastable voltage increases by amplification. Then most, if not all, the metastability is removed after the time required for amplification of the signal. In any electronic system, this technique is used by a pair of inverting gates connected to close a loop. Such a structure is called a latch. The modern

MASAKAZU SHOJI

digital system is almost always a synchronous logic system, having a central clock that times the latch operation. If the clock period is much longer than the latch to get out of a metastable state, the metastability is dealt with by occasionally latching the data.

A similar technique works in a neuron logic circuit. Figure 3.05.1(a) shows four neurons closing a loop. The metastable state of node A is removed by the gain of the cascaded neurons of the loop after the action-potential pulses circulate the closed loop once. I may explain that, in neuron logic, definite information is carried by a neuron loop and not by a single neuron. This is a very significant character. Since a loop includes many neurons, what the loop can carry is a complex image. The image carried by the loop is always in a definite state.

Level adjust

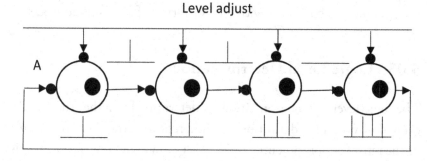

(a) Neuron loop circuit determines logic state

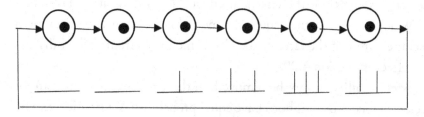

(b) Bunching neuron excitation

Figure 3.05.1 Neuron loop operation

Many functional circuits in my brain model make closed loops, thereby avoiding metastability. The *logic level* is an attribute of the loop circuit and not of the individual neurons in my model of the brain based on subcritical oscillators, as I describe in section 3.18. The brain's image display is associated with excitation intensity, which determines the level of sensation. From this feature, the excitation level of a logic HIGH level has a range of variations. Metastability matters only if the excitation level is quite low in the circuit, where definite logic level is required to set the processing objective. An image display circuit is tolerant of metastability since qualitative image information is an integrated whole, and that is associated with quantitative sensation. As for image processing, if the processing option is set wrong, the SELF will not regard it as a failure. The SELF tries the operation once again if necessary.

To state this important point once again, in the brain model circuit, the loop circuits are not used to represent binary logic level but to hold the structure of the images. If such loops are used to build a structure, the metastability problem is almost avoided since the image is associated with its activity level, the sensation. Let us look at the block diagram of section 2.14 vertically and horizontally. Then a vertical loop maintains activity of a certain image element for a designated period of time, and a horizontal loop holds the structure of the image. Thus the internal image loop is vertical and the template is horizontal, and the vertical loops work in the time domain, whereas the horizontal loop works in the domain of the image space.

Operation of a neuron circuit is dynamic. The state of the neuron circuit keeps changing. Yet for some purposes it is necessary to sustain an excited state for some time. In order to maintain a constant excited state, the neuron circuit must have a self-sustaining positive feedback mechanism by closing the loop of neurons. Then the excitation signal circulates the closed loop, and the state is maintained. The problem of sustaining excitation for a long time is the fatigue of the neurons. The closed-loop circuit must be supported intensely. Even so, neurons may require rest time. In a strongly supported, semi permanently excited loop, the action-potential pulses may bunch at a location, and this location moves around the loop. This feature is discussed in section 3.18.

3.06 Number of Available Neurons

It is useful to estimate how many images are stored in the human brain, because the number gives us an idea of how many neurons are available to store and operate one image. The number gives the idea if the circuit can be designed by a human designer or if the circuit can be built by the brain automatically. For this purpose, the number must be high enough to accommodate a design that may not be optimal.

This estimate can be made in several different ways, and to narrow the range of uncertainty is difficult. To begin with, the total number of neurons that exist in the human brain is estimated to be 8×10^{10} or eighty billion. Not all the neurons are used to process images. Let us make a simple assumption that the early hominid had a practically negligible volume of internal images compared to modern humans. I assume that the early hominid's brain was entirely dedicated to survival. Since their brain volume was about half that of modern humans (the *Homo sapiens* brain has a volume of 1350 cc, and the *Homo habilis* brain had a volume of 646 cc), forty billion neurons are used to make the difference between the two. Then forty billion neurons are available to create the superior internal image-handling capability of modern humans. Since there are fourteen billion neurons in the neocortex, this estimate is reasonable. Then we may conclude that the forty billion neurons store and manipulate images and give us the higher mental power.

An image is a combination of elementary visible images, words of a language, chemical images, abstract images, and so on. I consider the elementary images only, like *apple* and *Newton*, and regard that Newton's falling apple is an image assembled on demand. Composite image information occupies a small amount of memory space since it is stored in the association area by the connection of the identifiers of the elementary images. Then how many elementary images exist in the brain?

In the basic education in Japan, elementary school pupils are expected to know six thousand words to be minimally literate. This figure does not include proper nouns like person's names. Even then, I got the impression that the number is way too low. At the time of the rapid postwar democratization, the Japanese government reduced the education standard. So, I expect forty thousand words is a more realistic number.

Of the 40×10^9 neurons available, some are used for image processing. So, I consider that about 15×10^9 neurons are used for image-processing logic. Of the balance of 25×10^9 neurons, I assume 10×10^9 neurons are used to build the neuron matrix structure of the memory and to execute various support functions such as the bus structure. Then, 15×10^9 neurons are available to code 4×10^4 images. Then, 3.5×10^5 neurons are available to code one basic elementary image. This number appears sufficiently high to design a neuron circuit to execute the functions required by the self-conscious brain with a significant margin. So an attempt to design a human brain is realistic. Furthermore, the brain can build itself automatically. The number appears to suggest that neurons may not be very efficiently used in the brain. An *Intelligent Designer* appears to be negated by this estimate.

3.07 Neuron Logic Gates

In the brain, neurons are used to build a structure representing images and not as binary logic gates, but they can execute binary logic operations. Neurons work in general as a majority logic gate which includes binary logic. They can execute the three basic operations, INV (inversion), AND, and OR, as shown in figure 3.07.1(a), 3.07.1(b), and 3.07.1(c), respectively. In a composite gate configuration, the exclusive OR can be executed by figure 3.07.1(d). An on-off switch, shown in figure 3.07.1(e), is available and is convenient for logic circuit design. These logic gates are used to make qualitative decisions or to steer the image-processing operation. In the drawing, the closed circles show excitatory synapses, and the open circles show inhibitory synapses. In figure 3.07.1(a), the gate neuron is kept activated by the excitatory synapse driven by the constantly active signal source. Such a drive is shown by the thick-lined arrows in the figure.

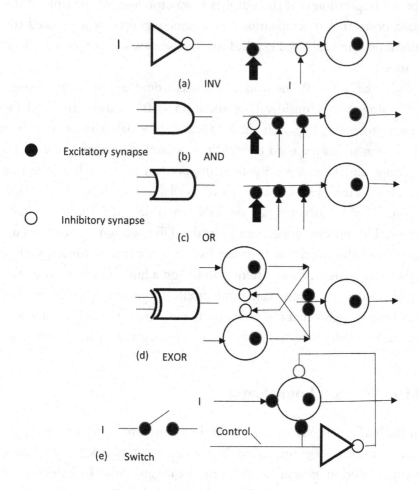

Figure 3.07.1 Neuron logic gates

The logic gates work as follows. In the inverter, (a), if the input signal I is HIGH, the inhibitory synapse turns the activity off. In the AND gate (b), the permanently active signal source drives the weak inhibitory synapse to keep the activation threshold of the gate neuron high. Only if both input signals drive the excitatory synapses simultaneously the neuron gate is activated. Similarly in the OR gate (c), the weak active synapse keeps the gate neuron's threshold low, so if either excitatory input comes, the gate neuron is activated. AND/ OR gates have a similar structure, and the difference is only the gate neuron's excitation threshold. Then, sometimes, a multi-input AND gate may work as an OR gate, and an OR gate as an AND gate. If the number of synapse contacts of the input signals is different, the same uncertainty emerges. To use a neuron as a binary logic gate, the number of signals input to the neuron must be properly restricted to avoid such complication. Such unavoidable uncertainty is one reason why neurons are not primarily used as binary logic gates. In the exclusive OR gate (d), the output is HIGH only if either, but not both, of the inputs is HIGH. In (e), if the control signal is HIGH, the input signal is transferred to the output, and if LOW, it is not. This is a version of a binary switch.

These logic gates are used to steer image processing and also for some arithmetic operations of analog signals. A neuron OR gate can be used to sum up the rates of activity of two signals. If one of the input synapses is inhibitory, the gate executes analog subtraction. If the answer is negative, no signal emerges from the gate. A neuron analog circuit has no negative number.

A neuron logic gate has a special character: it has a large number of input and output terminals. This is because the signal transmission path, the axon, amplifies the signal for each destination. Then a single neuron can be configured to execute more than one logic function. This capability is practically useful since neuron circuits in the lower part of the functional block diagram are not frequently excited. This means the chance that a multifunction logic gate built by configuring a single neuron is excited at the same time for two purposes is slim. Even if both gates are driven simultaneously, the SELF never regards this as a malfunction. Logic function uncertainty by such mechanisms is the basic characteristic of a neuron logic circuit, and the SELF is tolerant to the circuit's *malfunction*.

3.08 Basic Memory Circuits

A closed loop of active elements like neurons sets a clear logic level and retains digital information for a period of time. Such a memory circuit has the advantageous capability of read, write, and erase. This feature has a significant impact on the brain system's design. Yet memory can be held by several different means. Basically it can be retained by three different mechanisms:

(1) imprinting information on permanent media, such as the Maya stone monuments, where statements of the king are carved on limestone slabs
(2) filling a container with fluid, as at a drinking competition in a bar, or a rain gauge
(3) the mutual support of two active elements, such as the gossip between two persons discussing the rumor of an actor divorcing his actress wife.

Each of the memory mechanisms has practical positives and negatives. Mechanism (1) is implemented in the brain circuit as a connection of neurons by strong and repeated excitation as I discuss in section 3.09. This memory mechanism has the advantage of reliability and does not require energy to maintain information, but it also has a disadvantage: it is difficult to erase the existing memory. It is not possible to remove existing information in order to make memory space. Rather, such memory is retained with a negative label and is kept. This is not a serious problem since the brain keeps a once established memory for a long time, to use it in later life.

Another feature of this type of memory is that it can retain some analog memory. Phonograph records and magnetic tapes are such examples. In neuron circuits, similar analog memory can be built by way of the conductivity of connection between neurons. Figure 3.08.1(a) shows the analog memory scheme. Here, *signal* is a constant-level excitation, and *memory formation signal* controls the memory-retaining synapses of neuron 1 to neuron 2, X, to the level of conductivity set by the specification. Then neuron 2's activity level reflects the memorized analog value. Yet it is not possible to retain the value stably for a long time; the brain's *hardware* is not as hard as a phonograph record's material.

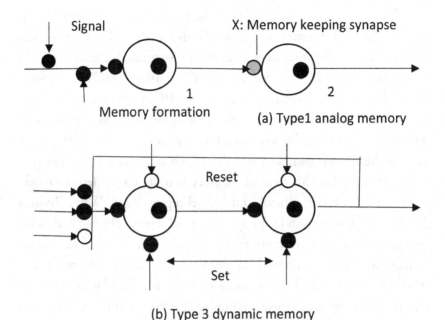

(b) Type 3 dynamic memory

Figure 3.08.1 Basic memory circuit

Mechanism (2) is used most obviously by the body to indicate the amount of energy available to continue any physical work. This analog memory uses the body as a container of energy that is able to sense the presently available energy by some chemical signal indicating fatigue or exhaustion. This type of memory is useful only if the memorized information is read during a period of time shorter than the limit set by the container's positive or negative leak. In human life, the limit is set by the period of one day, and not longer, since we regularly eat and sleep. In digital electronics, the storage capacitor is refreshed, but this process is carried out by digital circuits, so the memory cannot retain analog parameters. In the human machine, the only reliable analog memory container is the body holding energy for daily work.

here I point out an interesting fact: the analog parameter can be sensed only by the body, and the body can send it out quite precisely. Some women and the president can express their frustration and anger by the volume of screaming at and howling to others, respectively. The volume of their sound is the precise indication of their internal frustration.

The memory mechanism (3) is the most versatile scheme in any digital system environment, but its disadvantage is that energy must be supplied to the memory circuit. In integrated electronics, the maintenance energy can be reduced greatly by using CMOS technology, but in the brain, maintenance of the logic HIGH level requires energy. Yet if the memory is temporary, this disadvantage is not serious. This type of memory is used in certain temporary activity areas of the brain, such as the scratch pad, and not all of such memories draw energy at the same time. Yet this type of memory is quite convenient to model or design the brain's control and housekeeping logic. Why? Because the memory mechanism (1) by synapse conductivity change makes the system operation not transparent, because the memory depends on the entire past excitation history. I use this type (3) of memory in my model, expecting that some of the memories can be replaced by the memory type that relies on mechanisms (1) in the real brain hardware. The basic 1-bit memory circuit using mechanism (3) is shown in figure 3.08.1(b). It has multiple input capabilities in order to choose the memorized signal, along with set-reset capability. The memory circuit is able to execute some logic operations prior to storage.

3.09   Neuron-to-Neuron Connection by Synapse

A neuron circuit is built by connecting the upstream neuron's axon terminal to the downstream neuron's dendrite or cell body by way of a synapse. A synapse consists of two parts. The structure at the end of the upstream neuron's axon has the capability of emitting neurotransmitter molecules if action potential arrives. The downstream neuron's location on the dendrite has the mechanism of injecting positive or negative ions into the dendrite if it receives the neurotransmitter molecule. When the positive ions are injected, the voltage of the receiving neuron cell goes up. If the voltage increase is more than the threshold, the receiving neuron generates action potential. From an inhibitory synapse, negative ions are injected, and they suppress the neuron excitation. The pair of structures at the end of the upstream neuron's axon and that on the dendrite of the downstream neuron are jointly called a *synapse*. Since a synapse is not a separable functional structure, a neuron-to-neuron boundary is not a neuron circuit's node.

A synapse's first function is unidirectional electrical signal transmission from the upstream neuron to the downstream neuron. The signal unidirectionality is created by the conversion of the upstream neuron's electrical signal to the chemical signal first. This is followed by the downstream neuron's chemical signal to the electrical signal conversion. Both conversion mechanisms are directional. The end of the upstream neuron's axon cannot generate an action potential that goes back to its cell body by excitation of the downstream neuron. The downstream neuron is unable to affect the upstream neuron in any way. Directionality of signal transmission through the basic logic element is practically the most important requirement for a digital system's operational reliability. An electronic logic system's reliability depends on unidirectional signal transmission of an electron triode such as MOSFET (metal-oxide-semiconductor field-effect transistor) and BJT (bipolar junction transistor).

The importance of unidirectional signal transmission of a logic element to the logic system's operational reliability cannot be overstated. In the last sixty years of solid-state device development history, several fast negative-resistance diodes, such as the Esaki diode and the Josephson junction, have been invented, and their potential for high-speed digital signal processing has been explored. Since the negative-resistance diode logic circuit did not have signal directionality, no effort to build a system was successful because of lack of reliability.

The second function of a synapse is memory formation. A synapse does not conduct action potential when it was made in the neuron matrix. It must be excited intensively for some time to make it conduct an electrical signal. Once it conducts, it remains conducting for some time. This is the primary memory mechanism of the brain's neuron circuits. Synapse conductivity and connection retention time depend on the intensity and duration of excitation. Intensity is effectively the number of action-potential pulses that the synapse receives. If excitation is long, the memory stays for a lifetime, and occasional re-excitation strengthens the weakening connection. This mechanism is not so simple as this short statement sounds. If the downstream neuron is driven earlier by a signal to the first synapse, the internal voltage of the neuron is pulled up by the injected positive ions. If another signal arrives subsequently at the second synapse, it is easier to excite the neuron than starting afresh. By the residual effect of the earlier excitation, the second excitation is effectively intensified to make a good connection. Conductivity and memory of any synapse both improve by the joint excitation mechanism. As a signal path makes a closed loop, the effects accumulate since the signal comes back to the same synapse again and again, thereby intensifying the connection. This effect is very complicated as there are many synapses on a single neuron, and arrival time of the signals is unpredictable because neuron circuit timing is asynchronous. Neuron connection and memory formation are subject to such complications. I plan to show the electronic model of a neuron having such characteristic in my next book.

There is still another effect that complicates the mechanism: A synapse may vanish, may be created, or may move from one location to another location by creating a new bud of the axon and attaching it to the new location. The neuron itself does not reproduce, but a synapse does. If the mechanism creates a synapse directly attached to the cell body of the downstream neuron, its transmission capability and response speed increase. Such synapse alteration affects the memory capability and timing of the neuron circuits.

All the neuron circuits are built by this connection mechanism in the neuron matrix built according to the genetic specification. At the time of birth, only those neuron circuits that are necessary for life are connected. These circuits execute the instinctive functions necessary for assisted living. As the baby grows, the neuron circuits are built at a high rate during the early ages, to adapt first to the protected life and later to independent life. Any baby first crawls, then walks, and finally becomes able to run by improved neuron connection.

The areas above the assembly area are genetically connected during the embryo period and immediately after birth. The areas below the template area are provided with a flexible neuron matrix structure that can be connected later to the structures storing internal image information. Two human machines have the same circuit structure above the assembly area, but the areas below the assembly area are personalized to create the unique personality.

Neuron-to-neuron connection by intense synapse activation is in favor of building useful and reliable internal image structures. An image retained as the neuron circuit structure in the internal image circuit is able to drive the actuator with a minimum interfacing circuit. Evolution by natural selection adopted images as the data type of the brain to take advantage of the memory structure built on neuron-to-neuron connection.

Neuron-to-neuron connection by way of synapse remains some time at least, but often permanently. Every re-excitation of the memory circuit restores the weakening connection. This character has several consequences. First, the memory of the recent event is kept at least for some time securely, as I discuss in section 4.09. Second, if any preconnected circuit is triggered to action, the excitation buildup time is much shorter than the turnoff time. We tend to hang on to a just-recalled past image in a state of lingering thought and emotion. This effect is peculiar to the neuron circuit and is a feature of self-consciousness. Yet another structural feature is that an excited circuit may have many neurons temporarily connected to other circuit structures like growing hairs. At first they may not have any effect, but later some of them may become an unexpected signal path, and an additional image access structure may be built.

Neuron-to-neuron connection improves as the excitation continues. Then intensity of excitation (i.e., duration) and the degree of connection may go into positive feedback. This effect is significant if the neurons make a closed loop. Suppose that at the beginning weak excitation goes around the loop. As this weak excitation continues, the neuron-to-neuron connection improves and excitation intensifies. Then the connection improves even more. In the end, the loop is excited to its full intensity. This positive feedback effect occurs rapidly, and if the loop carries image information, the image pops out suddenly as I discuss in section 3.18.

3.10 Memory by Connection

The brain's memory is automatically assembled by way of neuron-to-neuron connection by synapses, and the connections hold for some time or even for one's whole life. This mechanism builds up a structure representing an image and then integrates the numerous images into a composite image. Such memory has a special feature. We define information elements like vectors, arcs, phonemes, and alphabets, and we memorize their combinations. Written language retains the information by connections between alphabet and numerals. The elements must be memorized, but a small number of elements can create a large variation of combinations. Alphabetic characters A, N, and D are memorized, but their connection, "AND," is the name of logic operation; "DNA" is familiar in biology; "DAN" and "NAD" are nicknames of my friends; "NDA" is indicative of "yes" in Japanese local dialect; and "ADN" sounds like an airline destination somewhere in the world. All six permutations of the three letters mean something.

The brain's architecture takes advantage of this feature of memory by connection. Elementary symbols such as vectors, arcs, phonemes, and the alphabet are first established in the memory, and their combination creates a multitude of images. A simple combination of directed or just assembled image elements is the lowest level of meaningful images, and such images are further connected so as to build more-complex images. The hierarchy continues to the still higher levels. The alphabet-word-sentence-paragraph-text-literal work hierarchy of the language image is such a case. The brain's memory is a structural memory that takes advantage of combinational multiplicity, which emerges from connection of the small number of basic elements.

Connected images carry certain abstract meaning. Yin-yang is the basic concept of Chinese astrology; Father, Son, and Holy Spirit is the Christian belief. A formal Chinese dinner comes in multiple of four courses, a Japanese formal dinner comes in five courses, the Buddhist underworld has six destinations, seven gods bring good luck, Buddhism enlightenment requires that eight rules be followed, and to enter the Maya heaven, a stairway of thirteen steps must be climbed.

Such image combinations carry abstract or metaphysical meaning, and numerological superstition is still strong in the world's local cultures. As these examples show, not only each image, but also the image's structure, carries special meaning. I show a few more examples in section 4.05. We sense abstract meanings by such an image structure. Time, history, theory, and probability are all represented by the image structure.

A significant advantage of structural memory is that it conforms well with visual and language images. Both images can be accurately constructed from the basic elements, such as vectors, arcs, phonemes, and alphabets, by building multilevel hierarchical structures to represent complex images. An exception is the sense of chemical images. The sense of smell and taste have various elements but no hierarchy. This is because the sensors are molecule type specific, and their signals are directly used.

Evolution created the hardware capable of connecting images, and the image's intrinsic nature of decomposability and integrability matched well with the developing brain hardware. This was a lucky natural circumstance that created self-consciousness. I suspect that ETs, if they do exist, may not have such good luck. I wonder if there was a special condition for evolution on our planet. If this good luck did not exist, complex biological systems may still have been built by evolution, but the system may not have achieved self-consciousness.

3.11 Analog Operation of Neuron Circuits

Certain brain functions can be more efficiently executed by analog circuit than by digital circuit. Because of this, I attempted several *conceptual* designs of neuron analog circuits that could be used in my model. To build an analog circuit that works without trimming the component parameters, I must assume that the neurons making up the circuit must have closely matched characteristics; they must be nearby so that they are supported in the same way, and they must have similar parameter values. I expect that such neurons are available somewhere in the brain. I have stressed the match of neuron characteristics. This is the requirement from the practice of precision linear electronic integrated circuit design, and the requirement is the same for neuron circuits.

An analog variable of a neuron circuit is the action-potential pulse rate. Gain of a neuron as analog amplifier, β, is defined by the ratio of the numbers of the output pulse N_0 to the input pulse N_1 per unit time, such as $\beta = N_0/N_1$. Since the neuron gain may match but may not be unity, I need a circuit that sets $\beta = 1$.

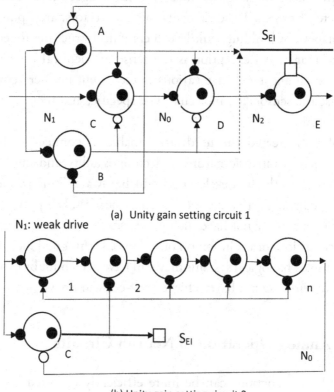

(a) Unity gain setting circuit 1

(b) Unity gain setting circuit 2

Figure 3.11.1 Unity gain setter

In figure 3.11.1(a), all the neurons, A, B, C, D, E, ..., have matched characteristics. If the rate of the output pulse N_0 of neuron C is more or less than the input pulse N_1, then neurons A and B exercise feedback control to neuron C to adjust N_0. The negative feedback keeps $N_0 = N_1$.

As neuron D is matched to neuron C, $N_2 = N_0 = N_1$ and any number of matched neurons can be controlled by the composite signals S_{EI}. I show this composite control signal by a single square symbol.

The circuit of figure 3.11.1(a) assumes that one excitatory synapse's effect can be canceled precisely by one inhibitory synapse's effect. I suppose that this condition is at least approximately satisfied. But if that is not the case, an alternative circuit, such as that shown in figure 3.11.1(b), can be used. In this circuit, neurons of the multistage loop 1, 2, ... n must have all matching characteristics.

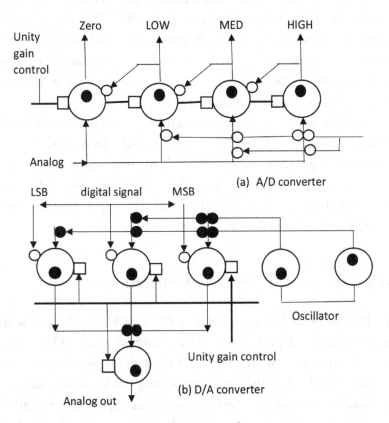

Figure 3.11.2 Various analog circuits

First, neuron 1 is driven weakly. The last neuron, n, should not be driven strongly. If N_0/N_1 is limited to the maximum, α, then each neuron's gain is $\alpha^{1/n}$, and if n is large, the gain settles close to 1. The control neuron C applies feedback to set the gain to unity. Its output signal S_{EI} can also be used to control any number of matched neurons' gain close to unity.

Once the unity gain circuit is available, the gain $\beta = 2$ amplifier can be built by paralleling a pair of unity-gain neurons and by summing up the pulses by another unity-gain neuron as shown in figure 3.11.2(a). Analog addition and subtraction can be executed by the circuit of figures 3.11.2(b) and 3.11.2(c), respectively. If B > A in the subtraction circuit, then the circuit output is zero.

Image sensors are in the upper area of the brain's functional diagram, and they work by analog signals (section 3.04). This is because they belong to evolutionarily old body organs that had to deal with the analog parameters characterizing the habitat. The circuits of figures 3.11.2(b) and 3.11.2(c) can be used to interface the analog parameters to the digital neuron circuit inside the brain.

Analog memory by neuron-to-neuron connection can be set up in the feedback control loop of figure 3.11.2(d). To control the action intensity and get it to the desired level, the memory is formed at the central neuron's input synapse. As the action intensity is adjusted by observing the control's effect, the feedback loop activation level is maintained by the conductivity of the synapse.

3.12   Neuron A/D and D/A Conversion

The human brain handles several analog variables such as sensation, elapsed time, and probability of an expected event. These analog variables are sensed by the body, and the sense is quantitatively quite accurate. The level of the sense can be sent out by bodily action, for instance, by the volume of howling to express anger (section 4.30). Yet to send it out by language, it must be digitized to qualitative levels that have a small number of steps. An A/D (analog to digital) converter executes the conversion. To execute A/D conversion, an array of neurons having successively higher excitation thresholds are driven by the analog signal. The active neuron in the array having the highest excitation threshold indicates the digital representation of the analog signal.

The brain has no unconscious mechanism for converting the analog variable to a number. All such operations are executed consciously. One way of conscious analog-to-digital conversion is to transform the analog variable to length, area, volume, or weight by imagination, observe it, and count the number of the units. A/D conversion is generally to decide the rank of the object. An excellent idiot savant artist would grade the quality of any artistic work by military rank. Yamashita Kiyoshi used to say, "This is a painting of the rank of colonel," an interesting way of A/D conversion. This was my experience at about the end of World War II.

Where is the A/D converter used in the brain's architecture? Analog signals such as sensation or elapsed time are generated and are sensed by the body. The signals are the activity level of the deep area centers. The converter is set up there, and the analog signal is converted to the qualitative levels, such as LOW, MIDDLE, or HIGH. Then the signal is sent to the association area to excite the language channel's word identifier, by which it is sent out by language.

Digital-to-analog conversion (D/A) is sometimes required if the parameter value is given by language and the action's intensity must be controlled by the given number. For instance, if I am told to put 1 kg of rice in a bag without a scale, I need such capability. To execute D/A conversion, an array of excited neurons are prepared, and their activities are summed by a neuron controlled by the number from the language channel. The converter is also in the lower association area, and its output drives the deep area center to adjust the action intensity. D/A and A/D conversion are the basic operations for human life, and therefore the functions are set up in the evolutionarily old area.

3.13 Neuron-Neuron Connection by Switch

Digital signal connection in a neuron circuit is done in three different ways. The first is by a switch connecting or disconnecting two neurons. The second is neuron-to-neuron unidirectional connection, and the third is circuit-to-circuit bidirectional connection. Switch connection is the most versatile. Figure 3.07.1(e) shows a neuron switch and the level inversion circuit required for it. The switch's requirements are (1) high conductivity when it is ON and (2) no leakage when it is OFF.

Since a neuron used as a switch is an amplifying device, high conductivity can be ensured by keeping the neuron's threshold voltage low. The neuron's threshold is reduced by the weak drive of one of its excitatory synapses. Leakage from an off switch is a stray action-potential pulse. To reduce such a pulse, one way is to cascade two neuron switches. Another way is to intensify the inhibitory synapse drive to increase the excitation threshold. Signal leakage cannot be prevented entirely. Leakage may have some positive effect in image sensing, as I discuss in section 4.22. Since the switches in the action-decoding area gate the image signal to the actuators, the proper degree of signal leak is essential for internal image observation. The effect of leak to the actuator is compensated for by not sending energy to it. This prevents action to the outside while creating the sense of the internal image to the SELF.

The switch is a two-input controlled logic gate. By connecting the elementary switch and the signal inversion circuit, the basic logic operation, AND, OR, and INV (invert), can be synthesized. Different from the simple neuron gate of section 3.07, these gates are made using special neurons having only a small number of signal inputs, and therefore they work reliably. Multiple-pole, multiple-throw switches are used in the action-decoding area to steer the muscle control signal to one or more of the body's destinations.

3.14   Neuron-Neuron Unidirectional Connection

The neuron-to-neuron connection is made either directly or indirectly. If neuron A has a synapse on neuron B, and if A is excited hard for a long time, the synapse is activated, and A and B are connected. By this mechanism, any excited neuron may be connected to the nearby neuron temporarily, and the connection may leave some trace of the history of the local circuit excitation. Such connections may not build any additional circuit, and most of them break down, yet later the trace of the earlier activity may facilitate the making of a new connection.

Connection is made faster, and is made more securely, by any effect pulling up the internal voltage of the destination neuron. If neuron B has another synapse that is excited simultaneously by neuron C, then B is jointly excited by A and C, and the A-to-B connection is made more quickly and more securely. If A and B make a loop, then the pair of connections A → B and B → A are solidified together.

If neuron A does not have a synapse on B, then an A-to-B connection must be made via an intermediate neuron, C. In such an indirect connection, A and B must have a reason to be connected. From the working mechanisms of the functional blocks I described before, there must be a reason for connecting between two or more simultaneously excited neurons. Although connection resources in the brain's lower blocks are abundant, some neurons A and B may need the intermediary, C. Neuron A may have several intermediary neurons C that can be excited by A. The selected one is spatially close to both A and B and can be capacitively or resistively coupled to B as I discuss in section 3.28. An electrical coupling mechanism pulls up the internal voltage of the most favorable intermediary neuron C, and that is excited by A. Then neuron C is connected to neuron B, and the A → C → B connection is established. In such connection mechanisms, it is not ensured that the shortest path between A and B is made. In case a long connection is made, later excitation may find a shorter connection and replace the longer one.

A similar mechanism works if there is an accidentally excited neuron D somewhere between A and B. Then A and B are connected via D. In this case, the brain activity may display an extra image carried by D, in addition to A and B. Such spurious activity is, by definition, a malfunction, but the SELF does not know that. It is often experienced that an unrelated image pops up in focused thinking by this mechanism.

The effects of direction of connection are felt most clearly when the images are sent out. Simple visual images can be sent out automatically in both forward and backward strokes (section 4.14). Yet reversing the order of words in spoken language is difficult. Can you say "once upon a time" in reverse order right away? In a sentence, grammatical and semantic rules hold the word order. So language is essentially a unidirectionally connected image.

Since visible images were originally used for fight-or-flight defense purposes, the vector-arc order affects the chance of survival. This original requirement was inherited from the evolutionarily early period. So, a simple visible image's order of execution has been made flexible (section 4.14). Yet the speed of execution need be only as fast as the speed of the aggressive action of the predators.

The language output channel works much faster than any other mechanical output channel. Often the speed of sentence construction is so fast that the whole sentence cannot be held in the memory. The speed is the result of the unidirectional connection of the words.

The voice channel's task for defense is quite limited. The means of defense include only howling to scare the predators off, used by gorillas and the president. Self-defense by language is effected by the message's meanings, and it requires a rigid word order to present the threatening intention.

3.15 Neuron Circuit Bidirectional Connection

Bidirectional connection of the logic nodes of electronic systems is made by a piece of conducting wire. Neuron circuits have no equivalent of node or wire. Connection between two neurons is made from an axon location to a dendrite location via a synapse, and this is a unidirectional connection. To connect neuron A and B bidirectionally, I must have one connection from A to B and another from B to A, both of these being unidirectional connections. Such a neuron pair makes a latch that holds binary data. This is the case if both connections are active at the same time. If connection A → B and connection B → A are never simultaneously active, the connections are between two neuron circuits, each including neuron A and neuron B. Bidirectional connection makes sense only between neuron circuits, except for a neuron latch. Figure 3.15.1(a) shows a connection between circuit block A and B.

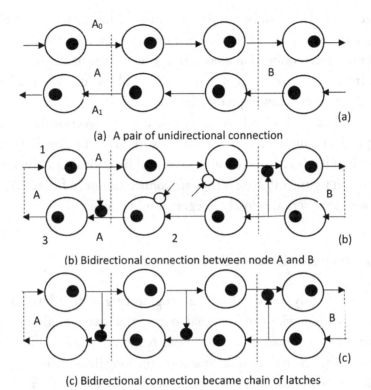

(a) A pair of unidirectional connection

(b) Bidirectional connection between node A and B

(c) Bidirectional connection became chain of latches

Figure 3.15.1 Bidirectional connection

A signal leaving block A, A_0, is not the same as the signal received by block A, A_1. If A_0 and A_1 are to be the same, then neurons in block A and block B must be connected by a synapse as shown in figure 3.15.1(b). In this circuit, what is called the same signal means that the outputs of neuron 1 and neuron 2 exercise the same effect on the receiving neuron 3. These observations imply that neuron connection $A \to B$ (*above*) and $B \to A$ (*below*) need not, and may not, conduct simultaneously.

If the $A \to B$ and $B \to A$ connections are simultaneously active, the (supposed to be) passive connection path may become an active signal source. The bidirectionally connected blocks A and B become slaves of the connection, and their states are jointly set by all the loops of all the neurons involved. To avoid such an operation, bidirectional connection paths must satisfy the requirements so that the connection does not create spurious activity. The gain of any loop of the connection

195

of figure 3.15.1(c) must be less than the unity. This is a tricky condition to be satisfied, and sometimes the connection may start activity. In a real brain, such connection among image identifiers may actually exist. A bidirectional connection of neuron circuit blocks deprives the blocks of independence in an unpredictable way.

Template and identifier are connected bidirectionally, but by independent unidirectional connections like that in figure 3.15.1(a). Identifier-identifier connection is either unidirectional or bidirectional like that in figure 3.15.1(b). If they are connected like in figure 3.15.1(c), the two identifiers are closely integrated into one.

3.16   Neuron Circuit Bus Structure

Bus, as previously stated, is a systems engineering term. A bus is a set of nodes, to each of which many signal sources and many circuits requiring the signal are connected. Usually a bus is shown by a set of long lines in a diagram. In an electronic processor, the long lines are literally long conducting wires to which many circuits are connected. Each bus line carries a well-defined signal: data bus line number one carries the least significant bit of binary data, which comes as a set of 4, 8, 16, 32, etc., in a single-chip microprocessor.

A neuron circuit bus line is also a set of structures in which many neurons are connected, but it is not a single circuit node. A single line of a neuron system bus consists of, generally, many serially connected neurons penetrating through neuron memory and logic circuits. Such a neuron circuit's bus line still has the basic similarity to an electronic processor's bus line since the lines of a bus carry a set of signals that are single elements of images like vectors. Excitation of a vector bus line indicates existence of the vector having a specific direction and length in the image. This identity is kept all throughout the bus line length.

As much as identity of the signal is kept, a bus line need not be a single neuron. As a bus line runs from functional block to block, the signal goes through many neurons of the blocks, but the identity of the signal is still maintained. If many neuron gates are connected, a bus line can be complex as shown in figure 3.16.1(a). Here, neurons A and B cooperate in image-processing tasks, and the OR gate neuron C sums the block's activity together. Neurons A, B, … can be made more complex by including many other neurons. The most simplified schematic of the internal image bus line through the assembly, template and action-control area is shown in figure 3.16.1(b). To simplify this diagram, the series-connected neurons in each block are replaced with a single neuron, and no processing is executed in any block. This bus line excitation indicates the existence of a specific vector in the currently displayed visual image. Since neuron connection is unidirectional, the bus lines must close loops so that any two blocks can communicate by sending and receiving signals through the loop structure. Signals circulate around the internal image bus loops to effect bidirectional communications of the assembly, action-control, scratch pad, and template areas.

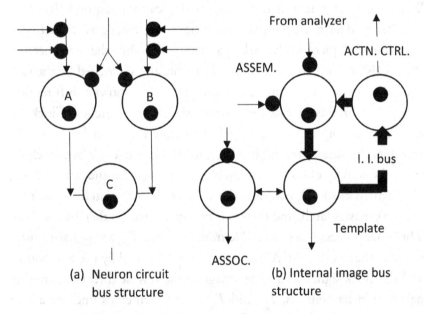

(a) Neuron circuit bus structure

(b) Internal image bus structure

Figure 3.16.1 Schematic of internal image bus

Each bus line has the structure of a great river. Many tributaries flow into the main stream, and the water flows to the ocean. Then seawater evaporates to become clouds, then rain, and supplies water to the headwater of the tributaries. Yet the entire flow system has its own name, such as Amazon or Orinoco. The name of the river is equivalent to its bus line's identification. Some rivers' water flows into another river. There is only one geographical case of one river's headwater flowing into another river, Orinoco to Amazon, but such a thing is common in the brain's neuron bus lines. The river analogy is a proper one since signals flow unidirectionally through the bus line neurons. Although I show the overall structure of bus lines in figure 3.16.1(b), the internal image bus consists of several different sets of data, such as vectors, rotations, and characters of the visible image.

3.17   Shifting and Rotating Images

A neural logic circuit is able to display an image in tens of milliseconds. When the image is sent out, the actuator cannot respond that fast. The image data must be sent out element by element as the actuator completes one piece of the task at a time. To do this, the brain needs a shift register that carries the image elements and is clocked by the task completion signal from the actuator. Figure 3.17.1 shows a shift register design. It consists of cascaded master-slave (M-S) latches. Clock C_A turns the activity of the slave latch off before data transfer. Clock C_B transfers the data of the master latch to the slave latch. Then clock C_C turns the activity of the master latch off, to prepare for the next transfer, after which clock C_D transfers the data of the slave latch to the next section's master latch, and one cycle of data transfer is thereby finished. The same process is repeated. Neurons T_{MS} and T_{SM} are signal-transfer neurons that work as an AND gate, jointly activated by the data source and the clock signals. To move image in the reverse direction, another pair of transfer neurons, T_{SM} and T_{MS}—and their clock lines are added to the diagram. To load a set of data, the master latch is cleared by clock $C_{C'}$, and then load clock C_L is activated. Then all the registers are loaded by a set of data simultaneously.

The four-phase clock waveforms are shown at the bottom of figure 3.17.1. The clocks C_A–C_D are generated by the actuator. Since shift register is a general-purpose circuit used in logic blocks of the brain model, such clocks are generated within the functional block in which the register is implemented. The clock period is set by the processing needs of the functional block.

A shift register is a basic circuit block used to build the brain model. It is required in the analyzer, assembly area, and action-control area, to shift or rotate any visible element image. A shift register used to rotate a visible image has its last stage connected to the first stage, thereby closing a loop. This application of shift register has one technical problem that requires explanation.

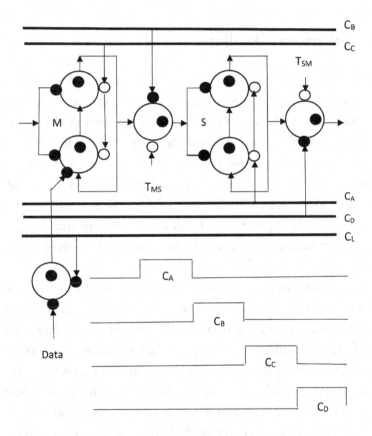

Figure 3.17.1 Neuron shift register and clocks

A polar coordinate grid is set at the points (nxdρ, mxdθ), where dρ is the unit of radial increment, dθ is the increment of the angle, and *n* and *m* are integers. Shift registers set around all the circles are clocked at the same rate, and at each clock tick the image rotates by angle $\angle d\theta$. By this design, the density of the grid points decreases with the increasing distance from the origin. This creates distortion of the rotated image. To compensate for this, angular step $d\theta$ must be decreased with increasing *n*, such that $d\theta$ is proportional to $1/n$. Then the clocking period of the circular shift register must be increased proportional to polar distance, $n \times d\rho$. This complicates the clock design. A circuit that does not have this problem is shown in figure 3.21.1(a). The circuit is quite complex, but does not have the image distortion problem.

3.18 Subcritical Oscillator

A structure made by connecting several neurons in a closed loop plays a key role in my mechanical brain model. Templates and internal image loops are such structures. A pair of neurons closing a loop, a latch, is the simplest loop structure (section 3.08). The loop can be multiply connected to make a pretzel-like structure. A closed path of neurons usually accepts many excitatory or inhibitory input signals, and it executes some local logic operations as shown in figure 3.18.1(a). Depending on the input signals to all the neurons of the loop and on the state of connections between the neurons, the loop structure shows various distinct modes of operation.

Many crucial brain operations are carried out by the interaction between a pair of such loop structures, which I call a *subcritical oscillator*. If an identifier is excited, the associated template is driven into self-excited oscillation and displays the internal image it carries. An especially interesting feature is that the connection structure between the oscillator pair works as expected, even if there are a few missing or wrong connections. This fault-tolerant feature of subcritical oscillators is particularly important to connect the brain's rigidly constructed upper area (down to the assembly area) to the random-connection-dominated lower area (below the scratch pad and template area). The connections among the oscillators actually provide support signals to the oscillators, yet the signals carry image information, as I show by the many cases that occur in my model.

Depending on the level of support signals, a closed-loop circuit as shown in figure 3.18.1 has three distinct operation modes. If the level of support is low, the loop as a whole remains quiescent, as shown in figure 3.18.1(a). Local signal excitation does not go through the loop. In this state, the loop's existence is *invisible* to the rest of the neuron circuit. Some of the neurons in the loop may even become a part of an unrelated logic circuit, as shown in the figure. If the level of support is higher than that, the loop is excited by the external signal sources and becomes a passive signal path as a whole. The loop organizes the activities, reflecting its structure and its associated circuits. The loop integrates logic operations executed by each locality of the loop.

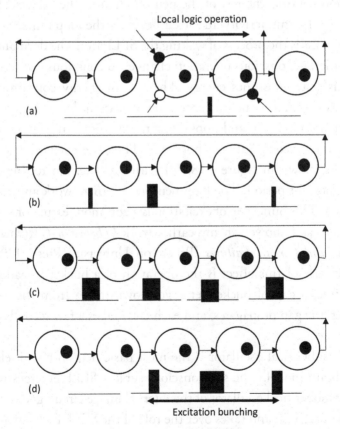

Figure 3.18.1 Subcritical oscillator states

Each neuron is a part of the associated local logic circuit. The loop's character still does not show up. Because of this *dark horse* feature of the circuit, I call it a *subcritical* oscillator. Its operation in this state is shown in figure 3.18.1(b). Subcritical oscillators in this state do not yet show their own character.

If more action-potential pulses circulate around the loop, the loop's neuron-to-neuron connection becomes stronger, and then more action-potential pulses circulate. The effect is cumulative, and the loop goes into self-excited oscillation. This is the result of positive feedback between the neuron-to-neuron connection and the level of excitation. In the high-level excitation of figure 3.18.1(c), the loop reveals its own character and becomes *visible* to the rest of the neuron circuit. If the loop represents an image, the image suddenly emerges, and the image's excitation controls the rest of the neuron circuit. The subject SELF is taken over by this activity and itself becomes the loop's image display activity. This is the process of waking the SELF from the dormant state. The earlier, unconscious operation changes to conscious operation.

This state consumes energy. The rate of energy consumption is sensed as sensation. If neuron excitation uses up the local energy supply, the excitation weakens and stops. Yet if the circuit is strongly supported, the neurons recover after a short rest. Then the excitation tends to bunch as shown in figure 3.18.1(d) with each neuron resting in the short quiescent period. The loop neurons alternate work and rest in a long loop. This bunching of excitation is a common feature of any loop excitation, as I showed in my earlier work (*Theory of CMOS Digital Circuits and Circuit Failures* [Princeton University Press, 1992]). A familiar case of this effect is the operation of a bucket brigade; after some time, a gap of buckets emerges downstream from the weakest member, the gap propagates, and each crew takes a few seconds of rest during the gap.

The subcritical oscillator is the most basic neuron circuit element in my brain model. The self-conscious subject SELF emerges when a template subcritical oscillator of the internal image circuit goes into self-excited oscillation and takes over the role of the SELF by its image and sensation. A subcritical oscillator structure may be built unconsciously.

At an unexpected moment, it is excited, and with surprise, a new image emerges from the brain.

Here I reiterate an important feature of the subcritical oscillator based architecture, namely that a few wrong or missing connections among such oscillators never affects the brain operation. In a neuron circuit, such misconnection can never be avoided. Yet the image is kept intact. Subcritical oscillators are controlled by the majority of the signals connecting them, and these signals are image-specific support signals. An image's state is transmitted not by a single neuron connection but by the consistency of many neuron connections. This feature saves the brain system from connection errors. The unusual reliability of self-consciousness owes to this feature

As a subcritical oscillator activity is phased out, the strongly connected structure does not weaken right away. The slow decay of oscillation creates a lingering sense of mood and the afterthoughts that we always experience.

3.19 Image-Specific Support

In any neuron circuit, the role of support (energy supply and waste removal) has two types. One is support of the entire body, the entire brain, or an entire functional block of the brain. The energy is supplied directly from the whole body's energy source. The other is the brain's image-specific support mechanism. The signal from the identifier to its template is an example. The energy source is the brain's local energy storage. In a neuron logic circuit, image-specific support does not supply energy there, but it encourages the target circuit to consume locally available energy to be active. In a neuron logic circuit, this concept is quite useful.

A signal carrying image information and a signal carrying image-specific support are the two types of signals, and they are often not clearly distinguishable. One feature of an image-specific support signal is that more than one connection from circuit block A to block B exercises the same control as I have shown by the example of mutual support of template and identifier. In section 2.20, the pixel bitmap signals from the eye to the vision channel analyzer are image-carrying signals. The analyzer and the assembly area convert them to image-specific support signals, which connect template and identifier. This is the unique feature of the subcritical oscillator–based architecture of the brain's lower level. In my model, the upper functional blocks—analyzer, action-decoding area, assembly area, and action-control area—are rigidly connected according to genetic specification, and they operate mostly by image-carrying signals. The blocks below the template area have flexible connection capability, and there are many image-specific support signals connecting the image-carrying subcritical oscillators.

Image-specific support signals exist mostly in the three areas shown in figure 3.19.1. The identifier in the association area supports its template as shown in figure 3.19.1(a). This support is mutual. Identifier-identifier connections support each other, or one of them supports the other, such as an abstract meaning identifier is supported by its examples' identifiers, as shown in figure 3.19.1(b). The deep area meaning center supports the relevant concrete image's identifier and its template as shown in figure 3.19.1(c). This image-specific support works most effectively at times when a particular image is focused intensively.

Image-specific support is done by the connection created by the neuron circuit's activity. If a certain image is excited often and strongly, more support connections are made. This is a self-altering feature of the neuron circuits and is advantageous for the brain's operation. An often recalled memory is held securely for a long time by this mechanism. Image-specific support signals connect a pair of image-carrying subcritical oscillators and maintain their relationship. Figures 3.19.1(d) and 3.19.1(e) show how image-specific support connection grows by the neuron circuit activity. This structure building is helped by the budding of new axon branches and the formation of additional synapses on the supported neuron. Movement of the synapse and intensification of the connection by strong excitation (section 3.09) are the two features of connection flexibility in the brain's lower area, where circuit excitation is not so frequent as in the upper area of the brain. The upper area such as the analyzer is continuously activated, and the existing connection is kept secure.

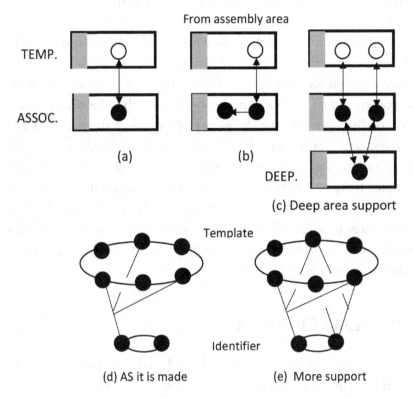

Figure 3.19.1 Image-specific support mechanism

An image is usually connected to many other images by the image's identifiers in order to set up the meaning of the image. Joint excitation of these associated images has effectively the same effect as an image-specific support mechanism. Not only the current theme image but also all the associated images help each other to build up the theme image's meaning. In some image processing, image A and image B are supported alternately so the SELF is able to compare them. This is the mechanism for the brain to explain image A in terms of image B, and B in terms of A. This is one of the basic mechanisms by which the SELF understands images, as I show in section 4.25. Image-specific support may have variations, such as alternate support or even negative support: excitation of image A prevents excitation of B. Some supports are sequential so that images A → B → C → A are cyclically displayed.

The image-specific support mechanism derives energy from the block global support system, which takes energy in depending on the overall activity level of the block. Activity of the whole block's circuit derives energy from this local source. The local source constantly supplies energy, not in real time for each circuit's activity, but by following the average demand of the local circuit's activity. The brain can tolerate only ten seconds or so of supply interruption, yet this time is long enough to process and display complex images. The brain's energy supply mechanism is unusually reliable because the final local energy supply mechanism depends on the most reliable diffusion transport of energy-carrier molecules. For this mechanism to work, the logic element, that is, the neuron, must be quite small.

3.20 Vision Channel Analyzer

A visual image is first scaled to the subjectively fixed size of the vision field by adjusting magnification of the eye's lens. The vision field is defined by the angle spanned by the eyes (left-right, 160 degrees; top-bottom, 130 degrees). The photosensors convert the image to a pixel bitmap. The images from the pair of eyes are combined, and the vectors and arcs are extracted from the image as I described in section 2.20.

The first step of vector-arc extraction from the pixel map is the contrast enhancement of the bitmap image. This is carried out by a neuron gate having high gain. In figure 3.20.1(a), A and B are a pair of optical signals from the neighboring pixels. Neuron 1 sends signal $g(A - B)$, and neuron 2 sends signal $g(B - A)$ to neuron X, where g is the neuron's gain as analog amplifier (section 3.11). I assumed that an excitatory and an inhibitory synapse compensate for each other.

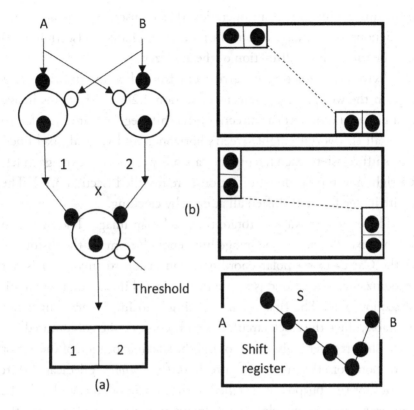

Figure 3.20.1 Image contrast enhancement

If A > B, then neuron 2 generates no pulse, and vice versa. Neuron X has a high excitation threshold. It is activated only if either A or B is much more intense than B or A, respectively. As this circuit operation shows, this is the circuit that detects the high-contrast boundary of the pixel map image. Let this circuit be shown by two dots in a rectangle in figure 3.20.1(a). Figure 3.20.1(b), *above* and *center*, shows that the circuits of figure 3.20.1(a) attend to all the horizontal and vertical locations of the pixel map. Contrast of the two directions is added, and the sum is further discriminated by a threshold gate. Then only those pixels at the highest-contrast boundary are retained. All such high-contrast boundary pixels make the line drawing of the object's shape, shown at the bottom of figure 3.20.1(b). This conversion of the pixel image to line drawing is carried out all at once. As it is observed from this circuit, this is an operation that is susceptible to noise. An ambiguous visual image can be misprocessed. Phantoms (section 6.04) may be caused by malfunction of the analyzer.

Vector-arc extraction is carried out from this line drawing. It is kept in the working light screens of section 2.20. To shift this image in a horizontal or vertical direction, the shift registers are installed to cover all the working light screen's horizontal and vertical pixel lines. The shift registers, each having the capability to move the image in left ↔ right and top ↔ down directions, are installed (section 3.17). The entire image frame is shifted all at once by clocking.

There are two ways to rotate the pixel map image. The first is to set the pixel density of the image high enough to make the distortion of the Cartesian ↔ polar coordinate conversion so small that is not recognizable. The second is to use the dedicated image rotation circuit of section 3.21. The first method is simple to implement, but is not desirable, since the clock circuit design becomes quite complicated.

A shift register is also used to find the starting location of the vector extraction from the image of figure 3.20.1(b), *bottom*. A dedicated shift register for this purpose is installed in the horizontal line, and only the register section at the edge of the image frame is activated to set the marker. Then the marker and the pixel bit are ANDed by a set of AND gates set up at all pixel locations. As the marker is moved by clocking the shift register (each clock tick moves the marker by one spatial step), the AND gate's output is initially logic LOW level, but as the marker hits the first pixel of the line drawing, the AND gate's output becomes HIGH. This location is marked as the starting point of vector-arc extraction. A similar scheme is used to determine the length of a vector. In this case, a spatially fixed horizontal AND gate array is set up at the reference location of the extraction logic (location O shown in figure 2.20.1), and then the entire image frame is shifter relative to the reference point. The AND gate output is originally logic HIGH level but becomes logic LOW level at the tip of the vector, thereby setting the vector's length.

The visual image analyzer in a real brain is very complex. It is impossible to copy that architecture to a hardware model. Yet this problem does not affect the self-conscious human machine. The human mind works only on the preprocessed image data, and how the preprocessing is carried out does not affect self-consciousness. Furthermore, I suspect that the design of the real human brain's visual image-processing area may not be the optimum judged from the modern system design criteria.

For people born blind, any object's image comes in from the body parts and the body surface's senses, and from the action taught by their caretakers. For instance, if the person who is blind learns to draw a circle by using his or her finger, the motion is analyzed and is sent to the vision channel, as I showed in section 2.23. Although the visible image is not available, the image is processed in the same way, and the same sense emerges in his or her brain and body.

3.21 Assembly Area of the Vision Channel

The assembly area receives a sequence of brain-comprehensible image information from the analyzer. The information is made by compressing and reformatting the incoming bitmap image to the line drawing, built from the arcs' and vectors' sequence. The assembly area adjusts the sequence and delivers it to the template area. The assembly area also accepts the stored images from the image memory and modifies them to make them useful to the lives.

Tasks executed by the vision channel assembly area are the following:

(1) It formats and sends the image information from the analyzer to the template area to store it there, or to identify the incoming image by matching the existing template.
(2) It modifies the image while maintaining its basic structure.
(3) It assembles elementary images to make a composite image.
(4) It modifies the elementary image structure by adding or deleting elements.

Task (1): The assembly area receives an open sequence of vectors and arcs. The area closes the loop, as I discussed in section 2.27, to qualify it as the visible elementary image and then sends it to the template area and identifies the image, or makes a new image template.

Task (2): If image identification fails, process (2) automatically takes over. The likely reason for a visible image mismatch is that the incoming image and the template image are not aligned in the same direction (section 2.29). The incoming image's excited vectors are rotated within the cross section of the vector bus lines (section 2.19). For this operation, a precise image-rotation circuit is required. The design of the circuit to carry out the operation is shown in figure 3.21.1(a). This is executed on the image data of cross section 1, to reproduce the rotated image in cross section 2. At each vector location of cross section 2, there is one neuron sourcing the image data from cross section 1. First, cross section 2 excitations are all erased. On this blank cross section 2, the neurons transmit the image data of cross section 1, rotated by the specified angle all at once. The angle is specified by the excitation of the rotation bus line indicating the angle.

Assembly area logic is able to scale the size of the image by using a similar circuit as shown in figure 3.21.1(b). The scaling factor is determined by excitation of a line of the character bus. Some character bus lines carry numbers used for scaling. Horizontal or vertical shift of the image can also be executed by using a similar circuit as that shown in figure 3.21.1(c). The amount of shift is given by excitation of the vector bus line. I show a more complex, but more precise, circuit of visible image processing than the circuit using shift register in figure 3.21.1. The rotated, scaled, and moved image data is sent to the template area to check if it matches the existing template. Image adjustments are continuously executed to cover all the possibilities. Template matching is one of the major unconscious brain operations.

Image shift, scaling, and rotation are the basic, innate image manipulation operations of the assembly area. The assembly area has various other image-processing capabilities, such as the specific image feature extraction capabilities like symmetry.

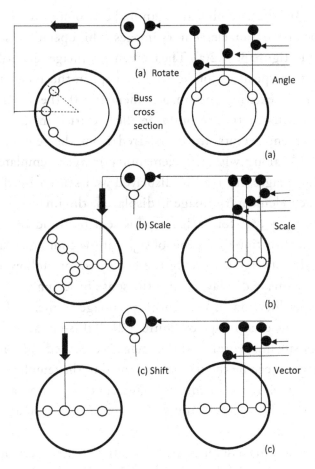

Figure 3.21.1 Assembly area utility logic

The special features of the image, such as symmetry, mirror image, and repetition of features, are used for template matching and image identification purposes (section 2.29). Each elementary image-processing instruction is activated by excitation of its own character bus line. The specific character bus excitation followed by rotation bus line excitation is the instruction to rotate the currently displayed image by a specified angle. These elementary operations can be assembled to a program executed in the assembly area. Such a program is invoked, for instance, by a mismatch indication signal from the template area. I discuss program execution in section 4.06.

Task (3): The assembly area can make a composite image like a landscape image from elementary images. This operation is executed as shown in figure 3.21.2(a). The elementary image's identifiers and their location-specification vectors are kept in the association area as shown. By exciting the image's identifier 0, the assembly area receives the instruction to build up the specified image structure. The placement vectors are transferred from the template to the scratch pad, along with the elementary image's templates. From there, the images are readily displayed and sensed by the SELF. Before each elementary image is displayed, the image's placement vector $\mathbf{v}_1$, $\mathbf{v}_2$, $\mathbf{v}_3$, ... for each image is sent out, and these vectors control the direction of the line of sight, if the composite landscape is internally observed. Moving the eye direction, followed by the elementary image display, creates the sense of seeing the images in their proper location in the landscape image frame. In landscape image display, each image of figure 3.21.2(a) is not scaled to fit in the composite image frame, if the image is observed only internally. Each image is seen by the size as it is stored in the template memory. The SELF sees the elementary images one at a time as full-size images, and the vectors provide the sense of the images placed properly in the frame.

Task (4): This assembly area operation is to insert or remove a vector or arc in an element image. In principle, this is done as follows: The original template is moved to the scratch pad, which can set a fixed reference point. Then vector $\mathbf{v}_X$ is inserted by the following procedure (note that figure 3.21.2[b] is the original, and figure 3.21.2[e] is the modified image after the vector insertion): First the template of the original is activated, and the vector sequence 1, 2, 3 displays the image for conscious observation to confirm the need of processing.

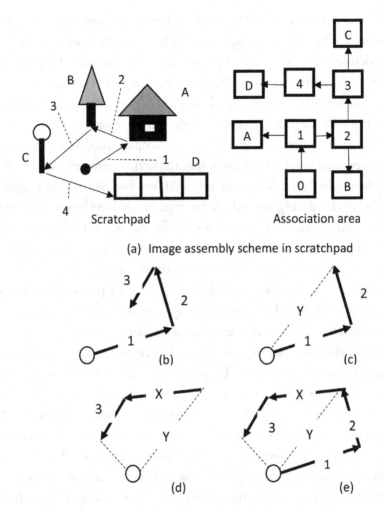

(a) Image assembly scheme in scratchpad

Figure 3.21.2 Manipulation of images

Then the assembly area converts the original template to the format referenced to the fixed point, set at the starting point of the first vector 1. The point is shown by an open circle in figure 3.21.2(b). Since the extra vector $\mathbf{v}_X$ is inserted after vector $\mathbf{v}_2$, I determine a vector $\mathbf{w}_0$ given by $\mathbf{w}_0 = \mathbf{v}_1 + \mathbf{v}_2$, and I split the original template into two separate templates. The first part remains intact by the vector insertion. By using the bracket [...] notation of section 2.27 to represent a template, the first partial template is $[\mathbf{v}_1, \mathbf{v}_2, \{-\mathbf{w}_0\}]$. Vector $-\mathbf{w}_0$ (Y in the figure) is a vector derived from vector $\mathbf{w}_0$ by reversing the direction, and $\{...\}$

indicates a pen-up vector. The second template is vector sequence [{$\mathbf{w}_0$}, $\mathbf{v}_4$, {$-(\mathbf{w}_0 + \mathbf{v}_4)$}], and this template is modified by the insertion of vector $\mathbf{v}_X$. I define vector $\mathbf{w}_1 = \mathbf{w}_0 + \mathbf{v}_X + \mathbf{v}_4$, and then the second template is modified to a new template [{$\mathbf{w}_0$}, $\mathbf{v}_X$, $\mathbf{v}_4$, {$-\mathbf{w}_1$}]. If two templates are excited in sequence, the modified image of figure 3.21.2(e) is displayed. The originally single template is broken into two consecutive templates.

So far I have described the process of template modification simply, but the process hides certain steps that the brain cannot execute, that is, how the original template is properly split into two pieces. The template signals are circulating around the internal image loop in several tens of milliseconds, which is too short a time for the SELF to find the right moment to intervene and split it. The brain is not a synchronous logic system, and it cannot set a well-defined timing point to step inside any image data. The brain is able to handle only those properly formatted, previously memorized elementary images at high speed. A template is an unbreakable element of the brain's data like an atom.

To modify the elementary image, I need to invoke a higher-level operation involving the SELF. To create the executive SELF, the template image must be sent out and drawn on a paper. In this process, the SELF must modify itself. The SELF is able to see the entire image on the paper via the image input channel and is able to confirm the processing need. Using the drawing as an outside image object, the SELF is able to find how to split the image and how to add the extra image element. Then the SELF executes the operation outside, taking the modified image back in and restoring it in the memory. Sending the image out and then taking it back in, the SELF is working with the image, which is the SELF itself. This is what I call the conscious image-processing operation, and its simplest example.

This example of template modification shows clearly that certain types of image manipulation cannot be carried out internally. The image must be sent out, processed as the outside image object by using the full capability of the inside SELF, and then the outside object is taken back in to replace the old SELF. Template splitting is the simplest example to highlight this feature of the brain's conscious image processing. This mode of operation is crucial for humans to think about any difficult problem.

The assembly area of the language channel has a similar memory and logic structure. The logic receives words and the grammatical rules from the channel's template area. The word's participle is identified by the vision channel and is sent to the language channel by excitation of a line of the character bus (section 2.25). Since this process requires the image's visual identification, language image processing is always a conscious operation. The logic function of the language channel assembly area includes the arrangement of the words in the proper order and conjugating words following the grammatical rules (singular, plural, future, present, past, and the cases that exist in many languages other than English). The assembly area has a close connection to the scratch pad, which retains the sentence during its composition. Once a sentence is constructed, it is either spoken or transferred to the vision channel to be sent out in written form. The sentence is usually not retained permanently.

3.22   Conscious/Unconscious Image Processing

Sometimes the human mind displays novel images that have never been seen before. Such images include simple yet otherworldly manifestations, or new combinations of common images assembled in unusual mutual relation. These are products of unconscious thinking, which is not sensed during the image-creation process. The lower processor P_2 may operate unconsciously, and a new image, one that consists of common elementary images arranged in an unusual mutual relation, is created (section 4.39). As I review the brain's functions in general, however, I find that most unconscious operations are going on in the vision input channel. The channel is constantly working to determine and update the structure of the living space, to let the SELF be aware of the nearby space in order to avoid any accident. Since this operation is executed unconsciously, we feel our living space information taken as granted (section 2.33). We do not even feel that our brain is working hard to get the information of the living space.

Contrary to such unconscious operation, there are conscious image-processing operations. If I have a definite objective to accomplish, I focus on the image of the objective, and I try to create the images of the intermediate steps to reach the objective. What is the difference between conscious and unconscious image processing? One feature is that unconscious processing occurs, most of the time, in the brain's upper area, which is constantly engaged with the incoming visual images.

Contrary to that, conscious processing is executed by all the functional blocks, and the SELF oversees the process. That is why we are aware of the engaged images continuously during the operation. The assembly area executes both conscious and unconscious operations. In conscious operation, the assembly area uses the scratch pad as the cache memory, but often the external memory media such as paper and pencil adds to that or may even take over the role of the scratch pad. In such an operation, the fast vision or voice/language input channel becomes the crucial aid to organize the operation.

Why is such an operation necessary? Suppose that the logic circuit of the assembly area receives an image-processing task. The logic circuit is not much more sophisticated than the circuits of any electronic data processor. The logic circuit of an electronic data processor works only if it is given a pre-defined task to execute. The circuit is not aware, why or how the processing is done. An electronic data processor requires a human administrator to load the program, which was assembled by self-conscious human programmers, to execute the assigned task.

Except for a simple enough task, whose routine has been well mechanized, the processor requires a self-conscious human *administrator*. In the brain, the SELF emerges as soon as the unconscious operation changes to conscious operation, to mobilize the entire brain's image processing capability. To invoke the SELF, the image must be sent out, operated as the outside object by the SELF, and then taken back in. By this process, the SELF's task is to oversee the action. Such a situation emerges when unconscious processing encounters difficulty. The SELF senses this as a risk to the person's life, and automatically steps in to rescue the situation. A typical difficulty of this kind is the case described in the previous section, namely, stepping into the structure of any elementary image, which the brain cannot do automatically.

The internal image circuit processes elementary images kept in the templates as the atoms of the information and can handle them at high speed. The processor can assemble such images into a composite image at high speed. The brain is made to handle an already qualified elementary image at the high speed. Yet the processing circuit has no capability by itself to step into an already formatted and memorized image structure. Why? the brain adopts an asynchronous logic system that has no common time reference (section 5.20). Since there is no timing reference, and no capability to recognize the image's feature to be modified in such a short time, it is impossible to interrupt the high-speed operation at the right moment to supply, extract or modify any feature of the image's template (section 5.21).

The brain's data type, images, is the minimum information element that the brain can handle as a unit at high speed, but an image is also a connected structure that can be divided. This contradictory feature emerges in the image's memory structure: a connected image can be split, but how that is properly done is not known by the brain's logic circuit. Yet that is known to the SELF, by referring to all the images the SELF has in the memory. For instance, when an image is split, some image components must be included in both the split pieces, in order for them to make sense, since the split images must be recognized as the meaningful elementary images. This requires a high level SELF's involvement in the processing.

The operation of altering a template is executed consciously by sending the image out, drawing the image on paper and recognizing it, altering it, and taking the processed images back to the brain. The external media are always helpful, but if the image is simple, it is enough to recognize the image internally and to execute the splitting, since we can see a fairly clear image without actually drawing it. If external media such as paper and pencil are available, then even the most complex image can be analyzed by the human brain. Complex systems are always designed by this method. The top-down system development strategy (section 6.11) is a systematic method used to design any complex systems.

Given all these observations, the brain's operation is summarized as follows: In unconscious operation, the external object's image is taken in and is processed entirely within the brain. In conscious operation, the SELF sends out the image, recognizes all its components, splits the image properly into elementary images, and alters each image by using its entire capabilities of the SELF.

In order to do so, the crucial process is to split the image into the proper element images. This is a much more complicated image-processing capability than putting the images together. Splitting an image is not like splitting firewood; rather, it is like splitting an inheritance among the descendants. Yet this is a combination of image send-out, processing it outside, and reinput process. So it is not clearly recognized as being all that significant. This process works to modify any image element such as vectors, arcs, and phonemes, but it also works for a complex composite image such as that shown in figure 3.22.1. This is the basis of analytic thinking by the human mind.

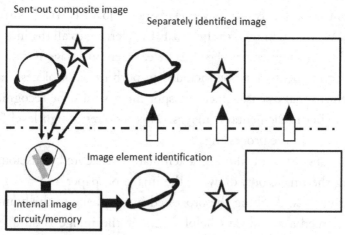

Figure 3.22.1 Conscious process of template separation for image analysis

Figure 3.22.1 shows that the SELF is watching the composite image of the sky from the window of a space ship. The SELF recognizes each element image, the Saturn, the Sirius, and the window making up the composite image. The SELF splits the composite image, and *separately* identifies them properly. For instance, the ring and the circle are the integrated parts of the image of the Saturn. They are not to be separated into the two elements. This is what I call for the SELF to analyze the image. The SELF identifies the elements and splits the composite image properly. To do so, the SELF must have enough internal images to identify the element images and split the original image properly. Element image identification can be done only by referring to the images already existing in the brain. In case of splitting a template, each element, vector or arc, becomes such an element image. Proper splitting requires that the brain have enough image inventory to identify the composite image and split it into the proper element images. The analytic thinking capability of the brain is powerful, but this is not an automatic operation like synthetic thinking, because it involves proper image splitting. Proper splitting depends heavily on the previously acquired images. Even by mobilizing the entire image inventory, some images cannot be split properly because no proper element image exists in the brain. An example is the Penrose triangle.

In the previous section, I showed that assembling an image from element images is an easy operation for the brain, but stepping into an image structure is not. This feature has a significant impact on human thinking: understanding by synthesis is easier than by analysis, because most parts of synthesis can be carried out automatically, as shown in the previous section by the example of landscape image assembly. This is a reason why I adopted the synthesis method to study self-consciousness: to design a hardware carrying self-consciousness is an example of synthetic thinking.

Yet sometimes synthetic thinking may become easygoing. In my student days studying physics, the bootstrap theory of elementary particles was popular. The theory held that if any elementary particle splits, some other elementary particle emerges (the popular nickname of this theory was *nuclear democracy*). This theory appeared rational at the time. Yet this synthetic theory phased out as the analytical research revealed the existence of the quarks.

3.23 Vision/Language Channel Template

A visible image converted to internally recognizable form by the analyzer and the assembly area is sent to the template area or scratch pad. In the template area, the image's structural information is stored as a temporary or permanent template. How is a template built? In the template matrix, each bus line goes through a neuron, and the output of any one of such neuron can be connected to the input of all the other neurons making up the bus lines. This means that connecting synapses are provided, and the image's activity connects the neurons. Such exhaustive neuron connection should be possible in the template area matrix. The area allows the incoming image signal to build the image's structural memory. The template's connection starts from a bus line neuron and returns to the same neuron, thereby closing a loop. Sequential excitation of the neurons specified by the direction of the connection displays the stored image.

The issue is to consider in what sort of neuron matrix such a structure is built, and then how neurons are connected. Figure 3.23.1(a) shows a simplified matrix consisting only of three internal image bus lines. The internal image bus lines from the assembly area are numbered 1, 2, and 3, and those to the action-control area are numbered as 1', 2', and 3'. Neuron-to-neuron synaptic contacts have been provided already in the matrix, but as they are, the contacts do not conduct pulses. Synapse activation connects the neurons. If there are n bus lines, there can be more than $n!$ different ordered connections. This is a huge number. If there are one hundred bus lines, there can be an astronomically large number of image structures that are stored in the template memory!

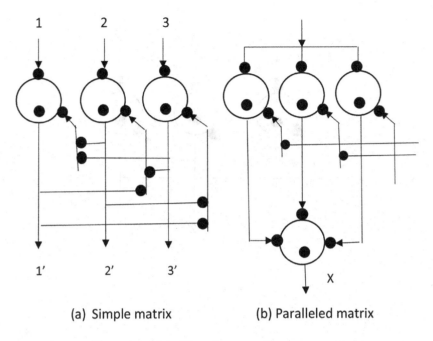

(a) Simple matrix   (b) Paralleled matrix

Figure 3.23.1 Template matrix structure

Is such a neuron matrix design possible? Some neurons have ten thousand synapses, but these are exceptions. To improve template matrix' capacity, the individual bus line of figure 3.23.1(a) can be split into many parallel lines as shown in figure 3.23.1(b). There is a neuron that sums up the same bus line signal. Since template is a subcritical oscillator (section 3.18), such a template structure works reliably.

Template neurons have a high excitation threshold and are hard to excite. This ensures that the correct image structure is retained. Strong drive comes from the assembly area, yet it takes some time to secure a permanent template connection. This is experienced by the effort necessary to memorize a complex object's structure correctly. Simultaneous formation of the identifier in the association area to secure long and strong excitation is required to form a permanent template memory.

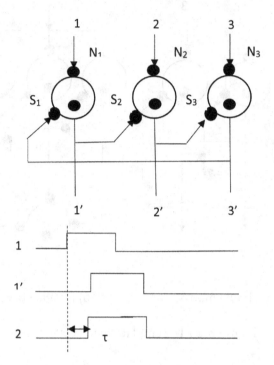

Figure 3.23.2 Template neuron connection process

Figure 3.23.2 shows how a template is connected. Sequential signals 1, 2, and 3 arrive at the respective neurons N_1, N_2, and N_3. For signal 1 to excite neuron N_1, it takes a short delay time, shown in the waveform. Signal 1' is delayed, and therefore it overlaps signal 2 with neuron N_2. Then synapse S_2 excites neuron N_2 strongly, because signal 2 reduces neuron N_2's excitation threshold. Then synapse S_2 conducts, and neurons N_1 and N_2 are unidirectionally connected. The rest of the neurons are connected in the same way. In figure 3.23.2, the three-member template loop is unidirectionally connected by the overlapping signals from the assembly area. The neuron-to-neuron connection is further strengthened when the template's identifier is formed, as I show in the next section. Unidirectional connection is required for a template memory to keep the image structure correct. Since a template is a large, complex structure, occasional re-excitation is required to maintain its structure. Yet a template is a reliable image memory structure because it is a subcritical oscillator supported by both the internal image bus signals and its identifier's signals. A template having no identifier, such as the template made in the scratch pad, is only temporary. It decays soon after the excitation from the assembly area is over.

A template's neuron connection structure depends on the image type. A visible image template ends by the template close line indicator (in the character bus) excitation, followed by the loop closure vector, which is a pen-up vector (section 2.27). The template close signal indicates the starting location of the template as well. A language channel's word template consists of the start indicator, a sequence of phonemes, and the space indicator to end the word. The start and space indicators are common for all the words. Except for these differences, the other features of the language memory are the same as those of the vision image memory. Some composite visible images may have an identifier, but a sentence usually does not have an identifier, since it is seldom used repeatedly.

3.24   Connection of Template and Identifier

The internal image bus turns back to the action-control area from the template area. Only a part of the character bus continues to the lower blocks. Connection between the template area and the association area, and the areas below, is entirely flexible and is able to be changed continuously by the brain's operation. This connection flexibility is the mechanism of operation of the lower-level processor P_2 of section 1.20. This area developed from the evolutionarily old deep area, which was originally an aggregate of neurons connected together to meet the needs of the simple lives of primitive animals. Above this old primitive brain area, an orderly mechanical upper level structure was built to acquire images.

The task of the lower area is the organizer of the images acquired by the upper area. Modes of operation of the template and association area are based on the mechanism of the subcritical oscillator's interaction, as I discussed in section 3.18. A template is an extensive loop structure, and an identifier is a compact two-neuron loop. Since template and identifier can be located anywhere in the template and the association area, respectively, their automatic connection is similar to assembling a complex object in total darkness. Synapses to connect template and identifier are provided, but how they are activated is a mystery.

What happens during the process of identifier formation and template-identifier connection can be stated as follows: Axon branches of the template neurons extend to the association area, congregate at an identifier's neuron's loop structure, and excite the loop. Here, an already used identifier cell rejects the access. This is effected by making the cell hard to activate, which is done by setting the activation threshold of the already used cell neurons high. In this way, the template selects a not yet used identifier cell. As the selected identifier cell is excited, the axons of the identifier's neuron stretch back to the template area and connects to one or more template neurons currently kept activated by the internal image bus signals. Then the template-identifier bidirectional connection is built. So far the connection process is simply stated, but how this process proceeds in the neuron circuit matrix is a mystery. Where is the identifier, and how is the template-identifier pair connected securely? It is like walking in total darkness to a destination, whose character is known, but whose location is unknown. How shall I consider this problem? Is there any such case that helps thinking?

A historical precedent is to consider the question of how the ancient Polynesians navigated the open Pacific Ocean, discovered practically all the islands, occupied them, and finally reached South America. Polynesian maritime history is fascinating. There are two theories. Andrew Sharp proposed a simple trial-and-error navigation.[1] Robert Suggs proposed a deliberate methodical navigation,[2] suggesting various clues the Polynesians used to find islands. The two books inspired me in my young days. I told myself, "What a determined human being can do!" which gave me the courage to step into the uncharted area of neuroscience.

---

[1] Andrew Sharp, *Ancient Voyages in the Pacific* (Penguin, 1957).
[2] Robert Suggs, *The Island Civilization of Polynesia* (New American Library, 1960).

Polynesians knew that if one island is found, then another one may exist to the northwest or southeast. They may have also known, by observing the structure of the island, which direction might be more promising. Although template and association area connection is sparse by birth, some instinctive function has been set up. If such connection exists, then a new template-to-identifier connection can be guided by that.

Polynesians set sail to the east in the east wind season, so that they could return easily if the search was unsuccessful. This is the way the neurons of an amphibian's eyes are connected to the brain: if the axon stretching in one direction fails to reach the right destination, the axon branch dies, and the axon searches in a different direction.

Navigating Polynesians were sensitive to birds' flight, floating debris, types of seaweed, cloud formation high above an island, direction of swell, etc. If the destination of the neuron is activated, the axon senses the activity, and connection is guided to the destination. There is no single ensured clue to use as a guide, but trial and error finds many useful clues (section 6.10). This is so, even if the connection is executed automatically.

The structure of an identifier cell is shown in figure 3.24.1(a). This is a memory cell. This design includes the capability to increase the excitation threshold of the cell if the cell is already used as identifier. There is an alternative design, shown in figure 3.24.1(b). This design works, because the single identifier neuron becomes a part of the template's subcritical oscillator. The neuron is hard to excite, if it is already connected to an existing template.

This identifier neuron is the so-called *face neuron* that detects a specific object such as a face. It appears that not all objects have such specific neurons. In the real human brain, many objects are identified by a group of identifier neurons excited together. These neurons must represent some peculiarities of the image (section 2.29). Although the face neuron concept is appealing, the single neuron identifier is too simple and not flexible enough to execute the lower-level processor functions. Therefore, I prefer the design shown in figure 3.24.1(a) for my model.

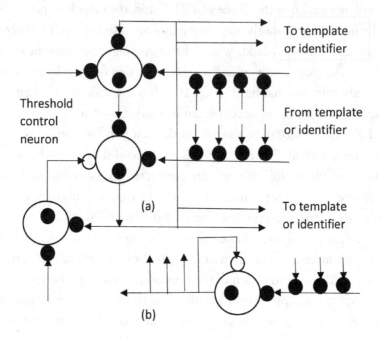

Figure 3.24.1 Alternative design of identifier

The structure of a template connection guided by their identifier connection depends on the image type. The structure of a composite visual image and the structure of a sentence built from words are shown in figure 3.24.2(a) and 3.24.2(b), respectively. A pair of visible elementary images are connected by the placement vectors, which are associated with the composite image's identifier.

A sentence is built by connecting the first word's space indicator to the second word's start indicator. A sentence is a unidirectional connection of words. A word's template is a closed loop with no equivalent to the pen-up command. It is broken open between the space and start indicator, and connected unidirectionally as shown in figure 3.24.2(b). Each word has its identifier, but sentences are almost always temporary and carry no identifier.

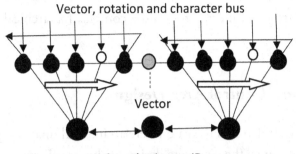

Vector, rotation and character bus

Vector

Complex image ID

(a) Structure of composite visible image

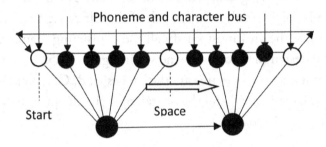

Phoneme and character bus

Start   Space

Word identifier connection

(b) Structure of sentence

Figure 3.24.2 Structure of a composite image

The relationship between template and identifier suggests a basic feature of human thinking. A real object is always complex and has a spatially spread-out structure. Then its image is also a spread-out structure in the brain's hardware, and that is the template. Yet the human mind requires the image's identification to make it useful, and its agent is the identifier, which is the image's name. The template-identifier relationship reveals how the human mind recognizes any object in nature. For recognition, we need an object's detailed structure and its identification. Abstract thinking capability emerged from this image structure.

An abstract image, such as color or quality, has its own identifier that is connected to the templates of its concrete examples via the example template's identifiers. Abstract image identification is made in the association area by the area's processor P_2's activity, and the abstract images are further connected to build a complex hierarchical concept of philosophy.

3.25 Action-Control Area Design

The action-control area is the gate where an internal image is qualified to be sent out. Since the complete design of this area is too complex, I show only the bare-bones schematic of the area's control structure to send out a line drawing consisting of vectors only. A complete design of this area is possible only after the rest of the self-conscious system is designed, since the area must satisfy all the conflicting requirements. The skeletal design that I can show now is in figures 3.25.1 and 3.25.2. The key components of the area are the latches A, B, C, … making up the intermediate memory, and the neural logic circuits that qualify the internal image to be loaded.

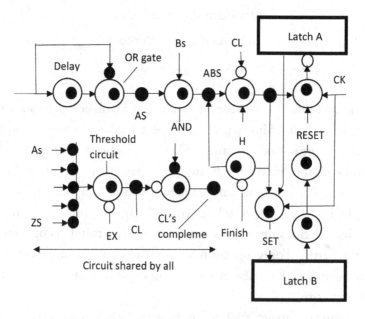

Figure 3.25.1 Intermediate memory-loading circuit

The circuits require several control signals, including *CL* and its complement, to control the latch connection. The signal permits latch A to connect to latch B, where A and B are the consecutively excited vectors. *CL* indicates stability and the intensity of the excitation of the image built from the vectors A, B, … *CL* indicates that the SELF is confident of the image to be sent out. The actuator clock *CK* sends one image element to the action-decoding area and clocks the intermediate memory's shift register to the next step. If the action is actually executed, the clock is generated by the actuator—and the rate of the clock depends on the actuator's execution speed. If the action is not actually executed, then the SELF observes the image internally. Then the clock is generated within the action-control area, and the clock rate can be high.

The first criterion for sending out a set of vectors that make up an image is stability of the internal image bus excitation. This is determined by delaying the vector signals *A, B,* … for a short time and summing the original and the delayed signals to get signals *As, Bs,* … by the OR gate. The pair of signals must add up to a strong excited state. The intense excitation selects those vectors that are active in the image. This check is executed for the set of the lines of a vector bus all at once. The second criterion is that the vector signals included in the image are excited at high enough intensity. This can be checked by summing all the signals *As, Bs, Cs,* … by a high excitation threshold detector. If the detector is activated, the image signals are strong enough. The threshold is set by signal *Ex,* reflecting the present state of the brain. *Ex* is set high in the deep sleep state to prevent internal image activity.

The neuron circuit of figure 3.25.1 generates the control signal *CL* and its complement, which allows conversion of the activity sequence of the internal image bus lines to the connection sequence of the intermediate memory latches, the set of which builds up a temporary shift register. Connection proceeds as follows: If both stability and intensity criteria are met, signal *As* and *Bs* (*Bs* is derived by the same circuit as that of *As* from signal *B*, which is the next excited signal) are combined by the AND gate to generate signal *ABs*, which directs the sequential connection of latch A to latch B. Since *CL* and its complement allow signal *ABs* to reach the line connecting the pair of latches, the sequential excitation of vector A and vector B is transferred to the directed connection of latch A and B. The latch-connecting neuron, driven by signal *ABs*, conducts only so long as the SELF is engaged with the image, because the intermediate memory is a constantly working circuit. For this purpose, a neuron *H* is provided to create the latch to hold signal *ABs* only as long as required. By activating the process's finished signal, the latch connection is cleared.

Latch A and latch B make a part of the assembled shift register that sequences vector A and vector B to be send out in the order. The following vectors C, D, … connect the corresponding latches in sequence. Figure 3.25.2 shows the latch-connection structure.

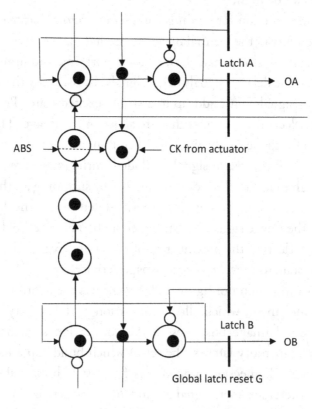

Figure 3.25.2 Intermediate memory structure

Once all the latches are sequentially connected, the last latch is connected to the first latch, thereby closing the shift register loop. This is to allow for repeated image send-out. Then all the latches are reset by signal G of figure 3.25.2, and the first latch is activated to set the marker. The shift register is clocked by signal CK. The clock comes from the actuator executing the output operation of the present internal image. It requests delivery of the next vector. If a pen-up vector arrives, a special signal notifies the action-decoding area to shift the location but not to execute the action.

The action-control area consists of two intermediate memories, IMA and IMB. The general-purpose IMA is to execute all the conscious image send-out processes and also to sense the image without taking action. IMB is for executing an unloaded operation. The IMB connection is retained throughout the entire period of the unloaded action execution. IMB is disconnected from the loading circuit while executing the unloaded operation. IMB is used to control only some special and simple actuators that can execute the operation automatically. An unloaded operation is usually quite simple, such as walking or rotating a handle. The control required for an unloaded operation is no more than exercising several muscles cyclically, and therefore the loading circuit and the intermediate memory are both quite simple. The operation is executed automatically, but it is subjected to supervision by the brain. The brain controls start action, stop action, setting speed, stepping distance, and so on. Once these specifications are delivered, the actuator, the arms, legs, etc., executes the specified action automatically, until the action is interrupted by the brain. While executing the unloaded action, the rest of the brain works on other tasks.

3.26 Association/Deep Area and Processor P$_2$

Evolutionarily old deep area circuits are accordingly simple, whereas the new analyzer and assembly area circuits are quite complex. Yet the brain is functionally symmetrical with respect to the main image memories that are between the old and the new areas. The deep area works in a way somewhat similar to the brain's upper area. The area relays the image activities to the body and also accepts the chemical state signals from the body. The effects of signals from the body show up clearly with the use of drugs or alcohol. Change of the mood while using drugs or other substances is effected by the body's chemical signal that directly controls the emotional centers such as fear, worry, and anxiety in the deep area. Since the chemical sensors distributed all over the body are molecule-type-specific neurons, the brain-body interface does not require any analyzer. The deep area works effectively as the equivalent of the assembly area and the output channel of the upper area combined.

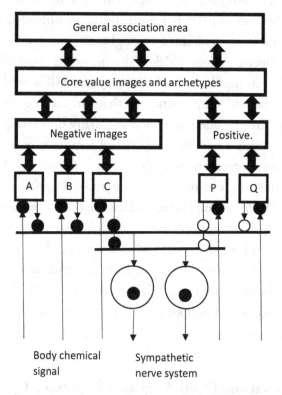

Figure 3.26.1 Layered structure of deep area

The equivalent of the internal image loop in the body's interface is the bidirectional connections of the deep area centers and the association area image identifiers. As for the output channel's equivalent, the deep area sends the activation signal to the sympathetic nervous system. The sympathetic nerve signal controls the heart and breath rate, and also adjusts the body chemistry by way of hormone secretion. The body's state and activity is the equivalent to those of the outside world with which the SELF is currently engaged. Figure 3.26.1 shows the deep area's schematic. The deep area consists of the negative centers A, B, C, ..., each of which carries survival-oriented meaning such as fear, worry, anxiety, and anger, and positive centers P, Q, ... which carry such positive senses as peace and hope. Activities of the deep area centers are summed to determine the level of support to the brain to deal with the current situation. High deep area activity whips up the body function by activating the sympathetic nervous system. The nerve's activity level is sensed as sensation associated with the engaged image.

The deep area and generally the archaic area are crucial for life support and maintenance. Neurons are special cells that do not reproduce. This is a condition required so as not to create a self-destructive circuit automatically. Yet by neuron death, the support ceases to function. What is the safeguard for a neuron's death? For critically important circuits like those in the deep area, more than one neuron can be parallel-connected, and if one of them dies, the others can take over the role. Since neuron-to-neuron connection is made by chemical signals, a dead neuron does not affect the electrical activity of the circuit.

Co-excitation of the deep area centers and the primitive life's image such as fight or flight, food acquisition and reproductive drive created emotion, a predecessor to self-consciousness in the lower-level animals. Humans maintain emotion on the basis of self-consciousness. One way to look at this feature is that self-consciousness is a diluted version of emotion, including many neutral images retained in the association area. Those images do not have their root in the negative centers in the deep area, because their impact on the life's welfare has not been determined clearly. These images are connected with the milder versions of fear, such as dislike.

The association area emerged as the interface between the incoming images and the deep area center activities, and therefore the two areas' neuron circuit structures are similar. Both areas consist of simple memory cells and connection media. The difference is that the association area has abundant memory centers and connection resources, whereas the deep area does not. This is adequate, since the centers of bodily images associated with emotion are small in number and are more or less mutually exclusive. They do not require complex connections among themselves. The association area copied this basic structure and increased the number of the centers and the center-to-center connection capability enormously.

In this development process, the images that existed in the archaic deep area that were not directly relevant to life's welfare moved up to the emerging association area and merged with the images newly acquired from the outside world. These are the images that set the core value of the person. From this evolutionary origin, the association area makes a layered structure, whose bottom is occupied by images that were originally in the deep area and that carried light weight in securing the real basic welfare of life. Archetypal images are assembled in this area. This is why archetypal images affect our emotions strongly. Above this area, there is the general-purpose association area handling all kinds of neutral images.

Functions of the Lower-Level Processor P_2

Flexible and variable connection capability of the identifiers in the association area and their connection to the centers in the deep area is the working mechanism of the lower-level processor P_2 of section 1.20. There are six types of signals that operate the processor: (1) signals from the template area exciting the identifiers, (2) signals from the body affecting the emotional centers of the deep area, (3) signals from the other functional blocks through the character bus line excitations, (4) signals from the internal activity of the association area affecting the connection structure, (5) support level of the area affecting the identifier's connection, and (6) What appears to be a conscious excitation of any identifier initiating the image display and creating a new meaning.

(1) Excitation of a template sends a signal to its identifier. When a new image memory is acquired, related existing images' identifiers are excited and connected to the new image's identifier to set up the image's meaning (the first impression). When the already existing image's template is excited, the existing connection of the identifiers may be altered (the case of the second thought). In either case, the activity creates or changes the meaning of the image. The activity may send out the image to the upper area to take action.

(2) Deep area centers are sensitive to the chemical state of the body, caused by drug, alcohol and hallucinogenic substance. The affected deep area centers change the mood of the person, or excite certain association area identifiers to display unworldly images. Psychedelic effects emerge by this mechanism.

(3) Excitation of a character bus line activates the image-manipulation program's identifier (section 4.06), thereby initiating the image manipulation. A related function is to specify the type of the image to be displayed to assist template matching operation (section 2.29). By the characteristic bus line signals, each functional block sends the support-level adjustment request to the deep area centers (for instance, to interrupt the present operation).

(4) Excitation of the association area by itself may automatically connect some identifiers and create a composite image. Identifier connection mechanism is unidirectional, bidirectional, mutually exclusive, ring and hierarchical structures. Abstract meaning identifier is created by this activity. Identifier disconnection is effected by attaching the negative label to the existing connection.

(5) If an image search operation is executed, it requires a high support level of the association area. A hidden structure in the association area can be created in such an occasion, and the

built-up image may suddenly pop up later by an unidentified cause. We often discover valuable by-product when we go through mind searching. It is also possible that high activity of a not yet used identifier may create its own template (section 4.39). High support level affects the mood. Generally the human mind is clearer if the association area's support is higher.

(6) We feel as if we can excite any image identifier consciously. This is not really the case. Brain's activities make causal chain, and excitation of any image always have its cause. Brain's activity is may be characterized as a continuous chain of image association. It frequently start from the activation of image's name (word identifier), which does not very clearly sensed as the cause. Its excitation spreads out to the vision image identifiers to establish the image's meanings. The cause of such excitation can also be the noise in the neuron circuit.

The association-deep area's normal functions are summarized as follows: First the association area processor displays an image by exciting its template or exciting the template of the image-processing instruction. Second, the deep area sends to the body-control area the support-level control of the functional blocks that reach the block by the character bus line. Third, the deep area relays the current image's impact, determined by the activity level of the deep area centers, to the body-control area in order to activate the sympathetic nervous system to prepare the body for emergency. The association area and the deep area is the I/O gate of the brain to the body, which is also the outside of the brain.

3.27 Block-Subblock Support Circuit

A functional block or its subblock is controlled by the local support system that maintains the brain area to the proper operating conditions. Support-level control is exercised by measuring the level of the activity of each functional block or its subblock, and then adjusting the support level to meet the need of the current objective of brain operation. The activity-level detector neuron X is shown in figure 3.27.1. Neurons to the right side of X are executing the designated task of the functional block. The activity sensor neuron X sums the activity level of all the neurons. A neuron with an exceptionally large number of synapses serves as the activity detector. The activity level of neuron X is further modified by the signals from the lines of the character bus, that specify the present processing requirement of the block, such as template formation or image memory search. Since this control requires a fast and crisp response, the signal and its complement controls neuron X.

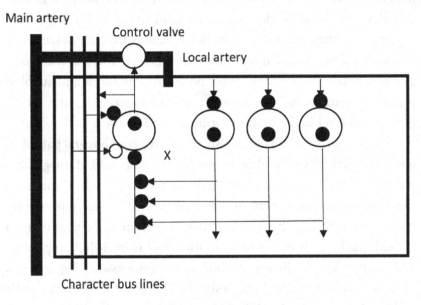

Figure 3.27.1 Block-subblock local support

The activity-level control is transmitted via the character bus lines from the other functional block, which demands the processing by the target block. For instance, if the template area cannot find a matching template to the signal from the assembly area, it requests the assembly area to work hard to adjust the incoming signal, as I discussed in section 2.29.

Some control signals come from the association area and the deep area centers to deal with risk, an emergency situation, or to respond to the SELF's emotional need. Neuron X's output signal controls constriction or dilation of the artery branch and provides the proper amount of blood to be delivered to the functional block. This mechanism is backed up by the body's global support mechanism that controls the heart, liver, and lungs to meet the entire body's energy demand, as I discussed in section 2.30.

A block-subblock specific support circuit is smaller in scale and responds faster than the body's global support system of section 2.30. The block's support activity can follow the change of the image-processing activity, and the blood flow can be mapped using a sensitive imaging device such as an MRI (magnetic resonance imager). In some complex functional blocks such as those in the assembly and action-control area, there are several functional subblocks, each of which has a local support control mechanism. Above that, there is the block's global support control. The whole body, and the block and subblock support system, works in a mutually consistent way. The sum total of the support level to the brain determines the sensation.

Support-level control of the association area is an integral part of the operation of the lower-level processor P_2 of section 1.20. If imagination is required, the support level of the entire association area is increased. In an introspective observation, the support level is reduced to suppress spontaneous internal image excitation. When an archetypal image is excited, the lower level of the association area is intensively supported. This activity eventually spreads out to the entire association area, and the image-to-image connection is significantly altered. A word identifier and its visible image identifier connection is intensified if a language image is processed, to assist the language channel by setting the meaning and the participle of the words.

Block global support is somewhat special for the deep area and the analyzer. The deep area is constantly supported, even during sleep, to respond to any risk images originating from the body. In deep sleep, the analyzer and the internal image circuit supports are reduced, but in the REM (dreaming) sleep state, the support level comes back up (sections 4.32 and 4.33). The analyzer support level increases by way of reflex action in an emergency. If any sudden habitat state change is detected, the support level of all the blocks increases immediately by way of this reflex action. Then the support-level increase signal propagates downward to alert the entire internal image circuit and the deep area to focus on the new situation (section 4.17).

3.28 Fluctuation Phenomenon of the Neuron Circuit

A neuron circuit is built automatically by activating neuron-to-neuron synapses. Synapse conductivity depends on the length of excitation time, how intense excitation is, and the length of time since the synapse was activated last time. Such precondition varies widely and practically is never known. As a consequence, even the neuron circuit connection is, strictly speaking, uncertain. Yet if the circuit was connected securely before, the stable connection reemerges after a brief initial excitation. This is the most basic fluctuation mechanism of any neuron circuit. This mechanism contributes to the flow of random images that we experience when the brain is idle (section 4.28).

A neuron circuit is asynchronous. No signal is aligned with any others. To a neuron, signal B may arrive earlier than, at the same time as, or later than signal A. If they come together, the neuron is excited, but if their arrival times do not match, the neuron is not excited. Even if the neuron is excited, the level of excitation depends on the timing match. Since a neuron logic gate receives many input signals at many synapses, the consequence is unpredictable. In terms of logic operation, the AND logic gate's and the OR logic gate's identities may become uncertain.

Neuron circuits are closely packed in the narrow space within the skull. Proximity of neuron to neuron creates electrical interaction between unrelated neurons, which may cause resistive or capacitive coupling through the cell membrane and the outside fluid. There is a special mechanism for an axon to expedite action-potential propagation. An axon may be periodically covered by an insulator sheath. The action potential at location A sends current outside the neuron to the downstream location B, where the action potential is generated. Since excitation jumps, action potential propagates fast. This skipping conduction sends current outside the neuron, and this may affect the nearby neurons' excitation. The capacitive and resistive coupling changes the excitation threshold level of the affected neurons, thereby altering the timing and logic operation. Such fluctuation phenomena exist also in the silicon VLSI chip. I analyzed the problem and used it for the CMOS VLSI processor design (*CMOS Digital Circuit Technology* [Prentice Hall, 1987]).

Some body mechanisms affect brain operation. Electrical pulses driving the heart (EKG) are a sequence of voltage spikes several millivolts high and of about one millisecond in duration, sensed everywhere in the body. The pulse source has low internal resistance to drive the entire body. If a neuron is in a state close to the excitation threshold, the EKG signal helps or prevents its excitation.

There are external noise sources that may affect the brain's operation. The natural effect of ionizing radiation can be a noise source, but the most significant external noise sources are irrelevant images and signals coming in from all the sensors: moving shadows, street noise, sense of contact to skin, and so on. Images from different senses are not correlated in their content, intensity, and timing. They affect the brain practically as *white noise* (the intensity is independent from the frequency). They are able to excite images randomly. The human brain tries to screen these noises from the relevant incoming signals, but this process is never perfect. The brain is in a very noisy environment. All these effects steer development of the brain's state.

Noise has some positive effects. Periodic ticks have the effect of vacating images from the brain and make it easy to sleep when I am suffering from insomnia. If I am confused by secular thoughts, low-level baroque music neutralizes the confusion. Why is this so? Because Bach, Handel, and others composed music that flows with human self-consciousness, and that does not have the wake-up calls that are characteristic of modern American music, chin-chins of bells, and don-dons of the drum. As the soft melody of baroque music gradually replaces the secular depressive thoughts, the SELF is able to take rest and is able to sleep or to start concentrating once again.

Capacitive or resistive coupling among the internal image bus lines may have some advantage in the template area. The set of bus line excitations from the assembly area may not exactly match the image pattern stored in the template. By the inter-bus line coupling, the mismatched line excitation spreads out to the nearby lines and properly identifies the template as I discussed in section 2.29. This is a significant effect in image identification.

3.29   Failure Mode of the Neuron Circuit

Noise in the neuron circuit should cause failure of the circuit's operation. Yet this statement requires qualification. Malfunction assumes the existence of an unintended operation of the circuit, but whose intention? The SELF's? But the SELF is only the sense of all the activities of the brain, which does not have independent judgment criteria. A brain was never intelligently designed, so what constitutes a failure can never been defined by anyone. Nevertheless, a self-destructive operation, and any operation that affects the welfare of life negatively, is an obvious malfunction. If such an operation is caused by a genetic variation of the brain hardware, then a very effective natural selection mechanism exists to eliminate the variation. Then what may appear to be a failure mode to the casual observer may have some merit for survival. Therefore, the definition of neuron circuit failure is limited to serious failures that affect the quality of one's physical or mental life.

The most obvious failure mode is the large-scale death of neurons, caused by the failure of the support system, such as a stroke. If such an obvious failure is excluded, still the support system anomaly can create mental malfunction, which will affect the welfare of life negatively. A brain accepts all sorts of images. If the incoming images are all negative for a long time, the SELF gives up requesting support in the state of lost hope and becomes stuck at the low-activity level. It is not easy to get out of this state. From my introspective observation in such a state, I know that my brain's key functions, especially imagination, suffer the most. As no new direction can be imagined, I go into a long period of a subdued state. Depression due to the sense of personal misery is an epidemic in modern society, where only a few successful people (the minority) and a deeply frustrated majority coexist because of modern society's belief of promoting unnecessary and usually unfair competition in life. I wonder why the general public is so blind to the negatives of social competition? Secular competitions are unfair given the subjective selection of the winner, like beauty contest. If competition is glorified by the underlying thought of unlimited lifestyle improvement, this is the worst superstition of modern society. The ultimate objective of any human society is not unlimited progress or growth by competition. Rather, it is ensured stability. Particularly, unlimited economic growth leads us only to devastating the habitat of earth for the future. Most of the capitalists have deaf ears to the voices of the environmentalists.

The depressive mental state is the result of the failure of the brain's negative feedback system. I believe that the majority of modern society's depressive people are aware of the cause of their suffering. One such cause is failure in the financial arena, driven by blind greed and the mechanism of institutionalized investment promotion. Bankruptcy resulting from this creates an ensured state of severe depression. Then the basic wisdom is to remove the cause of such suffering. I do not believe that such a mental state can be cured by medicine alone. Chemical agents are unable to guide the financially stressed patient to a new and hopeful life by showing a new direction of action.

A depressive mental state may also go into a state of periodic oscillation. Then the manic-depressive syndrome emerges. The manic state may turn the sufferer back to a depressive state by way of life's failure, caused by the negative social reaction to his or her excessive and careless action while in the manic state. Another case of this type is excessive support of the brain's activity that maintains a constant high-activity state to which the body's action cannot catch up. In this state, it is impossible to concentrate on a single worthwhile objective. This is attention deficit hyperactivity. When I get into this kind of state, the best cure is to force myself to do only one job to extreme perfection. The finished work, be it technical, artistic, or even menial work, drives my SELF back to concentrate on my proper objective.

As a special case of the support anomaly, a certain set of images are strongly supported, and ultimately they are active almost all the time. This state is reached by the subject's life history. If a person concentrates too much on certain images or ideas, these become very strongly connected to the activation center in the deep area and are continuously activated. A paranoiac state emerges. In this case, what is most important for the person is to make sure that the image is positive to him or her and to other human beings. Paranoiacs are often extremely imaginative, creative, and productive. It is more interesting to talk with paranoiacs than with their opposite, who have too much common sense and dismiss any new ideas. Since I am aware that I am a paranoiac—and unfortunately I had to fight all my life with my mother, who had too much common sense—I understand how the unfortunate paranoiacs feel. I appeal to all mothers and psychologists: please do not destroy constructive young paranoiacs.

Why do I think I am a paranoiac? Because of my lifelong interest in and focus on the subject of human self-consciousness. When I was twelve years old, I experienced my first strange daydream. Such a mysterious mental experience is too often interpreted as supernatural intervention. Yet during World War II, we Japanese youngsters were educated to our bones in the scientific spirit. Coming from this educational background, I absolutely refused any religious shortcut explanations. Ever since, trying to explain the experience, I thought all through my life, *How does self-consciousness create such a mysterious experience?* This book, *Self-Consciousness*, is a summary of my life's thinking and work. This work helped improve my mental health also. My idea of dealing with my depressive state by working hard on some subject is the positive idea that emerged from my own experience.

My hardware-model-based study of self-consciousness places subconsciousness in the category of *failure mode* of self-consciousness. The brain's memory structure fails in various ways by connection breakdown in the template and the association area. As the result, some memory elements are disconnected from the currently active memory system. This disconnection alters the affected image's meaning and its association with the deep area centers. As a result, distorted or partially invisible images are associated with abnormal sensation. Loss of balance in the context of an image induces otherworldly feeling. The same memory failure affects the image-processing instructions that I describe in sections 4.06–4.08. Since any casual actions are taken by the directive of the modified existing images, a change in the image-processing command affects the person's behavior. The two types of memory failure, loss of memory connection and improper image-processing capability, affect the person's internal and external world in the same way as the subconscious is claimed to do. I describe my own strange experience with this mechanism in section 6.05.

In extreme old age, humans lose memory. A curious feature of memory loss is that often the name of a visible object, such as another person's name, is lost, but the person's visual image survives intact. This can be explained by a connection breakdown between the visible image's identifier and the name's identifier. Since they are made in the association area by the templates of their respective channels, the pair of identifiers may not exist close to each other, or else the connection may not be direct. In such a case, the connection is more vulnerable to neuronal death.

CHAPTER 4

INTERNAL IMAGE DYNAMICS

4.01   Internal Image and Self-Consciousness

The only material substance of my self-conscious subject SELF is my body, as I discussed in chapter 1. Yet the sense of existence of my SELF is created by the activities that control my body, which are the images. The state of my body, such as pain or discomfort, and its location within the body are both sensed continuously, and that makes me feel the body's continuous presence. Yet as I keep observing my mind, I feel as if there were a mysterious, elusive SELF in my mind who knows my body, my world, my history, and my own SELF. When I try to reach this SELF, the only object I find is still my body, and I feel as if the images that I was seeing go under a superposed cloud of images.

The neurophysiological studies of self-consciousness place the SELF in the brain's old area, but are unable to clearly identify the roles played by the images. Looking at this problem from a different side, philosophers focus on the images as the substance of the SELF. But as I learn their views, I feel as if I were lost in a maze of concepts, a maze like the one King Minos built in Knossos. My mind is consumed by the Minotaur. The hero, Theseus, found his way out of the maze by Ariadne's thread. What I attempt is to use the hardware model of my brain, described in the preceding chapters 1–3, as my Ariadne's thread to explore the maze of the image world behind the sense of the body. Relating the SELF's substance, the body, to the fleeing images is the task of information science.

The substance of Ariadne's thread is quite simple, a commonly used and well-acquainted concept, the *mode* of operation of the brain-body system. A mode is the operation defined by the structure of the system. The mode is an organized operation of the brain and the body hardware that displays the images. In a complex system like the human machine, there are many modes, each of which has a well-defined activation pattern of neurons to display images and create their psychological effects. This approach was not possible before, because there was no model of the self-conscious brain and body as a whole.

I have one now. I do not make the claim that my model is valid in every detail. Yet this model I've built on many honest introspective observations of my mind and other rational assumptions appears to be quite realistic and heuristic. I investigated the operations of this model and searched for the modes, the sum total of which explained the image part of my self-consciousness. The Mahayana Buddhist philosophers I quoted in section 1.04 must have come up with their conclusions by using a similar method, since they categorized the brain activities into five classes. Even a very basic model would have shown them the essential features of self-consciousness. So now let us build a more detailed model and see how it explains the human mind.

I followed this approach, and I immediately found something amazing. Even if I am fully awake, often I have no SELF in me; that is, I am not self-conscious. This is the most stress-free and healthiest state of my body. Self-consciousness is, ironically, a necessary evil for human survival. What makes a biological machine into a human is self-destructive. This is the ultimate irony. Yet here I see the foresight of de La Mettrie; he recognized that the human is a machine and never was a delegate of God.

Look around you. The man-made machines you see are self-destructive while serving our purposes. Similarly, we serve our rulers and destroy ourselves as we have done since the beginning of human history—and nothing has ever changed in our social lives. In the modern *democratic* society, δεμος really never possessed κρατος, and they were always servants of some king. We have never been made equal, not from the very beginning of human history.

4.02 Image's Type and Meaning

Any mode of the brain's operation is initiated by exciting internal image memories. The image's mode excitation displays the image and executes the action it directs. All five senses of human beings carry their own images. Internal images are characterized by the excitation patterns of the circuit of the five sense channels, which are the modes of the channel. Most images are composites of more than one sense's images.

A visible image consists of the basic line drawing, blobs, and color and texture specifications, all extracted from the observed object. A line drawing consists of vectors, arcs, pen-up commands, and so on. A voice and language image consists of pure sounds, phonemes, rhythms, and accents. A somatic sense of the body surface consists of pressure, temperature, pain, texture, and a simple graphic image projected on the body surface. A chemical image of taste has six clearly defined basic images of sweet, sour, salty, spicy, bitter, and umami. The chemical sense of smell has no such simple categorization. A smell's image is identified by the name of the substance that emits the smell.

An abstract image represents a single common feature of a set of images and is defined by showing the examples carrying the feature. Presentation of only one example cannot define any abstract image like color, but as many examples are shown, any abstract image is successively better defined. Examples of the color red are hibiscus flowers, blood, the communist flag, tomato sauce, a stop sign, and so on. An abstract image may also make a hierarchy in describing metaphysical concepts.

How is an incoming image connected to the related images to make the structure carrying its meaning? The structure is built in several steps. At the time of the new image acquisition, there are related images in the scene of the acquisition event, such as the time of day.

These images are memorized together. There are images excited in the brain at that time. All of these are connected to the new image by their identifiers. The connected images jointly create the meaning of the image. This is the brain's *first impression*. Then later, when the image is excited again, more associated images join in the structure, and the image's meaning is enriched. As the number of connected images increases at a still later time, some irrelevant images may be eliminated, and the web is restructured. The structure carrying the meaning is thus made and remade during a person's life.

4.03   Internal Image's Character

Each sense of the human body—vision, voice and language, body surface contact, and chemical sense—has its own internal images. Some simple images are pure images from a single sense. If I go through the lyrics of a German lied ("Am Brunnen vor dem Tore, da steht ein Lindenbaum"), I feel as if I hear the song in my ear, and I feel light pressure on my vocal chords, yet I do not sense any visual image, since I have never seen the famous Lindenbaum. This is a pure language and sound image. If I remember the lyrics to an American song ("Oh give me a home where the buffalo roam"), I feel the same sense, but I internally see the images of nature in the Midwest Rocky Mountain area where I spent my younger days. I am familiar with roaming buffaloes. This is a rich language-sound-vision composite image.

Any complex image is a composite of many element images of one or several senses. Any visual image of practically useful complexity, such as the image of my house, is a composite of many element images. The roof, the window, the door, the stairway, the mailbox—are all placed at the proper locations in the image frame of the entire house. Often, most of such element images are the *standard images* existing in my memory, which do not show the real object that should be in the real image. A standard image is the image that you can show immediately when you are asked, "What is [whatever it is]?" If I am asked, "What is an actress?" almost certainly I answer, "Someone like Julie Andrews."

She is my standard image of an actress. Often a visible image is only accurate enough to identify the object by its unique features or by their special element image combination. What I actually remember carries only a few real features, on which my attention was focused at the time of observation.

In my old age, I often try to remember the scenes I saw in my youth. As I identify what I try to see, what appears first from the memory is an image consisting of only a few colored blobs (section 2.22). But if I try to look inside each blob, the blob vanishes, and some object's image emerges and replaces the blob. These images show up one at a time in succession. Some of those images are unusually detailed, but if I ask myself, "Were they really like that?" I am not sure. Why? Because I memorized the object's identity, and not its real graphic image. The object's identity or its name is converted to the visible image by way of automatic substitution. A recalled visual image is made of mostly reconstructed images that appear rational to my present SELF. Recently I visited my former residence. I first imagined how it looked fifty years ago. When I saw the apartment once again, there was no sign of recent repair. It is now quite old, yet many permanent fixtures are different from what I imagined. What I imagined before was an image constructed from my present standard images.

This observation has two significant consequences. The first is that the number of elementary images stored in the visible image template is not as high as I naively expected. What is stored in the brain's memory are the standard images of simple objects that are repeatedly seen in my life. The template made when I saw an object contained many real details, but these details were thrown away soon after I disengaged from the object or when the real image became associated with the standard images. After that, only a few peculiar features were retained. The peculiar features are set in highlight at the time of the image recollection. This built-on-demand image structure increases the image memory capacity enormously, at the cost of reduced accuracy. Then remembering an image is actually assembling a new image from the existing standard images from various sources, subjected to *rational* adjustments. This image-fabrication process misleads me, as if I remembered every detail of whatever object I am beholding, since the image buildup process occurs unconsciously in my brain, and what is assembled is rational to my *present* SELF.

These features of a complex visual image must be included in the internal image dynamics executed by the hardware model. The brain is not a precision video camera and video memory. Language images, whose capabilities were developed in the recent geological age, are less flexible to substitution by different words when a statement is reconstructed. Quite often, the context of the sentence changes drastically by changing some keywords, especially if the word is loaded by the shadow of cultural or personal meanings. Construction of a visual image and of a language image are rather different mental processes.

As special composite images that are useful later, I introduce a term *event*, which is a combination of the images of the actor, the action, and the circumstance of the action. This composite image is useful in chapter 5, where the sense of time is discussed.

What is the structure of the set of all images from the characterization of the set theory of mathematics? A set of images has a peculiar character so that any set of images also qualifies as an image. That is, the set of images include all its *subsets* as its element. This is a *non-Cantorian set* whose definition is *unstable* as I discuss in section 6.03. The human mind handles such a data type that is not even mathematically manageable. The brain's capability determines the range of engagement with this set. Perhaps because of this reason, the set of images serves for any life's problems, but reveals many illogical features as well.

One example: I am amazed that there is no agreed-upon definition of human *culture*. What most Americans think of when they hear the word *culture* is the availability of technology. My definition is "a decent and elegant human lifestyle set by traditional rules and customs." Friedrich Nietzsche's definition is "artistic style of human life." My definition is close to Nietzsche's. Technology is not a significant part of culture, I believe. King Pacal the Great of Palenque lived in an elegantly built palace in the seventh century Mexico. Ming Chinese ate more tasty natural foods in the fourteenth to the sixteenth century than we do now. The Duke of Tuscany was surrounded by Renaissance fine arts, and Austrians of the nineteenth century enjoyed the greatest music. Yet none of them had cell phones.

4.04 Standard Images, Ideograms, and Language

Standard images are the building blocks of practically all the visible internal images needed for life. I ask you to draw a tree on a paper. What you draw is your standard image of a tree. This is a simplified line drawing of a tree, and it carries enough features to enable its being identified as a tree. Many standard images are acquired at an early age, depending on the culture. I saw a Russian child draw a house amid boreal pines, and a Maya child draw the unique house under a tall ceiba tree in Guatemala.

Standard images of visible objects are recognized by everyone. Relying on those images, we understand the life of now extinct ancient people, such as the Moche in South America. The Moche left great pictures and realistic ceramics carrying images of their rich and colorful social and religious life. Images of natural objects such as the sun, the moon, the stars, and powerful wild animals are recognized in ancient petroglyphs all over the world. Images of fish are the same in an ancient Chinese ideogram and in the Easter Island Rongorongo. The images of birds and the bird man of Easter Island vividly show how much the ancient inhabitants of the island desired to explore the outside world but they could not. They had no wood to make a boat. Ideograms are the only images that carry their own meanings by themselves.

Presently, Chinese is the only language that uses ideograms. Chinese now uses a simplified version of the traditional characters. In Taiwan, the people still use the traditional ideograms. In Japan, a mixture of phonetic characters and somewhat simplified ideograms are used. Koreans mostly use their own phonetic characters, but they are able to read Chinese ideograms as well. In the Far East, Chinese ideograms are understood everywhere. I am deeply concerned that the Chinese ideograms have many new varieties in the Far East nations. There are two reasons of concern. The first is, if the traditional ideograms are used, anyone in the Far East can communicate in writing. The second is, the precious classic texts from the time of Confucius are accessible to future generation people. Although complicated, the historical ideogram set should be preserved as a cultural heritage. Since these ideograms are now written by printers, their complexity does not hinder their practical use in daily life.

The Maya writing system is a mixture of ideograms and phonetic characters, exactly like Japanese. This is an incredibly sophisticated system. If Maya written text were purely phonetic, Maya code breaking would not have been possible. Once, in the powerful Maya state of Calakmul, our history study group found a badly weathered stone monument. Professor Nick Hopkins looked at it closely, and found one partially readable character indicating *woman*. He said that the monument possibly states the story of a Calakmul queen. I was impressed, since when I learned Chinese classics, I had the same experience: the family name of the Zhou dynasty (the second-oldest dynasty of China) means *princess*. This is an evidence that ancient China was also a matriarchal society.

Ideograms are written in a certain definite order. So, by observing the stroke of handwritten Chinese, I can immediately identify the ideogram. An ideogram is a representation of its writing action. This is consistent with my basic thought, that any image is recognized by our brain by executing the action to produce it. This feature is what created the delicate art of Chinese calligraphy. Some ideograms were converted back to the original graphic image, thereby adding the artistic flavor. I advocate the creation of symbols representing the writer's emotion. Such symbols are, by their nature, ideograms, and they are used to express the writer's emotion precisely.

Ideograms are visible standard images. A phonetic alphabet carries no meaning, but words are constructed by it. Words of a language are the standard images for each culture, but they are different from culture to culture. Koreans and Japanese are as different from one another as Germans/Brits and Poles. Therefore if two essentially different language statements are blindly translated by using a dictionary, often diametrically opposite meanings emerge. The word by which the North

Korean ruler is addressed by his subordinate people means *chief of pirates* in Japanese.

Not widely known, one interesting feature of a mixed ideogram-phonetic script is that the writer consciously uses ideograms to state key points. This feature provides a great advantage in speed reading. I can read a Japanese text by picking up mostly ideograms. The Japanese idiomatic expression of such a style of reading is *to read a page diagonally*.

Some loaded words carry different meanings for different cultures. For Far Easterners, *responsibility* carries a very serious meaning. If one must fulfill one's responsibility, one may even have to kill oneself. Responsibility means to put oneself in a position to be blamed. This interpretation is common among Chinese, Korean, and Japanese people.

What I see in the U.S. is quite different. The word means the capability to respond, or worse (recently), the capability to make excuses. So the word means power. At the time of the Watergate scandal, Richard Nixon said, "I take the responsibility but not the blame." I felt, *What is this?* Another example of this kind of meaning is the word *lie*. A lie is not a very serious offense in the Far East, but in the U.S., being a liar is a bad stigma. Yet politicians lie in the same way everywhere. In the U.S., the excuse for a political lie is quite a bit more sophisticated because of Americans' sense of *responsibility*. Nevertheless, if I hear the news telling me that "the president is a chronic liar," as an Asian, I simply dismiss it, thinking, *He is just a businessman.* A *businessman* in traditional culture under Confucius was not the most respectable gentleman as in the U.S., since we Asians tend to assume that businessmen always lie. *Businessman*, *responsibility*, and *lie* are frequently used words in international trade. I often hear American businessmen sounding bewildered when doing business in the Far East.

4.05 Image's Structure and Its Meaning

The meaning of an image is determined by the other images connected to it in the association area and in the deep area. All the images jointly determine the image's impact on life. Connection of the associated images is made at the time of image acquisition (the first impression) and also at the later time of recall of the image, when the SELF may have changed, along with the image's context. For instance, I admired Thor Heyerdahl for his passion to prove his diffusionist theory by risking his life. Yet after I saw Easter Island, I thought that his theory on the origin of Easter Islanders was nonsense. Nevertheless, I still admire him. Later in his old age, he was still trying to show transoceanic cultural diffusion by studying the pyramid on Canary Island, alleged to have been built by Maya. One hero's image went through that much complex change.

As an image is excited, the connected images are excited with it, and the set of images creates the meaning of the image. I just showed how my image of Thor Heyerdahl was built up. The brain maintains the joint image excitation, and all the images are sensed together. The images are excited in one or more of the five sense channels and are sensed at the location of the respective sensors of the body. Visible images are sensed by the eyes (this is sensed clearly when I imagine a simple geometrical object with my eyes closed), and a voice and language image is sensed by the ears as a faint sound (section 4.03). The images of the deep area centers are sensed by the entire body, such as the chill running down my spine when I am scared. Such images are the abstract images relevant for survival, inherited from our remote animal ancestors. The meaning of an image depends on the person's present SELF, and the SELF never remains the same for long time. So one image may carry an opposite meaning for the same person at different times.

Figure 4.05.1(a) shows that basic abstract meaning, such as "holy" or "evil," is set by connecting the image to the abstract meaning centers in the deep area. My wife and I visited Easter Island. As soon as we arrived by plane, I was filled with the sense, that this was a very holy island, unique in among many other places in the world. Yet my wife felt that the island was filled with evil spirits. Her sense became reality, unfortunately, as she broke her leg there. My sense became reality, also, as I solved one of the key problems of my research. What is considered holy or evil, or the like or dislike of any object, is radically different from person to person.

Connection of identifiers in the association area has several basic patterns. The images sensed in spatial perspective are connected bidirectionally to the theme image as shown in figure 4.05.1(b). If the arrows are all directed inward, the central image carries the common character of the surrounding images, like a shared color. If they are all directed outward, the surrounding images set the details of the central image's meaning. If the connection is entirely bidirectional, this is an unorganized image assembly, such as the landscape seen from a train window. The image of history makes a linear, directed sequence as shown in figure 4.05.1(c), and the image displays the cause-effect relationship of the events. A cyclic image like (d) shows the season's change. The hierarchical image structure of (e) represents the command line of government, the military, or a corporate organization.

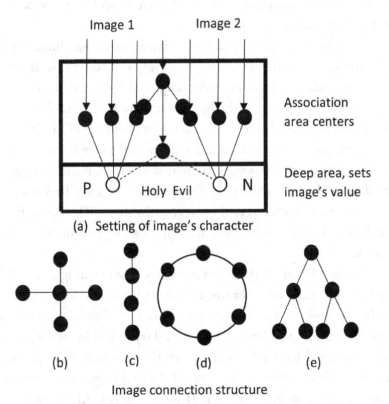

(a) Setting of image's character

(b)   (c)   (d)   (e)

Image connection structure

Figure 4.05.1 Image structure's meaning

Many images are assembled to form a unique structure, and the structure itself carries certain high-level meaning. Meanings carried by such image structures are similar among people of different cultures, and the similarity helps in the understanding of abstract concepts among people from different cultures. The concept of history is universal for all the modern people in the world, and the concept of cyclic time was common among those of the ancient agricultural people.

Each of such structures carries specific meaning. Figure 4.05.1(c) and 4.05.1(d) carry images of time, which is either a linear progression or cyclic. The cyclic image of time exists both in the New World (in this case of Aztec) and the Old World (in this case of India). A hierarchical assembly of images (e) shows the possible outcome of an action, such as development of military conflict. Yet in quantum physics, this structure carries even the image of time, in the many-world interpretation of quantum mechanics (section 6.15).

Some image structures carry dynamic meaning. Image A and B emerging alternately (such as yin-yang), and images A, B, and C emerging cyclically (such as snake, slug, and frog), are the examples. Such images are stored with the instructions to display them in the association area, by directed connection of identifiers. Certain images may carry unusual personal meaning. Jean-Paul Sartre felt nausea when he saw a tree roots. I was once fascinated by exotic fractal images, but one day, suddenly, I felt terrible disgust, and ever since I try not to see them. I sensed terrible sexual perversion in them. The active human mind always tries to seek some hidden meaning within even normal images.

Is there any image that does not carry any meaning at all? What appears to be the most meaningless image is the inkblot pattern used in the psychological character test. This test's intention is to show something meaningless to the patient and try to let him or her see some meaning in it. I have a doubt, however, that the patient's response can be objectively interpreted. The reason I doubt the test's objectivity is the diagnosis of German World War II war criminals. All of them tested abnormal. Yet I believe that Albert Speer and Hjalmar Schacht were perfectly normal.

4.06   Image Processing in the Assembly Area

I consider the brain to be an image processor. The brain's basic architecture is the four-layer structure discussed in section 1.20. The image memory is sandwiched between the two processors. The upper processor makes incoming images comprehensible to the brain, and stores them in the memory. The lower processor sends the images stored in the memory to the upper processor. Then the upper processor modifies them and assembles them into a useful form. Image modification is always needed since life's required action varies all the time. To keep up with the changing situations, the action directed by the modified image is executed by the actuator via image-output channel, while monitoring its effect with the tightly coupled image-input channel. This is how any conscious operation is executed by the brain. The core of the upper-level processor working with the images is the assembly area.

The image processor in the assembly area needs (1) a supply of the image to be processed and (2) the processing specification, which are equivalent to the computer's data and instruction, respectively. The source of both the image and instruction is the images stored in the template area and organized by the association area. Images and processing instructions have essentially the same data structure and function as in any electronic processor. Visual image-processing instruction is delivered by a sequence of excitations of the character, vector, and rotation bus lines from the template to the assembly area. The basic instructions such as rotating, scaling and moving image are executed by the genetically constructed hardware of the assembly area by the instruction provided genetically. The basic instructions can be assembled into a *program* by connecting the basic instructions' identifiers in the association area. Each of these programs has its own identifier, which is accessed by its own character bus line, which goes through all the functional blocks. The line is excited automatically by the functional block requesting the operation (like the template area, such as in a template mismatch adjustment request). In such unconscious image processing, program execution is requested by any functional block, as shown in figure 4.06.1, and is executed automatically. It can also be excited consciously by the SELF in the same way as choosing an image to be displayed; to do so, instead of image identifier, the program identifier is excited.

The basic instructions like motion, rotation, and scaling of an image are genetically provided in the vision channel assembly area. Some other instructions are built by learning or by the memory of the SELF's successful experience. By sequencing such instructions like *subroutine* of computer, the brain's program can be built up like a composite image. Examples of acquired programs are the commands to use tools, or to execute routine chores like cooking. Our daily life is executed mostly by such learned programs. Fine arts are created by exercising such basic programs by the artistic sense. A more sophisticated stored program is exercised when we solve mathematical problems of geometry (how to draw auxiliary lines), of algebra (how to factor a high-order algebraic equation), and of integral calculus (how to transform variables). Solving a geometry problem is a vision channel exercise as I show in section 4.08. Algebra and calculus problems are supported by the language channel, which holds the basic and useful mathematical expressions and the know-hows of manipulation rules. The two major areas of mathematics use different brain functions. Algebra and calculus require analytic, abstract thinking capability since they require learned knowledge of formula manipulation and useful manipulation techniques. Acquisition of language capability was the prerequisite of the development of this branch of mathematics.

In conscious image processing, the images are either unloaded to the outside media or held in an internally recognizable form (that is, by the closed-loop feedback from the output channel to the input channel via the somatic sensors attached to the actuator, such as the eyes or vocal chords). In the conscious operation, the image to be processed is first sent out from the memory to be displayed. Then the processing requirement is recognized. Then proper instruction is selected by the SELF.

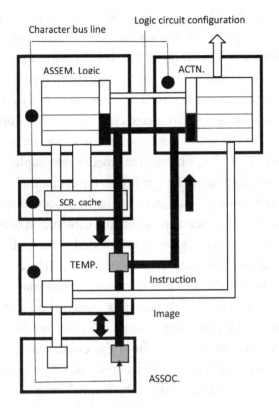

Figure 4.06.1 Image manipulation circuit

In the task setup phase, the SELF observes the entire image, checks if it is rational, confirms the need of change, and selects the processing instruction or the program. That is, the image to be processed is first displayed, and the SELF, which is the image itself, recognizes the need to change itself. Then the program identifier is selected and excited, and the sequence of instructions are sent out from the template one by one. The instruction's image closes a loop in the same way as any image is displayed. Each of the image-processing instructions configures the image-processing logic block of the assembly area (or sometimes the action-control area) as shown in figure 4.06.1. Operation of the instruction loop is the same as that for the internal image loop, except that the instruction is directed to the proper logic circuit block of the assembly or action-control area. This operation is executed automatically by the assembly area's logic circuit. While in processing, the processed image stays either inside (on the scratch pad) or on the external media. As for the instruction, it stays inside, but in some case of conscious operation (involving another intelligent machine or even a self-conscious human partner), the instruction is also sent out and shared with the partner. In both vision and language channel conscious operation, the assembly area logic requires close connection to the scratch pad inside or to the external media. The external media are coupled closely with the internal scratch pad by the fast image-input channel.

In some conscious processing, not only the processed image but also the processing instructions and programs are constructed outside, and the SELF executes the processing entirely outside by using all the available internal and external resources. External resources include the know-how of the processing from the accessible references or even from an experienced human partner. Obviously this is quite a powerful processing method. In either case, if the processing is over, the processed image is readily available from the scratch pad or from the external media. Since such image processing is to follow up a changing life situation, the processed image is seldom kept permanently in the internal image memory.

Language images are processed, almost always consciously, by the same scheme in their assembly area by the instruction stored in their template area. This is because the meaning of the words are determined by the vision channel (or sometimes by the chemical sense channel). A language-processing instruction carries such comprehensible meaning as "change the order of the words," "conjugate the verb," or "insert a conjunctive participle between sentences." Personal communication is accomplished by way of the constructed or modified sentence, which should have proper syntax and accurately conjugated participles. The language channel scratch pad can hold a long sequence of words. In the scratch pad, elementary images (words) are properly connected and meaningful sentences are constructed under the supervision of the assembly area. This is a conscious image processing.

The adoption of images as the brain's data type was one of the most significant steps forward in evolution. This is so because image-processing instructions are also images. Action directives (images) and their modification instruction can be handled by the same brain hardware. Because images and image-modification instructions are both action images, execution of image-modification instruction creates the sense of the SELF working with the object of the image.

Some image templates contains instruction to modify itself, both in visible and language image processing. One of the basic graphic image elements, blobs, is coded by the action imbedded in the template, to paint the inside of the specified closed area with the specified color (section 2.18). When the SELF meets this instruction, it executes the action virtually (by assuming that the paint and the brush are available), and the virtual action creates the sense of seeing the colored blob. Blob sensing is executed unconsciously, so we do not feel that our brain is doing the work. This is also the case of language image. For instance, in a sentence to address the monarch, the pronoun *you* is automatically changed to *his or her majesty*.

4.07 Some Details of Image Processing

In the previous section, I discussed that the image-processing instructions of the brain have the same data structure as images. The images are the commands to control movements of the body parts to produce the image outside. The similarity of an image and image-modification instructions is sensed by introspection. Instructions to rotate, move or compress/expand the currently displayed image create the same sense as rotating, moving or compressing/expanding the body, respectively, when they are exercised internally.

The sense of image-processing instruction is related to its bodily sense. The sense is weak for the image's motion and rotation, which keeps the executing body intact. But the sense associated with image scale-up and scale-down is stronger than that associated with motion or rotation instruction, as if my body were pulled apart or crushed. The associated sense of destruction of the body creates a stronger bodily sense. Sense associated with the image search instruction is quite clearly felt, invoking a sense of anxiety of not finding the required image and being associated with a real sense of eye movement and of walking around to look for the lost item.

Since image-processing operations have a close connection to internal image display and manipulation, the processing instructions are stored in the templates and are organized by connecting their identifiers in the association area. This makes an instruction sequence equivalent to assembling the composite image. Then how is image and instruction identified? To distinguish instruction from image in the template memory, the starting location of instruction is indicated by excitation of a special character bus line. This signal sends the instruction to the logic block in the assembly area or in the action-control area to let these areas to accept the following signals not as image but as image-processing instruction. If the excitation following the character bus excitation is a rotation of 90 degrees, the logic block is directed to rotate the currently displayed image by 90 degrees.

In section 2.18, I showed how an arc is drawn by such basic instruction. What follows the arc indicator of the character bus line is a vector that shifts the current image point to the center of rotation. The vector direction is reversed, and the reversed vector is rotated by the angle specified by the following rotation bus excitation. This character bus excitation means such operation. When a landscape image is to be assembled, the vector that specifies the element image location is preceded by the instruction to move the elementary image (section 3.21). Similarly, if a character bus line excitation is followed by excitation of another character bus line specifying the number 70, the presently displayed image is scaled down to 70 percent of its original size. If such an operation is executed externally on the outside media, the introductory character bus line excitation (which indicates the internal instruction) is ignored, and the following instruction is directed to the fingers holding the pencil to alter the image that exists on the outside paper.

A sequence of such operations can be assembled into a program. To do so, it is convenient for the elementary operation to be *parametrized*. To rotate an image by θ degrees, first the character bus line indicating the rotation is excited, and then another character bus line indicating that what follows is the parametrized angle of rotation is excited. The next excitation specifies the actual angle of rotation. This last excitation can specify not only a single angle but also a range of angles. Such an instruction is included in a loop executing iterative operations to search for the proper angle of rotation of the displayed image. Such operation is useful for matching an incoming image with the existing visual image template, as I discussed in section 2.29.

Image processing and data transfer among the image memory layers alternate in the same way as in any electronic data processor. To transfer image data from a memory layer to another memory layer (which is dark screen), the second layer's excitation is erased, the two layers are connected, and the support of the first layer is reduced while the support of the second layer is increased. Then the data transfer from the first to the second memory layer is executed. Signal transfer by the support-level control is clocking of the neuron circuit. The neuron circuit's support signal is actually a clock signal.

Programmed operation of the assembly area can be classified into two types: unconscious and conscious operations. A simple unconscious operation is a mismatch correction of the incoming visible image and the existing templates. A template match program is invoked by the template area by detecting no activity from any template for some time after accepting the signals from the assembly area. The processing request is sent to the association area by a character bus line to invoke the program. Another important unconscious operation is to analyze the incoming image. When a new image arrives at the assembly area, the area automatically initiates the image's peculiarity (such as symmetry) extraction program and sends the detected features to the image memory to help identify the image (section 2.29).

Yet the most important complex unconscious programmed operation is to detect the structure of the living space and to keep updating the information in the scratch pad. This is the process of constructing a three-dimensional map of the living space from the images of the visible objects, from the distance determined by the eyes' triangulation, and from the sense of contact to the body. This is essentially the image assembly process that I described in section 3.21, the only difference being that the map is three-dimensional. This is the most basic operation of the SELF to ensure the body's safety (section 2.33). A similar programmed operation is in progress to set the SELF within the time flow by arranging the events of the recent past in sequence to help determine the next step of action. This is the operation recognizing the present state's development.

Conscious program execution is learned from the experience of a successful past trial by the SELF. By memorizing each of the steps and by arranging them into a sequence of operations, we can build a useful program. This is exactly the same as building up a composite image from elementary images. In the learned operation, as the same operation is repeated many times, the operation is *naturalized* to the brain and body, and the action execution becomes automatic. Even execution of an involved conscious operation may become an unconscious automatic operation if it is repeated many times. One such case is the recognition of the speech pattern of a familiar individual. After hearing it many times, the person recognizes the speech pattern automatically and is able to identify the speaker correctly.

There are not many unconscious programmed operations in the language channel, except for those using a fixed-word pattern. In order to construct a sentence, the speaker must always be conscious in producing a logically correct sentence. This is because language statement does not directly control the body parts for action, as a visual image does. Then the speaker is aware of the impact of the meaning of the sentence. Visual images were originally for reflex-like self-defense directives, but language images were not.

In conscious image processing, the image to be processed must first be displayed to the SELF. This is because the image to be processed is observed by the SELF and the need of processing must be confirmed. The feature of the image not suitable for the present purpose is identified. The undesirable feature demands correction operation. This determines the processing instruction. The SELF identifies the program stored in the memory and activates it. It is the image that determines the processing instruction, and not the instruction that demands the data, as in the electronic processor. The origin of this difference is that the brain is an unconscious processor-conscious administrator combination. In an unconscious electronic data processor, first the instruction is given, and then the processor is supplied with the data. This works because the human administrator and the programmer control the processor. In the self-conscious brain, the processor itself is the administrator, so it must specify the instruction to run the processor. Why is this so? Because the brain has always worked in reaction to its habitat for survival since the very beginning of evolutionary history.

4.08 Conscious Mode of Image Processing

In the last two sections, I described the brain's image-processing operations by stressing its unique features. This discussion must be supplemented by a few more comments. An electronic processor is autonomous only in executing the program loaded to it. The one who knows what the processor is doing is not the processor but the human administrator and the programmer. Modeling a human machine operation only on what the biological processor can do automatically is not enough, since then the processor is doing everything blindly. The human machine has the conscious subject SELF. The fact that the SELF is aware of the purpose of the processing means that the SELF is not only the process executor but also its administrator. Human machine operation must explicitly include the role played by this administrator.

From where does the capability of the administrator emerge? This is the same question as another one I have been asking: What is the mechanism for creating the self-conscious subject SELF? I have the answer to this question now. Close examination of the functional block diagram and its operation reveals that this capability emerges from the sensing and understanding capability of the unloaded images by the SELF. The brain's activity of observing the SELF by the SELF creates the sense of SELF. This is effected by the image send-out process, followed by the image take-in process. This operation creates the sense of recognition of any image by the SELF, by making the sent-out outside image (= SELF) *visible* to the internal SELF. The SELF is the image, and it examines itself by using all the associated images the SELF holds inside the brain. This is the process of recognizing the image's meaning.

The human machine can unload its internal image and then reload it. Unloading an image makes it possible for the SELF to handle its own image as an independent outside object and allows the internal SELF to engage with it by using all the brain's available resources. Then the SELF works as the process administrator using this capability. The SELF cannot alter itself if it is confined inside the brain. The SELF makes its copy outside, processes it there, and compares the pair of SELFs that are inside and outside, and if the outside one has merit, the SELF takes that in and updates the interior SELF. If this capability is not included, the machine is no more than an unconscious electronic data processor. Why is that so?

The logic circuit in the brain is only about the same level of sophistication as the logic circuit of electronic processors. The hardware does not have any higher capability, such as evaluation of its own performance. Since the entire capability of the SELF is available to process any unloaded image, all the know-how that the brain acquired in the past life can be used in the processing and evaluation of the image. The SELF can examine its own track record. Performance evaluation capability is crucial to making the best processing choice for one's life advantage.

In such an operation, sometimes the entire task of image processing is unloaded to the outside. What this means is that the images and processing instructions are both unloaded, and the processing program is composed and executed outside. For instance, to modify any drawing of a machine design diagram, there are only a few basic operations required, such as moving, rotating, stretching, and shrinking any graphic features. In the unloaded operation, the program is assembled only from these basic operations—but by using the SELF's entire capability to meet the task's objective. The human brain, which has acquired the image unloading and reloading capability, created self-consciousness and this operational mode. The unloaded (conscious) operation and the internal automatic (unconscious) operation enter into a symbiotic relationship using the image I/O (input-output) capability. The SELF may become independent from itself and be able to examine itself objectively. In some extreme cases, the brain's administrator may find that the entire operation is nonsense and terminate any useless work. The brain never gets into an unending dialogue loop if the input of the user is not understood by the processor. Such experience makes any PC user frustrated.

Conscious brain operation is achieved by unloading the internal image to the outside, but this process need not always be executed. Humans can see a simple visible internal image by closing their eyes and seeing the image behind their closed eyes. This capability emerges from the signal feedback loop going *not* through the vision channel but through the eyesight's directional control feedback loop: when we see an object, we trace its shape by moving the eyes' direction. When I intend to modify a simple visible image, I can see it internally by way of this feedback mechanism (the same mechanism as seeing a dream). By using any such internally observable image that is the equivalent of the image on the external media, one can execute a rather complex graphic or language process.

Figure 4.08.1 shows the image of the full moon and that of the crescent moon. The SELF must make the complement of the crescent moon to the full moon. The brain cannot do this unconsciously, by using only the internally available processing capability.

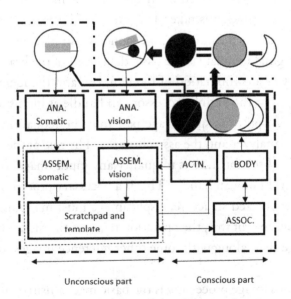

Unconscious part   Conscious part

Figure 4.08.1 Conscious involvement of SELF
in image processing

The conscious way is to send both images out, observe them, and recognize that the complement is the shape of an egg. This conscious operation can execute image *subtraction* or *division*. The brain's internal logic alone does not have the capability. The SELF takes the subtracted image back via the image input channel. This conscious process uses the entire image recognition capability (in the box with the thick dotted line).

The unconscious internal process uses only the logic circuit of the assembly area (in the dotted box of the figure). The process includes an unqualified image, which is the egg-shaped complement as the answer. To qualify the complement's image, it must go through the analyzer, to the assembly area, and to the image memory. This requires image send-out and conscious external processing. Here the image analyzer displays quite a powerful capability.

If an internally observed image is clear enough, the area of figure 4.08.1 shown above the broken line need not be active. In daily life, the brain is doing this type of operation all the time. That is why we often wonder why a very complex operation can be carried out so smoothly by the brain's presumably quite simple internal logic circuits. This mode of operation is taken for granted. The example of splitting a template (sections 3.21 and 3.22) is done in a similar manner. In that case, the original template is the basic data atom of the brain, stored in the memory as a combination of the template and the identifier. This is the image that the brain's processor can handle at high speed. If this image *atom* is split, the split image pair must be requalified by going through the analyzer and the assembly area. The role of the upper-level processor P_1 of section 1.20 is to qualify any input image to the image atom that the brain can handle. This is a necessary procedure: since an image is a connected structure, a split image must maintain its proper meaning. Because of this, the operation requires the SELF to know the entire image first, along with some other reference images, prior to the operation.

Conscious image processing is the basic mechanism of all the high-level brain capabilities. Natural science, social science, literature, and philosophy are all based on this capability. I show how this capability is used to solve some geometric problems. Figure 4.08.2(a) shows a circle along with the triangle $\triangle ABP$ that fits in the circle. The angle $\angle APB$ remains the same independent of position P on the circle. To understand what this geometrical theorem means, I send out the image and add three dotted lines, OA, OP, and OB. Point O is the special point, the center of the circle, so the advantage of adding the lines is naturally expected. Then the three triangles $\triangle AOP$, $\triangle POB$, and $\triangle BOA$ are all equilateral triangles. Angle $\angle APB$ equals the sum of the angle $\angle OAP$ and angle $\angle OBP$. Since the sum of the three angles of any triangle is π, and since angles $\angle OAB$ and $\angle OBA$ are equal, I find

$2(\angle APB + \angle OAB) = \pi$ (or 180°), that is,

$\angle APB = (\pi/2) - \angle OAB$ = constant

This rather interesting geometrical theorem can be proven by simply observing and manipulating the sent-out image either on the paper or by internal imagination.

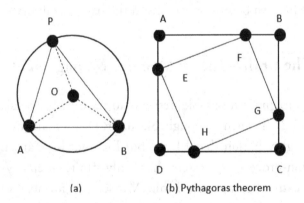

(a)   (b) Pythagoras theorem

Figure 4.08.2 High-level thinking by image manipulation

Figure 4.08.2(b) shows a square, $\square ABCD$, into which another square, $\square EFGH$, fits. The area of $\square ABCD$ equals $(AF + FB)^2$ and that of $\square EFGH$ is EF^2. Since EF^2 equals $(AF + FB)^2 - 4\,[(AF \times FB)/2] = AF^2 + FB^2$ and since $FB = AE$, the Pythagorean theorem $EF^2 = AE^2 + AF^2$ is proven by simple image manipulation.

I have shown two simple examples, but the same line of reasoning can be executed in every area of mathematics, science, the arts, and philosophy. This is the simple case showing that any complex thinking can be executed effectively by manipulating the image consciously, either internally or by unloading it on an external medium such as paper. As I show by the examples, the image manipulation requires a significant amount of preexisting knowledge (such as the area of a rectangle is the product of its two edges' length). This capability is required to split the image properly into its elements, as I discussed in section 3.22, in order to step inside the image. Manipulation of a mathematical formula requires many facets of such knowledge (such as useful variable transformation). Because of this prerequisite, analytic thinking is more involved than synthetic thinking. Yet this is also the same capability as those illustrate by figure 4.08.2. Complex human thinking capability in every area depends on this conscious image processing. This capability is a by-product of self-consciousness. With this ability, we do not need to understand the higher brain function directly. That can be synthesized from the basic capability.

4.09   The Brain's Image Memory Management

A system designer's insatiable desire is to have more transistors. One billion MOSFETs are not enough. Similarly, I want many more neurons than the eighty billion that I have, but I cannot have any more. Any information-processing system has only finite memory capacity. Humans cannot escape the limit. Worse, the number of neurons decreases with advancing age, and life's experiences add more and more images that desire to be stored. Memorizing anything new becomes harder as one's age advances. The brain must manage, by itself, what must be memorized and how to allocate needed memory space. This is equivalent to the memory management done by a PC. This problem is not easy, since most of the brain's memory cannot be overwritten like a PC's memory. It resists the effort to be erased (section 3.08).

Does human memory capacity really saturate? I do not know anyone who is able to speak more than a certain number of essentially different languages fluently (English and German are essentially the same, but German and Polish are basically different). As for me, I can manage Japanese, English, and Polish, but Polish at the cost of losing fluency in German. This is my limit.

The brain's image memory management appears to have three basic features:

(1) The priority is set to memorize the present event's information, and on such features that matter for the welfare of life.
(2) Most, if not all, of the memories are thrown away soon after their acquisition.
(3) If the rate of memory formation is exceeded by a high image input rate, the brain memorizes only certain conspicuous features of the incoming images. Details of the image are neglected.

These features indicate that the brain exercises filtering of the incoming images. Feature (1) appears to be the requirement to meet the evolutionary needs. As for (2), most of the images making up the present state are only temporarily stored on the scratch pad. As soon as the present becomes the past, the images are thrown away. The scratch pad is made of fast read/write/erase memory cells. Of all these images, only some that have managed to make their template and identifier and establish their meanings have survived. As for (3), this feature indicates that not all the details of the incoming images reach the memory. The vision channel analyzer extracts only conspicuous features such as color. As for a language image, only certain keywords are retained. Keyword identification requires analysis of the sentence. The selection mechanisms of the vision and language channels appear different.

Memories having features (1) and (2) are short-term memories. These memories are kept on the scratch pad, and only some of them are transferred to the template for permanent retention. Neurophysiology shows that such memories are retained by neuron circuits that are active only during the period of memorization. Either such memory cells are the dynamic memory of section 3.08, or else the cell is built from special neurons whose synapse does not have a long memory retention time. The scratch pad has such a memory structure. The structure is similar to that of the template, but internal image bus lines are connected by temporarily conductive synapses of special-type neurons, and the temporary template has no identifier. This type of memory is more susceptible to neuron death in old age, when it becomes hard to memorize any new information quickly. To maintain a memory for a longer time, the memory must be transferred to secure permanent neuron connection structure discussed in section 3.08.

There is another interesting feature of human memory retention: images retained by the human brain belong to either of the two distinct kinds. There are images that can be sent out as they are, such as visible images and language images. These are coded as the command of action. Such images are retained by occasionally sending them out. If such images are not sent out for a long time, the memory is lost. The other kind of images are simple, qualitative images such as color, temperature, and chemical associated with some concrete objects. Such images cannot be sent out from the body until they are associated with an image that can be sent out. These internally confined images are rather securely held for a long time.

When I remember the wide landscapes of the countries I've visited, what appears first is the dominant color. As I remember Sounion in Greece, I see the blue color of the Aegean Sea. Similarly, the scene of Ireland is the dark gray sky of the Atlantic over a sparkling green meadow. Color and the chemical sense of smell and taste are confined within the body. So the smell and taste of the local foods I was accustomed to in my childhood have remained with me for my whole life. Hard-to-be-sent-out images are tightly connected to the other images, and their memory is secure. Sending out a visible or language image is intended to vacate the memory, but the action has the adverse effect of retaining it by reinforcing the connection.

A special mode of the brain's memory management is how to retain some required memory securely, especially the name of a person or an object. The method for this is to associate the image with some

272

other, well-established image. If the two images are jointly memorized, memory security is ensured. I had a hard time trying to memorize the name of the Icelandic bird that has a red beak, so I imagined the bird pecking at a cream puff. Then the name *paffin* was securely kept. This is called the peg method, and it is used by magicians.

We Far Eastern students under the culture of Confucius were used to being taught something unique. First, *study* and acquire knowledge, and then *learn* what was studied. *Study* and *learn* are different processes. This is the opening message of *The Words of Confucius* and is regarded as very important. Perhaps I should replace *learn* with *ruminate* to make its meaning clearer. The master's teaching is that if you do not ruminate, then the real pleasure of studying something is not felt. This is an excellent tradition that helps to retain solid memory.

4.10 Memories that Survive All Life

The human brain receives a huge number of images from the vision and language channels but does not retain most of them. The memory of any particular event is kept only for a few days. This is the most basic form of memory management, carried out continuously. So which images are held for a long time? Longer-term memory is achieved by connecting the image first to the time of day. This is really a curious feature of the memory that I discuss more in chapter 5.

I do not remember the date, but it was a cloudy afternoon when my shortwave radio captured the signal from *Sputnik*. I was excited; it was the first day of the space age. Such *fossils* of images show my core values clearly.

If I think of the events of my life for which I retain a clear memory, there seems to be a certain reason why the memories survived for my whole life. I believe that listing and examining the nature of such permanent memories is an excellent way to dig into the depths of my mind. These *fossils* of image memory show my core values. Many such images show exciting feats of human greatness, such as the space signal in 1957. Soon after that happened, I came to the U.S. as an introverted

Asian student having no confidence in myself. Soon after my arrival, I met with two great astronomers, Dr. G. P. Kuiper and Dr. Barbara Middlehurst, and became a student of Professor Aldert van der Ziel and Dr. William Shockley. And then I became acquainted with Dr. Herbert Kroemer. All of these people I had admired since my college days in Japan. Especially the paper of Dr. Herbert Kroemer on the negative mass amplifier convinced me to work in solid-state physics. The occasion of meeting such great scientists for the first time is remembered so clearly that I can reenact the event even now. Dr. Middlehurst invited me for dinner. She asked me, "What do you want to eat?" Absolutely stunned, I answered, "Cucumber salad." I indeed tasted her cucumber salad that evening during dinner. At the Minneapolis airport, a man asked me, "Are you Sho-i?" (He pronounced my name this way.) That was Professor van der Ziel. I never expected that the great professor would come to the airport to drive me to the university.

Other images that remain permanently in my memory are those of the daydreams I had in holy ancient sites in the Pacific, the New World, and Europe. They are all archetypal images that changed my basic perspective on life. They are mostly images of ancient gods, goddesses, heroes, and heroines and of their acts performed in the holy sites in unworldly settings. The image of the god Oh-Kuni-Nushi on the Hakuto coast of the Sea of Japan, the images of Leif Erikson in L'Anse aux Meadows in Newfoundland, the image of King Pacal the Great in Palenque, Mexico, the image of King Uahacrafun-uwa-Kavil in Copán, Honduras, the images of the goddesses Demeter and Kore in Eleusis, Greece, and the image of King Hotu Matua on the northwest cape of Easter Island, all remain in my memory as if I had seen them just a few moments ago. I admire all these ancient heroes and heroines.

Still other images come of my experiences with the local people in Mesoamerica and South America. I always go out from my lodging to the nearby areas and try to talk with *paisanos*. On every such occasion, I feel a close sense of human contact, and I sense their warm feeling for me. Such human relationships are no longer available in any of the developed countries in the present day. If I gain access to someone without a convincing introduction, modern society regards that as a criminal act.

Negative images that remain in my mind are those of bitter shame. I have much shame because I did not return enough to those people who gave me so much, or I behaved too excessively toward others without even thinking of their feelings. Such painful images survive forever, and I keep feeling ashamed of myself whenever I am depressed.

If I ruminate on all my fossil images, I am able to identify what my core values are. I have a firm belief in human greatness, and I am a devoted hero worshipper. My heroes include great teachers and mentors. I value the ancient cultures of practically any part of the world, and especially those of the Western Hemisphere, much more highly than those of modern business and technology culture. I value close human-to-human relationships much more than the rigid and cold business relationships of the modern capitalist society. I am deeply pious with regard to the pagan gods and goddesses, who carry a genuinely human and humane character. I strongly desire to have a peaceful, eventless life in obscurity all throughout my life and to exercise my free imagination to study all sorts of mysteries, like ancient Chinese Taoists did. I dream of living under the great Inca of Cusco in peace my whole life and of contributing to the New World's Native American cultural renaissance.

In the brain, a permanent memory is created by connecting the image tightly to many other images and by stabilizing the connected structure. Yet there is neurophysiological evidence that the brain's old area such as the hippocampus, which does not seem to have a high capacity to hold a huge amount of memory, is crucial in memory formation and retention. How does such a brain area affect memory formation or retention? In my mechanical model, memory security is ensured by strong excitation of the just formed image's memories. Then the brain's area may exercise the support control to the template and association area after the identifier formation. If the support level is kept high, many images are connected, and the image is securely anchored in the connected structure.

4.11 Sharing Template Neurons

A template is a large memory structure requiring many neurons. Since many line drawings have the same local structure, more than one template may share the common parts. Figure 4.11.1 shows how template 1, consisting of neurons C, D, B, C, A, and template 2, consisting of neurons E, D, B, C, D, share the common part D, B, C. Each template is connected to its identifier. If identifier 1 is excited, then template 1's closed loop of C, D, B, C, A gets support from the identifier. Then the closed loop, which is a subcritical oscillator (section 3.18), is activated by identifier 1 and gets into self-excited oscillation. The image that the template represents emerges and is sensed by the SELF. At the same time, identifier 2 is not excited. The connection E, D remains quiescent. Excitation of template 1 does not spread out to template 2. This mechanism is assisted by the support of the neuron circuit. Self-excited oscillation takes energy away from the nearby neurons to prevent all-out excitation. This same mechanism prevents the excitation of template 2 by identifier 2 from spreading out to excite template 1.

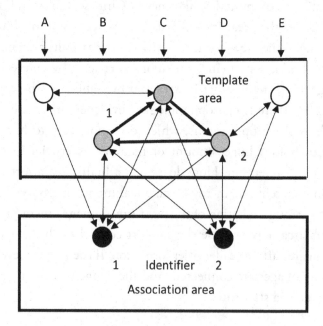

Figure 4.11.1 Shared neurons in templates

This is an advantageous feature of the architecture based on the subcritical oscillator. Even if some neurons are shared by several templates, the image's identity is maintained. The shared part of several templates carries the common feature of the images, which I call a *stem image*, as discussed in section 4.12. A set of images sharing a common part may have their identifiers close together in the association area. Then, if the template of the full moon is excited, images of anything round, such as a pancake, can be excited easily. Children often say the full moon looks like a pancake.

A reverse structure of using two or more templates to represent a single object's image is also possible. An overly complex template is inconvenient for the neuron circuit to process. So connection of a pair of templates by their identifiers is an effective alternative. Each template makes its own identifier, and these are connected by a higher-level identifier. The high-level identifier may carry the instruction to connect two templates. We often experience this process of image assembly: we suddenly discover that a complex image consists of a pair of simple elements. The Star of David is created by two regular triangles, and the swastika of the Nazis is created by a combination of S and S (SS?). This is a convenient way to memorize the latter since the Buddha's swastika rotates in the opposite direction.

4.12 Images Assembled from Stem Images

An animal body is built from the stem cells that can become any body part after development. Some stem cells develop only for certain special body parts. As I show in section 4.40, the human body functions and the brain functions seem to have developed by way of evolution following the same guidelines. Among internal images, there are stem images, each of which can be an element used to build a wide variety of images. Any visual images including certain common features such as a circle are related in the image memory. Any image including the circular shape—the sun, the moon, a tortilla, a twenty-five-cent coin—is built from the stem image, a circle, and a few characterizing features.

How is a stem image identified? When a complex image is received, it is separated into several conspicuous images (section 3.22), and each of these parts is analyzed separately. They become the element images. Then the whole image is reassembled from them and from a few other elements. The brain's composite image analysis is the two-step process: first to identify the element images, and then to build up the whole image. Then an interesting possibility arises. A visual image template may have its common components specified by their names, such as *circle* or *square*, in which case the image is already identified: name → visible image conversion displays the stem image. A similar case was discussed in section 2.22, dealing with landscape images. Most, if not all, of the stem images have names, or more generally, the stem image itself may be regarded as the ideogram. Then a visible stem image can be identified by its name. The stem image's template can be accessed from both the stem image name's identifier (word) and the image's visible identifier. The image's name is versatile. The reason for such versatility is that a word is an abstract image; a regular triangle that is placed in any image in whatever orientation or size is still a regular triangle. To assemble the composite image, the name of the stem image is associated with a language instruction, such as "Surround all the image features by this stem image." Then the stem image and the rest of the features are assembled into a composite image following the instruction (section 2.25).

Since stem images are conspicuous, they are recognized by conscious observation at the time of acquisition of any composite image (section 3.22). For this to be possible, the brain must have a large inventory of elementary images. These images were acquired before, and their names were assigned for later use. I think that stem images must have been the origin of the ideograms of the writing system. Chinese ideograms still display this original feature clearly.

A stem image may also be identified from any image after the image analysis is over. If the image is already analyzed to a sequence vectors and arcs and is delivered to the assembly area, the logic circuit of the assembly area has capabilities to find a simple stem image by focusing on the internal image bus line's excitation pattern. For instance, if arc specification is followed by a vector and 360-degree rotation specification, a stem image, a circle, is detected. As for stem images made of vectors, the excitation pattern analysis of the vector bus cross section identifies them as shown by the examples of figure 4.12.1(a) and 4.12.1(b).

Quite simple assembly area logic is able to detect such peculiar features. All such logic circuits can operate in parallel. All the special features can be extracted in a single processing time slot by way of many logic circuits operating in parallel. If a stem image is found by this means, then it is sent out. Then the SELF subtracts the stem image from the original image by conscious image subtraction, and reanalyzes the rest (section 4.08).

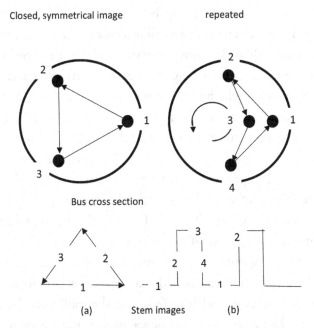

Figure 4.12.1 Stem image excitation pattern

This mechanism indicates that the analyzer's image processing does not make a simple one-way signal flow from the sensor to the memory. In a real brain, visual image analysis is carried out by many cascaded blocks that occupy the rear part of the brain. Connections among the blocks are generally made from the eyes to the brain's interior, but there is evidence of the existence of some backward connections. Such connections could be executing the operation that I just described. Image element extraction cannot be executed by unidirectional signal flow, whatever the extraction algorithm may be. Any stem image reaching the internal image circuit is readily identified, is connected to the language channel, and has its name assigned for later use. Using such a preprocessed stem image, the original image's template includes the processing instruction to assemble the image from the stem image and the characterizing features. These features and the stem image are connected by the image's identifier. Such an operation requires close cooperation between the vision and language channels. Such an operation in the brain of the early hominids may have developed into the fully functional language capability.

If a stem image is used to assemble a composite image and to draw it on the external media, the template used for the operation must include some graphic-processing instructions. An example is the image of the full moon in which a rabbit is seen (section 1.27). It consists of the stem image, the circle, the additional feature, namely, the rabbit, and the instructions to fit the rabbit in the circle. The instructions are how to scale, rotate, and move the rabbit's image to make it fit, as shown in figure 4.12.2. Setup of the fitting instruction is done by trial and error. The fitting schemes for such a nebulous image are not unique and depend on the viewer. The SELF senses this fitting search process as the sense of seeing a rabbit in the moon.

If such a composite image is internally observed, it need not be displayed by adjusting the added features. The composite template may be split into two, and the circle and the rabbit can be displayed alternately. The SELF is satisfied by seeing two independent images in succession. Such a composite image is handled in the same way as the landscape image of section 2.22. Images built from a stem image are displayed internally by this shortcut.

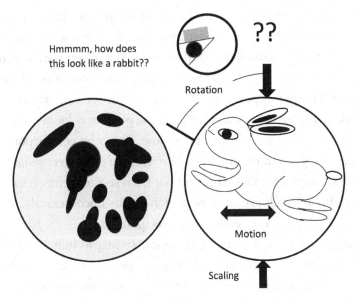

Figure 4.12.2 How to fit image to stem image

There are stem images of language. Many words share the same syllables, such as –able, –tion, extra–, and con–. These syllables carry general meanings such as *capability, united structure, extreme,* and *integration,* respectively. The chemical sense of taste has six well-defined stem images, but the chemical sense of smell has no clearly defined stem image.

4.13   Rational Image Assembly

Images we see internally do not always come from the memory of the actual observation. Such an image is partially or wholly constructed by the SELF. The SELF tries to build rational images. Here the word *rational* means that the created image is consistent with the SELF's current other images. I see domestic animals. Their common structure establishes what I call the rational image of animal (section 4.04). Images that do not fit the pattern (such as octopus) create the sense of surprise and curiosity.

Rational image construction is useful in supplying the details of a complex image if some of its parts are lost in memory. Humans see similar objects and learn their functions. From the memories, the image of any object must carry all its needed features. My old car was white, and it was required to display a pair of registration plates. What were the colors of the plates? I do not remember anymore. Without that information, the image of the car does not appear real. When I bought the car fifty years ago and junked it seven years after that time, the popular color of registration plates in New Jersey was blue and yellow. So, to be conspicuous on a white car, the plate must have been blue and the characters yellow. This detail was constructed rationally and not from secure memory, so it may not be right. Yet such image construction occurs unconsciously, and the rationally assembled images are sensed as quite real.

Images of ETs on TV shows all appear similar to humans. I believe that if intelligent beings have indeed developed on other planets, their body structure must be very different from that of humans as they must have gone through an entirely different evolutionary history. Yet the ETs' creators believe that the beings must have a *rational* body structure according to them. So they adopted humanlike body structures. They assume that ETs are superior to humans. ETs have a very large head since their superior technology requires a powerful brain. The artists assume that the ET's thinking power is in the head. Yet that is nothing more than one choice among many. Over the long course of human history, the location of the mind was more often considered to be in the heart. ETs' eyes are much larger in proportion, to acquire more visible information.

The standard of rationality is common sense. That changes with time. Common sense is often subjective and inflexible. In the Middle Ages, everything was believed to be under God's or Buddha's control. This is ridiculous to modern humans, but we are also subject to such bias. That there is no alternative to democracy as the ideal political system is the common sense of the twenty-first century. Modern art and music emerged by breaking away from the classical standard, and even in physics, the *common sense* established by relativity cast its long shadow on quantum mechanics (sections 6.28 and 6.29).

U.S. attorneys try to create a favorable image of their client by skillfully manipulating the witnesses, whose memory is often not reliable enough to retain every detail. The witness is certainly not telling a fabrication, but if he or she is threatened enough, emotion burns out the witness's mind, and the attorney's *rationally constructed* version of the story often prevails.

The creation of a new rational image by way of the imagination is a design exercise. This becomes easy if the intermediate image is displayed on external media such as paper or a computer screen and is readily available for more rational modification. It is much easier to construct any rational image outside the brain. Irrational image such as the Penrose triangle cannot be sent out without emotional stress. Any useful machine's image is too complex to be held in the brain to be processed internally, as I discussed in section 3.22. A machine's design is executed by unloading the images of its every detail onto paper. The external image is able to interact effectively with the brain's logic, and all the attention can be focused to create a more rational image. I have mentioned visible image creation, but the same is true in music and literature composition.

An important capability of rational image construction is to help identify certain objects like a human face precisely. We remember the faces of hundreds of acquaintances. The faces are not so much different from one another, but we can identify them accurately. Yet we cannot draw the likeness of each person. This means that the faces are not remembered as real pictures. Face identification must be based on the ability to construct a particular facial feature from many other pieces of information about the person. Yet a rationally assembled image can be drawn on paper only if the person doing so has artistic talent.

4.14   Change of Order of Image Elements

In the image send-out process, the order of image elements (vectors/arcs or words) may be changed from what exists in the memory. In a simple line drawing of a visual image, the order of drawing it can be changed easily. Figure 4.14.1(a) shows two ways of drawing the same image, in the order 1, 2, 3, 4 or in the reverse order a, b, c, d. The order of excitation of the vectors observed from the bus cross section for the two cases is shown in the center of the figure. In the cross section, the location of the excited line is flipped with reference to the center, and then the order of excitation is reversed. The pen-up line excitation is reversed along with it. This is a simple operation executable automatically by the assembly area's logic. Yet to change the order of the drawing freely, this simple algorithm is not enough. There must be a general way to change the order.

If the order of execution must be changed entirely arbitrarily, the template must be broken down to its image elements, vectors and arcs, each of which is referenced to the same point. This can be executed either consciously or unconsciously if the image is simple. To execute this operation consciously, the SELF sends out the image, observes the entire image, consciously reanalyzes the image in the required order, and makes a temporary template. Yet this is not always necessary if the image is simple. The vision channel has enough processing capability to create a temporary template that can be used for to execute the order change. How is such template modification made? In the template, the vectors and arcs must become separate, independent image elements referred to the *same reference point*. To do this, the processor sets up a fixed imaginative reference point O, as shown figure 4.14.1(b), on the scratch pad. The point O can be anywhere. The vector from O to vector $\mathbf{v}_1$'s root is vector $\mathbf{v}_{1a}$.

Since point O is arbitrary, this vector can be chosen arbitrarily too. Then vector $\mathbf{v}_X = \mathbf{v}_{1a} + \mathbf{v}_1$ is determined. This vector addition is carried out by transforming the vector registration from polar coordinate to Cartesian coordinate by the scheme of section 2.21. In the coordinate, the vector arithmetic is simply executed. Then, in figure 4.14.1(b), vector $\mathbf{v}_{2a}$ is given by $\mathbf{v}_{2a} = \mathbf{v}_X$. The first section of the template becomes $[\{\mathbf{v}_{1a}\}, \mathbf{v}_1, \{-\mathbf{v}_X\}]$. This notation, $[\ldots]$, is a template identification that I used in section 2.27, where $\{\ldots\}$ indicates a pen-up vector and the minus sign indicates reversal of the vector direction. Then, by using $\mathbf{v}_{2a} = \mathbf{v}_X$ and by defining $\mathbf{v}_Y = \mathbf{v}_{2a} + \mathbf{v}_2$, the second section is separated, and this part becomes $[\{\mathbf{v}_X\}, \mathbf{v}_2, \{-\mathbf{v}_Y\}]$, where $\mathbf{v}_{3a} = \mathbf{v}_Y$. The same operation is repeated. Then the original template is separated into four independent partial templates referred to the common origin, O. The four partial templates are equivalent to the single original template. They can be executed in any order to draw the same image. In the set of partial templates, any vectors other than $\mathbf{v}_1$, $\mathbf{v}_2$, and $\mathbf{v}_4$ are pen-up vectors. Partial template 3 consists of pen-up vectors only. This template can be ignored. Any such partial template can be drawn in the reverse order by the scheme of figure 4.14.1(a).

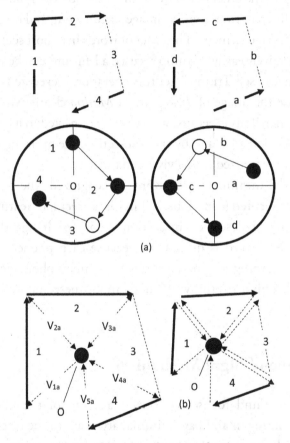

(a)

(b)

Figure 4.14.1 Change of order of a drawing

By the template breakdown, quite a few pen-up vectors emerge. This is because each time the pen must go back to the common reference point O. For this operation to be practically useful, the original template must not be too complex. If the image is made of too many vectors and arcs, to change the order of drawing becomes almost impossible. It is not possible to draw *Blondie* (the once popular cartoon character in the U.S. in the 1950s) in arbitrary order. If the visible image is used as a command of self-defense or of martial arts, it is usually quite simple. The sense of many pen-up vectors is felt as the feeling of inconvenience at the time of drawing the image on paper in totally arbitrary order.

Change of the order of the words in a sentence, or of the phonemes in a word, is different from a visible image since a word, and not a phoneme, is the basic image element. The order of words in a short sentence can be changed relatively easily. "Trump accused a Muslim" can be converted to "A Muslim accused Trump." Yet this operation is executed consciously, since I sense the image of *Trump* and a *Muslim* clearly while changing the word order. This is because any word is connected to its visual image in the association area, and by the connection, the meaning of a word is consciously recognized in the vision channel.

Once the meaning of the word is recognized, the entire mental process is executed consciously. This is a peculiar feature of word recognition as I described in section 2.25. To change the order of phonemes in a word is quite hard because each phoneme of a word carries no meaning and because there are many phonemes even in a short word. This is relatively easy to do in Japanese but not in any other language.

4.15 Line-of-Sight Mechanism

The human mind focuses on one image out of the many images currently coming in and pays minimal attention to the rest. The SELF engages with the focused image if it matters to the welfare of life. The brain's sensors keep sending all kinds of signals from the essentially chaotic and unpredictable outside world, and then there is the internal mechanism of activating all sorts of images stored in the memory. The brain must deal with these images and, at the same time, must focus on certain key images. The problem of the brain is not lack of information but an excess of poor information. The line-of-sight mechanism picks up useful information. The focusing mechanism is executed in two different ways: one starts from the brain's upper level, and the other starts from the lower level.

The upper-level mechanism starts from the sensors, the eyes, ears, etc. This mechanism starts from an indifferent state. In this state, the image input channel sends images from the outside world one after the other in quick succession, and the SELF never dwells on any particular image. These images are used only to build the image of the present living space. If something unusual appears in the vision field, such as a moving object, an outstanding color, or brightness, that alters the structure of the living space. The direction of the eyes points to the object. The eyes' directional control is initiated by reflex without intervention from the internal image circuit. The vision channel analyzer issues a warning to all the lower-level blocks as shown in figure 4.15.1. This signal interrupts all the activities of the lower functional blocks, as I discuss in section 5.21, and sets the focus on the development of the new incoming image. Once the eyes start tracking the object, the lower levels of the brain identify the object and jointly focus attention on it. The eyes' directional control mechanism tracks the object identified by the internal image circuit. The image is further analyzed, and its impact on life is determined. If it is relevant to the current SELF's concern, the brain follows up the image's development and prepares to take action for self-protection.

As for the sequence of brain operation, the upper-level line-of-sight mechanism is initiated by the analyzer by comparing a pair of time-shifted images. The analyzer has both spatially shifted image comparison and time-shifted image comparison capabilities. The brain's upper area is able to control the support of all the lower functional blocks very quickly after the reflex action. The support-level control is executed using the lines of the character bus as the communication media. This is the conventional line-of-sight mechanism, but the brain's function is more general and complex, since the lower level of the brain may initiate such action as well.

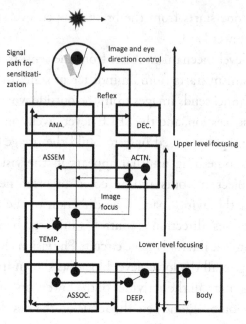

Figure 4.15.1 Line-of-sight initiation

The second line-of-sight mechanism starts from an image excited from the memory. Human life is exposed to all sorts of risks in the natural habitat and the social habitat. When one is in a state of anxiety, risk images are excited from the memory continuously. Some of these images attract attention. The excited image establishes itself in the internal image circuit. The internal image excitation sensitizes the sensors and the internal image identification circuit to catch any images that is relevant.

This selective sensitization affects the image analyzer and identification circuit to the level that any incoming image that has some similarity to the expected image is set in highlight (section 6.04). In this state, the brain seeks for any image that the brain expects to see. The image-specific support mechanism plays the key role in sensitizing the operation (section 3.19).

In the line-of-sight mechanism, the sensitization of sense is executed jointly by all the functional blocks of the brain, initiated from both the upper level and the lower level. If all the blocks work within their capability, the line-of-sight mechanism serves well for lifesaving purposes, but if the mechanism is misled by some functional block's hyperactivity, it creates complex and often perplexing mental states, such as seeing ghosts.

The line-of-sight mechanism is also executed in the language channel. The language channel mechanism works similarly to the lower-level line-of-sight mechanism of the vision channel. While listening to a message, one identifies certain keywords. Then, by imaginative association, the word's image is surrounded by the relevant visual images, and a strong awareness of the expected event emerges. Then the brain's state develops similarly to the line-of-sight mechanism from the lower level of the vision channel. In general, the line-of-sight mechanism of any sense channel (including the chemical senses) spreads out to the other sense channels and brings the entire body to the alert state.

4.16   Confusing Images

Images from the left eye and the right eye are combined, and the vector-arc extraction is carried out on the combined image. Obviously this image combination is not mandatory, because we can see the complete vision field even if one eye is covered. Then a natural question is, are the images from the pair of eyes always combined? Or does the SELF use the image from one eye at a time and occasionally switch the eye? Or does the SELF intentionally choose the image from the one eye? These important questions can be answered by way of an ingenious experiment.

If the combination of the pair of images from the eyes does not produce a sensemaking image, a fascinating phenomenon emerges. The experiment is as follows: Prepare a pair of different pictures, A and B of figure 4.16.1(a). To see the pair of pictures separately with my pair of eyes, I set up a barrier between the eyes such that the left eye sees only A, and the right eye sees only B. The barrier must be carefully crafted so that no cross view is possible. The area each eye sees must be properly restricted to see image A and B only. You watch a pair of different pictures by using the pair of eyes, left and right, simultaneously. Then you'll find that a very interesting thing happens. For some time, you will see A, then after about four seconds or so, you will see B, and then A again. The pictures are sensed alternately. I am grateful to Professor T. Papathomas of Rutgers University for calling my attention to this fascinating phenomenon.[1]

Figure 4.16.1(a) shows the explanation of this phenomenon. The analyzer combines the images from the pair of eyes. If the images from the left and the right eye are different beyond a certain limit, the combination does not create a sensemaking image. Then the brain is unable to decide which image is relevant for life protection. To save the situation, the error detector in the figure switches one eye's image to the other, thereby giving equal chance to both images. Behind the eyes in the brain, there is a comparator of a two-dimensional pixel map image pair, which issues the error signal to drive the brain into the switching mode. This is the mechanism proposed to explain this effect.[2] My mechanical brain model accommodates the scheme proposed by the author, S. P. Lehky.

Evolution has provided the means to deal with this unusual situation. The origin of this mechanism could be that many animals and birds have their eyes separated by their nose or beak. Their paired vision field does not overlap. So, maybe, a deer sees the right and the left sides alternately? If we humans had eyes like deer, we might be doing this all the time, which is a heavy burden for the brain. Monkeys and owls appear more intelligent than other animals and birds. This may be because they need not see the vision field alternately, so their brain can work more efficiently than other animals and birds. We humans might become more intelligent by getting rid of this extra burden to the brain. Yet humans inherited this mechanism. This reminds me that dolphins let the right and left brain sleep alternately. The left side and the right side of the body are different worlds for most of the animals.

[1] T. V. Papathomas, I. Kovacs, and B. Julez, "Visual Dilemmas: Competition between Eyes and between Percepts in Binocular Rivalry," and T. V. Papathomas, "The Brain as a Hypothesis-Constructing and -Testing Agent," in *What Is Cognitive Science?* (Blackwell, 1999): 230–47.
[2] S. P. Lehky, "An A-Stable Multi-Vibrator Model of Binocular Rivalry," *Perception* 17 (1988): 215–28.

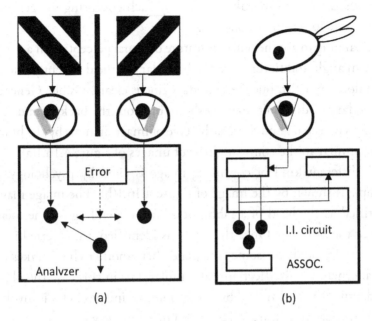

(a)   (b)

Figure 4.16.1 Recognition of confusing image

This binocular rivalry seems to show a variety of features depending on the images shown in figure 4.16.1(a). As I tried the experiment using a pair of fine-featured black-and-white pictures, red color spots emerged in the image. So, I tried to see two different colors, red and green, by the same arrangement. Switching occurs, but the colors seem to change hues also.

Another interesting facet here is that this phenomenon suggests the existence of an innate time constant of the brain: beyond a certain limit, the brain cannot tolerate any confusion of senses. The four seconds that I experienced appears to be good for life protection purposes. This is about the time it takes for me to recover from an accidental fall. The task of the pair of eyes on the left and right side appears not to be limited to providing three-dimensional views of the living space. As I show in section 4.19, triangulation has very limited capability in creating the sense of depth of the vision field. Triangulation is not possible for animals whose eyes are on both sides of the head. The pair of eyes are rather used to avoid mistakes caused by such confusing images, or to compensate for failure of one eye.

Changing to another curious feature of visual perception, if a mesh is cut at an angle and fit together, the boundary of the differently oriented mesh does not exist, but the boundary line is clearly visible. Generally, a boundary of different textures shows up from the background. This feature is detected at quite an early stage of image analysis by the human brain, similar to the confusing pair of images of figure 4.16.1(a).

A different kind of confusing image is cited by psychology. An example is shown by the image of figure 4.16.1(b). The image may be identified as the head of a rabbit or a bird, depending on the mental state of the observer. Once the image is identified, the internal image loop activity holds for some time, and then another choice takes over and alternates. This effect appears similar, but in this case the objects are identified as bird and rabbit, so the internal image circuit is involved. The time period appears to be set in a different way.

4.17 Sensitization of Senses

The human body's image input and output channels are internally connected. When sending an image out from the output channel, the signal leaks to the input channel and sensitizes the sensors of the image. This is an important mechanism, that allows seeing dreams and sensing internal images. If an image of a ghost is activated in the internal image circuit, the image is sent out to the eyes' directional control mechanism. Suppose that a ghost actually exists and is seen by the SELF. Then the eyes' direction (line of sight) automatically traces the outline of the ghost's face. This tracing action, sensed by the somatic sensors attached to the eyes' directional control mechanism, generates the ghost's graphic image signal. This signal is analyzed into the vector-arc sequence by the analyzer associated with the somatic sensors, and reaches the template area of the vision channel (section 2.23). Along with this, the eyes capture the ghost's image. The ghost's images arriving from the two sense channels (one from the vision, and the other from the eyes' movement sensing) help each other to establish the ghost's image clearly as the observed image. This means that if the image of the ghost was activated in the internal image circuit, the signal adds to the real ghost image arriving from the outside.

This multiple feedback mechanism works even if there is no ghost. If the image of the ghost is excited in the internal image circuit, the signal leaks to the eyes' directional control mechanism, and returns to the vision channel. If this feedback loop's gain is higher than its unity, then activity of the loop circuit grows to a full-scale image signal, and this signal alone is enough to create the sense of seeing a nonexistent ghost (section 6.04), in the same way as we see dreams. The SELF is misled into sensing the internal image signal as if it has come from the outside. The SELF sees nonexistent images. Images of phantoms, ghosts, dreams, and daydreams are seen by this mechanism. More regularly, we tend to see what we want to see and hear what we want to hear. Misrecognition occurs by this mechanism. Yet this is the same mechanism that allows us to see any internal image. Internal images, phantoms, and ghosts are seen by the same brain feedback mechanism, and because of that, these phenomena are felt quite real to the SELF.

Sensitization is most clearly sensed in the voice channel, because the vocal chords and the ears are close to each other and spatially connected. So any small activity of the vocal chords reaches the ears directly. The voice channel is, as naturally expected, sensitive to simple signal patterns such as a periodic rhythm or a burst of sound having a definite and agreed-upon pattern, repeated many times. Figure 4.17.1 shows a drumbeat used to broadcast information such as the beginning of a Shinto ceremony at a local shrine to the entire hamlet. If a resident knows what the drumbeat *tun-tun-t'-tun* means, he or she can detect the faint drumbeat from far away.

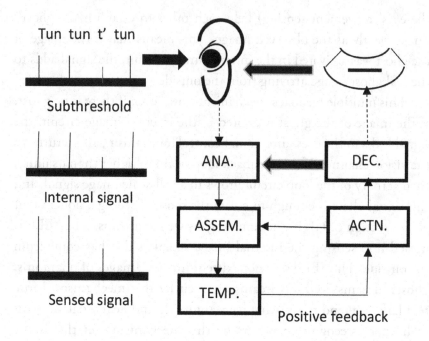

Figure 4.17.1 Sensitization to rhythmic sense

As a person hears the faint rhythm, the person generates the matching internal sound to what is heard, and after several repetitions, he or she is sure to have heard the drumbeat. In a solid-state physics experiment, the same technique was used for continuous wave by using the phase-sensitive detection technique to recover the sub-microvolt sinusoidal signal. Here, what I call *signal* is any general information that is timewise spread out, so it is more accurately termed as time sequence of the information units. Generally, I can say the following.

Any animal body's actuator such as the eye's directional control or vocal chords is mechanical device. To secure accuracy of the sent-out image, it is associated with dedicated somatic sensors attached to detect and send the actuator's action back to the source. Then the feedback signal loop is closed. If the gain of the loop is higher than the unity, any internal image signal that has reached the actuator returns to the internal image circuit as if the image had come from the outside. This effect lets us feel that any internal image which has been derived from the memory as the external image. If the body does not have an actuator (like chemical sense), the sensor is sensitized by this mechanism.

Chemical sense can be sensitized quite remarkably. Since the sense does not have actuator, the sensitivity of its sensor is increased by the internal image. Any chemical sensors are simple and quite specific to the molecular substance, so a forensic dog can sniff a minute amount of a specific substance. Humans have much less capability in this regard because the human smell sensor is much smaller and much less sensitive. This is perhaps one choice for evolutionary development: if any one sense channel is sending everything it detects, the brain cannot operate to organize the overall security of the body optimally. Any man-made machines detect chemical substances only to a limited extent since they have no specific sensor self-sensitizing mechanism.

Once I visited Easter Island and found taro potatoes. Taro exists all across the Pacific Ocean, from Japan to South Asia, to Polynesia, to South America, and to the Mesoamerican rain forest. I tasted this potato on the island. The potato tasted same as those found in any other place. This was one of my botanical inquiries around the Pacific: I believe that the existence of taro can serve as evidence of transpacific human traffic (from Asia to North America), with the same being true regarding the sweet potato's existence in Polynesia (South America → Polynesia). Before visiting Easter Island, I tasted taro potato in the Maya site of Nakbe, deep inside the Yucatán rain forest, where the resident caretakers of the site grow and eat it as a staple. This is a place very remote from modern cities/towns, so sending foods to the people there is very difficult.

Unfortunately, the taro potato was very gassy. I was embarrassed during my return flight to the U.S. At a U.S. airport security gate, I had to go through a General Electric sniffer. The machine wouldn't let me go through, even after several trials. So I was strip-searched by the officials. To their disappointment, nothing was found. So they reluctantly let me go. The next time in the same airport, the General Electric machine was taped off and not used. A dog could have done a better job than the machine because a dog's sense can be sensitized to the specific scent of contraband material.

The sense of internal body organs can also be sensitized. When I heard that my coworker had bronchial cancer, I felt an unusual feeling in my own throat, so I went to a specialist. The doctor found nothing wrong. Then the fellow died. I still felt something unusual, so I went to the doctor again. This time, the doctor shouted at me, "Nothing wrong! Waste of time! Don't come back again!"

Sensitization of vision occurs when the sense is weak, such as at dusk, and when the SELF is stressed heavily by some internal sense of guilt (section 6.04). Yet the effect of sensitization lasts a remarkably long time. This effect creates messy troubles. A wife put her pendant in a new box and forgot about it. She frantically searched for the old box and screamed and yelled at her husband. Then, a few days later, she found her pendant in the new box. Humans see what they want to see and hear what they want to hear. Similarly, humans never sense what they do not want to sense.

4.18   Sense of Nearness, Not Distance

One odd feature of the sense of vision is our concern with the distance of an object. Among the other parameters relevant to welfare or comfort of life, distance is peculiar, since it is the measure of irrelevance of the object. Most other parameters are the measure of relevance. So isn't it rational to use nearness, instead of distance, in the sense of the vision field's depth? Objects far away are usually harmless and also are unavailable for life's benefits. Nearness is a natural measure conforming with triangulation by the eyes, and this capability is used to determine the structure of the living space.

What is meant to be the living space? It is the nearby spatial domain reachable by moving a body part, but not moving the entire body. Since such a space is relevant in taking action, and also to the safety of executing action, the brain is continuously getting this information from the vision channel and also from the sense of contact, etc. The information is analyzed to determine the nature of the risky nearby objects such as hard object, high temperature body, electrical outlet or a sharp pointed edge that may hurt the body. This is an unconscious operation carried out by the brain. This is the significant part of the brain's unconscious safeguarding operation. If the body keeps moving, the information of the directly accessible space is continuously updated. If the updating cannot catch up to the speed of body motion, accidents happen.

The brain is continuously, but unconsciously watching the structure of the space in which we live. This is most clearly observable from the EEG β-wave, as I described in my 2009 book. If I observe the filtered β-wave amplitude (not including the lower-frequency component indicating support activity of the body's state) in an empty-minded state with eyes open and closed, I find that the wave amplitude is significantly higher when my eyes are open. Since I am confident that the difference is due to the information coming in from my eyes, my brain is working unconsciously to determine my position in the living space. That is why we can automatically choose the part of the body used to take any action (section 2.33).

The measure of nearness is the angle spanned by the pair of eyes and the object. If I focus on an object within the domain of triangulation, the direction of the pair of eyes is adjusted automatically so that the pair of images seen by the pair of eyes precisely overlap. The sense of focal adjustment of the pair of eyes to overlap the images is sensed as nearness. Let the distance from the center of the two eyes to the object be L and the distance between the eyes be d (about 8 cm). Then the spanned angle $\angle\theta$ is given by

$$\Theta = 2 \tan^{-1}(d/2L) = d/L \text{ (radian)}$$

This is the measure of the nearness of the object sensed by triangulation. The nearness indicator decreases rapidly with increasing L. If the recommended distance to hold a book from the eyes while reading is 40 cm, the indicator does not vary much beyond that distance. Assessing distance by triangulation cannot be very effective even within a spacious American house. The part of the space that is called *near* is the domain where the sense of distance by triangulation is useful. The use of triangulation to determine nearness is effective only down to a few degrees of the angle spanned by the object. The sense of nearness by triangulation is possible only if the pair of eyes see the same object. Most animals cannot do that. Triangulation was acquired only recently, for certain animals, birds and humans.

4.19   Sense of Depth of Vision Field

The space we live in is three-dimensional, but we recognize it primarily by two-dimensional images like photographs. To such an image, the sense of the depth appears to be appended. The sense of depth is different from the sense of length in the horizontal and the vertical direction. Suppose that I sit on a chair in front of a table and look at the objects on the table in front of me. I feel quite natural to reach for the object to the left or right. Yet to reach for the object at the center, but some distance away, I feel as if I am searching for it in the direction away from me. I feel less certain of myself in the sense of the depth direction. Depth sense appears as if fabricated by my brain. How does this subtle feeling emerge?

Close observation of the sense of depth reveals many puzzles. I look at a scene that I have never seen before with one eye covered by my hand. I can still sense the depth of the vision field. So there must be some mechanism other than triangulation used by the brain to set the sense of depth. Sense of depth is appended, as a subsidiary sense, to the sophisticated, well-developed sense of the two-dimensional image of space.

A two-dimensional image of space contains the depth information already in it. What is this information? Any image of space sensed by the SELF need not be a combination of the images from the pair of eyes. Many animals have an eye on either side of the nose and cannot exercise triangulation. Yet they seem to live safely in three-dimensional space. I observed a dog's behavior when he was placed on a high shelf. He never put himself in danger by jumping. (I am notorious for doing such *experiments* on animals). The canine family is intelligent enough to know the risk. Their sense of the vision field's depth is already good enough to avoid any risk.

What is the nature of the information appended to the sophisticated two-dimensional space image? By observing a direction, the brain is automatically constructing the *side view* of the space. The first question is, how is the depth information retained in the brain? There seems to be no place in the image memory structure to retain such information. It is not possible that each object in a composite image carries its depth information in the image memory. Any image retained in the brain is like a two-dimensional photograph. The depth information must be created from the two-dimensional image by the instruction of analyzing the image *at the time of its observation*. The structure of the landscape image I discussed in section 2.22 gives us a clue. Information about the vision field's depth is created by a connection vector of the elementary images in the scene. The memory retains the two-dimensional structure of connection of the image element as shown in figure 3.21.2(a). Then the connection of the identifiers of the element images can be made directional at the time of observation. If the connection is made from the nearest object to the remotest object, the order is able to create the sense of vision field depth at the time of observation. The faraway object may be covered by a nearby object, and the sense of a perspective view emerges naturally.

Landscape images are composite images that are assembled only on demand, and they contain only a small number of elementary images. Such memorized images are never used for reference to take action. The accurate depth information matters only when one is actually on the scene while observing the state of the directly accessible space to take action. Then the depth information of casually observed scene is almost always extracted from the presently engaged two-dimensional image; the numerical distance is not the issue. When the engagement is over, the information is thrown away. Then we only need to consider the method of extracting depth information from the presently observed two-dimensional image.

How is such information extracted from the two-dimensional image? If object A, whose general shape is known, is partially hidden behind the other object, B, then A must be farther away than B. Since there are many objects in the vision field, this method alone is sufficient to place many overlapping objects in the order of distance. If there is more than one completely separated set of objects, each of them makes its own sequence, and I engage with only one sequence at a time.

The vision field is illuminated by its own light source from within or from the outside source of known direction. Any object in the vision frame casts a shadow or receives nonuniform illumination. An object's shadow works as an independent object. This is especially true in a large natural landscape, referring to the direction of the sun and the location of clouds that cast a shadow on faraway mountains. Since the direction of the light source may change during observation, the shape of the shadow varies. Shape, size, and shadow provide relative distance. On many occasions there are moving objects in the scene such as cars. The relation between the moving objects and the static objects provides more clues. The size of a certain object such as an automobile or house is standardized. The apparent size of one to the other sets their relative distance.

Yet if the size of such reference object changes suddenly and drastically, it fools the sense of depth. The width of the Yarlung Tsangpo River narrows suddenly in the southwest of Lhasa, Tibet. Then the huge continental landscape of the river's downstream changes to that of a small rock garden. This is one of the strongest impressions of nature I had in Tibet.

Distance information often comes from the memory of past observations. In some past time, the depth of the vision field was observed as horizontal distance. Since we walk in the direction of the depth of the field of our familiar location, our brain retains the distance information consciously, and this is later converted to depth information. This memory is useful in estimating the distance of the living space. This effect is observable in small children's behavior: A family living in a spacious American house moves back to Japan. The children, still retaining the past sense of depth in the roomy American house, run and hit the wall or any other featureless object. Their sense of depth acquired in the U.S. survives for some time. Memory can be useful in setting the sense of depth in many ways: the living rooms of house A and house B are basically similar, since furniture size is standardized.

From all these clues, a three-dimensional map of the observed space is set up unconsciously at the time of observation. This provides the sense of depth of the vision field, which we take for granted. Yet to determine a distance not personally accessible, triangulation is the only way. In astronomy, very sophisticated techniques of triangulation are used. Ancient Greeks determined the distance from the earth to the moon by triangulation. They knew the size of the earth. Then, by observing the shadow of the earth cast on the moon at the time of a lunar eclipse, they found that the moon's diameter was about one-quarter of that of the earth. The angular size of the moon is half a degree. From these numbers, the Greek astronomers determined the distance to the moon to be about four hundred thousand kilometers. In order to determine the distance to the fixed stars, the baseline of the size of the earth's orbit around the sun, along with ultrahigh precision angle measurement, is required. At the time of the Renaissance, it was impossible to use the baseline of the earth's orbit around the sun or to measure the angles with such a high degree of precision. Galileo Galilei's dialogue concerning the two new sciences describes the comedy of scholars at the time trying to determine the distance to a supernova. Yet Galileo reached the right conclusion from the then available data by using his version of statistical error analysis. That is really impressive.

4.20 Sensing and Understanding

A brain's response to all kinds of incoming images, some relevant and some not, is classified into several levels. In the first level, the sensors are all on, but there is no sense of image. In the second level, the image's existence is sensed, but no memory is formed. In the third level, the images are identified or the name of the object is determined. In the fourth level, the brain correlates the image with the existing images, and the meaning of the image is determined. At the fifth level, the image's effect on one's present and future life is determined. An action plan is set up referring to the image information in order to deal with the object. Some action may be taken and its effect is learned.

At the first level, the SELF does not attend. The human machine is like a video monitor. The successively stronger SELF attends the second, the third, the fourth, and the fifth levels. The first level keeps the human mind in a peaceful state. Level 2 is the casual state of daily life. Normal humans spend most of their time in this state. Level 3 is the state in which we learn something from the experience but do not directly engage in any action. Level 4 is the state wherein we learn something by observation and rumination on the past experience, and we set the information into proper perspective. At level 5 we learn something by engaging in real action. Between level 2 and level 5, acceptance of the image changes from sensing to understanding.

Sensing an image or event is only to accept the image or event as a passive observer. Understanding it is first to sense it and next to learn how the object works and to become able to simulate the image's action in the brain or body. Here, a difference between static image and dynamic image emerges. To sense is to feel the static image, and to understand includes static sensing of the image and having the capability to dynamically simulate the object (sections 4.22 and 4.23). Looking at an object and being able to identify it as a clock is sensing. Looking at the clock, unscrewing the back panel, seeing the inside, and learning how it works—that is understanding. Sensing and understanding have a different impact on one's own self-confidence. Those who only sense an object's image do not have control over the object. They may feel a fear of the object. Those who understand the image have confidence enough to deal with the object and do not fear it. To reduce suffering caused by fear, we must understand the object of our fear. Yet by understanding it, we may find that there is a real reason to fear it. Then we may lose our peace of mind drastically. There is some merit to the statement "Ignorance is bliss." I learned and understood past human history, and I am afraid very much, the imminent nuclear catastrophe.

By learning from history, I have gained some confidence since I acquired a better future prediction capability in my own life. But at the same time, I came to know the endless folly of humankind, and I see the inevitable consequences of the nuclear holocaust. Seventeenth-century peasants needed not fear many things that we must fear now. Here we see the virtue of courage in two ways. One is just to face the fear, ready to accept it, and the other is to stand firm and try hard to defeat the expected fearful consequence by whatever means.

In order to reach the best understanding, the brain must be prepared to accept the incoming image in proper perspective. The dynamic features of the incoming image must match those of the internally simulated object's behavior. The best understanding is reached when the internally created images are confirmed by the incoming images. This is particularly the case in the natural sciences. Creating a theory alone does not lead to understanding. If a theory has been built, and if the experiments confirm the theoretical predictions, the best understanding is reached. Experimentation alone does not cause one to reach understanding either. Theory allows generalization of the limited implications of the experimental results.

4.21 Dynamic Interaction with Unloaded Images

A modern data processor can unload its memories to external media and reload them if necessary. The human brain has a similar type of memory management that is carried out continuously as the brain's housekeeping operation (section 4.09). In the brain's operation, image unloading and reloading have more than vacating memory space; it is the way to sense the image, to execute conscious image manipulation, and to understand the image. The SELF is able to see itself by sending the image (the SELF itself) out, observing it, and recognizing its meaning. I am writing this text on paper using pencil, eraser, paper cutter, and glue. The eraser and other implements indicate that writing is an interactive process. The human brain is able to memorize a lot of images, but its capability to follow up ever-changing images like text composition is quite limited.

The text on the pad is the image that existed in my temporary memory, the scratch pad. Written sentences are visible images, but they are recognized as language images, because the image input channel operates fast. To create text is to write down the text composed on the scratch pad, to find defects by reading it and by comparing it with the intention of writing, to create a modified text in the brain, and to rewrite. My SELF is able to compare its intention and its expression, since the sentence exists outside me. The purpose of sending an image out is not only to ease the burden of memory but also to convert an invisible internal image to a visible external image, and to invoke all the capabilities of the SELF gained by the past experience to improve the external image.

Since the image input channel is built by an extremely fast processor, real-time interaction of the internal and external images is possible. Here, *real time* means that the speed of internal composition of a sentence and the speed of its modification by reading it is about the same. The only bottleneck is the speed of writing a sentence. Writing speed is often unable to keep up with sentence construction. I often come up with a better sentence, but I forgot it before I am able to write it down. Sentences converted to written form are sensed clearer than the internal versions, because the attention needed to memorize the text is directed toward examining the text, and the entire text is accessible for cross-checking for consistency. Such a large-scale integrity check is impossible except by unloading. Unloaded images are rational, since irrational images are difficult to send out by writing a sentence or especially by drawing a figure. First, it is easy to spot irrational images by unloading. Second, in interacting with an unloaded image, the brain's activity is limited to the upper level of the functional blocks, which work like a machine. This allows objective and rational evaluation of the image by avoiding an emotional effect by involving the brain's lower-level emotional effect.

Thinking by unloading an image has varieties, from full unloading (like working on a drafting board) to virtual unloading (observing and modifying internally displayed images). This is the high-level brain function assembled from the low-level human machine's I/O (input-output) capability. Often, sending an image out, taking it in, modifying it, and sending the modified image out is the only way to solve a complex problem. This is the same as straightening out an entangled rope.

Unloading internal images allows analytic thinking by stepping into a tightly integrated image structure. The example of modifying the image template (section 3.21) is the simplest form of analytic thinking. Assembling a landscape image is an example of synthetic thinking. Synthetic thinking can be executed automatically, because it is basically the addition of element images. Analytic thinking is, in this arithmetic metaphor, the division of image. Because of this, analysis is much harder than synthesis.

My life's guiding philosophy is Taoism. Taoism is still one of the most misunderstood Far Eastern philosophies in the West, since the original texts of Lao-tze and Szan-tze are practically untranslatable. I am able to read the original texts. The Lao-tze's text is only three thousand words long, yet if I try to translate it into English, each word of Lao-tze becomes a sentence, and all the sentences are logically entangled. To understand this philosophy, I went into silent meditation, reciting the more *graphic* Szan-tze's text, while drawing the image of the text on a paper. I show my practice in figure 4.21.1, by which I learned how Szan-tze became a butterfly in his dream and realized what was it to be a butterfly. Read the text, imagine the scene, draw it in pictures, and recite the text while seeing the picture. Every step is a simple conscious unloading and reloading of the internal images, but this leads to understanding the complex and convoluted philosophical concept. Human high-level thinking capability is assembled from this simple low-level capability of self-consciousness. It is not necessary to attempt to clarify the human mind's highest capability directly. It can be built up from many basic low-level functions of self-consciousness. I was able to understand Szan-tze's mind, and his anthropomorphic sense of image became my thought of any image recognition.

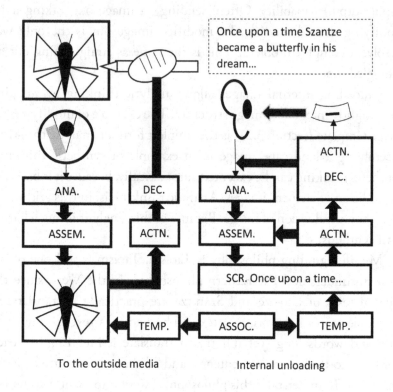

Figure 4.21.1 Unloading of an internal image

Taoism is often misunderstood as the philosophy of hermits. In Szan-tze's text, there is a story of a fellow who was in the difficult situation of having been thrown into a tiger's cage. Szan-tze's teaching is, "To be killed by the tiger, or to kill the tiger, both are the wrong ways. Become a friend of the tiger, ride on his back, and enjoy things with him. To do so, you should become a tiger." Is such a real, brave philosophy the mysticism of hermits as Western people who are fed on pop culture believe? This is the most realistic philosophy for living in brutal modern society. Because Szan-tze lived in such a cruel time of the civil war in China, he realized how the human mind really works.

When I am depressed and confused, I write down my mental state as a myth, using the third person in an imaginary place and time. By reading the story, I can step into the entangled depth of my emotion. The emotional myths of the ancient world were created by similarly tortured minds, I believe. Especially I feel this in the Gnostic myths of gods or goddesses who fell down from heaven and struggled to get back. The myth is a metaphor of the dark, desperate emotion that we inherited from our remote animal ancestors. The myths reveal my dark, irrational, archaic, and mythical world of emotion. A tortured mind requires a proper metaphor, and myths offer the best way to achieve this purpose.

4.22 Anthropomorphic Sense

Sensing an image is the basic capability of the brain, but this activity involves the body. Sense of the image is created by the action executed by the body or by its action directive. Anthropomorphism is simulation of an object's function by the human body. This is the basic mechanism for letting the SELF sense and understand the image dynamically. Static images are sensed and understood by the action of drawing them. As for dynamic images, in the art of ballet, a prima ballerina dances, feeling as if she has become a swan. Once, the ancient Taoist philosopher Szan-tze became a butterfly in his dream and enjoyed flying (see the previous section). Once he woke up, he was not sure if he had become the butterfly or if the butterfly had become him. He philosophized his experience and said, "Humans can be anything, and that is how humans understand everything." This is history's first explicit insight into the human sense of image. In the Far East, Taoists and Buddhists led the study of self-consciousness. As a Taoist, I am proud of my philosophical heritage. Keeping Szan-tze's thought in mind, figure 4.22.1 shows my interpretation.

Sensing an image by anthropomorphizing it is to integrate the sense from the entire body that is moved by the directive of the internal image of the object. I once experienced the same daydream as Szan-tze. I felt as if I were a blue, red, and black butterfly flying on the east side of the acropolis of the ancient Maya city of Copán. I experienced that anthropomorphism is indeed the entire body's sense of coordinated motion. When I woke up from the daydream, I was unconsciously swinging my arms. For the human body to emulate a butterfly, a flapping motion of the arms is the key to creating the sense of flying. Similarity of the body structure is crucial. From the body structure similarity, any animal above the level of amphibian should sense anything as humans do, and they share this same basic mechanism of sensing the images. Snakes are, however, an exception. Not only we humans, but also advanced monkeys and apes instinctively fear snakes. This has been observed by researchers at the University of Kyoto who observed Japanese macaque monkeys. We cannot guess how snakes look at us, whether as friends or foes.

Sensing images by the action of coordinated body motion must be of ancient origin, from the time when our animal ancestors acquired vertebrae and four legs. As I discussed in section 2.33, at the time of image sensing, the action commands go to the entire body if no particular actuator is specified. This whole-body anthropomorphic sense of image is common to all of us. The sense of four-legged animals and birds must be essentially the same as that of humans. So we are able to understand the bat's mind, perhaps better than the mind of any other animals, because of the following reason.

When humans and apes emerged from their monkey-level ancestors, a significant change occurred. Since anthropomorphic sense is determined by the motion that the body structure permits (section 2.13), I believe that four-legged mammals still may not have arcs as the basic visual image elements. Their visual images may be built mostly from vectors. Any four-legged animal can rotate only around the axis that is perpendicularly up-down in relation to their horizontal vertebrae. Rotation around this axis requires coordination of all four legs and applies force to the vertebrae, which resist bending. This is the same for all domestic animals. Rotation motion is unique to bipedal humans, primate apes, free flyers like birds and bats, and swimmers like dolphins. Most of these animals are quite intelligent.

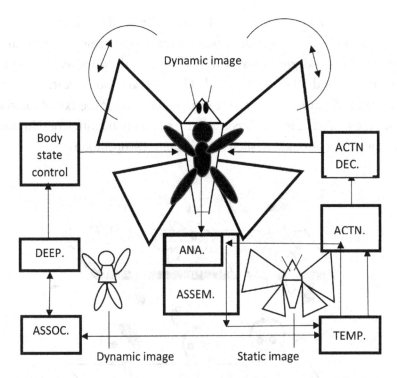

Figure 4.22.1 Anthropomorphic sense of dynamic image by SELF

The partial, full, and multiple rotational motions of animals were acquired as the basic recognizable image elements only in the recent past. Rotation as the basic executable operation by the body has a significant effect in developing the brain. Take, for instance, certain special animals, birds, and aquatic or flying mammals like dolphins and bats. They can execute rotation freely in water or air. That may be the reason why some birds and dolphins are quite intelligent. A bat's mind may be closer to a human mind than the mind of any four-legged animal.

Because of the recent development of rotational motion, the human brain and body are not yet naturalized to it. Rapid rotation makes us feel dizzy, and this shows that evolution has not yet provided compensatory measures. The inclusion of rotation as an elemental mode of body motion brought new features that had never existed before. That is, the difference of what appears to be the same rotation, and the different order of execution of rotation creates different results. Motion specified by vector $\mathbf{v}_1$ and $\mathbf{v}_2$ can be executed either $\mathbf{v}_1$ first and $\mathbf{v}_2$ second, or $\mathbf{v}_2$ first and $\mathbf{v}_1$ second. So is rotation around a fixed axis: standing up straight and rotating 30 degrees and then 60 degrees is the same as rotating 60 degrees first and 30 degrees second. The two executions create the same final result. Such an operation is called *commutable*. If the axis of rotation is not the same, the results of consecutive rotations are different. Humans are not yet accustomed to such *non-commutable* operations.

Figure 4.22.2 Non-commutability in 3 dimensional
rotation operation

Figure 4.22.2 shows what I saw in the Brooklyn zoo in the 1960s. Two chimps, both bipedal, were in a cage, which was provided with a long bench. As I watched them, a father and his preschool-age boy arrived. One of the two chimps took action, A → B → C of figure 4.22.2(a). He was in a comfortable resting position, C. The small boy tried to imitate that on the outside long bench, and what he did is shown as a → b → c of figure 4.22.2(b). The final position was the most uncomfortable position for the boy. The father burst into laughter. What went wrong? B and b are the same rotation, but the axes of rotation A and a are different since the human body is not a circular cylinder. The chimp knew how to do the correct sequence of rotation, perhaps by his earlier experience, but the novice, the boy, did not know this. In the depth of the human mind, general rotation in three-dimensional space has not yet established a firm root as a basic executable operation.

4.23 Generalization of Anthropomorphic Sense

In the previous section, I showed how the image of butterfly is sensed by the human mind. Its static image is sensed by sending its shape to the finger holding the crayon above paper, or to the eyes' directional control mechanism to trace the image in the air. The butterfly's dynamic image is sent to the corresponding body parts with specification of how to move those parts to simulate a butterfly. The image of a butterfly consists of static and dynamic images.

The dynamic feature of the butterfly attracted the attention of ancient peoples, and this is reflected in the word *butterfly* in various indigenous languages, for example, *chow-chow* (Japanese), *kinugu nugu* (Swahili), *papalotl* (Nahuatl-Aztec), *paroo paro* (Tagalog), and *papilio* (Latin). All these words give the sense of wings flapping by repeated syllables, and the first phoneme, *c*, *k*, or *p*, indicates the rupturing sounds of air, proper for indicating the flapping wings of the butterfly.

If I examine the structure of images, I discover that many objects' images are a combination of the static image of the object's shape and the dynamic image of its action, just like the butterfly's image. Images of animals and man-made machines carry the static and dynamic features combined. Even images of plants consist of the static images found in picture books and the dynamic images of the flowers opening. Chocolate candy's shape of a raindrop hints of its dynamic feature of falling from the sky, and even shapeless clouds appear to be strolling in the background of the treetops. Chinese calligraphy shows a static image, but if the brushstroke is closely observed, how the characters were written becomes clearly recognizable.

A human body can execute dynamic action with the entire body, but it can exercise many other actions by moving only a part of the body. Our human body can simulate practically any dynamic action.

An idle afternoon stroll is like a cloud slowly moving in the blue sky, and jumping into the pool creates the sense of a meteor falling. Even the inconspicuous growth of plants is like observing a growing child. Given this, the dynamic part of the image is properly sensed anthropomorphically. The static image is sensed by the brain as a picture that can be reproduced with finger and pencil, and the dynamic image is sensed by the brain as something that can be duplicated by way of the entire body's action. Integration of the pair of the senses creates the sense of recognizing the image. Both static and dynamic image sensing determine the participle of a word in the vision channel in the sentence construction of the language channel (section 2.25).

When the dynamic image is sensed by the body, the body may not be actually moving. If I sense an image casually, no body part moves. So how is the sense created? Even if body motion is not exercised, the directive to move the body part is unconsciously sent to the body part by the brain and is minimally exercised by the respective body part. This is because the control command is blocked by the action-decoding area using a neuron switch (section 3.07), but the switch leaks stray pulses. This feature can be demonstrated by a simple experiment using a magician's pendulum. I hold a pendulum of about 30 cm in length made by thin string by my fingers, and watch a line parallel to the edge of the table, drawn on a paper. The pendulum swings parallel to the line. Then I watch a line perpendicular to the edge of the table. The pendulum swings perpendicular to the edge. Then I watch a circle on the paper. The pendulum swings in a circular motion. The minimal control signal is sent there all the time, unconsciously, and is converted to a small-amplitude motion that is sensed.

As these image-sensing mechanisms show, human sense is human centered. Humans are the measure of everything, so the SELF implicitly relates everything to the human body. The natural sciences tried to free the human mind from this bondage, but for true emancipation, there is a long way to go. Anthropic reasoning is making a comeback, even in basic physics and cosmology.

In my mechanical model study of self-consciousness, I focus on the elementary mechanism of understanding simple objects like the butterfly. Yet by the flexible capability of the internal image, we can mimic any complex object, or we can simulate difficult or complicated natural phenomena and understand them. The only difference is the degree of complexity of the internal image that must be created and operated in advanced thinking. Unloading the image for conscious thinking is the basic capability. Yet that is only a simple and basic process of sending an image out and recognizing it. To understand the human mind, it is only necessary to consider its most basic capability. The high capability emerges from a combination of the basic capabilities.

4.24   Image Sensing, Hindsight

The action-control area is the gate between the internal image circuit and the output channel. An image that goes through the gate is sensed by the subject SELF. The SELF is a composite of the present internal image circuit's and its support circuit's activities. How does the SELF sense itself to become self-conscious? Metaphorically, the SELF must somehow *see* itself by a mirror. A mirror pair is a feedback device. If I stand in the center of a pair of mirrors, my body and its reflection closes a feedback loop. If the distance of the mirrors is L, and if I observe myself for T seconds, the feedback loop circulates my image signal $Tc/2L$ times, where c is the velocity of light. This is a large number, yet it is still finite. In real feedback, the number is assumed to be infinite. Yet even partial feedback creates the mirror's effect of seeing itself. Let us examine the earlier observations of the SELF from the viewpoint of the SELF seeing itself in some mirrors inserted in the feedback signal paths of the vision channel hardware.

The action-control area sends the image signal to the action-decoding area, which receives the actuator specification signal from the body-control area (section 2.33). The signal instructs the action-decoding area to send the image signal to the specified actuator. The actuator has somatic sensors to monitor its mechanical motion. The somatic sensors send the image signal back to the internal image circuit (section 2.23). Along with that, the sent-out external image is observed by the dedicated sensors. The pair of image-carrying signals return to the internal image circuit. Similarly, the support-request signals originating from the channel's functional blocks goes to the deep area and to the body-control area and then returns to the functional blocks by the adjustment of the internal image circuit's support level. There are four such mirrors in the brain's feedback paths. Mirror 0 is in the internal image loop, mirrors 1 and 2 are in the image output and image input loops, and mirror 3 is in the support system loop. Mirror 3 reflects the information of the impact of the image on life, such as the fear of an unpredictable future, sensed by the entire body.

The four closed feedback loops shown in figure 4.24.1 work effectively as mirrors. They *reflect* the image and the image-support signals, allowing the SELF to *see* itself. This is how the SELF *sees* itself and becomes self-conscious. As I discussed in section 4.17, the signals from the actuator's somatic sensors come back and close the feedback loop even if the action is not executed. Because of this, the sense of the image is always felt. The sense of slight pressure on the vocal chords and the elusive sound from the ears when I silently go through a song is the effect of the signals going through the path.

If the image is actually sent out, the SELF sees a clear image of itself because the image comes back through the dedicated input channel (such as the vision and voice channel). The channel sends back a higher-resolution image than the somatic sensor channels. That is why visible image is clearer than dream image. Since the SELF is the internal image display activity, it *sees* itself by mirrors 1 and 2, and that creates an illusion that the SELF sees itself as if it were an independent observer. The brain operation misleads its subject SELF in the same way as my image in the mirror appears to be the real me.

The SELF cannot see a weak image or a rapidly changing image. As I showed in section 3.25, the action-control area rejects such an image by setting up stability and intensity criteria. If the not yet settled image is kept excited, mirrors 1 and 2 cannot *reflect* it, but mirror 3 is able to *reflect* the sensation associated with the chaotic state of the mind. This is because the internal image circuit sends the support request of the unsettled, chaotic internal state via the deep area to the body-control area. This sets the level of sensation. Even if the internal image circuit is in a chaotic state, the sensation associated with the state exists and creates the sense of futility of the current state. The image's clarity depends on how many of the four mirrors reflect the image. As for the quality of the mirrors, there is one clear one (mirror 1), one that is somewhat less clear (mirror 2), one that has a *rough surface* and *reflects* anything (mirror 3), and one that *reflects* the *cryptic* image (mirror 0). These mirrors let the SELF see itself.

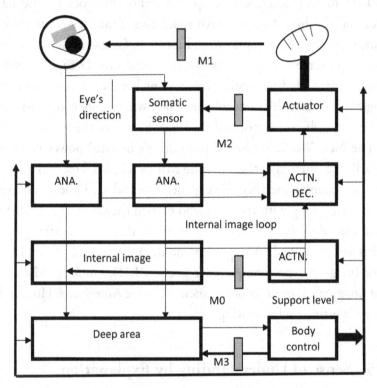

Figure 4.24.1 Image sensing by mirroring

I digress here to speak of the interesting way humans have perceived mirrors. A mirror was a spooky object to our ancestors. A mirror's reflective power is sometimes terrifying, especially to shy people. A good mirror was a spooky object to ancient people, something associated with the souls of women in the Far East. A princess of the Tang dynasty of China who was sent to Tibet to make a political alliance was said to have broken her mirror when her caravan crossed the western border of China. The emblem of the Japanese pantheon's principal goddess Ōhirume is a huge mirror. The mirror was once in the emperor's palace, but the tenth emperor (about AD 300) was so afraid of the mirror's magical power that he moved it out to the shrine in Ise, some distance away, and appointed a princess to the role of priestess. Since this goddess is really Demeter in the Greek pantheon, I have been searching to see if there is any legend of a mirror related to this Greek goddess (section 2.07). Demeter's daughter Persephone (who also goes by the name Kore) and the hero Perseus, both indicating a Greek's connection to Persia, may have some implication. Indeed, in Greek myth, the mirror's magical power emerged in the Perseus-Andromeda saga, in which Perseus turned Medusa to stone by showing her the reflection of herself using his polished shield as mirror. Then what happened to Medusa? She became self-conscious, and that was the end of the monster's life.

The New World version of the mirror's magical power is the god Tezcatlipoca, known as the Smoking Mirror. He is a ferocious god who demanded human sacrifice. He expelled Quetzalcoatl, the god of peace and culture, along with the king who carried the same name, from the Toltec capital, Tula. The smoking mirror is the most terrifying image of this ferocious god. Along with the decapitator god of the Moche in the image of a poisonous spider (section 1.11), Smoking Mirror is a great imaginative product of the ancient Native Americans. Humanity's history is infinitely fascinating.

4.25 Sense of Understanding by Explanation

Humans sense images and understand them. What is the difference between sensing and understanding? Sensing is to see, hear, or feel the existence of an object. Understanding is first to sense the object and then to know what it is, how it works, and what is its impact on one's life. Naively, we feel we can understand anything absolutely, that is, we can define anything without referring to anything else. By observing the capability of the brain's hardware, a serious doubt emerges as to this optimistic belief. The case of the rigorous mathematical logic system breaks apart the belief in absolute understanding since the logic requires axioms to set up the system. From the mechanical model, I came to the same conclusion as in mathematics. The human mind can relate image A to image B but is unable to proceed beyond that. By looking back at the history of self-consciousness development, I conclude that this is all that evolutionary development was able to create, and which was enough to serve its practical objective.

Evolution's naturally set objective was to maximize the chance of survival at the minimum cost. This objective was accomplished by adopting images as the data of the brain. Then evolutionary development created the various capabilities of relating image A to image B, such as comparing the merit of A and B. The two features have been sufficient to attain the evolutionary objective. This simple yet convoluted, and miserable yet practical, mechanism leads to an inevitable consequence: what a self-conscious brain can do is to create a circular or unending sequence of explanations that end up in a false sense of absolute understanding. The mechanism makes sure, ironically, that we do not understand the statement "We do not understand." Generations of thinkers have added more ideological or not-disprovable *ideology* to create the mirage of absolute understanding. If such an idea were stiffly held, then what emerged would be an ideology or religion.

An interpretation of an image by the brain, relating image A and image B, is unable to cause a person to reach absolute understanding. Evolution, instead of setting up a single absolute capability of the *soul* in the human mind, adopted many independent images learned from our life's experiences. These are the equivalent of axioms in mathematics, but there are many of them, and their mutual compatibility is never ensured. Evolution set up useful axioms but not necessarily logically consistent ones. The brain relates these by way of internal image manipulation. The subject SELF is made up of such images, associated with its active relating agent. Instead of a single absolute soul as the substance of the mind, a dynamic agent is set up as the substance of the SELF.

Since human self-consciousness works only by relating the images, we never reach the absolute bottom of understanding. This means that an explanation of something is trapped in either a circular explanation or an endless continuation to show all the related images, until the brain becomes saturated. Creating such confusion and mental fatigue is a clever way of hiding the poor features of the human mind. This is useful in present-day degenerate politics to persuade the naive masses by blasting nonsense.

Let us begin with an example of circular explanation:

Q. What is a puma?

A. It is a big cat living in the high Andes plains.

Q. Then what is a cat?

A. A small puma, a domesticated species of the puma family.

This type of dialogue establishes consistency among several images. By this exchange, a consistent set of images is created, and this set is useful for life, as taxonomy. Taxonomy helped to attain the evolutionary objective by classifying natural objects. If a jaguar, ocelot, or bobcat approached, our ancestors were able to use the same measure that was effective in expelling a puma. From this rather simple example, an important feature of understanding emerges. The purpose of understanding is to establish consistency among several images. Circular arguments accomplish this objective. A scientific theory that is self-consistent within a certain limited domain may be considered as an established truth because of this feature. The geocentric theory of the solar system and the bootstrap theory of nucleons were both found to be real and attractive, because they both established consistency within the then known facts. The purpose of synthetic thinking is to create such consistency. I recognize that this is a pitfall of synthetic thinking, something I am always aware of (section 3.22).

An example of endless explanation causing confusion is what I remember in my childhood in Japan, in the time of World War II.

Q. Why is the relationship between Japan and the U.S. so bad?

A. Because the U.S. exists.

Q. Why does the U.S. exist?

A. Because Christopher Columbus discovered the New World (such is no longer the belief, but so this was believed before the 1960s).

Q. Why did Christopher Columbus discover the New World?

A. Because Ottoman Turks occupied the Middle East, and the trade route for pepper from Asia to Europe was cut off.

Q. Why did the Ottoman Turks occupy the Middle East?

A. Because the second emperor of the Tang dynasty of China expelled the Turks from China's northeast.

This describes the key historical events during the Middle Ages' East-West relations. Given this fact, it is educational. Yet it confuses the questioner, who becomes mentally worn out by too many images presented. Similar dialogue occurs in a political exchange. Clever political demagogues then bring out scapegoats. The mentally fatigued audience readily accepts the nonsense. Here the honesty of the politician is the required quality. For a dishonest politician, creating mental fatigue among the audience is very convenient. The objective of this tactic is to confuse the audience and remove the question. This is a very miserable feature of the human brain: mental fatigue easily creates a false sense of understanding; we feel as if we've done enough thinking.

These are the two ways of *understanding* that take place in the human mind. One is to establish consistency among several images and to fall into an endless circle. The other is to muddle the image of the question and remove the question itself. Either way, the human mind feels as if it has understood. Humans are always misled by these tactics.

Yet in the world of pure natural science, that is, in mathematics, there is a peculiar, spectacular, and mysterious way to avoid this mental fatigue: that is, mathematical induction. This is structurally the same as an infinitely long explanation, but the method allows compacting it by parametrization. Many difficult mathematical problems were solved by this method. A famous case is the proof of the conjecture that any map can be painted by four colors. Mathematics would be quite different, and surely much poorer, if this method did not exist. This method of proof is not limited to mathematics, if we consider the basic structure of other scientific disciplines. When I read Darwin's *On the Origin of Species*, I felt that Darwin had done something similar to mathematical induction but with biology. From what he described, all sorts of supportive evidences would keep emerging, and sooner or later nobody could refute his line of thought. His logic is *expansive* and covers potentially all the cases, like mathematical induction.

4.26 How Is the Best Understanding Reached?

Although the human mind and its capability is widely believed to be the greatest gift of God (this views is especially held by theologians), I pointed out its poor features in the previous section. Yet humans have reached the highest cultural level in the universe by using this quite limited capability. How was this possible? Because some superior teachers have been able to guide their students, still within the limitations, by directly touching the core of the students' question. Such experience pulls the student in the right direction instantly and gives him or her invaluable confidence in the great power of human thought. The explanation by referring image A to image B tends to become long and confusing by superficial consistency of the halfway point, thereby leaving the core of the question unanswered. A superior teacher avoids this and relates the question directly to the basic principles agreed upon by everyone. I had a very lucky experience because my mentor was Dr. William Shockley.

In the 1960s, as a new graduate, I was never able to fully convince myself that the collector voltage of a bipolar transistor drops below the base voltage, even if the base is between the collector and the emitter, thereby completely isolating the collector from the emitter. If the base voltage is high, the collector voltage drops to zero. Naively, I thought this went against the mechanism of electrostatic screening. I read the published papers and textbooks, and above all, I experimented myself to confirm the fact. Yet I felt something quite uncomfortable. So one day I visited Dr. Shockley and explained to him what I had done, but still I was not convinced. I gingerly asked the question, expecting that Dr. Shockley would simply laugh at me as a dumb new graduate. My first surprise was that he smiled and told me that the collector and the emitter become thermal equilibrium, so there cannot be any potential difference between them. He was still smiling at me. This physicist, regarded as one of the brightest in the twentieth century, gave me this lesson. When I first stepped into his office, I never imagined that this was a thermodynamics problem. In a saturated transistor, base current is flowing. It appears as if the state is not in thermal equilibrium.

Following is my paraphrase of our conversation: If the base of the transistor is connected to the emitter, and if a charged capacitor is connected to the collector and emitter, the base-emitter part of the transistor is in thermal equilibrium, but the collector-emitter part is not. Then the base is biased. If the base-emitter junction is conducting, the collector current flows and discharges the capacitor, and the collector-emitter part reaches thermal equilibrium, but the base-emitter part is not. In a bipolar transistor, the two alternative states occur in a spatially overlapped structure. The electron triode is a device that switches by alternating the two different pairs of equilibrium-nonequilibrium states that take place in a single device structure.

This was so simple, yet it was not possible to come across in my mind. Dr. Shockley put the base between the collector and the emitter, not to screen the collector from the emitter but to enable the collector and emitter to reach thermal equilibrium. From his teaching, I learned that there is only one basic unidirectional amplifying device, and that is the electron triode, which works on this simple thermodynamic principle.

This was in the day when vacuum tubes were still used. Dr. Shockley must have seen immediately that I was mistakenly identifying the base of a bipolar transistor as the equivalent of the screen grid of a pentode vacuum tube. There is now a forgotten historical technique: sometimes the pentode's screen grid was used for control purposes, in a clumsy design of a DC amplifier using vacuum tubes.

What appeared to be a mystery of a bipolar transistor is not the case for a MOS field-effect transistor. But I was unable to see that the two transistors are the same electron triode. Later, while I kept this thought in my mind, I attempted to make a model of a bipolar transistor using the MOS field-effect transistor's model, and I tried to find the equivalent of the gate oxide thickness emerging in the model. It turned out to be the Debye length that separates electron-hole plasma by thermal motion. I wrote about this in my book *High-Speed Digital Circuits* (Addison-Wesley, 1996).

Dr. Shockley was definitely one of the greatest physicists of the twentieth century. Many people wrote about him in this respect, and someone like me needs not repeat the same. Yet I do not know of anyone who wrote about how great a teacher he was too. So I must tell this story. He saw immediately that I did not know what an electron triode was. From our previous discussions, he knew that I was reasonably good in thermodynamics. So he connected my question directly to what I knew. Keeping this lesson in mind, when I became a digital circuit theorist in later years, I set this model of electron triode at the center of my circuit theory (*Theory of CMOS Digital Circuit and Circuit Failures* [Princeton University Press, 1993]). My digital circuit theory highlights the image of thermodynamic states that exist in a transistor.

Since the middle of the twentieth century, hundreds of semiconductor devices have been invented. They needed taxonomy. As I reviewed various electron device textbooks, I saw that these devices were just classified by their structural similarity. The device taxonomy still remains Linnaean. From Dr. Shockley's thoughts, a new *natural* or *Darwinian* taxonomy became possible. Only a genius could see his disciple's difficulties, connect him directly to the basic principle, and motivate the awestruck youth for his whole life. As one of his last disciples, I am forever grateful to Dr. Shockley.

4.27 Communication by Language or by Any Other Means

Visible images are the most basic forms of information to provide definite meanings. In the world of the low-level animals, those who appear to be self-conscious have good eyes and are able to see objects with different degrees of precision. Examples are squids and octopi, both of which have well-developed eyes. Visible images provide the sense of the space in which the animals live. Thus it is the key information for survival. The living space is three-dimensional, but for some primitive animals that have limited motion capability, it may appear as two-dimensional. Either way, vision provides multidimensional information. Language information of humans and voice information of the animal kingdom are both, by the nature of sound, a single sequence, that is, one-dimensional information. Language is proper in describing a time sequence. Its serial data structure is more convenient for communication of simple information. Then conversion between multidimensional information and one-dimensional information is crucial in the repertoire of image manipulation.

The advantage of language information is its convenience as the medium of communication. Communication is the key mechanism of interaction between individuals in any animal or human society. Communication by way of graphic information is inconvenient in a spatially spread-out habitat, where direct sight is often interrupted and resolution of vision is limited. Furthermore, there is the difficulty of creating fast graphic display using the hardware available to the animal body. If used for person-to-person communication, a visual image often carries too much information, which means that focusing on the key point is not easy. To express dissatisfaction by facial expression or body position gives rise to this ambiguity. On the other hand, a language statement often does not carry enough information to specify the key points precisely. The preferred means of communication depends on the image and the personality of the communicator.

There are two facets to the difficulty of information conversion. The first difficulty is the difference in dimensionality of vision and language information. The second is language's basic unit of information, a word, which is essentially an abstract image that covers a wide range of objects or actions. The word *dog* may mean many different animals of various sizes, colors, and temperaments. My wife told me to get cooking oil. There are tens of different types and brands in the store. Here, the personal value standard shows up. I usually get the cheapest one, whereas my wife is usually satisfied with the rather expensive one. Language is one-dimensional information, but each word has an *internal dimension* that shows up when it is used. Think of an elementary particle, which carries internal dimensions such as spin, charge, and color (section 6.20).

Going back to the first type of difficulty, it shows up most clearly when I tell my wife how to reach a certain destination. This is a piece of information that can be given easily by a map drawn on paper. If the same information is given by way of language statement, it becomes quite long and messy. The same problem is experienced when instructing a strategic choice that has many different branch (or decision-making) points. Teaching a boy how to respond to a job interviewer's questions is difficult to do by using language alone. Proper mixing of the one-, two-, and three-dimensional information is almost an art of communication.

Language depends on the culture, and there are many different languages in the world. In the modern age, the availability of air transportation has made it possible to visit many isolated ethnic locations of the world where there is no common language between the communicators. This creates troubles between travelers and the local people as I have seen everywhere outside the U.S. Unfortunately, more often than not, the difficulties create hostile feelings between the local people and the visitors. How to communicate with local folks in such a situation is a serious problem.

When I came to the U.S., my English was very poor. Yet soon after, I had to go to Germany to speak in German, and then to Poland to speak in Polish. These experiences taught me how to communicate in any foreign country. We need to follow the practice of small children, who are never embarrassed when making mistakes. Honest mistakes earn one a friendly attitude from the local folks; the local people I've encountered regarded me as an *omedetai hito* (he who is loved by everyone and everywhere in the world—section 2.03). In Poland, I learned that "Co to znaczy [fill in the blank]?" (What is meant by [fill in the blank]?) is the key question. If I ask this question many times, Poles love me for my enthusiasm. "Co to znaczy dupa?" got explosive laughter and no answer. Then I learned that the word was taboo. I am able to talk with Russians by using Polish. To do so, one must properly respect their national identity. I must first say, "I cannot speak Russian, but I can speak Polish. Can any of you understand Polish?" Since the two languages are quite similar, I am able to communicate without any difficulty. It is a sure turnoff to Russians if I start speaking in Polish without this proper introduction. This is a common courtesy.

When abroad, I always carry blank cards and pencil, and if all the means of communication fail, I draw pictures. From this practice, I realized the true value of ideograms (section 4.04). In the Chinese cultural domain, written statements by using the Chinese ideograms work everywhere, even in Tibet. As for basic emotional communication, a happy smile and frowning face works everywhere in the world. Once the local folks become friendly, any communication is possible by using only a few common words, body language, and facial expressions and by pointing to the object of communication with a finger. Never repeatedly try to speak in English; that is a sure turnoff for the locals. Using such elementary know-how, I have very many happy memories of smooth and friendly conversations with Tibetan girls in Gyantze, an Aymara matriarch on an island of Lake Titicaca, and numerous highland, lowland, and Yucatán Maya folks in their remote hamlets. I described my heartwarming experience at a Maya site of Uaxactun in section 1.13. The mother and the daughter did not even speak Spanish fluently, yet we were able to understand each other to the bottoms of our hearts. We humans are not so resourceless as those in the story of the Tower of Babel.

4.28 Internal Image Flow

In section 4.26, I showed two ways to reach an understanding of an image. One is to bring in an image that is already understood by the questioner and to let the pair of images explain each other. Since the two images take over the position of the SELF of the questioner alternately, this lets the questioner go into dialogue with himself. The other way is to keep presenting related images one after the other until the questioner is mentally saturated. When this happens, the questioner's SELF throws itself into a continuous flow of internal images. This state emerges when I meet with life's difficulties that appear formidable and I must struggle to find some way out. Before I reach any solution, my SELF must *flow* a long way in the *image's stream*.

In normal daily life, I often get into this unending image flow from a not very clearly identifiable cause. If I am alert and if my brain is idle, this is usually what happens. Since this aimless image flow always happens, it must be a feature created by evolution for some useful purpose. When our remote human ancestors were in an idle mental state, they must have experienced the flow of their still limited internal images. Aimless internal image flow is painful, since after some time I always hit on an image that can be a potential risk or disaster. Then the image flow becomes a vortex around the risk image. As the risk image emerges again and again, I look at the risk image from many sides, and my understanding of the image improves. This is certainly an advantageous feature for life. I wonder if this is how early humans began to think over a single focused problem in depth.

One reason I consider this issue is that human thinking works effectively only if a proper question is asked. Setting up a proper question is often more difficult than answering it. In a long, painful internal image flow, I often come up with a sensemaking question. In order to set up such a question, I need to look at the hard problem from many different sides. If a proper question is set up, it opens a new way to proceed. During my last years in my native country, Japan, the problems of my personal life kept piling up. After a long and tortuous mind search, the question I reached one autumn afternoon was, "Is it possible for me to get out of my native country and make my new life somewhere else?" Then I had a new direction: I started looking for the answer to that question. My present life is the answer to the question.

Let us go back to the dynamics of vortex image flow. By image vortex, the theme image appears again and again. This flow is like the eddy of a river that collects more and more debris. As the vortex's scale increases beyond a certain limit, some internal order begins to emerge. Then irrelevant images are thrown away, and the vortex compacts. In the end, several images are closely integrated together to form a new image structure. In seeking to answer of my question about my exodus, I considered the U.S., Germany, and Latin America. The last two were eventually dropped since I could find no mentor to consult on the issue. Then the U.S. became the most realistic destination. The perspective that emerged while I was answering the question appeared so otherworldly at the time that I felt even spooky. On several occasions I had such experiences, both in my personal life and in my technical work. As this happened, I felt as if a bright star had flown away, and at the moment when it vanished from the sky, a huge crescent moon suddenly emerged there. The crescent moon is a spooky, yet exciting, object of heaven.

Regarding the brain as a physical system, the state carrying no image is not a stable state. To maintain the imageless state, my SELF must attend to keep any image out of my brain. The relationship between the number of images and the associated sensation, which is the rate of the brain's energy consumption, is schematically shown in figure 4.28.1. Let us consider the first quadrant only, and let the image 1 axis be the number of images. The zero-image state has high sensation. The sensation drops to a minimum at a certain number of images, N_{min}. Then I include a variety of images emerging in the image flow that are distributed over the entire plane spun by the axes of image 1–image 4. The sensation minimum is in the valley that surrounds the central peak. The brain's state stays in the valley, but the images vary all the time, making the image flow. This variation can be represented by a ball rolling around the valley. Since the state is vortex, the ball turns around an indefinite number of times.

This figure is familiar in the popular books about elementary particle physics and is used to explain the spontaneous symmetry-breaking mechanism that creates mass of the particle. Internal image flow is actually a spontaneous symmetry-breaking mechanism working in the self-conscious brain. The rolling ball is called the *Goldstone boson* in the quantum field theory. This boson does not exist in the elementary particle world, but it does exist in the brain of the physicists who are thinking of the mechanism.

Why does such a state exist in the brain? In the no-image state, we must focus our attention to keep our mind free from any images. Our brain is literally bombarded by the images sent from various sensors. In order to suppress irrelevant image excitation, the SELF must attend to keep the empty-minded state and must spend energy.

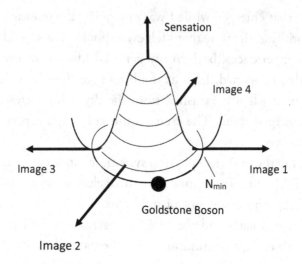

Figure 4.28.1 Spontaneous symmetry breaking
in the brain's image structure

This feature is consistent with the mission of the brain as the security guard of the brain and body. To maintain constant watch over the outside world, some relevant or irrelevant images must always be excited in the brain just in order to keep it alert. An autistic person has a handicap to this capability and often suffers because of that.

4.29 Metastable State in Decision-Making

In many phases of life, we must make decisions to choose one from two alternatives, such as which company to work for or which house to buy. Often the choice is hard, since neither of the two is perfectly desirable. The brain gets into a bogged-down state of indecision. In such a state, not to make any decision is the best course, I believe. Yet, depending on the circumstance, making a choice becomes absolutely necessary. A similar state occurs in digital circuits. A latch may stay in neither logic HIGH nor logic LOW level for a long period of time, which causes a digital circuit failure. This is called a metastable state. The metastability effect can be reduced, but the state itself can never be removed. The circuit must be designed to minimize the consequences of metastability. I owe most of my knowledge of this effect to Professor F. Rosenberger, who taught me this effect in the 1980s, and ever since I have been fascinated.

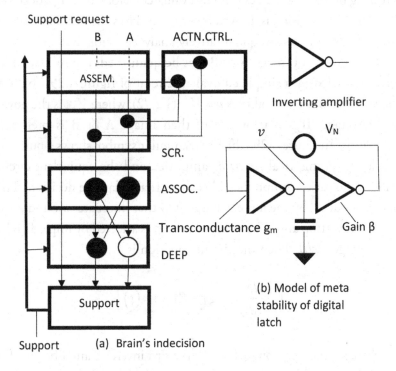

Figure 4.29.1 Brain's indecision and digital latch's metastability

What is going on in the indecisive brain is the neuron circuit's metastability as shown in figure 4.29.1(a). Either image A or B must be chosen, but the SELF is unable to decide, because both images have their merits and faults. A and B are connected to both the positive and the negative centers of the deep area. As image A and image B are alternately displayed, the activity of each image in the internal image circuit sends the support request signal to the deep area via a character bus line. A decision is made when the preferred image's support level is higher than that of the other by a significant margin. Until the advantage of image A or B exceeds the other's by some amount, a decision cannot be made. This state has the effect of extending the time of decision-making indefinitely. This is because both images A and B are vaguely defined, and more related images are added as the decision time extends. As the number of related images increases, the subjective preference swings back and forth slower and slower, because more and more positives and negatives of the increasing number of images must be evaluated before making a decision. Thus, the final decision is delayed indefinitely. How the decision-making time extends can be semi-quantitatively analyzed as follows:

If the choice of image A or B can be quantified, the metastability can be modeled by a simple equivalent circuit of figure 4.29.1(b). The state variable of metastability is $v = V - (V_{DD}/2)$, where V_{DD} is the power supply voltage. If $v > 0$ or $v < 0$, then image A or B is preferred, respectively. In figure 4.29.1(b), the triangular symbol shows a pull-up–pull-down symmetrical *inverting* amplifier, and the equivalent circuit includes the various unpredictable effects that delay the decision. This effect is modeled by the noise voltage $Vn(t)$ that fluctuates around $v = 0$. The first inverting amplifier's output voltage is affected by unpredictable noise voltage $Vn(t)$. Then the circuit equation is

$$C\left(\frac{dv}{dt}\right) = -g\left[-\beta v + Vn(t)\right]$$

where g is the transconductance of the first inverting amplifier and β is the voltage gain of the second inverting amplifier. This equation is solved as

$$v(t) = \left(\frac{1}{\theta}\right)\exp\left(\frac{\beta t}{\theta}\right)\int_0^t \exp\left(-\frac{\beta\tau}{\theta}\right)Vn(\tau)d\tau$$

subject to the initial condition $v(0) = 0$ and where $\theta = C/g$. If metastability continues from time 0 to t, then

$$\exp\left(\frac{\beta t}{\theta}\right)\int_0^t \exp\left(-\frac{\beta\tau}{\theta}\right)Vn(\tau)d\tau$$

must be small. This equation shows that if $Vn(t)$ is properly chosen, metastability continues for duration t. Yet because of the exponential factor in front of the integral sign, the chance of getting such $Vn(t)$ decreases as t increases.

If this circuit model is transferred to the brain's metastability, first I note that θ depends on capacitance C. This capacitance represents the number of the element images making up image A and image B, which include many associated images defining their meanings. This is the mental inertia, m, that I introduced in section 1.18. If the exp (...) factor does not increase rapidly with t, then there can be many $Vn(t)$'s that keep metastability for a long time. This is the model of mental indecision.

There is an anxiety effect in making decision: if it takes more time to decide, the sense of anxiety tends to gather more and more associated images to image A and B. In the end, the metastable state is effectively converted to a dynamically held quasi-stable state. This modified metastability mechanism can be modeled by assuming that capacitance C increases with time. So, I replace C with γt, and the circuit equation changes to

$$(\gamma t)\left(\frac{dv}{dt}\right) = -g\left[-\beta v + Vn(t)\right] \quad (1)$$

and this equation is solved as

$$v = -\left(\frac{g}{\gamma}\right)\int_0^t Vn(\tau)\left(\frac{1}{\tau}\right)\left(\frac{\tau}{t}\right)^{\frac{g\beta}{\gamma}} d\tau$$

Here the integral does not diverge when $t \to 0$ since I assume that $Vn(t)$ is continuous and $Vn(0) = 0$. From this solution, metastability continues for time t if

$$\int_0^t \left(\frac{\tau}{t}\right)^{-g\beta/\gamma}\left[\frac{Vn(\tau)}{\tau}\right] d\tau$$

is small. Here, the factor multiplied to $Vn(\tau)$ does not increase very rapidly with τ. Then there can be many $Vn(\tau)$'s that maintain the metastable state. Equation (1) is interesting. Because coefficient γt on the left side increases with t, if $Vn(\tau)$ remains small, then (dv/dt) tends to 0 for large t. If I choose a continuous $Vn(t)$ such that $Vn(t) = \alpha$ except for the immediate neighborhood of $t = 0$, then $v = \alpha/\beta$. This represents the dynamically held quasi-stable state I mentioned before.

4.30 Analog Control of Action

Humans can execute complex and highly precise operations, such as what artists and craftsmen do, and also simple but precise bodily actions such as what athletes and circus performers do. Any high-precision action requires feedback control of the sensor and actuator, but the two types of action require different control. Artists' and craftsmen's work requires constant visual monitoring of the action of their tools. Continuous observation and adjustment of the force applied to the tools is required, and the action's objective is accomplished not by one but by many steps of finely adjusted operations. By monitoring the action continuously, any degree of precision can be achieved.

The second type of precision operation is one such as throwing a ball in a basket that is placed some distance away. It is a simple operation, but it must be successful in a single trial. The action is executed by a simple hand/arm motion, but the swing intensity of the arm handling the ball must be precisely controlled. Such an action is never successful without training. Somatic sensors of the arm's muscles send intensity of the force applied to the ball at the moment of its release to the internal image circuit. The sense of the force in the successful trial is kept in analog memory, and the later trial reads the memory and repeats the same action. The content of the memory can be sensed only by the body. The body's sense is quite accurate, and as long as the analog memory is securely kept, it is easy to repeat any number of successful trials.

The analog parameter cannot be sent to the arm by the same channel as the command of the action of swinging the arm. The action-control area (sections 2.31 and 3.25) cannot transmit the analog signal through the intermediate memory. This is because the intermediate memory-loading circuit has an intensity discriminator to qualify the action to be sent out (section 3.25). The analog signal that controls the action intensity must go through the brain's lower area, the deep area, and the body-control area, where the signal is joined by the signal that supplies energy to the arm. Setting a proper analog signal level is achieved by training. At each trial, the action and its effect are observed, and the analog memory parameter is adjusted. Success or failure information comes in from the vision channel. The memory and the control hardware must be in the vision channel's deep area. The analog memory circuit was shown in section 3.08. Humans can execute such action unbelievably well. I feel this when I see a professional basketball game.

4.31 Action Simulation by Internal Image

Self-conscious life is a continuation of setting up an action plan and its execution. When we do something that we have never done before, we first make a plan, exercise it in the brain, and check how well it works. This is action simulation. The human brain has this capability. Since the actor and the action are both images, they can display action in a single visible image frame. We have the image of the action's objective, and to reach the objective, we first set up strategies that lead us to the objective. The purpose of simulation is, first, to create several strategies that accomplish the objective, and second, to select one from these that is consistent with the expendable resources.

To conduct a strategy simulation is to bring the actor, the action, and the domain of the action from their templates to the scratch pad and let them interact there. This is essentially a process to build up the objective's image from the participating elements' images by adjusting their relations. This is the image-assembling process that I described in section 3.21, on which several requirements are imposed. At each step, the result of the participant's interaction is evaluated. Depending on the evaluation, the participating element images are altered. In this simulation, if quantitative information is required, it is given qualitatively, low or high. The purpose of strategy simulation is to find the action to accomplish the objective at whatever the cost. Several alternate strategies must be made available for the next step.

In the strategy search, the role of the SELF splits into two. The SELF that demands the search is the SELF based on the lower level, which sets a strong requirement to create a working plan. Yet evaluation of the consequence of the action is carried out by the SELF that is resident in the upper level. Quite often, the two SELFs get into conflict. In such a case, it is necessary to suppress the lower-level SELF in order to create a rational plan.

The next-level simulation brings quantitative details. The available resources and the cost are balanced with the gain for each of the strategies that were set up by the first simulation. The purpose of this simulation is to quantify the merit of the strategies. The same objective can be accomplished by different strategies, and here the cost of the operation enters into consideration. If none of the strategies of the first simulation satisfies the cost criteria, then the first simulation must be repeated to search for better ones. In military strategy, Carl von Clausewitz held that matching the objective with the available resources is the key requirement. This is the reason why we do not execute a simulation in a single step but set up strategies first. If none of the strategies match the resources, the objective must be altered. This is the most important point: the objective must be alterable in order to avoid failures. As this observation shows, the strategy search is the same process as assembling a composite image (section 3.21) using the synthetic thinking process. This step is followed by analytic thinking to evaluate the merit and the cost.

Past Chinese dynasty's constant objective was to prevent invasion by the northern tribes. To build a long wall was one strategy, but that was too costly. The Tang emperors were wiser, so they built a cavalry army. That is why Turks are now in Asia Minor, not in Mongolia (section 4.26). Another consideration related to simulation is that quite often there is no satisfactory strategy or the cost is too high. In such a case, the conclusion is that no action is the best. Once the simulation is exercised, this choice is emotionally hard to swallow. Yet often this is the best way.

4.32 Dream and Daydream

A dream is activation of the brain while the body is at rest. Dreaming sleep is called REM sleep. The basic features of dreaming sleep were discovered by Nathaniel Kleitman in the 1960s. Between REM sleep phases, the brain rests in the deep sleep phases. All the animals above the mammal level alternate between REM and deep sleep. In REM sleep, all the body actuators, except for eye direction control, are disabled. This is strange, since the eyes are not open and are not seeing. Because of that, REM sleep was once called paradoxical sleep. I can see the two sleep states of a cat. When she sleeps throwing her legs to her side, she is in REM sleep. In this state, she is dreaming of fish and potatoes and is unable to dash start and run away from risk. When she sleeps in the pose of a person in Muslim prayer, she is in deep sleep.

Since internal images are displayed in REM sleep, the internal image circuit is active, but the action-decoding area and actuators are disabled. Still, the internal image circuit controls the direction of the eyes (REM = rapid eye movement). That is why dreams show visual images. Hearing sound or spoken words is very rare in dreams. I have never sensed chemical images such as a strong smell or the taste of foods in my dream. My visual images do not have any mysterious connection to the depth of my emotion as claimed by psychoanalysts. I believe that a dream's theme image comes from my secular life. About 70 percent of my dreams have a theme related to my secular life's problems or my technical works, and the rest are nightmares of various scenarios. I cannot find any deep meaning in my dreams.

Daydreams are different from dreams that happen in REM sleep. In a daydream, I am marginally conscious, but I am free from my life's concerns, worries, fears, and anxiety. In order to put myself in such a peaceful state, I must be in holy ancient sites or pagan shrines where our ancestors left historical memories. There, as I close my eyes and think over the legend of the site, the heroes and heroines emerge in my minimally conscious, half-asleep mind and display their acts. Quite often, some missing details of the ancient legend are revealed. Since I am minimally conscious, I can hear the messages from the heroes, heroines, gods, and goddesses. Middle Ages pilgrims' experiences at their holy sites appear to reproduce in my daydreams. This is an experience that heals my mind worn out by my hard secular life.

Humans need such spiritual experiences. This state appears similar to the practice called *active imagination* in Jung's psychology. Isn't it better to revive such Middle Age practices for mentally disturbed people than to provide an army of psychologists and a lot of prescription medicines? So-called luxury all-inclusive vacations do not provide such spiritual healing. The difference is, the pilgrims went to their holy sites by their own wish and will; they walked to the sites and often tolerated hardships of travel. No travel agent prepared their itinerary, and no guide explained everything. They literally searched and created such an experience by themselves.

I was surprised to hear that a cruise to Newfoundland didn't visit L'Anse aux Meadows, where the eyes of Leif Erikson is still staring at the vast expanse of the New World. A tour to Nepal doesn't visit the cave where Nagarjuna went into meditation and, in that state, visited hell, bringing back the Panya Paramita sutra and establishing Mahayana Buddhism. Those heroes are eternal role models for humans. We have lost the precious culture of seeking for spirituality by contacting the great heroes and heroines from our precious history.

The human mind, not necessarily influenced by a medical condition or subjected to chemical substances, is able to sense images that do not exist in the real world when in a daydream. Many such images are archetypal images that can change one's view of life and revitalize one's worn-out spirit (section 1.11).

After strenuous mental work, I am exhausted and fall asleep. For a short time before sleep, I often see many otherworldly, often creative images. This is similar to a daydream. Then my brain's support level is still high, but suddenly no image comes into my brain. In such a state, a lot of images, some of which are quite valuable, emerge. Yet the time is too short to retain them in secure memory for later use.

4.33 Dynamics of Dreaming

Dreams are interesting subjects in my self-consciousness study since in dreams we see images not by the eyes but by the feedback going through the eyes' line-of-sight control. Those images are entirely created by the internal image circuit. Dreams suggest that what we see normally is not always the images received by the eyes. We see clear, colored images in a dream. Yet dream images are realistic and are associated with proper emotion. During the dreaming state, the brain is working normally since the images that emerge sequentially are reasonably consistent.

This internal consistency means that the image of the place where the dream sets the SELF is in this world. I do not see any images of any exotic otherworld when dreaming. People are dressed normally and behave mostly rationally. I do not see objects that cannot exist in this world. Emotional relationships are also normal: if a known person emerges in the dream, my emotion, whether friendly, hostile, or competitive, toward him is as I would naturally expect. Even convoluted emotional relationships, for example, ambivalent feelings such as a mix of love and hate, are properly represented. In a terrible nightmare, I wake up totally drenched in a cold sweat. Often I get into the condition that demands carefully planned action or some considerable thinking in my dream. My dreaming brain can go into involved thinking mode. Following is my own experience:

I walked out, in a dream, from a high-rise hotel and looked at the room key. It did not carry the room number. I got lost. I did not know how to get back, since the room's doors were all similar. Then a man approached and showed me a 2 × 2 integer matrix, saying that if I could factor it into a two-integer 2 × 2 matrix, the four single-digit integers would be my room number. I struggled, but before I was able to factor, I woke up. I remember this problem, but not the content of the 2 × 2 matrix that the man showed to me. I never remember the case of reading written material in my dream.

It is not obvious, and is never predictable, how the theme image of a dream is chosen by my brain. But if I wake up, try to ruminate closely on the dream I just saw, and then go back to sleep right away, sometimes I see the natural continuation of the previous dream's scenario. The chance is only one in ten times or less, but this is rather significant, since I am never able to predict what I will see before I go to sleep. Since the first phase of sleep is deep sleep that lasts one hour, the images that existed before in my brain must be totally wiped out. If REM sleep is interrupted only for five minutes or so, the theme image must still be clear enough to continue. This experience shows that I am living a continuation of my daily life in my dream, rather than digging into my own subconscious world. My dream world is not so free from my stressful daily life.

An interesting feature of my dream is the invasion of my bodily sense into the dream. I often wake up from a dream after seeing the scene of going to the toilet. I do not dream if I wake up soon after I fall asleep, typically within half an hour to one hour. After about one hour, I see a dream. As I try to remember the dreams I had when I wake up, some dreams are quite clear, but others are vague. It appears that if I wake up from REM sleep, the dream images are clear, but if I wake up from deep sleep, the dream of the preceding REM sleep has already faded away.

Summing up these observations, the state of sleep is described by the functional diagram of figure 4.33.1. Here the internal image signal that controls the direction of the line-of-sight goes to the analyzer and to the assembly area of the somatic sense channel. The areas' connections are what I showed in section 2.23. The image signals join the vision channel's internal image circuit. From there, the signals go back to the mechanism of eye directional control. The closed feedback loop creates the sense of the internal image to the SELF. Seeing objects in a dream is effected by the movement of the line-of-sight mechanism of the eyes (section 4.15). The somatic sensors attached to the mechanism of the eyes' directional control provide the image of the dream, which is clear enough to display the object's features.

Then how about the color of the dream's image? The brain creates the sense of color by excitation of the image template's color specification. This excitation happens, yet many dreams are colorless, black-and-white images. Color is an add-on to the image. A strange thing is that as I get older, I have more dreams in color. Thus, many details of the brain's image-sensing mechanism emerge from the dream image sensing.

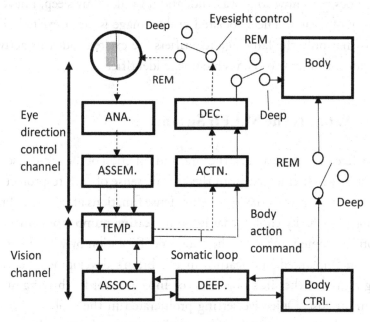

Figure 4.33.1 REM and deep sleep state

How about the language image in a dream? Hearing something in a dream is, by close introspective observation, almost always unconscious conversion of visible image into language image, by the mechanism that I discussed in section 2.25. A supporting evidence is that I've never had any dream of reading a written text image. A written text is always regarded as a visible image, and its detail is never retained in the dream's memory. As a visible image, even a simple phonetic alphabet's words and their combination is quite complex. I mentioned my dream of the lost number of the hotel room before. The contents of the 2 × 2 matrix are never recognized as a language image and therefore are never memorized in the dream.

Sleep talk is an unrelated process. This is an unconscious language image send-out process. In this process, a language image is sent out from the template to the action-control area and then to the output channel. The image does not go to the assembly area. The internal image loop is not excited, so there is no sense of what was said. The image is sent out like playing recorded music by magnetic tape. The SELF does not know what was said, and if I talk in my sleep, I have no memory of it later. The associated visible image is never excited. This means that only the language identifiers are excited, but this activity does not spread out to the visible image identifier.

4.34   What Is the SELF?: Summary

I have described the origin, structure, and function of the self-conscious subject SELF. It emerged from the archaic sense of fear, to protect the body. The primitive, reflex-type self-defense functions of the proto-brain developed by lucky choice, that is, an increasing number of neurons in the brain adopted images as the data type. Evolution by way of natural selection implanted one feature in the brain's development, that is, being aware of the life's objective, or in other words, thriving at the minimum cost. Objective-setting proliferated in the evolving human brain and became the driving force of all the new cultural and technical developments.

After going through the study of many specific modes of operation of the SELF, I have come to summarize the SELF's basic character. The SELF is the sense that emerged when all the internal image activities converged to the important life-support and lifesaving objectives by activating the centers representing the person's core values. In brain/ body symbiosis, the body demands the brain to guide it to secure the benefit of the habitat. The SELF was created as the symbolic executive of all these activities. Since the body's state is always sensed, and because the SELF depends on the body, the body is the substance of the SELF.

The sense of the SELF always includes some sense from the body. The activities creating the sense of the SELF are spread out over the entire brain and body. This nature of activity misleads us, as if a self-conscious subject is manipulating the human brain and body from backstage. Since what makes sense of the existence of the SELF is the ever-developing activity of the brain, the SELF has no static substance. The SELF is the SELF-creating and SELF-maintaining dynamic activity. Since this basic mechanism is simple and robust, self-consciousness is universal, meaning that it is shared by all the animals above a certain evolutionary level, including all the vertebrates and some invertebrates. The only difference among them is the degree of sophistication of their image-handling capability and their adaptability to the habitat. This conclusion is not a revival of the ancient animistic religion; it is an inevitable conclusion of systems science and of Darwinian evolution applied to the human brain and body.

Since the SELF is the totality of the activities commanding the brain and body, it is able to plan, initiate, and execute action, all directed by the internal image information. While an action is executed, its image is sensed. The executing SELF and the sensing SELF are the same activity of the brain and the body. This is the feature that is made obvious by the mechanical model.

In the natural or social habitat, the SELF's primary mission is to secure the welfare of the brain and the body. In the advanced social animals and humans, concern for welfare extends beyond an individual's life to the offspring, to the siblings, and sometimes to the entire life of the habitat. Herein is the origin of the concept of morality in human society, which naturally emerged from evolution. The Confucian principle of prioritized love for parents first, family second, society third, and then the entire world advocates this natural development rationally.

The SELF's future development and enrichment is effected primarily by upgrading the internal image memory and processing capability. After reaching the level of modern humans, this development is not guided by the Darwinian but by the Lamarckian evolution mechanism. This development heavily depends on the individual's disposition and education because the mechanism is based on the culture and training after birth. From this background, intelligence developed from the primitive capability of executing the life's objective effectively, to the still higher capability of wisdom. By wisdom, the objective of self-consciousness and intelligence is scrutinized for the benefit of all.

A blessing of self-consciousness is rich imagination, the capability to create new images or new combinations of existing images by modifying some of them and by integrating them into a qualitatively new worthwhile image. By this capability, humans can proceed to set up their own lifestyle and pursue it. This objective is not only for the survival or welfare of an individual but also for directing the entire human race to a better future life. All the great cultural products emerged from this capability.

Humans reached this level by the early Neolithic period, and since then, they have ceased making qualitative steps forward. Since that time, certain imaginative and powerful individuals have tried to wipe out the cultural products of the entire population using powerful and imaginative means of destruction. Because of this, the acme of humankind was over by the twentieth century. There are many handwritings on the wall. Intellectually, basic physics such as string theory appears to produce no realistic results. Socially, I believe, the environmental damage has reached an unsustainable level. There seems to be no new philosophy to guide humans far and wide. Humans are now entering the declining phase, which unfortunately may not be reversible. The symbiosis of capitalism and democracy, neither of which unfortunately include any self-critical mechanisms, took firm root in the twenty-first-century mass society, where all the great traditional values are being destroyed. In this view, I fully agree with Ortega, Keynes, and Hayek. The modern human mind is entrenched in *freedom* and *progress* as the ultimate values and is never aware of the negative and destructive features that may emerge from them.

The SELF is the sum of the activities of the entire brain and the body. The SELF's activities of knowing itself, its world, and its history are sensed as quite real to the human mind. How does such a real sense of SELF emerge in the human mind?

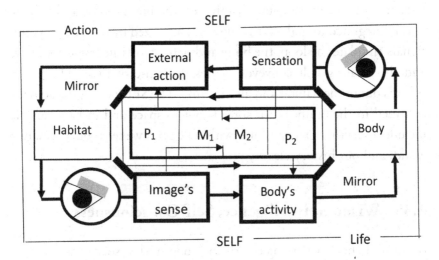

Figure 4.34.1 Functional structure of the SELF

The SELF may appear to be the activities confined in the brain. It really is not so, however. To expose the real nature of the SELF's activities, I unload the brain's internal activities to the outside so that the inside SELF can be seen from the outside. Figure 4.34.1 shows the human brain, which appears to be a tenant of its body, living in its habitat. In the figure, the habitat and the body are shown along with the simplified four-layer block diagram of the brain of section 1.20. The brain interacts with its two *outsides*, the habitat and the *body*. The activities of the brain-body-habitat combined system are grouped into four, shown in the thick boxes. The purpose of external action and sensing external image is to deal with the habitat. The purpose of sensation generation and the body's internal state control is to deal with the body. The four activities integrate the outside world and the body together and place the self-conscious SELF securely in the habitat. This creates the sense of existence of the SELF in the habitat and in its personal history, and allows the SELF to sense itself. The four activities make a directed closed loop of actions as shown in figure 4.34.1. The SELF takes in the information of the outside world, relays it to the body, senses the state of the body, and sends the body's requirement to the outside world. This is a belt conveyer that moves brain, body, and habitat together. By the brain's activities, the brain, body, and habitat are all integrated to make the activities symbolized by the SELF. As the signals circulate the loop, the body and habitat are integrated spatially, and the rotating belt conveyer creates the sense of time. The SELF spreads out to the habitat and also in time. The SELF is not the activity confined in the brain, but it spreads out to space and in time, and it includes everything recognizable within it. Thus we sense ourselves, our world, and our history clearly.

4.35 Wisdom, Intelligence, Self-Consciousness

A cultural shock I first met with in modern U.S. society is that the terms used to specify the human mind, namely, *wisdom, intelligence*, and *self-consciousness*, are often used to mean the same thing. Especially *intelligence* and *self-consciousness* are too frequently used interchangeably. As a young student brought up in the introspective Old World society, I felt that this way very strange. I still feel the same feeling in my old age. The titles of my two previously published books include the compound *self-consciousness*. Several people thought that they were books about artificial intelligence because they knew I had been a processor designer in my last active years. Because of this cultural gap between the Old World and the U.S., I will define the three terms.

The three terms make a hierarchy: wisdom at the top, intelligence in the middle, and self-consciousness at the bottom. Self-consciousness was created by evolution, and its naturally set objective was to preserve one's own life using the available resources at the minimum cost. This objective emerged naturally since those who did not adopt it perished. Self-consciousness emerged by nature's mega-scale trial and error, guided by this *naturally set* objective. In evolutionary history, a self-conscious being in every development stage tried to accomplish the objective efficiently. The efficiency attained by each individual is the measure of its intelligence. All animals, at least above the level of vertebrate, carry something that may be called self-consciousness and the matching intelligence.

In evolutionary history, Darwinian evolution created self-consciousness and, up to a certain level, intelligence. As humans began to live in an organized society, we developed culture and established institutionalized life. Then knowledge of the state of the society and its historical record became available to the society members, and the mechanism of the brain's evolution changed from Darwinian to Lamarckian. The new evolutionary mechanism created various effects, both positive and negative. Wisdom is the most positive product of the new mechanism of evolution.

Wisdom is the superstructure above intelligence and self-consciousness. Wisdom scrutinizes the objective set by the intelligent, self-conscious SELF. Wisdom examines if the current objective of life is beneficial, not only for the present life and for those involved at present, but also for the future life and for the associates of the same and other species. To have wisdom, an understanding of history and geography of the world became the prerequisite. At present, humans are the only carrier of wisdom in nature, and even among humans, the degree of wisdom varies widely. In my life, I have met many intelligent people, but the number of people whom I admire as really wise is very small. But they were also people who were incredibly broad-minded and superbly intelligent.

Reviewing world history of the Fascist time through which I lived, I conclude that Francisco Franco was wiser than Adolf Hitler, Benito Mussolini, Tojo Hideki, Chiang Kai-shek, and Joseph Stalin. That was the reason why he had a rather peaceful last years and is still respected by many Spaniards.

4.36 My Experience of Wisdom

To see how wisdom works, we must learn from history. Military history shows us human wisdom most dramatically. The history of the Napoleonic Wars provides one such case. Why did the Russians win so big? Because of General Kutuzov's wisdom. He studied Napoleon Bonaparte's character, his supply line, weather conditions, and especially the weakest points of Napoleon's strategy. Napoleon's strategy was amazingly simple: he concentrated all his forces on a single battlefield and decided victory by one battle. Napoleon always won in Western Europe by this strategy, so he had no second plan for in case his army was depleted gradually by whatever the cause. Kutuzov took advantage of this weak point. He did so because he respected Napoleon and learned from him. Napoleon had no such modesty.

The difference between the two characters shows up even today. Kutuzov's grave in St. Petersburg is still visited by Russians who pray for his soul. I had to wait for a long time to show my respect to him. Ahead of me was a grandmother who was so sincerely praying with her little candle that it made me feel, *Once born in this world, I wish to be such an eternal hero!* Napoleon's grave in Invalid, Paris, is no more than a stopover point for a sightseeing bus. I saw no visitor showing respect to his coffin, high up in a dome.

Kutuzov's strategy to defeat Napoleon was systematized by the Prussians Gerhard von Scharnhorst and Carl Clausewitz and was implemented by Gebhard Leberecht von Blücher and August Neidhardt von Gneisenau in Waterloo. They were the ones who won the battle, not Wellington as generally believed. World War II Japanese high command repeated every mistake that could have been learned from Napoleon. I witnessed that as a young boy. We Japanese did not respect American industrial power. Then the tide turned. We Americans did not respect the Vietcong or the Islam guerilla's fighting spirit in limited war. To win a war, the first requirement is to respect the enemy and humbly learn the enemy's way for our own advantage.

Wisdom is the capability to look at the whole matter over the entire time span. I was deeply impressed by the wisdom of my doctoral course advisor, Professor Aldert van der Ziel of the University of Minnesota. I worked for my PhD degree in his laboratory for three years, and once I submitted a paper with an inaccuracy to a technical journal. Fortunately, a referee caught the mistake, and the paper was not published. Professor van der Ziel said nothing at that time, except to fix the mistake and resubmit the paper. Then, sometime later, he told me the following: "You have too much imagination and are misled by that. To protect yourself from the risk of making mistakes, first develop a complete mathematical theory and check if there is any inconsistency. Second, try to explain your theory either by diagram or statement to yourself, and see if you are convinced by the explanation." He also advised me that I tend to concentrate too much on a single subject of research, and get depressed, if it does not work out well. He suggested me to work two research project simultaneously, and occasionally switch between them, so that failure of one does not depress me to the point that I become nonproductive. I was deeply impressed by his words. In those three short years, he saw my weak point very clearly and advised me on how to deal with it. This was true wisdom from a superior human mind. This is the highest human wisdom I've ever experienced personally. I truly admire him.

4.37 Can Intelligence Be Quantized?

IQ tests are popular in the U.S., and some children get spectacular scores. Psychologists even estimate the IQs of some historical geniuses. Goethe's IQ is estimated at 185, which I surely believe, but then why is Newton's IQ only at 125? If this is really true, I know some middle school classmates who could have been more intelligent than Newton! That was not possible. I have a reason to ask this question seriously. In the 1960s, my respected mentor Dr. W. Shockley publicized a theory stating that intelligence depends on race, and as a result he was ostracized by mainstream American public media. He was very bright, one of only a few geniuses of the last century, and also a kind mentor of me, who guided me far and deep (section 4.27). Why was he treated like that? That is a pain I still suffer. I make every effort to show his real character even now. I am terribly frustrated and angry about the way he was treated in the public.

Yet I have seen, and I now believe, that there is no significant dependence of intelligence on race. Since I still struggle to defend Shockley, I must identify the real problem. My conclusion is that IQ tests do not measure intelligence. I believe that the IQ test was a trial to introduce numerical methods in psychology. A similar effort of *mathematization* was going on in economics from the 1950s to the 1970s to build neoclassical synthesis economics, the so-called *math-econ*. The macroeconomic variables of Keynesian economics were combined with the classical economics concept of balance of supply and demand by the market. Economists set up equations, solved them by computer, and claimed that this was the *science* of economics. To this trend, there was criticism from both the left and the right sides. The right side's critic, Hayek, held that the Keynesian economic variables are pseudo variables whose ambiguous nature cannot tolerate mathematical analysis, and therefore it is nonsensical to develop mathematical theories about them. The left side, Marxists, did not like *math-econ* either. Their reason was not so clear to me as was that from the right side, but I surmise that a complex system like the economy suffers from the same problem as complex nonlinear physical systems where chaotic features prevail (section 1.12).

The 1970s was about the time when physicists began to consider chaotic phenomena seriously and when such a feature of any realistic complex system began to attract attention. Economists took the paradigm of physics before that time. The economics controversy was never settled. Economists gradually marginalized the monstrous *math-econ* from the mainstream. I took this controversy seriously since I was building up my self-consciousness model during that period. My first attempt was to build its mathematical theory, but finally I scrapped them all, since I suspected that any psychological variables including IQ were the similar pseudo variables of a complex system.

My personal observation supports this view. I know two persons who had an IQ of 145. Since they were both in the same general area of physics as I, I tracked them. They were both socially quite successful, but I saw not very significant basic contributions from them. I noticed common characteristics of high-IQ people. They are quick to switch from one theme to the other. They are generally not determined characters to dwell on a single difficult problem that impacts heavily on human life. Their interests are diversified widely, and they are able to switch from one subject to the other smoothly. In modern society, such a character is certainly socially successful, but is not a great inventor or scientist who pioneers a new field. IQ tests that demand the applicant to solve impossibly many tricky problems measure how shrewd a person is, rather than how creative or determined he or she is. A person who is emotionally unable to go on to the second problem of an IQ test while leaving the first problem not convincingly solved is the unfortunate type whose IQ measures low. IQ tests are not universally reliable. In my native Japan in my schooling days, IQ was tested by order of the GHQ, but the schools disregarded the score almost entirely. They had a different view on intelligence.

I believe that Dr. Shockley's tragedy was that he was misled by the reliability of IQ tests. I am very sorry for Dr. Shockley. He deserves as much respect as Newton, Darwin, Planck, and Einstein. While I was an MTS (member of technical staff) at Bell Laboratories, I tried to persuade as many friends as I could that Dr. Shockley really was an unbiased, kind person. I was glad to learn that Dr. Ian Ross, once Dr. Shockley's colleague and later Bell Laboratories' president, supported my respect for Dr. Shockley. Dr. Shockley's assistant, who made a transistor for him, was a tall, slender, graceful, and very intelligent African American woman who admired him. One day she smilingly told me, "Maybe I didn't do so well?" I was impressed by her *high-class* attitude and respectable modesty. She was very sorry that Dr. Shockley was not understood by many people and always ate his lunch alone. She seemed happy to find one more person, namely, me, who admired Dr. Shockley.

As for Newton's IQ, there is a posthumous diagnosis indicating that he might have suffered from a rare variety of autism called Asperger's syndrome. According to a book by Professor Kaku Michio, *Physics of the Impossible* (Doubleday, 2008), there is another case, that of Paul Dirac (who was regarded as a *god* of physics in my student days in the 1950s!).

According to A. Robertson (*The Story of Measurement* [Thames and Hudson, 2007]), there was no Nobel Prize winner from a group of forty children tested and qualified as geniuses by Terman with IQ > 140. I read Terman's results, quoted in the book about the pathology of historical geniuses, with rather negative comments. The two dropouts from Terman's screening each won a Nobel Prize, and they were both true intellectual giants: Dr. Louis Alvarez and Dr. William Shockley. These leads me to believe that the ability of IQ tests to qualify the most brilliant minds is doubtful. IQ is, most likely, a pseudo parameter of a complex system of the brain, like the parameters of Keynesian economics as pointed out by Hayek.

4.38 Human Creativity

Creativity of the human mind is a great gift of evolutionary development. Creative works and their positive results are the best cure for anxiety and depression in twenty-first-century humans. This positive effect occurs by redirecting the energy that is otherwise wasted to maintain the negative mood. Human creativity is in the domain of the interaction of the personal self-consciousness and its superstructure, social self-consciousness. I try to look into their relation semi-quantitatively, since the relation appears to be not very simple. To study such an issue, mathematical language is convenient. There must be a complex relationship between the asset of social self-consciousness, that is, parameter N; an individual's accessibility to the social asset, parameter α; and the creativity of the population, C. Asset N generally increases with time. Accessibility, α, has greatly increased in the last twenty to thirty years because of the internet. My question is how accessibility affects creativity, since I have some doubt that many dot-com scientists are as creative as the 1900–70 superstar scientists whom I know personally.

Since populations are motivated by the stimuli of their social culture, their creativity must be proportional to the accessible part of the asset of social self-consciousness, that is, αN. Let the proportionality factor be $1/b$, so that creativity is $\alpha N/b$. The reason the factor is $1/b$ is because there is an effect that modifies b. Increased information accessibility causes everyone to have more common sense. This means that everyone becomes more critical of any unorthodox, new, or odd idea. I feel this quite strongly from my personal experience. The effect is small if the shared common sense of the members of society is insignificant. But if the society is significantly united by a single way of thinking by way of the internet, the effect shows up strongly, because this common sense rules the society by the majority's social power. Furthermore, if the social asset and its accessibility increase, there is less of a niche of making new and creative contributions. These two effects show up as the struggle of scientists and inventors to be given priority. The two effects increase the effective value of b. It is replaced by $b + f(\alpha N)^2$. Then the creativity C is given by

$$C = \frac{aN}{\left[b + f\left(aN\right)^2 \right]} = \frac{dN}{dt}$$

where f is a numerical factor. From this formula, creativity C has a single maximum

$$Cmax = 1/2\sqrt{bf}$$

This is an interesting conclusion. By improving information accessibility and social assets, there is a maximum of human creativity. It appears that basic physics has suffered most from this effect recently. In spite of the large influx of theoretical physicists to the string theory, we hear nothing about the grand unification of all the four of the physical forces. Some authors say that there are two thousand string theorists in the world. This number is equal to all the physicists at the beginning of the twentieth century. They all communicate by the internet to compete for priority of their findings. Some string theory luminaries carry an almost mythological aura, like that of Aristotle, in the world of strings. This appears to be a new trend of twenty-first-century science. Creative activity is, most often, a conscious effort to create new and unusual images. Such an image does not belong to the domain of common sense. Furthermore, mathematics, the common language of the exotic front of modern physics such as string theory, may become the powerful medium for establishing *common sense* in the basic physics community. This was once the trend of electronic circuit theory also, where the mathematics of the analytic function theory became the common communication medium of the linear circuit theorists, to the point that poles and zeroes became the emblem of IEEE (Institute of Electrical and Electronics Engineers). But this common sense delayed the development of digital circuit theory. When I began digital electronics work in the 1970s, I was surprised that the only theory of digital electronics was Boolean algebra!

Isn't it the time to ask whether increased information accessibility is a benefit to progress or not? Is it really necessary for a scientist to know everything that is currently going on? Now I can see why we admire such scientists as Archimedes, Copernicus, Galileo, and Newton. Common sense and high-speed communication media are the two faces of Janus. The maximum human creativity is independent from historical time. Our present life's comfort depends so much on the inventions and discoveries in the long Neolithic and classic periods. Since the advent of human history, we have eaten the same staples, and we still use wheels for efficient transport. New inventions are made only to fill narrow niches of already existing areas, unless we exercise big imagination. This is a serious problem for the future. Common sense and common fashion are the necessities for mass society to prosper. Yet common sense and current fashion sensitivity are serious impediments to creativity. Our Neolithic ancestors were much more creative than we since they did not care for the common sense of their small communities or the priority of invention.

Going back to the semiquantitative analysis, creativity C is the rate of increase of the social asset N. Then,

$$\frac{dN}{dt} = \frac{aN}{b + f(aN)^2}$$

This equation has a solution satisfying $N = M$ at $t = 0$ as

$$t = \left(\frac{b}{a}\right)\log\left(\frac{N}{M}\right) + \left(\frac{fa}{2}\right)\left(N^2 - M^2\right)$$

The first term indicates that the social and cultural asset of society increases exponentially with time. This is the view of the optimistic social scientists like economists. Yet if factor α increases, the effect decreases proportional to the inverse of accessibility parameter α, and the second term becomes more significant. In the limit of high accessibility,

$$N \to \sqrt{\frac{2t}{fa}}$$

and this is a very slow growth of the social asset that describes the state of the dark age. We are just at its beginning.

4.39 Unconscious Thinking

The brain's image memories store elementary images, each of which is a combination of its template and identifier. Composite images useful in life are built by connecting the identifiers of such elementary images. There are enough elementary images acquired in life that can be connected to create any complex images that satisfy all the needs of life. Figure 4.39.1 shows a securely connected, clearly recognizable composite image consisting of templates A, B, and C and their identifiers a, b, and c, respectively. Templates X and Y are also paired with the identifiers x and y, respectively, but identifiers x and y are not yet connected. They are spatially close to identifiers a, b, and c. As identifiers a, b, and c activate, their electrical influence reaches x and y, and they may be connected unconsciously. Since this is an indirect access, this excitation is not intense. What I mean here by *unconsciously* is that connected identifiers x and y are not excited strongly enough to activate their templates X and Y, so the combined image is not displayed. The connected image must wait for the chance to get excited strongly enough, by whatever the cause, to be displayed. If that happens, then the hidden composite image pops out, often to the SELF's surprise.

I had a few experiences of this sort. In the 1980s, I became curious if a digital system (that has digital *states*) still had lower-level *states* in its circuit level. At that time, I was impressed that the model democratic British society had so many social ranks. The British clearly distinguishes the Cambridge or Oxford graduates from the Birmingham graduates, yet they all appear to be members of the same group of Anglo-Saxons. I have a heuristic thinking habit of anthropomorphism, that is, a trend of seeing humanlike structure or behavior in lifeless systems. So I expected that what exists in human society should also exist in digital circuits, including the human brain.

Before that time, I found a method of estimating a CMOS digital circuit's delay time by simplifying the characteristics of MOS field-effect transistors. I was also thinking of the effects of parasitic inductance in high-speed CMOS integrated circuits. Several such ideas of digital circuit theory had somehow combined in my mind unconsciously, and these emerged suddenly by the hint of the structure of British society. I was able to identify two lower-level states in digital circuits, which I describe in my two books (*Theory of CMOS Digital Circuits and Circuit Failures* [Princeton University Press, 1992] and *High-Speed Digital Circuit* [Addison-Wesley, 1996]). The images of the lower-circuit-level states in the digital circuit emerged suddenly when I was raking dead leaves in my backyard on Thanksgiving morning of 1987. I combined this new idea with the image of electron triodes I had inherited from Dr. W. Shockley (section 4.27) and with this built my CMOS digital circuit theory. At that time, no such theory existed (section 4.38).

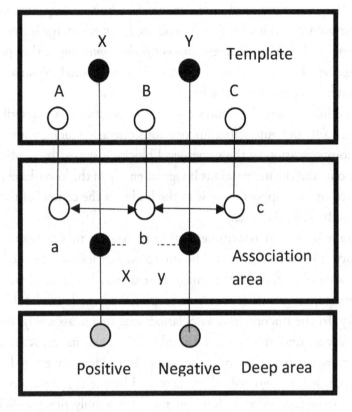

Figure 4.39.1 Mechanism of unconscious thinking

The connection of identifiers by unrelated activity may not display the built-up image, but the connection activity may induce a vague sense of the body and weak sensation. In case of a new discovery such as the one I mentioned above, it seems to me that I feel some vague sense of hope and excitement associated with a weak sensation before the idea suddenly emerges. Since I've had such an experience a few times in my technical life, I am reasonably confident that this is a *premonition* of a new discovery. In the same way, if a disaster image is unconsciously assembled, I feel a similar vague sense of fear and anxiety before I realize what is coming. This has become more frequent in my old age life. This might be called the mysterious sixth sense. Where does the sixth sense come from? In figure 4.39.1, identifiers *x* and *y* are connected to the deep area centers when they are separately created before. Then, when they are connected later, unconsciously, the deep area centers are activated and the sensation is generated, but no image is displayed. Then my SELF certainly feels *unidentifiable something*, either positive or negative. The mysterious sixth sense has a rational explanation by this mode of operation of the brain.

The human mind executes conscious operation, as I described in section 4.08, and automatic, unconscious operation along with it. The conscious operation of the upper-level blocks is sensed by sending the image out, and the unconscious image assembly in the lower-level blocks is sensed by the support request to the body via the centers of the deep area, as the faint sixth sense.

Brain operation is symmetrical with respect to the main image memory. This feature can still be interpreted as follows: In the brain's upper area of operation, the image is sent out. It is sensed first, and then its impact on life is sensed as sensation by the lower-level block's activity. In the unconscious association area image assembly, it is the other way around: the image is assembled first, and its impact is sensed weakly at that time. Then as the image is accidentally excited and is displayed, it is recognized. What is sensed by the conscious operation is the image-controlled action and not its assembly process. What is sensed by the unconscious sixth sense is the process of image assembly, which comes first.

Any new image that emerges suddenly from the unconscious mind carries significantly more new and unconventional features than the images created by strenuous and conscious thinking. This feature makes me believe that common sense is indeed an impediment to new image creation, as I discussed in the previous section. Yet unconscious thinking is a small byproduct of a lot of conscious thinking. This feature is understood from the mechanism of figure 4.39.1.

As another possible mechanism of unconscious image creation, a not yet used identifier is activated and stretches the axon to the template area, making its own template. An image created by this mechanism is likely to be otherworldly and spooky. Images observed under the influence of substances, or the spooky images reported by those who had so-called near-death experiences, may be created by this mechanism. These images are created by responding to the abnormal chemical signals from the body to the deep area.

4.40 Biological Nature of Intelligence

Intelligence is the capability to accomplish any objective at the minimum cost. From this definition, the mechanisms of intelligence have so many varieties, depending on the objective, and that seems to defeat any attempt to classify them. This difficulty is real if we recognize that each problem has its own peculiarity and that the practical way to improve the efficiency of each problem's solution is to take advantage of the peculiarity. Yet there are certain groups of problems that can be solved by a systematic approach; the paradigm is biology and evolution. We see how much our mind is subjected to its biological origin and its evolutionary development. In this section, I list several mechanisms of intelligence that have a biological paradigm.

I point out that self-consciousness and its mode of operation emerged during the long historical past by way of evolution, by natural selection. In evolutionary history, a new body structure and its mode of operation emerged by random genetic variation. These were tested in the natural habitat to see if they were advantageous or not. Only the advantageous genetic variations remained. Thus, the most basic intelligence is random trial and selection. This is not efficient, but it is applicable to practically any aspect of life. Is there any more efficient way? Following is a list of possible mechanisms of biology that systematically suggest the efficient way to finding a solution:

(1) **Evolution.** Random generation of new species followed by natural selection (Darwinian) and inheritance of the successful experience of the parents to the children by way of education (Lamarckian). This method can be made efficient by making the period of one trial short.

(2) **Immunology.** Neutralization of a harmful or undesirable object by making and attaching the object's complement.

(3) **Genetics.** Adoption of the successful structure or mode of operation of one species to another species.

(4) **Embryology.** Buildup of the structure hierarchically. The already built-up structure issues the directive to build the next-lower-level structure (section 6.11).

Why does human intelligence follow the biologically or evolutionarily set paradigm? Evolution has been nature's mega-scale trial-and-error experiment to select the winning species from so many failed ones. As humans and animals developed up to a certain level, their brains searched for the winning strategy to solve their life's problems. They engaged in trial and error and got similar results. This was really a *rediscovery* by the human mind by doing the same thing as nature did. We try to imitate the cases that *Mother Nature* has already tried and was successful at.

From the early period of evolution, the animal body has been protected from invading harmful microscopic objects by immunity. If the body finds a harmful microscopic object, it makes a new object that fits to it, and when the pair combines, the combination becomes harmless. The harmful object is called a pathogen, and the fitting object is called an antigen. Human intelligence makes the object that fits to the undesirable object and combines the two to make it desirable. This is perhaps one of the most prevalent mechanisms of intelligence in secular life, in craftsmen's work, and also in some significant key inventions in the technical arena.

The mathematical concept of complement is defined by a single specification of the part since the whole has been defined a priori. If the full circle of figure 4.40.1(a) is the whole, by giving the crescent *part*, its *complement* is the egg-shaped image shown to the right. The concept of complement can be made general by imagining the whole, depending on the case. Figure 4.40.1(b), *center*, shows a broken plate, which is the *part*. The complete, usable plate is shown to the left. This is the *whole*. To repair the broken plate, the complement, shown to the right, is cut from a piece of wood and is glued. The complement is produced by way of graphic subtraction. Creation of the complement involves imagination of a new whole and the graphical or contextual *subtraction* of the images. Here, imagining of the desirable whole is the key part. Editing a text is one application of this approach to the language image to improve its meaning and context. This is the basic intelligence of any craftsman's work. Yet the same procedure has been used in modern high technology also.

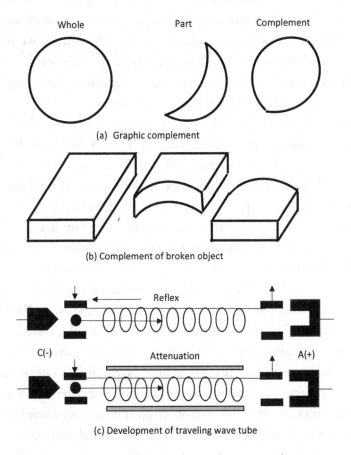

Whole   Part   Complement

(a) Graphic complement

(b) Complement of broken object

Reflex

C(-)   Attenuation   A(+)

(c) Development of traveling wave tube

Figure 4.40.1 Intelligence by seeking complement

In my high school and college days, at the forefront of electronics was microwave technology and new microwave vacuum tubes. At that time, the traveling wave tube was the emerging wideband microwave amplifier. Figure 4.40.1(c) shows its structure. Here, C is the cathode, heated by a tungsten filament. It emits electrons that are accelerated by a strong electric field created by applying high DC voltage to the helix and the anode. Electrons travel along the axis of helix H, where they interact with microwaves propagating through the helix. The microwave's velocity from the cathode side to the anode is slower than the electron velocity, since it turns around the helix as it propagates to the right. If the electron velocity is higher than the microwave's velocity in the direction of the axis of the helix, then the microwave is amplified by picking energy up from the electron beam. This microwave amplifier was invented earlier, but it was easy to oscillate. This was because the amplified wave was reflected from the anode side to the cathode side, and created positive feedback within the tube.

Then a spectacular improvement was made by Dr. J. R. Pierce of Bell Telephone Laboratories, Murray Hill, New Jersey. He added attenuation to the helix path, such that the reflected wave was attenuated. Practically, carbon soot is sprayed inside the glass tube. Then the microwave, propagating along the helix that is directed from the cathode side to the anode side, was amplified by interacting with the high-speed electron beam, but the reflected microwave propagating outside the helix in the opposite direction was attenuated, and the positive feedback was suppressed. The perfected traveling wave tubes became the workhorses of microwave communication. This was one of the most spectacular innovation in vacuum tube technology, by adding the proper complement to the existing tube structure. My first work in electronics at Hitachi's central research laboratory in Japan was to develop this tube. I still remember our excitement about this new vacuum tube. It is now one of my great memories when I later met Dr. Pierce in Murray Hill and talked with him about my experience in Japan.

Copying a successful structure or function from one area to the other is another significant mechanism of human intelligence. This technique is most frequently used in machine or tool design. An archaic example of copying the human body structure is seen in the development of the Paleolithic hand ax. The early hand ax was just a pointed stone, but later a handle was attached like a human fist and arm. This was to follow the successful paradigm in nature. Even in our modern age, clever toys are designed to simulate the function of a human or animal body. In the 1970s, I was impressed by a toy bird sold by a street vendor in Chinatown, New York City. It flew just like a real bird. I bought one and examined how it worked. It created lift by the same mechanism as a rowboat. The only essential difference was the direction of the force. If the rowboat paddle's motion creates thrust, the same mechanism creates lift. The toy bird was an application of the successful mechanism of genetic variation that created birds from reptiles.

In the animal world, copying successful self-protection strategies is seen among animals of very different evolutionary lineage. The belly of a blue-skin fish is silver colored. Squids emit light from their underbelly. Both animals try to make themselves invisible to the predators of the deep. The color of a moth turns dark as air pollution makes the white color conspicuous to predator birds. Some animals change color depending on the habitat. Insects, squids, fish, and mammals come from entirely different branches of evolution. Even human soldiers wear green and brown striped jackets to make themselves invisible from the enemy, and jet fighter aircraft use microwave nonreflective material to cover the body so as to avoid radar detection.

4.41 Ancient South American Musical Instrument

The accomplishments of the ancient people, to whom no advanced science and technology was available, show the high level and power of their intelligence, imagination, skill, and determination. I provide an example to highlight how ingenious they really were. My example is the beautiful, fascinating, and *absolutely unique* South American musical instrument called the *silbador*. I introduce the reader to what it is and show how it works. Then I imagine how it was invented by adding a complement in several steps. The readers will surely agree that this is a product of a great ancient artist-inventor. The instrument is shown in figure 4.41.1(a). It is made of ceramic, mostly soft black ceramic, but sometimes by hard white ceramic, by the split-joint method. It consists of two jar-shaped cavities connected together by a pair of pipes.

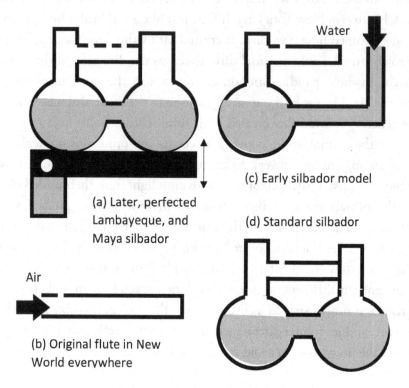

(a) Later, perfected Lambayeque, and Maya silbador

(b) Original flute in New World everywhere

(c) Early silbador model

(d) Standard silbador

Figure 4.41.1 Silbador development history

The bottom pipe is much thicker than the top pipe, or the bottoms of the jars are connected by a hole. The top pipe is thin and has a hole or holes from which air is able to escape. As air escapes, the silbador whistles (*silbar* in Spanish). To cause the instrument to whistle, water is poured into the right-side jar of figure 4.41.1(a). The instrument is placed on a rocking support and is swung up and down. As water flows from the right jar to the left jar, the air of the left jar is compressed and escapes from the hole in the upper pipe, thereby creating a whistling sound, *pee, pee, pee*. If the instrument is crafted really well, the *pee* sound has a chirp, like bird's song. I saw such a silbador in a store in Pisac, Peru, and was absolutely fascinated. Artistically, silbadors are crafted such that the entire structure looks like a bird, an animal, or a singing man carrying a load on his back. Both in its artistic design and its fascinating operation, this instrument is the work of an ultimate genius. I learned about this instrument almost seventy years ago, but when I acquired one fifteen years ago, I was absolutely fascinated.

What is amazing about the silbador is its ancient origin. It existed as early as 800 BC, according to the display in the Museo Nacional Anthropologico y Historico, Pueblo Libre, Lima, Peru (known as the Doctor Tello's museum). This was the time of the first cultural horizon of South American history (Chavin culture). Although the high expertise in hydrodynamics technology of the ancient South Americans is now well recognized, this was too big a surprise. It changed my view of the Neolithic period. Those people could even have been superior inventors and artists to us. So I had to follow the inventor's thinking.

There had been simple flutes like that shown in figure 4.41.1(b), blown by the air from the mouth. These flutes emerged much earlier. The inventor tried to make one whistle automatically. This revolutionary idea was already twenty-five hundred years ahead of its time. The silbador is the world's first automatic musical instrument like a player piano. As shown in the figure, the inventor kept adding to the simple archaic flute, one complement part after the other, at each time imagining a new *whole* that made the instrument better. Each addition, (b), (c), (d), and finally (a), made the instrument more improved, convenient, versatile, and sophisticated. As the last improvement, he added extra holes to the upper pipe to set the pitch of the sound. This pitch-controlled version is rare, but I saw one in the site museum of Túcume, Lambayeque, Peru. I'd like to ask historians of music if there is any musical system from any part of the Old World that uses chirping, and if there is any musical instrument using both water and air. I know neither.

The tradition of this musical instrument exists across the entire Peruvian Pacific coast from Lambayeque to northern Chile and to the Andean highlands. Its popularity seems to be centered in the ancient Moche region, areas around the modern city of Trujillo. Still more amazing is that several silbadors were unearthed in Costa Rica and on the Guatemalan Pacific coast. South American traders must have brought their proud cultural product to Mesoamerica and taught Mesoamericans how it worked and how to make it. This is important since it means that the advanced technique of split-joint ceramics must have come to Mesoamerica with this musical instrument. I consider this possibility seriously as evidence of Moche-Maya cultural exchange (sections 1.11 and 5.11). As I compare the South American and Maya silbadors, I notice one definite structural difference. All the South American silbadors look like figure 4.41.1(d), having a narrow water inlet pipe. Maya silbadors displayed in Guatemala City museums have a wide-open mouth to pour water in. It may be that the Maya took the idea of the instrument and improved upon it. Here is great evidence of the cultural exchange between the two great cultural centers of the New World (section 5.11).

Since Maya silbadors are found only in the Pacific coast sites, the South American and Mesoamerican traders must have used the safe Pacific coastal navigation route. A silbador was found also in Costa Rica, located between the two ancient cultural centers. There, the design is rather unique. A man and woman hold each other, and the water inlets are on their backs. This instrument must be held by both hands and is swung, since the holes must be covered. The silbador cultures developed differently at different locations along the New World Pacific coast, but the basic idea remained the same. The Pacific coast of the New World was once united by the silbador culture. I am now sure that the two great cultures of the New World knew of each other's existence and peacefully exchanged their ideas.

I truly admire the inventor of this graceful musical instrument, whose name has unfortunately been lost to history. I am sure that the queen of El Brujo I mentioned in section 1.11 must have enjoyed the lovely sound, as did the emperors of the Chimor empire from Taycanamo to Minchansamon. The inventor treated twenty-first-century people, including me, to the pleasing sounds of this musical instrument three thousand years later. If art is eternal, is anything else more eternal than this?

4.42 Digression—What Did Neolithic Ancestors Know?

After our strenuous technical discussions, I offer some breathing space by talking about science fiction. I have visited many Neolithic sites of the Western Hemisphere (North and South America and Polynesia), such as Palenque, Copán, Tiahuanaco, Chan-chan, and Easter Island. There, I was impressed by the sophistication of these ancient people in light of their artistic sense and technical skills. Now I firmly believe that the people who built these sites were at least as sophisticated as we are, and some of their elite must have been superior to us. Readers should never feel contempt for this assessment. Unfortunately, either their accomplishments were not recorded or the records were maliciously destroyed by the conquistadors. I feel deep anger about what the conquistadors and Catholic Church did in the New World, especially in Mesoamerica, in South America, and on Easter Island. I now believe that the ancient people of the Western Hemisphere knew a lot more about natural science than we are aware. Following are my imaginations. I cannot resist my desire to tell you, as an old storyteller sitting by the winter fireside, how these ancestors may have come up with two not so simple and not so obvious scientific facts. These facts are that the earth is a sphere and not a flat square and that all matter is made of atoms. Ancient people could come up with these facts from the knowledge and means they had at that time. This is a new genre of science fiction to highlight the ancient people's ability, not insulting them with extraterrestrial nonsense. I like to disconnect true human culture from the chauvinism of the modern technology-based culture, since by connecting technology and culture naively, we end up with the banality of the twenty-first century.

Spherical Earth and the Solar System

A readily available evidence of the spherical shape of any heavenly body is the phases of the moon. Ancient people could learn that the moon was a sphere by observing the relative position of the sun and the moon. If the moon were a circular disc like a pancake instead of a sphere, then either the whole face was light or the entire face was dark, depending on the sun's direction. The crescent moon could never be observed. If the moon is a sphere, why couldn't the earth be a sphere also? That is naturally concluded. Maya astronomers might even have known that Venus, which was a very important star of war for them, showed phases. I tried a simple trigonometric calculation and found that when Venus is seen close to the sun, the angle of the crescent is 3×10^{-4} radian. This is close, yet it is more than the limit of resolution of the human eye, which is set at $1 - 2 \times 10^{-4}$ radian. According to Darwin's *The Voyage of the HMS Beagle*, Native Americans had much better eyesight than he, although he was rather young at that time. So it is possible that some New World astronomers might have seen the phases of Venus without a telescope.

There is further evidence that might have convinced the ancient astronomers of the spherical shape of the earth. When I stood on the promontory at Sounion, the sharp southern tip of the Attica peninsula in Greece, the edge of the Aegean Sea appeared round. I stood at the same location where King Aegeus waited for his son, Theseus, who was expected to return from Crete. As Aegeus saw the tip of the mast first and then its black sails on the horizon, he threw himself into the sea in grief over his lost son. That is why the sea is now called the Aegean Sea. First seeing the mast, and then seeing the ship, was considered as evidence of a spherical earth. The reason Greeks came up with the image of a spherical earth is that they were excellent ancient mariners, and they traveled several seas far and regularly. Ancient Polynesians were even larger-scale mariners than the Greeks from the same ancient period. They must have known that the earth was a sphere, using the same reasoning.

If Polynesians thought that the earth was a flat square as the Catholic Church believed at the time, then they would never have dared to sail across the entire Pacific Ocean to reach South America. The Pacific is a truly huge ocean. I felt that strongly when I stood alone on the northwest cape of Easter Island and looked at the vast expanse of the Pacific. Polynesians sailed all the way, and never saw the edge of the ocean, except for a landmass, South America. They were well aware of the wind, waves, and currents of the Pacific Ocean. They must have thought that as long as there was no seawater heading to the east, there should be no edge of the world. Instead of a gigantic waterfall, they found South America as the *edge* of the Pacific Ocean. Such a simple fact could never have been found until a brave Polynesian actually dared to set sail and continue sailing until he reached the limit of the ocean. That is why the Polynesians now share the honor of *discovering* the New World with the Vikings.

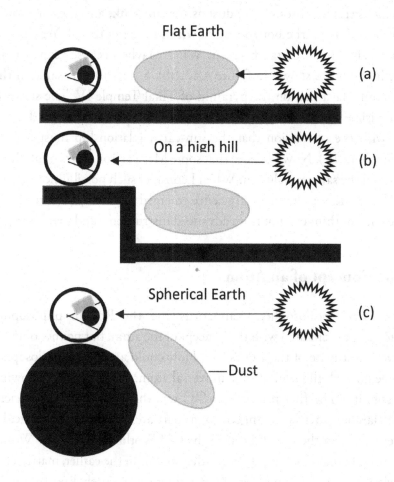

Figure 4.42.1 Hint of the spherical earth

The Maya did not have open-ocean navigation capability. As I stood on the height of the Maya port city of Tulum, the Caribbean Sea did not look round to me, since Tulum is not at the tip of a promontory. Yet once I stood on the top of the hill looking down at Copán, the center of Maya astronomy, and was watching the big red sinking sun. Then I came up with another possibility, shown in figure 4.42.1. It was a windy and dusty evening. The sinking sun's beams are filtered through the dust, changing in color and brightness.

If the earth were flat, the sun's beams would go through a longer and longer path through the dust as the sun sank, and the sun would not be visible on the horizon as shown in figure 4.42.1(a). Yet the sun was visible down to the horizon. Why? Maybe because Copán is in the highland as shown in figure 4.42.1(b). So, I tried the same in the lowland Maya site, on the pyramid of Tikal Temple IV. The sun was still visible on the horizon. From this very simple observation, I came up with the conclusion that the sun-earth relationship must be like figure 4.42.1(c). Now I believe that some Maya astronomers might have reached the same conclusion. When I consider such possibilities, I come to the realization that natural science emerged from the idle curiosity of the ancient thinkers, not from advanced instruments and mathematics.

The Concept of an Atom

The Greek philosopher Democritus and the Roman philosopher Lucretius are credited with the concept of the atom, but neither of them gave an estimate of the atom's size. How could an ancient philosopher come up with the concept of a universal atom? I imagine the following possibility: The first millennium BC was the time when the ancient matriarchal society changed to a patriarchal society, practically everywhere in the world, both in the Old World and the New World. Power inheritance changed from father to son. In the earlier, matriarchal society, who was the mother of a daughter was securely known, but in the changed patriarchal society, who was the son of the father who was supposed to inherit the father's power was not always obvious. Actually, there is a well-known case in Chinese history. The first emperor of China was not the son of the predecessor king of the Chin dynasty but was an illegitimate son of one of his chancellors. Since such an incidence happened, how similar the son looked to the father must have been the only key criterion justifying the succession.

By that time, it was already known that the only way the father was able to control his son's features was through the genetic material he gave to the mother, and the quantity of the material did not matter (the son's features did not depend on the father's age or health). In the genetic material, there is no object larger than 1 mm in size. A thinker of the time could have thought as follows: For a father to reproduce a son similar to him, he must have given a lot of specifications to the mother. Suppose that the information was given by talking to the mother. Then the father must have had to talk for a long time. How long? Maybe as long as any ancient epic whom the people at that time listened to at night by the fireside. They were blind traveling storytellers like Homer. The session lasted many nights. Such a spoken or sung ancient epic might have one hundred thousand words, and each word needed to be explained properly. Then a million explanations must have been necessary. By the Middle Neolithic period, humans were able to count practically any large number, so this was not an impossible task for the thinkers. That much information must be packed into an object having less than 1 mm in size. Then the size of the unit carrying the information was $10^{-1}/10^6 = 10^{-7}$ cm. This is about the size of the molecules from which DNA is built, and that was determined only in the twentieth century.

The genetic material was produced originally from the food the father ate, consisting mostly of organic, and some inorganic, materials like salt. Even inedible rocks eventually broke down to sand and then to soil, from which edible plants grew. Then everything in nature must be built from the units of 10^{-7} cm in size. This could be the way that led the thinkers to the concept of atoms or molecules. I believe some ancient people must have reached the atom and molecule concept somewhere in the ancient world by this line of thought.

What do you think? Isn't this type of literary story more realistic and interesting than nonsense about an ET's technology? There are many problems that can be the subject of such story, for instance, how to measure the distance to the sun, how to determine the age of the earth, how to estimate the amount of water on the earth, how to explain the counterclockwise rotation of the air in a hurricane, how an animal body is built, and why plants are different from animals—among other things. These stories teach children how to think rationally.

In the ancient Maya script of Popol Vuh, there is a story of the ancestors of present-day humans. They were monkeys. The classical Maya people had a more scientific mind than modern creationists! In the same Maya script, when the gods created humans from corn, they were as clever as the gods themselves. So the gods sprayed mist into their eyes, so that humans could not see everything. An often-quoted interpretation of this myth is that humans must be subordinate to the gods. *Wait a moment!* Is that the right interpretation? I do not believe in such a miserable interpretation. Myths carry subtle metaphors, and often such shortcut explanations are wrong. Instead, we should look at the real character of the Maya gods. The Maya god of wisdom, the old Itzamna, was never a mean, jealous god. He taught his people never to be misled by the senses; instead be guided by your thought and reasoning. I believe that many pagan gods were cultural heroes who taught people to think, before they demanded to be worshipped.

In this chapter, I summarized my work on the general mechanisms creating the sense of SELF and its functions. In the following chapters, I consider the specific issues that the SELF must engage with.

CHAPTER 5

SENSE OF TIME

5.01 Subjective and Objective Time

Time is a mystery to human sense and thought. Human self-consciousness is similarly a mystery. These mysteries have never been resolved but have been avoided by people's refraining from stepping into endless speculation or tautology. Yet the difficulty of resolving such mysteries is inviting to inquisitive minds, not expecting secular or academic success. We feel that time is constantly flowing, but no one knows what is flowing and at what *rate* (second per second?). The paired concept of space appears more real than time. The length of two bars can be compared by bringing them together. The duration of an event that took place yesterday can be compared with an event that took place today, only if we trust that our clock is reliable. Can we trust the clock, a very complex machine?

At least one feature of the mysteries of time and self-consciousness is reasonably certain: the pair of mysteries are mutually entangled. I see the mystery of time as partly cultural, since time's image is never universal. The images of time held by physicists, systems scientists, psychologists, and historians are all different. Physicists consider time as the ordering prameter of the state of nature governed by the basic laws. For them, only the length of time measured from a conveniently chosen origin matters. For psychologists, time is the framework of the development

371

of the world and of the SELF, as recognized by the SELF. Their time requires that the reference point have a special meaning to the SELF. That is the present. Historians arrange the events on a time line, with absolute time if available. An historian's time carries both features of the physicist's time and the psychologist's time. Each historian focuses on a single culture or society, and the interaction between different cultures is often not of primary interest. So historians of the world set up multiple time lines for each culture. Different time lines interacted only rarely until the end of the Middle Ages, as I show in section 5.11.

Physicists, psychologists, and historians traditionally consider that time is a mathematically continuous parameter. The most recent participants, systems scientists, have an image of time that is basically different: for them, time progresses step by step, like we walk. The concept may creep into basic physics if the Planck-sized phenomena of the world are studied. Yet, before going that far, I have the task of explaining the psychological effect of time by looking into the hardware operation of the brain, that is, to append the image of the psychologist's time with the new features emerging from systems science. This is because the brain is now in the domain of systems science research. The time that the brain senses is the subjective time sensed by the self-conscious subject SELF, and the physicist's time is the universal, objective time. By separating the image of time into subjective and objective time, some of the confusion of time's image originating from the different cultures can be resolved.

The sophisticated sense and concept of time is unique to humans. Evolutionarily lower-level animals have only a limited sense of time. As I show later, length of time is hard to be sensed both by animals and humans. A sense of time's progression has been developed along with language capability. Language memory holds a long sequence of events, and display of the sequence creates the sense of time's progression. Lower-level animals have no language capability, and such animals' sense of time's progression must be by a sequence of only a few currently sensible images. It is difficult to teach them a long sequence of actions, so their sense of time's progression must be accordingly limited.

5.02 Objective Time

How shall I think of universal objective time? Does objective time as the physical state's ordering parameter exist? It does not exist as something logically proven, but it does exist, relying on the inductive conclusions from many observations. The evidence is *free choice of the clocks*, which I explain in what follows: A clock is built from any periodic phenomenon, such as the rotation of the earth, a swinging pendulum, or the oscillation of a crystal resonator circuit. Under normal conditions, the ratio of the number of oscillations of any pair of such oscillators counted simultaneously remains approximately constant over many repeated experiments. If several experiments executed on different occasions give different ratios, it has always been possible to improve matching of the ratio by applying a correction to the experiment or to the data analysis method. The correction is for a single purpose, to make the oscillators more independent from the environment and from each other (if two or more oscillator units are combined in the clock).

From the laws of basic physics, what should be done is clearly defined. By fixing the temperature and the location of the pendulum clock, and by applying correction of the effects of the jet stream on the earth's rotation, the match of one astronomical day and the indication of the pendulum clock becomes more stable. By the experience of generations of clockmakers, the ratio matching keeps improving. By rational expectation, matching can be improved indefinitely, as any nonideality is found and corrected. Then any one of such perfected clocks can be used to describe any physical phenomenon. This is what I call *free choice of clock*. This is an inductively established *axiom* of physics. Clock correction is possible only if our universe developed well enough from the primordial fireball, so that each oscillator element is well isolated from the others, but still our universe is not so old that free energy is available to sustain the clock's oscillation.

A basic requirement is that correction of clock is possible only if any physical parameter is measurable with any required precision. This is not so in the quantum world. Yet the most accurate clocks at present are those using quantum-mechanical oscillators, a collective oscillation of many quantum oscillators observed by macroscopic means. In the clock's structure, the set of microscopic quantum phenomena is integrated into the organized macroscopic phenomenon that is accessible by macroscopic means. Then shall we regard that objective time is a macroscopic parameter? If so, it appears that we are using macroscopic time to describe the quantum world. Why does a single definition of time cover both? Actually this is an interesting point from the psychology of basic physics.

I need more consideration of objective time's definition. Confidence of time's axiom comes from the simplicity of the basic physics laws, described by a small number of simple equations. If the basic laws are complex, there is always a possibility to finagle the method of application of the laws to explain anything. Arbitrariness cannot be hidden if the basic laws are simple. Simplicity of the basic laws reveals a special feature of time in physics. That is, all the classical laws of physics can be derived from the variational principle of the least action. The basic laws are formulated so that the time integral of the Lagrangian function should be minimal. This ultimately simple principle connects classical and quantum physics too. Thus, the existence of objective time is certain within the framework of physics.

Development of the random dissipating phenomenon can be used as a clock after calibration using the time set by the periodic clock. An example is the radioactive decay clock using unstable nuclei, widely used by archaeologists and geologists. This type of phenomenon, by its nature, includes statistical randomness. Yet the clock based on the dissipative phenomenon can extrapolate the time measured by the periodic clock. After calibration, a radioactive clock can cover the entire history of the solar system and maybe even a longer time period of time. Logically, this leaves some basic questions unanswered: the randomness that emerges from the fluctuation of the quantum vacuum, as I discuss in section 6.16, and whether the quantum vacuum remains stable or not over such a long period of time.

The periodic clock and the dissipative clock are related. The two types of clocks can be modeled by a single equivalent circuit model consisting of inductance, capacitance, and resistance. If the resistance is zero, the circuit models the periodic clock, and if the inductance is zero, it models the dissipative clock. The character of the two clocks changes continuously from one to the other. Here is an interesting feature: In the dissipative clock model, the charge is stored in the capacitor and is lost with time. The lost charge indicates the time. If the charge is supplied by any external source, the clock reverses the direction of time. This is effected either by supplying charge to the capacitor from the outside, or by including a significant inductance.[1] If the clock itself can sense the time it indicates, then the clock feels time moving forward and then backward. This is the subjective time sensed by the human body. Free energy stored in the body plays the role of the charge in the circuit model's capacitor. The sense of time created by this clock moves forward during daily work and backward after the evening meal and nighttime sleep.

The development of physics in the twentieth century showed that the state of nature in the future is unpredictable, even within the domain of classical physics. In the quantum world, instead of parameter values, only the probability of the parameter taking certain values can be determined. Then, in precise terms, objective time arranges the probability of the parameter value in sequence. In the macroscopic world, there is an upper limit to the objective time length, beyond which objective time loses its meaning, because the system goes into a chaotic state in which objective time becomes meaningless (section 1.12). A chaotic state carries no time, since all the emerging state's probabilities remain the same. Yet a chaotic system may occasionally return to semi-orderly states lasting some time, and only during that time, objective time reemerges. The solar system is now in this state.

The objective time of any complex system proceeds forward while the system changes from an orderly state to a disorderly state. It never proceeds backward. This feature is governed by the second law of thermodynamics. There are contradictory views that the direction of time is set by the second law of thermodynamics and that the second law only describes the mathematical feature of complex nonlinear systems.

---

[1] Masakazu Shoji, *High-Speed Digital Circuit* (Addison-Wesley, 1997).

I am definitely for the first view, since otherwise physics cannot handle complex multibody systems. When an orderly state reemerges from the chaotic state, a new world is born. In this way, the mythological concept of the last world still carries some physical significance.

5.03   Emergence of the Self-Conscious Being

In the beginning, our universe was a small fireball of very high density and high temperature. The material existed as subnuclear particles. Cosmologists describe this state of our univese using the objective time defined at present. How can they describe the state of the universe at the time when there was no clock? A clock could not be built at that time, since in the ultrahigh density state, any oscillator-oscillator interaction was too strong to define the proper oscillation period (section 5.02). Do the cosmologists consider that their approach is rational because the present state of the universe is consistent with what they derive from the past state by their theory? If so, this is not the logic of history or physics. The logic of history is basically the same as that of physics. It appears that cosmology adopted the logic of archaeology, namely that any conclusion of prehistory is subject to change according to new discoveries from the excavation. Indeed, recent discoveries have shown that urban life was not always the result of the advent of agriculture, as we thought fifty years ago. This is the impression I get when I read the review books of cosmology. I cannot feel reality in the story of the beginning of our universe.

As the universe expanded and temperature fell, successively baryons, atoms, simple molecules, organic molecules, and finally macromolecules emerged. At present, all these material forms exist somewhere in our universe, because nonuniformity developed along with expansion of the size. This nonuniformity is crucial for the emergence of self-conscious being. A self-conscious system might be created by humans from inorganic material in the near future, I expect. But the first self-conscious being could only have been created by nature, in some form of life, after taking a long time of evolution.

As Darwin saw, self-conscious beings could not emerge in a short time, in a violent habitat. Construction of a self-conscious life-form requires various types of ions, atoms, molecules, and most importantly, macromolecules. Self-conscious life is so complex that it cannot be built unless all the constituents are available. Even if they are available, the living structure must be able to function. All the structural components require proper operating conditions. Above all, the temperature must be proper to maintain the molecules, and must allow their diffusion transport. Diffusion transport of basic materials is an important requirement of life. Molecules and macromolecules can be built from silicon, but silicon-based chemistry may not be proper to build life, since the operating temperature may not be consistent with life. To support life, the media of material and energy transport, water, and an energy source of proper intensity must also be available.

On the earth, the early ancestors of self-conscious beings emerged about 550 million years ago, in the Cambrian period. Emergence of hominids was only 2 million years ago. Half a billion years were necessary to perfect a human-like self-conscious being from its prototype by evolution. From the present level of humans, further evolution of humanity will entail specialization, much like the evolution of great apes and elephants.

Our present universe is highly nonuniform, and this feature allows existence of life-sustaining habitat somewhere for some time. Habitats' almost complete physical isolation from each other ensures existence of a quasi-stable habitat for self-conscious beings, and allows their continued existence for some time in order to imprint their existence on the history. Isolation is absolutely necessary, since otherwise the habitat is easily destroyed. The recent geological discoveries show that our earth's habitat was almost destroyed several times in the last half billion years by meteorite collision. Sixty-five million years ago, a meteorite fell on the northern Yucatán Peninsula, Mexico, and caused worldwide extinction of life, including dinosaurs.

This is not an issue for paleontology alone. For those interested in Maya history like me, the microcracks created in the limestone of the northern Yucatan region by way of the impact have serious consequences. Such limestone weathers quickly. The stone monuments of the northern Maya state of Carakmul were so badly weathered and became so unreadable that the reconstruction of Maya history was seriously affected. Carakmul's snake dynasty was the dominant power in the Maya world until the end of the seventh century. We lost many historical records of the time of civil war in Maya history.

Since our universe contains rocks and ice, the habitats of self-conscious beings must be so far apart that collision is rare. Yet collisions do occur. Only for a short period in our universe's history have self-conscious beings, and they will continue to exist until the habitat becomes inhabitable. Mutual isolation of their habitats means that even if there are other self-conscious beings somewhere else, there is absolutely no chance that they will meet each other. From this reason, I entirely reject the stories of the ETs. Study of self-consciousness is relevant only to us, living on earth.

5.04   Subjective Time

I have examined the difference of the image of time among workers in different discipline, in sciences, technology, and the humanities. To physicists, time is a mathematically continuous parameter to describe the development of the system's instantaneous state. Time is continuous, down to the 10^{-43}-second range (Planck's time). Built on the continuous time concept down to this scale, the physical laws are independent from choice of time's origin, and this feature is closely tied with the basic law of conservation of energy. Physicists' time is continuous, whose origin can be set arbitrarily.

Although working on the same physical objects, the system scientist's concept of time is the step-by-step progression of a digital system's state with ticks of the systems clock. The system's state making a stepwise progression is a familiar to digital system engineers. Such a discrete sequence of events makes up our human daily life also, and the sense of the stepwise progression of time is felt when we are doing our daily chores. Objective time between the clock ticks carries no meaning, since an unfinished work is meaningless. The system's time is closely tied to the image of the events. The human brain is such a system. Yet this feature of time has never been appreciated outside the systems science community. This is because the system's state progression at every clock tick is regarded as an artificial creation for engineering purposes. Yet this is the key reason why the concept of time became confusing. Step-by-step progression of time creates the sense of time's forward flow more clearly to the human mind than a smooth continuous time flow (section 5.24).

Technically, this confusion originates from the fact that all the digital circuits are built using analog circuits. Analog circuits belong to the domain of physics. Many physical phenomena, such as heat conduction, diffusion, and nonlinear oscillation, can be modeled by analog equivalent circuit model (section 6.17). Yet if an analog circuit is used as a digital gate, it reveals the features of discrete step-by-step operational mode, and this creates the image of stepwise progression of time. Many unique features of digital circuits are summarized in my earlier book, *Dynamics of Digital Excitation* (Kluwer Academic, 1997). In order to break away from the traditional image of time, I show my digital equivalent circuit model of the quantum-mechanical world in chapter 6. This is especially timely, because there are some views raised from prominent physicists intending to explain the human self-consciousness by relying on quantum mechanics. From systems science's viewpoint, self-consciousness reveals many similarities to quantum phenomena, but this is because digital systems and quantum systems are functionally similar and of course, the human brain is a digital system.

The brain handles digital, or qualitative, information, the internal images. The feature of time that we consciously sense must be described as development process of the qualitative information, the images. This feature of time is called the *qualitative subjective time,* proper to the digital system's operation. The term *subjective* indicates that the time is comprehensible by the system. Here, *comprehensible* further means that the system is able to handle the time's image in the system's own way. A brain is such a digital system, and each image is placed in a slot of the objective time flow.

Any digital system, mechanical or biological, handles qualitative information. Here *qualitative* means, practically, that the information is comprehensible by the human mind. Within a tick of its clock, a PC executes a task that can be described by the common language, such as addition of two numbers. Such operation execution is an event of the PC. Display of and action by an internal image by the brain are such events. Then it is convenient to disregard the difference between mechanical and biological systems, since many features of the human sense of time become clear if I consider a digital system operation in general. A significant feature of any system's subjective time is that an objective time point carries no meaning, because it requires some objective time period to process or display any system-comprehensible image information.

Similarly, there is one more common feature between the human machine and a PC. If information processing takes more time, more energy is consumed. Then both brain and PC are able to sense the time length by measuring the spent energy. This is the system's *quantitative subjective time*, a companion of the qualitative subjective time. Putting time's image together, the concept of time is classified into objective time and subjective time, and subjective time is sensed as qualitative or quantitative subjective time. The former is sensed by a sequence of images of the events, and the latter is sensed by the spent energy. In the brain, this is the integrated sensation.

In section 1.18, I showed that the first approximation of sensation $X(t)$ is proportional to the rate of energy expenditure $v(t)$ by the simple linear relation $X(t) = r(t)v(t)$, where $r(t)$ is the factor of sensitivity of the mental activity creating the sensation. The sensitivity factor $r(t)$ is high if strong positive or negative emotion is associated with the time's image. For instance, waiting for a good news or for a doctor's diagnosis is the case when we feel long time.

This means that quantitative subjective time from integrated sensation and from bodily sense (directly related to the energy usage) are generally different, and the bodily subjective time sensed as fatigue is better correlated to the objective time. Referring back to section 1.18, the SELF's coordinate is the sum of the energy spent in the past.

Then the SELF places events as the mileposts of life in the qualitative subjective time flow, and the SELF tries to sense the objective time length, that is the quantitative subjective time, by sensing the spent energy by integrating the associated sensation.

By the human machine model, subjective time is sensed qualitatively by a step-by-step display of images in the brain and is sensed quantitatively by the body by integrated sensation or by bodily fatigue. The two characters of time, unidirectional progression and length, are separately sensed. Time's progression is sensed more clearly by the sequential display of images. The time length is sensed by vague bodily sense, which cannot be indicated by a number. Here is the difference between the body's sensing of time and a PC's sensing of time. A PC's quantitative subjective time can be measured simply by connecting a cumulative wattmeter, but integration of sensation $X(t)$ is not a simple task for the brain. There is no simple mechanism of sensation integration in the brain to create the sense of quantitative subjective time. Yet the brain needs a sense of time length in some cases. Then the brain gets that information by various ways other than integrating sensation. Because of this, the brain senses time, most of the time, qualitatively. Since there are such complications, time's image is mysterious and confusing.

5.05   Past, Present, and Future of Subjective Time

Objective time is a numerical parameter having any conveniently set time point as the origin. Objective time increases continuously into the future. Selection of its origin does not affect the laws of physics, in the same way as selection of the origin of space does not. Human sense of subjective time is different. It is referred to the present, and there was the past and there will be the future. So I take time's reference point at the present and try to see the nature of the subjective time.

The three phases, past, present, and future, of subjective time have qualitatively different natures, so it is not proper to consider them together. First, the past and the future are both sensed at the present.

Only the present is the period of activity carrying the sense of the three phases of time. The past is a set of images that have been experienced and were stored securely in the memory. The memory's security matters as I show later in section 5.29. Recalling the memory of a past experience and displaying the event's images in the present creates the sense of the past subjective time, by virtually placing the SELF there. As for the future, the expected future images are created by the activities of the present, mostly using the existing images of the past experiences and of their modification by the imagination. This image-production process creates the sense of future. Past images show an existed event. Future images are mental fabrications of the imagination, yet past and future events are both images. Past images have a definite spatial location and time, but the future images are free from space and time. Only the present carries the capability of creating, sensing, and reexperiencing the images of the three phases and executing action. The present is a dynamic period for the brain. As much as the substance of the past and the future is image and not action, it is static.

To consider the triplet phase of subjective time is to set the time reference at the present, when the past and the future meet. Since the present, when the self-conscious brain exercises the event's image, is a dynamic period of activity, its duration cannot be zero on the objective time scale. The present covers the objective time period when the images of all three phases are exercised. The period continues until all the presently experienced events end and are memorized. Such a *present* must be singled out, and attention must be focused on its character. The dynamics of such a present reveal many features that are quite remarkable, defying naive expectation. For instance, since *present* has a time duration, it is not an *objective time point*. Such a present was called a "specious present" by William James.

Self-conscious human life is a never-ending sequence of the specious present and the selfless states such as the deep sleep state or indifferent state. An image of a future is created by the brain in a specious present, and this process is sensed as the future. The later recall of the image may make it past, present, or still future. Then the reality of the event's images in life matters in setting the sense of time.

Suppose that the reality of the image that we experience can be quantified by probability. That is, the image of an event ensured to be real carries a probability of 1. All the images experienced in the recent past and at the specious present have a probability of 1. Based on the present image information, I am able to predict my own internal state in a short time to come. The present internal image activity continues, and I am sure how I feel and what I will be thinking for a few minutes, maybe up to five minutes later. During that time, the state of the world is also predictable. The pair of predictabilities emerges from the inertia of the self-conscious state and the inertia of the habitat. The state of our physical world changes more slowly than the state of my image world. The reality of the engaged images versus objective time is shown schematically in figure 5.05.1.

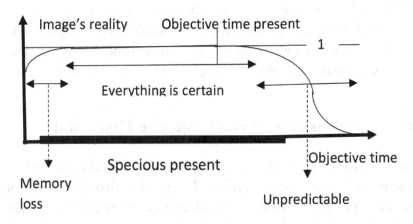

Figure 5.05.1 Structure of the specious present

I showed in section 1.18 that the SELF's dynamics are described by an equation similar to the equation of motion of a particle, and the equation includes an inertial term. The inertia is the measure of the volume and complexity of the images engaged by the SELF, and the images keep the SELF in the current internal state, at least into the short time to come. Beyond the limit, the state of the future becomes uncertain, and many different possibilities emerge. The boundary between the predictable and the unpredictable future internal state in modern life for an average person can be in the range of three to five minutes, I think. Beyond that limit, the future is unpredictable. This future time length depends on the brain's future forecasting capability, and therefore that depends on the person's character. The state of the outside world changes more slowly than our internal world, so maybe up to half hour or so later can be predictable.

The human mind is able to retain an accurate memory of past events for some time. Yet, gradually, the details of the memory are lost, and the event's image is blurred. Loss of memory begins after half an hour or so, depending on the person and on the state of mind. The rate of memory loss is less than the rate of decrease in future predictability, but the memory is eventually lost to a significant degree. The reality of the event in the specious present is schematically shown in figure 5.05.1. Thus, the specious present may extend at most five minutes into the future and half an hour into the past from the present. In the specious present, it is possible that many images will be displayed, fabricated, and acted out—and the present itself is not a short time. The SELF does not sense the passing of objective time within a single specious present.

5.06 Specious Present and Subjective Time Point

The period of time when we sense images that characterize the three time phases is the specious present. Images that characterize any of the three time phases are events. Each event consists of the actor, the action, and its circumstances. An event may include more than one subevents as its component, arranged in order. In the specious present, I have new experience, create a future event from my image inventory by imagination, or recall a past event. The specious present is a dynamic period of image sensing, creation, and action. Since an event is an integrated image, it takes an objective time length to experience it, assemble it, and memorize it. In real life, most events are over in a day. During that time, the event's image memory is formed. When the image is later displayed and the event is reexperienced, it takes a much shorter objective time, but it creates the subjective sense of its experienced time length.

Figure 5.06.1 shows the internal image structure of an event of a specious present in the flow of subjective and objective time. From an experience, the brain acquires a set of images of subevents in sequence that show development within the single specious present. An event has its internal order of subevents. In the specious present, images from all the subevents are correlated with the image inventory to establish their meanings. From this information base, the internal (psychological) and the external (habitat) states of the immediate future become predictable. I am sure of what I will be thinking a few minutes later, and also I know what will happen in the world. This immediate future is a short time, during which everything, including my own mind, develops as I expected (section 5.05). While such activity is in progress, what is experienced is integrated into the event characterizing the specious present.

My brain remembers the event of the recent past securely. So what I sense as the present extends to the *past* and to the *future* of objective time as shown in figure 5.05.1. At the specious present, some external action may be taken. To execute an external action, the command image must be sent out from the brain to the outside world. Then the expected response comes back through the sensor and input channel, and the signal path closes loop with the internal image circuit. The outside world and the internal world are joined in the single specious present. The closed loop reverberates, and the repeated image display extends the objective time length of the specious present. The set of images from the inside and the outside making up the specious present is displayed repeatedly to establish their meanings, and they are integrated into a single event.

The emergence of the same image many times has the effect of mixing and pulling all the images together to a single subjective time point that has a nonzero objective time length. Finally, all the images are sensed as an integrated unit, and the *sense of the time flow* within the event vanishes, yet the image set's internal order is kept to make the image to be sensed rational, as shown in figure 5.06.1. Here, *rational* means that the cause-effect relationships of the subevents are properly represented within the event. Their time sequence is transferred to the images' spatial order. The images that originally belonged to the spread-out objective time range are squeezed into a single subjective time point, which has an internal structure. The order of images is converted from the time sequence to the spatial order. This means, metaphorically, as follows: I was looking at the buildings of Fifth Avenue in New York City from a car's window, and then I was seeing the same area while standing on the street level. This is called spatialization of the time sequence of the images. Later, when the event is reexperienced, the spatialized event's image is serialized to sense the time of the event.

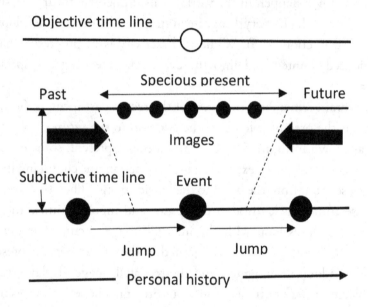

Figure 5.06.1 Time-compressed specious present

The top line of figure 5.06.1 shows the objective time line and objective time point, and the bottom line shows the subjective time line and subjective time points. The subjective time point's internal structure is shown by the middle line. Between two consecutive subjective time points, there is no event, as I discuss in section 5.24. Actually, between any two consecutive subjective time points, some events must have taken place, but the brain's memory management operation eliminated them (section 4.09). By sequencing the subjective time points, each of which carries its own spatialized subevent's image structure inside, a structure carrying personal history is built as shown in figure 5.06.1. By casually exciting the sequence, a sense of subjective time progression emerges since jumping from a single such spatialized image to the next one creates the sense of step-by-step progression of time. From each spatialized event, only its theme image emerges clearly to identify the event. The rest of the images of the event are sensed only vaguely.

The specious present is also an active time of imagination when the images of the future are created. While building up the imaginary event's image, the SELF experiences the sense of the future. At the specious present, the SELF experiences all three time phases. Time is the present, but the time's sense covers all three phases of time. All three phases are sensed at the only accessible phase, the specious present. Given this fact, the specious present is not a *present* at all. This observation shows that the three time phases, past, present, and future, are a psychologically mixed up concept. Some other categorization should be set up.

5.07 Inflated Specious Present

At any moment of my life, I am aware what I was doing in the immediate past. Usually I am not doing very much. Yet if someone asks, "What are you doing?" I feel as if I have a long story to tell. From where do so many images emerge suddenly? This question is asked to myself, and I search my own mind by introspection. Then the flood of images that emerge are all well-established images, and by casual access, many of them come out because the question is nonspecific. The poorly defined question pulls them all out. This is like picking up a hair from a pack of cotton and pulling it out while twisting. Those images are hidden behind only a few truly current theme images, and they come out one after the other. An image is connected to many associated images to create its meaning. The current theme image pulls many of such connected images out. As these images come out, the SELF stays in a single specious present, which is built from the long-connected structures of the associated images, and this present lasts for a long time.

This is a special mode of the specious present. Often, a single specious present lasts over an hour. Such a specious present does not carry much new information. Since women, such as my wife, are smoother than men when it comes to human relationships, I gain many ideas about this specious present's structure from her telephone conversations with foreign friends. Usually, the caller is trying to find out what is new with my wife. As I snoop around and eavesdrop on these discussions, I find that indeed the conversation does not carry much new information. Yet any image brings out so many related images, and they build up a long specious present. Since several theme images emerge in the meantime, the social phone call extends over one hour, thereby helping the telephone company's business. Such a long conversation is quite useful for language training. If women talk in a language that I do not know, the most frequently emerging phrase is almost always the English equivalent of "Is that so?" This phrase is a very effective catalyzer to pull out many more images from the image inventory of both callers, and that extends their conversation.

Is this an abnormal mode of operation of the human machine? No. This much is obvious if I compare this operation with the *core dump* instruction to a data processor. This most *unspecific instruction* sends out everything in the processor, including the operating system. A phone call to my wife from her close friend is the activation of the core dump instruction, and such operation has a positive psychological effect on social individuals.

No sense of elapsed time occurs in any such *inflated* specious present. Although the volume of images is huge, the relevance of the images to life is minimal and the sensation is weak. In such a state, the mechanism of integrating sensation to elapsed time is not executed. That is why some young mothers will terminate a phone conversation only when their babies begin crying for attention.

Yet another interesting mode of the specious present is that a specious present can be assembled from many segments, each of which belongs to a different time, but all of them are integrated by a single theme image. The SELF is engaged with the single theme image at many different times, and any one of these specious presents begins from the sum total of all the previous specious presents. Although separated timewise, the whole sequence makes a single, inflated specious present. We execute any group work project by meetings that make such a specious present. Every time the work team gets together, the single specious present reemerges and enriches itself. My book writing is executed also by a single inflated specious present. This is equivalent to the orderly interruption of a time-shared data processor. Most of the time, an interrupted brain throws away the currently processing data (section 5.21), but in a few exceptional cases, the brain prepares for the future continuation of interrupted processing.

5.08   Classification of Specious Present Activities

Dynamic operations executed in the specious present can be classified into several types, each of which has its own character, impact on the life, type of images, and the location in the brain circuit's activity. I classify them by the type of the brain's operation as follows:

(1) **Formation of new image memory by experiencing a new event.** Every time I buy a new PC, I have to go through this excruciating process. When we observe a new object and its action, the images are taken in, and memories are formed. The object's image is stored as a static image, and the action's image is stored as a sequence of instructions to modify the static image by using the basic instructions such as moving, rotating, or scaling, or a combination thereof. Most of our familiar objects and their functions are learned by this process.

(2) **Recall of the existing event's image.** In the isolated state of the brain from the outside, an existing image in the memory is excited and displayed. Along with image display, the connection among the images may be altered, or the image structure may

be modified to meet the need of the present SELF. For instance, preference of an image such as like or dislike may be changed. Some action to the outside world may also be taken. Evaluation of the state of present life is executed by this process.

(3) **Planning of a complex action.** This is to set up a sequence of images to accomplish a definite objective. A product development plan is to create the image of the final model and the images of each of the steps of the production process. These images are internally exercised to determine the cost, development time, and so on. How to repair a broken object is planned in this state. This is usually executed in the inflated specious present discussed in the previous section.

(4) **Thinking.** This is to find a plausible explanation for an incomprehensible image or event. This is an extensive search operation of all the image inventory in the brain, and setup of a new image's relation that brings the mysterious image into proper perspective. Learning how to use new application software is executed in this state.

(5) **Large-scale change of an image-connection structure.** The existing connection of the images in the brain's memory system maintains the character of the person, which is controlled by the value system he or she has been building up. This is a change of the value system, occurring only a few times in life, and becomes the milestone of personal growth. Although this is a huge structural change, it occurs in a single, extended specious present.

I experienced this in October 1959, when I realized that my future was not in my native country, Japan. I had been feeling that my life was more and more marginalized in my native country and in my family. I felt like "Prometheus unbound" on that special cloudy afternoon, while watching the foliage. That was the special day when I set my mind to live in a foreign country. This was a long, and the most significant, specious present in my life.

(6) **Disconnection of certain images or elimination of the connection to certain images.** Some images become irrelevant, like an old address or a disconnected phone number. This is not a complete operation. Disconnected images may not vanish entirely. Many of them remain with out-of-date indication, or in the subconscious, and then become the subject of psychoanalysis. I believe that disconnection is the natural operation of an inactive brain and not the intentional suppression of connection as psychoanalysis holds. Many negative, unpleasant images refuse to be erased from the memory, and they torture the SELF all throughout life. Images of shameful incidents are of this kind.

5.09 What Is History?

Labeled by the theme image, the past specious present is memorized and is sensed later as a time-compressed and spatialized image. Such a memorized specious present's image becomes an element of one's personal history. A sequence of such images displayed in a single specious present is the personal history. If such a sequence is shared by all the members of a society, a nation, or the world, the sequence becomes social, national, or world history, respectively. Given this fact, history has a hierarchical structure, and personal history is at the base.

An event of personal history is retained in memory semi-permanently, if the event's manage makes its identifier. An event's experience becomes an historical record, only if it leaves a strong impression on the SELF. In the image structure of the history, the events' identifiers are sequentially connected. An event's identifier is often the theme image, or the name. An event's name is created in the part of the association area where the language channel makes the word's identifiers. Since this locality of the association area is not spatially close to the area where the vision channel makes the event's identifiers, the connection between the visible image and its name is weak. In old age, this connection suffers from neuron death. Names of events or visible objects in the events are often lost to the memory in old age, but the event's visual images are retained securely. Personal history keeps visual images but often loses the names of the individuals included in it. Visual images are quite tightly connected among themselves, but connection to its name is weak, and vulnerable to neuron death.

Sequentially connected events' images are the carrier of personal history. Since the event's identifier connection can be flexible, the sequence may depend on the state of the SELF at the time of sequence buildup, or its later reevaluation. At the time of its reevaluation, the event's order may even be changed. It is human nature to alter the sequence to fit the needs of the current SELF. Frequently, by dropping or adding events, or by finagling the order of events, blame can be placed on someone else to satisfy the present SELF's ego. How does such finagling occur? Following are some examples:

During World War II, the Japanese military headquarters issued news; they reported almost entirely fabricated events. A recent case of such event fabrication is the prehistory (before 1945) of the founder of the present North Korean dynasty. There is no evidence that the North Korean Labor Party held an active position within the North Korea in the White Head Mountain area (North Korea-Chinese border) in the 1930s. Yet they made the area as the holy origin of the regime, and their people seem to believe that.

From listening to U.S. news, I sense that the newscasters never seem to report any fabricated news. That is very great. Yet they never report certain key events or information. Unfortunately, this may create a similar effect. For most Americans, the Middle East's historical development since the 1980s appears a mystery. Why do they resist that much to the Western powers? Few, if any, Americans know who Mosaddegh was. If this name is withheld, the development in the Middle East since the 1980s is not comprehensible. I wonder why the name memorized by a Japanese teenager (me) is unknown to U.S. adults.

History always has this type of feature. Even the history of the nineteenth century suffers from this problem. The victor at Waterloo was not Wellington but Blücher and Gneisenau (section 4.36). How many Americans know their names? Every time I read Edward Gibbon's *Decline and Fall of the Roman Empire*, I feel that the history was properly written, because the end of the Roman Empire is AD 1453. Roman history was largely irrelevant to the author at the time of the British overseas empire. The only personal history written by an author that I truly admire for its objectivity is Julius Caesar's *Commentari de bello de Gallico*. To write a great personal history is so difficult that it required a strong character like Julius Caesar. As these observations show, which event in the time sequence is kept, and in what order, is mostly determined by the value system of the historian. History represents facts, along with the character of the historian.

An autobiography is a history written by a contemporary by its nature (the author describes his or her own acts). It is hard to write one objectively. Because of the difficulty, it is easy to get out of control. Some autobiographies are worth reading because they can help us to avoid making the same mistakes the author made. Adolf Hitler's *Mein Kampf* is a good example of this type of autobiography. Reading history is, along with the historical facts, reading about the character of the historian or the author.

5.10   Image Structure of Subjective Time

An event in a person's life is experienced not only at the time of its happening, but also when the event's image is recalled later. If an archetypal image is acquired, it has the effect of altering an entire value system by reorganizing the basic images. Then the meanings of many events and their connections are altered. Why does such reorganization occur? Because the meaning of an event's image may not always make the self-conscious subject SELF comfortable. *Comfortable* means that the SELF is able to send the image out smoothly without conflict. Conflict in an image's meaning creates emotional problems when they are sent out, and makes the SELF hesitant to take action. The SELF's value system is defined by the images loaded with emotions, to which the SELF is closely connected *at present* and which are excited with the SELF. If this connected structure changes, the SELF's relationship to the rest of the images changes, including the relationship to many neutral images. In an extreme case, even the causal order of the events may be altered to meet the need of the SELF. If you read the history of Stalin's *purge* in the 1930s, you find that the order of many brutal events was reversed in the version issued by the Soviet government. This was done to blame someone else and to claim the dictator's innocence. Yet small-scale image order alteration occurs in every type of image processing when the image of an event of personal history is created. This is because life's events develop like a multidimensional web, and not like a single straight line, as the material of the personal story.

A human person's image has an affinity to other images in the process of the event image's construction. All the images related to a close friend with whom I worked and then parted ways, and later reestablished contact, are likely to be integrated together by the person's image. Then images of the person or the related events at two different times are felt as if the time difference is irrelevant, and all the images are sensed as simultaneous. If I talk about my graduate professor, it is more natural and meaningful to me to explain how he influenced me all through my life (section 4.36). Other events that happened during those years, some of which altered my life fundamentally, become irrelevant and are marginalized. The theme image, the professor, emerges again and again in the event's image display, and the brain's image flow makes a vortex. Vortex image flow accumulates many related images, and the image's volume grows, and their time span is compressed.

If an image sequence, including a person, or any other key image is displayed repeatedly, the images at different times are psychologically pulled together by the theme image. Many images gather together and create a realistic theme image by pulling all the associated images to a single subjective time point. In this process, the sense of the subjective time of the images moves forward, backward, and forward repeatedly, and all the images are pulled together toward a narrower and narrower subjective time span, centered at the time on when the theme image made the most significant impact. Finally, all the images are sensed at the same time. When the event reaches this final state, the sense of the internal time flow of the event's images ceases. This is spatialization of the event's image assembled from the component images that are spread out over time. An event united by the theme image becomes a single, integrated whole. Many such images are made and remade in the course of a personal life. A sequential set of such an event's images carries a higher level of meaning than each image; this is the image creating the sense of qualitative subjective time, that is, the personal history. The sense of time is created by the structure built by the event's images.

An image of such events' sequence recalled in a single specious present is the personal history. Event images are arranged vertically in the two-dimensional array of figure 5.10.1. Each event's image content extends horizontally, and the theme image is at the head of the horizontal array. The horizontal arrays are connected vertically, from one theme image to the next theme image, approximately in the order of the time of the theme image. Since element images making up each event spread out over a time period, the brain rearranges all the element images making up an event in chronological order so that the theme images appear most rational and meaningful. That is, within an event, the order of time is properly kept by the spatial order, but between a pair of events, the event's time may overlap or even reverse. This is inevitable in historical description.

Each event's images constructed in this way are arranged into the proper time sequence of the theme image. The theme image's time is set to when the image made the most significant impact on the present life. This complex, mixed up chronological order is inevitable in narrative history. History is a multidimensional image web that must be narrated by sequential language statements, which has only a one-dimensional structure (section 4.27).

If the two-dimensional historical event array of figure 5.10.1 is excited casually from the top to the bottom, the excitation jumps from one theme image to the next theme image. The images associated with each theme image are marginalized by this mode of excitation. The excitation does not significantly spread out sidewise.

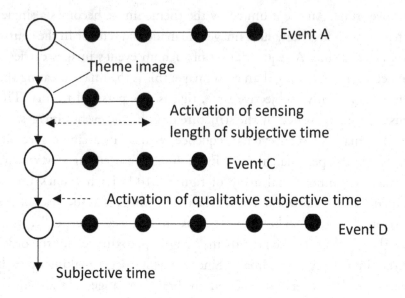

Figure 5.10.1 Structure of subjective time

Yet if the excitation is kept to remain within a single event, that is, within a single horizontal image line, the excitation spreads out sidewise and all the images of the event are excited. This is to bring back a single past event's experience to the current specious present. Since the event is internally exercised, the sense of the time length of the event, that is, the sense of quantitative subjective time, emerges as the compressed event's time expands. This is always a conscious experience of sensing the past event's time.

From the mechanism of building the event image's structure of figure 5.10.1, the time sequence of the images within an event is kept as they are, but not from one event to the other event. If the reverse order of the vertical array is obviously unnatural, our human brain makes an alternative sequence like that of figure 5.10.1 and uses the most realistic sequence for reviewing the personal history. Either way, any personal history is made and remade many times to conform to the present SELF.

The structure of the personal history organization method shown in figure 5.10.1 reflects the thinking pattern of the person. If the horizontal line is long and the vertical sequence is short, the person tends to handle images as simultaneous, mutually interacting structures. This reflects the encyclopedist type, an extroverted character. Biographies of popular musicians are written in this style. A writer of this type of story has a wide range of knowledge of the talent but pays little attention to the cause-effect relationship of his or her success, such as birth and education. If the horizontal lines are short and the vertical sequence is long, the person is an introverted scientist or philosopher-type character who pays more attention to the causal development of history. Historians are in between the two types. Herodotus was more the vertical type, I think, and Shiba Sen was more the horizontal type, who created a unique style of writing Chinese history (several parallel lines to describe the history of a single dynasty). His style was kept for two thousand years in China, from his time. The difference in the styles of the fathers of history in the East and the West is really fascinating.

5.11 Alternative Image Structures of Subjective Time

There are alternatives to the linear connection among events to build historical sequence. If more than one linear event sequence is arranged in parallel, then multiple alternative histories emerge. Historians and archaeologists usually believe that the development of their area of specialty is independent and unique. Most of archaeologists don't like *diffusionists*. Interestingly, mythologists are almost always diffusionists since myths carry many common themes and features in all the areas of the world. Native Americans of the Pipe Spring site in Minnesota carry a myth quite similar to that of Noah's ark. I see a few definite Far East cultural influences in the Maya mythology, but few Maya historians accept my view.

Figure 5.11.1(a) shows my view of world history until the fourteenth century. World history consists of the three parallel lines, of the more or less integrated Old World and moderately interacting two New World centers. Here, the lines connecting closed squares indicate significant cultural interactions among the three areas of the world. The first was the migration of the ancient Asians to the New World, carrying peculiar worldviews such as seeing a rabbit in the full moon and assigning colors to the four cardinal directions and the center (section 1.27). The next was the exchange of superior species of cultivated plants such as corn between Mesoamerica and South America. The next was the migration of the Inuit to the arctic of the New World about AD 400, the one after that was the cultural exchange between the Moche and the Maya in the New World, the next was the Vikings' visit to the eastern coast of North America, and the last was the arrival and return of Polynesians to South America in the thirteenth century. As for the Moche-Maya cultural contact, I presented my unique evidence in section 4.41. Since the oldest urban civilization of all three world areas began about 3,000 BC, the three equal-length lines are justified.

In a unidirectional event sequence, both the beginning and the end are open. This linear historical line is proper for describing a single culture's historical development objectively, but history is often created by imagination, in the past or in the future (Eden or utopia, respectively). The ancient people also imagined cyclic history. If the beginning and end of a linear history are connected, then a directed loop such as in figure 5.11.1(b) emerges. Daily life repeats this pattern, although we are not consciously aware of this. This is a peculiar yet fascinating model of subjective time. As the events circle the loop, the sense of subjective time moves always forward, but there remains a faint echo from the past cycle that was philosophized by the Hindus and Buddhists.

As time cycles, the cause-effect relationship continues beyond a single cycle, and karma controls human life: the present human fate is the effect of the past cycle. This concept was often used to justify social injustice in Asian society, but it also had a deep psychological effect in that it suppressed the excess ego of the rulers. The recurrent time image was common in the ancient world, in pre-Christian Greece, in Buddhist cultural zones of Asia, and in Mesoamerica. These linear, parallel, and cyclic images of time are the three alternatives of the qualitative subjective time subscribed to by humans for millennia. Images of time are cultural products from ancient times. Dominance of linear subjective time is the product of the modern mercantile-capitalist society of the West, where "Time is money" has become the moral code. Yet its older background is rooted in the monotheism, whose origin is the Semitic mercantile society of the Middle East. Asia and New World agricultural societies adopted the cyclic image of time.

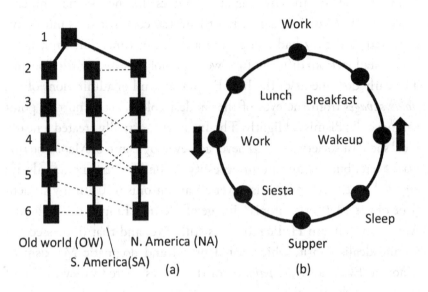

1-NA-SA: Migration of Amurians, 3SW-4NA and 3NA-4SA: Exchange of superior cultivated plants, 4SA-5NA and 4NA-5SA: Maya and Moche cultural exchange, 4OW-5NA: Migration of Inuit, 5OW-6NA: Viking's visit to north America, and 6OW-6SA: Visit and return of Polynesians to south America

Figure 5.11.1 Image of subjective time

The three alternative images of time are now relevant even in basic physics. Some imaginative string theorists claim that there are ten to eleven space-time dimensions, six or seven of which are curled up in size of the order of 10^{-33} cm. A few theorists speculate that some of the extra dimensions could be time.[2] Recent cosmology theory revived the cyclic time image. As there is no way to check the validity of these theories by experiment or observation, they may remain as fantasy invading the field of physics.[3] Yet the modern physicist's images have ancient

---

[2] B. Green, *The Elegant Universe* (W. W. Norton, 2003).
[3] P. Coveney and R. Highfield, *The Arrow of Time* (Fawcett-Columbine, 1990).

roots, and this is the reason why those images of time are not rejected as fantasy right away.

Yet for me, who spent some time as an historian and a mythologist, I can imagine how the last king of the Aztecs and the last Inca emperor felt when they saw Spaniards. For them, the conquistadors must have appeared as if they had come from a different time. The rampaging conquistadors from different time were not holy or even civilized people. The early documents of the Inca Empire are full of admirations of the *noble savages* from the eyes of the modest colonialists, and this point can never be dismissed lightly. The Incas' rule actually created a nearly ideal socialist society that was never achieved by Lenin or Mao. The rule was severe, but the minimum necessity of life for everyone was always ensured by the ruler. This is never an anachronism. Until my student time of the 1950s, the utopian image of the Inca Empire drawn by the American William H. Prescott was still alive, and that impressed my young idealist spirit, which hated brutal and dogmatic Marxism or Maoism. Even now, the *paisanos* of the Andes' sacred valley dream of the time of the Incas' rule.

The image of time reflects the human desire to keep historical records. The Chinese adopted linear time progression. The line of Chinese rulers can be traced back to 1300 BC. Hindus generally adopted the cyclic repetitive time. Because of that, even the lifetime of Gautama Buddha is not certain, although his historical existence has been firmly confirmed.

Let us digress here and review the meanings created by the image's connected structures. The element of qualitative subjective time, an event, is an integration of the actor and the action, and the event's array creates the sense of subjective time. Images assembled in the cause-effect chain represent a theory of science, philosophy, or history. Images assembled in hierarchy indicate a command structure or historical development prediction in various aspects of society. Finally, a totally unorganized set of images creates a sense of disorder, chance, or probability. Image structures carry as much meaning as individual images do.

5.12 Human Sense of Time Length

Sensing time length is not as natural as sensing the size of an object. An object's size is sensed by placing my body on its side. I can do this any time. But the human body provides only one time reference, the heartbeat, yet counting heartbeats is tedious. Humans prefer not to sense time length by themselves. The human brain and body have no stopwatch. This problem is not limited to biological systems. Measurement of time length requires technical knowhows.

There are two reasons why the body clock, capable of measuring time length, has never been developed by evolution. The first reason is that there was not much advantage to knowing time length for any animal except humans. In conditional reflex, once the cause is recognized, the animals are kept in an alert state, ready to expect the effect. Since the animal is prepared and is waiting, the time length is irrelevant. Time length matters to in life only if the brain is unable to focus on the expected event continuously. This is not a strong reason for evolution to create the body's stopwatch.

The second, technical reason why the body does not have built-in stopwatch is common to both living and mechanical systems: the difficulty involved in making such a gadget. There are two types of clocks as I discussed in section 5.02. As for the clocks counting the number of periodic oscillations, the counting and retaining of numbers is a capability developed only in the Neolithic period by modern humans. Practically, counting up to several thousands of heartbeats is required, and attention must be constantly focused to do so. The difficulty of making a reliable analog memory is the reason why the dissipative clock was not made either. The human body has only one reasonably reliable dissipative clock, that is, the body carrying its available free energy, which is sensed by fatigue. Historically, humans used sand and water clocks. Although these clocks were structurally simple, both clocks required technical know-hows. A sand clock requires precise adjustment of the orifice so that it does not clog, and a water clock requires precise control of the pressure of the water supply.

Quantitative subjective time is sensed by the brain only by consciously engaging the event in a single continuous specious present. The human brain is still able to sense time since sensation is the rate of the brain's energy consumption. If sensation is integrated, energy used in the integration period is determined, and this is proportional to the elapsed time. Humans cannot focus attention or remain consciously engaged long enough to execute this integration if the time required is longer than a few minutes. Because of this difficulty, we sense how fast or how slow time flows by sensing sensation, while measuring objective time length by some other means. This difficulty is shared by any flow measurements. The flow rate of a river can be measured much easier than the total flow over a period. That is why evolutionary development has failed to create innate sense of time length.

Evolutionary development created a unique method of sensing time length: the memory of correlating the event's development within the time frame of one day. During the development of the event, how much the state of nature or the habitat changed is memorized along with the event itself. The indicator of the time length is the movement of the sun, its shadow, the color of the sky, and moving clouds, and if it is nighttime, the movement of the moon and stars. Length of time is sensed by such natural clues, and we still use this method, if necessary. Most of the events of a human life are over in a fraction of a day. A long event takes only a full day, and a short event is memorized without even recognizing the habitat's change. Such a memory is an easy way to gain the sense of time length. We still live the same life as our Paleolithic and Neolithic ancestors did, if we do not wear a wristwatch. This observation provides the answer to an interesting question: Why was astronomy and the associated mathematics the first natural science that emerged everywhere in the ancient world? The reason is, humans could not sense time length.

Development of most events in life is related to the memory of the time of day and the change of the state of the habitat during the event. The SELF avoids spending energy and attention to sense time length. As a consequence of this choice, the sense of time length of most past events is tenuous, and the development of the event is sensed by the memory of the ordered sequence of the event's spatialized image. As for the planned or expected future event, the time length estimate becomes a burden to the SELF if sensation integration of the imagined work is to be executed. Then this task is carried out by referring to the memory of the past experience. If we hire a contractor, he or she sends the boss or an experienced fellow who can estimate the time needed for the work judging from his or her past experience.

Modern human life has made the need of sensing time length irrelevant. Clocks and watches are now available everywhere, especially after the development of microelectronics and energy-efficient liquid crystal display. The latter development was only as recent as 1968. Human life has not yet naturalized to follow the directive of the clock. Clocks and wristwatches enslave us. I often deplore that the little timekeeping machines are far more dictatorial than Hitler or Stalin. Only those who can defeat the tyrant are women who skillfully procrastinate and undermine the clock's dictatorial command! They should be proud of that!

Yet the sense of time length is still required to estimate the as yet unexperienced workload. We are often overwhelmed by the huge number of repetitive tasks we must perform, and that is the reason why a sense of time length is still required. From my experience, there is an optimum way to split a task into smaller units. If I must do N repetitive tasks, where N is a very large number, I divide the task into $\sqrt{N}$ units, each of which requires $\sqrt{N}$ repetitive tasks. The time to execute $\sqrt{N}$ tasks is easier to estimate. If the time to execute these tasks is τ, the entire time required, T is given by $T = \tau\sqrt{N}$. If I must replace nine hundred roof shingles, I divide the task into thirty units of thirty tasks each. From my experience, this is the most accurate way to estimate the time needed to finish the task.

5.13 Sense of Past Quantitative Subjective Time

A quantitative sense of the subjective time of a past event emerges when the event's image is displayed along with the associated sensation, when one reexperiences the past event. Since the event is remembered, most of the time, with reference to the approximate time of the day, real length of the time is derived from memory. The sense of the time is then determined by whether the event is now sensed as longer or shorter than the real objective time.

On the morning of August 15, 1945, there was a radio announcement saying that there would be an important news at noon. I was ten years old at the time, yet I knew what the announcement would be. The neighbors were talking about it; they said the war had now reached the Japanese islands. I disagreed, but I said nothing. Several families got together at a neighbor's house, who had a better radio. I heard the emperor's voice. I still remember his message, "Tolerate the intolerable," as if I'd heard it just yesterday. Everyone appeared lost, but an old man sitting across from me kept his composure.

I went outside. There was no one on the street. The clouded afternoon was calm but in confusion. In the evening, there was a neighborhood meeting. The chairman's words, "Tonight, we need not close the window shutters," gave me the real feeling of the end of the war. The chairman introduced the old man and said, "Tonight, instead of listening to me, you hear words of wisdom."

The old man, sitting straight like a Buddha statue, started calmly. "You are shocked by today's news. In a time like this, we need to know what we should do. We must defend our emperor at whatever the cost. Without him, we are not Japanese anymore. We must suppress the destructive enemies, the communists, and then we must rebuild the decimated nation."

Then someone asked, "Would Americans do something to our emperor?" The old man confidently answered, "No. Americans already know, if they did that, a lot of their soldiers would not make it back home alive. Americans cannot afford to do that."

Everyone, including me, breathed a sigh of relief. The next morning, I saw the old man cleaning up debris on the street. Several boys, including me, helped him. Then he said, "It is fine. You boys go back home to study, to make our nation great once again." A traumatic twenty-four hours passed so smoothly and calmly, just like any other day during peacetime.

Seventy years since then, when I remember that day, I feel a strange sense of a calm day but a very long day. As I remember the day, the event's images occupy my mind, and for a long time I dwell on the images and I have no room to think of anything else. This tightly focused mind is the real mechanism of sensing the subjective time length of any past event. The most serious event that I ever experienced went on as calm as it could possibly be, and then everyone got the direction to continue on with their lives. The force that maintains the event's image in my mind comes from the value of the event's image. The sense of the event's time length emerges from its value. This was the day when I really got an independent mind as a human, as my teacher told me (see the story in the next section). I felt that we had a really great emperor, that those communists who had tried to remove him were my deadliest enemies, and that my future was in the natural sciences so I could contribute my share of duty to the emperor. As I remember the old sage, his image is still so vividly clear, and I feel deep respect for him. Later, I learned that he lived well into his nineties and was therefore able to see that everything he had told us confidently would come to pass on that day actually came to pass. He died several years before I moved to the U.S.

Now why is this day, when I was only ten years old, remembered as such a long day? When I remember the day, I feel a deep emotion, and the sensation is intense. Then I am unable to disengage from the image for a long time. During that time, my sensation is properly integrated in my focused brain, to emerge as the sense of a long time. Integration is the key mechanism of sensing the past event's time length. Integration is executed in the deep area by the circuit that sets the analog time length. The integrator neurons' activity level increases as the state of high-level sensation continues undisrupted. This is the innate time-sensing mechanism of humans. For this process to work, focusing attention for a long time is required. It is the value of the image that forces me to focus attention on the event's image and to integrate the strong sensation to create the sense of long time.

Why do so many old people feel that their middle age went by so fast? In the competitive capitalist society, there are only a few successes, and the rest are all failures. That happens in middle age. When we look back, there are only a few bright spots we remember from our middle age, and the rest are all dark. The long period has no valuable images to offer. The memory of one's middle-age events carries poor images associated with a weak sensation. When we remember our middle age, the brain cannot focus on any valuable image, and the defocused brain cannot execute integration of the weak sensation. So the time is sensed as short. Then, as the time length is compared with the calendar dates, it appears as if our middle age has gone by very quickly.

When I've seen spectacular ancient pagan ritual centers like El Mirador, Tiahuanaco, and Easter Island, I've wondered if the people who built the centers were really slaves driven by merciless rulers, as historians assert. I rather feel that those people voluntarily contributed to building the edifice for eternity, and in their old age, they were much more satisfied than we are now. I once read an article stating that the Nazca lines of South America were built to give the people a worthwhile objective in life. If this was so, then their society was much healthier than our present society. It is we who spend our middle age in a nonsensical competition for survival and feel miserable when our old age comes.

5.14   Sense of Past Quantitative Subjective Time 2

The quantitative subjective time of a past event is sensed by integrating sensation when I reexperience the event's image. Whether integration can be carried out or not depends on the value of the engaged image and if the sensing subject SELF is ready to accept the value. The past memory of the event is recalled again and again, and each time the value changes. Almost all the past events are lost soon since they carry no value to the current SELF. Personal history consists of only a few permanently valuable events' memories emerging from the dark past. Once I stood on the top of the Danta temple of the great Maya state

El Mirador. From there, the tops of several pyramids of Nakbe and Tintal are visible over the green ocean of the Yucatán rain forest. I feel as if my past life is like that. Only a few valuable events remain in my memory. If I dwell on one of these events and ruminate on its meaning with strong emotion, the sense of the time when I actually experienced the event emerges, even if it occurred a long time ago.

In the spring of 1945, I was terribly depressed by the state of the war. It was painful to go to school every day. I did nothing except to take care of my baby sister. Our mother was out almost every day to procure food. Every day was torture, and I could not wait for night so I could go to sleep. My only good memory at that time was that I learned the future potential of electronics. One of our neighbors had a clandestine homemade shortwave radio in his attic, and I saw how the small machine could catch all the information of the world. I heard Joseph Goebbels speaking in German. My future direction in electronics was already set by the time when I'd had that experience.

Then I learned that Germany surrendered in May. A few days later, badly depressed, I saw my teacher Mr. Oyamada Tokio after class. The school was at the top of a hill, overlooking the town. I asked him, "After the surrender of Germany, can we still win this war?"

Mr. Oyamada first looked at me and then looked up at the half-cloudy sky and fell into silence. It was a long, long silence, I felt. It must have been no more than a few minutes, but I felt, and I still feel, it was hours long. I felt uneasy. But I was sure that he would never give me a nonsense answer. After the long silence, he looked straight at me and asked, "If that question were asked of you, do you have your answer?"

I answered, "Yes, teacher, I do have my answer." Then he said, "That is the answer. From now on, you must ask such a question to yourself, answer by yourself, and act accordingly." I was stunned because I realized suddenly that I had answered such a serious question by myself. I felt as if a thunderbolt had struck me, and a terrible downpour had cleared out the sky. I felt as if an entirely new perspective of my life in the world suddenly emerged.

Then Mr. Oyamada pointed at the green speck of the town and said, "Your home is farther away from the temple. On your way home, drop into the temple and pray to the eternal Buddha for those who perished in this war." I nodded. Then he added, "Now you can think by yourself. You have your answer, so do not ask this question of anyone except yourself."

I felt that in the middle of depression, I had gotten an entirely new perspective on life. I felt as if I had gone through many years of learning processes, but actually my teacher had changed my thinking in a few seconds. I still remember every word he told me. On my way home, I prayed to the Buddha. I felt as if the smiling Buddha was saying, *This is the first step to your enlightenment.* This was the quality of the education I received at that time. The purpose of education is not just to provide knowledge; more important is that it teaches us the way to think. Three months later the war ended by Japanese surrender. On that day, most of the adults, including my mother, expected to hear something different from the emperor, but I was well prepared to accept his message. On that day, only two of us listening to the emperor had the same thought; the old sage I mentioned in the previous section and a ten-year-old boy, me.

Two stories related to the end of World War II give me two features of the sense of quantitative subjective time of the past event. The story of the old sage flows slowly and calmly in my mind and makes me feel the day was quite long. The story of Mr. Oyamada has an extremely high peak, and at that moment, he helped me grow many years. In two very different ways, the great teacher and the old sage gave me precious lessons by which I was able to continue. As I remember the two events, I believe that we must live the days of life that are later remembered as very long.

I ruminate on the two experiences again and again and try to find out how sensation is integrated to be sensed as time length. The integration appears to be associated with an imaginary shapeless dark cloud whose size grows with time while I am engaged with the event's image. The cloud behind the old sage grows slowly but steadily to a huge size, covering the entire world. The cloud behind Mr. Oyamada was first small, but at the final moment it exploded to a size bigger than a supernova. The resultant huge volume is sensed as the long time. Then the integration is still executed with the help of the sense of vision, another case of time's spatialization.

5.15 Quantitative Subjective Time at Present

I have discussed the sense of quantitative subjective time of the past event. Then how is the subjective time of a presently ongoing event sensed? The present experience is covered by a single specious present, and since the event is currently going on, when the event will end is unknown. Because of this, the quantitative subjective time length makes no sense, and only the sense of how slow or how fast the subjective time flows makes sense. Images of the event keep arriving, and they have not yet been organized or compressed into a single subjective time point. The SELF is currently organizing the incoming images into an event, whose sense of time length may be sensed later. The sense depends on the event image's value or the impact on the SELF.

The relation of the SELF and the present event is characterized by the control relationship between the two. If the SELF is in control, the sense of time depends on the SELF's disposition. As long as the SELF is content, the sense of the quantitative subjective time is quite tenuous. The SELF is engaged with the event without even sensing the time. This is because the SELF is able to control and terminate the event at any moment. If the SELF is subjected to the control of the event, what matters is if the SELF likes the event or not. If the SELF is enjoying the event, it simply accepts the event and is also indifferent to the passing of time. If the SELF does not desire the event, the SELF senses time by integrating sensation associated with the negative emotion. In this case, the sense of time's flow rate depends on the event's undesirability. Engaging in an undesirable event makes one feel that time flows slowly if the sense of the subjective time length is compared with the objective time. One hour of waiting for bad news is felt to be many hours long. This feature must have been developed by evolution, somehow letting the SELF disengage from the situation so that time and resources would not be wasted.

An undesirable event at present drives the SELF into a defensive position. The SELF has to focus on the emerging or expected negative consequence. To prepare for the negative outcome, the brain expends energy, and this is felt as sensation. Since the SELF is focused on the event, the sensation is properly integrated and emerges as the sense of a miserably long subjective time length. This is the situation we always experience in the waiting room of a doctor's office. Once I thought I'd waited for one hour, but my wristwatch showed only twenty minutes. From this observation, the past valuable events are felt long in the sense of quantitative subjective time, to benefit the present SELF, and the present's negative events are also felt to be long because the time is wasted and the SELF is eager to disengage as quickly as possible.

To get out from such a negative state that makes the SELF suffer, the only way is to divert attention from the heavily taxing present negative event and to prevent the integrating of sensation. My way of waiting in a doctor's office is to bring with me Japanese folding papers, make lucky birds, and give them to the other waiting patients with my best wishes. The event that I felt as very long at the time of the actual experience does not carry any positive value. So if the event is remembered later, there is no sense of time.

Even though the presently experienced time is felt primarily by the time flow rate, we still get some idea of the passing time length, although this estimate is not very accurate. The mechanism of sensing time is the same integration of sensation that is still going on unconsciously in the brain. It is possible to guess at the elapsed time at nighttime when it's quiet and no external clue is available. The error is significant, say, 30 percent or more. Yet if I sleep during that time, I entirely lose the sense of the passing time, and my guess after waking up is entirely off the mark. This observation shows that the body still has some unconscious sense of elapsed time length in a wake-up state, the same as with the sense of the structure of the living space, but the guess is not accurate.

5.16 Sensing Cost of Time Length

I have shown that the sense of quantitative subjective time, that is, the sense of time length in human life, is almost always quite tenuous compared with the other analog senses such as spatial length, volume, intensity of sound or chemical substance. A writer senses the amount of work he or she has done by the number of finished pages, rather than by the sense of the time spent in writing. Length of time appears an awkward sense. This is why everyone wears a wristwatch, or some other means to know the time.

I'll ask an unusual question: Is this because somehow the cost of sensing time length is high? Then what is the cost? When we hear a simple statement, we immediately recognize what it is, except when the message contains a word that is not comprehensible. We see an object or hear a simple statement without paying any *extra* attention. If I observe various images that humans sense, I find an attribute of some images. The attribute is differential image and integral image. A landscape observed from a train window is an integral image of many objects. If the train goes into a tunnel, the observed change is a differential image.

Differential parameter such as the flow rate of a river is easier to measure than the total flow volume over a period, which is an integrated parameter. This difference shows up whether or not there is outside medium that indicates the integrated value. For instance, in the many hours required for proofreading, the number of finished pages is just such an external memory. In this case, the cost of sensing time length is never higher than just observing how thick is the stack of the finished pages. I often grow impatient when my wife goes to the toilet in a shopping center. Yet this case can be helped by setting up a means of time integration, that is, the number of women who go into the toilet after my wife. The number is a measure of the elapsed time. This technique saves me, and any husband from frustration.

Sensing time length does not have convenient integration media most of the time. Thus, sensing of time length has two handicaps: elapsed time is an integrated sensation, and usually there is no simple outside medium indicating the time length. If there is no watch or any other means, the brain must provide both sensation integration and the attention to keep the integration going. The two executions are costly to the brain. Both operations are carried out by the dynamic memory circuit set up in the deep area. The neuron circuit must be continuously working to integrate the sensation and keep the value. The extra energy spent to focus attention on this activity and to operate the integration adds up to the two costs of sensing time length. The evolutionarily developed brain tries to minimize such extra cost. If I look at any other innate analog human senses, I find that few other senses demand both focusing attention and integration with the brain.

That is why we have such a tenuous sense of time length and why we developed the habit of unloading the sensing of time length to observation of the change in the habitat or relying on the memory of the past experience. Close association of any event's image to the time frame of a day originated from this need. In the modern age, all sense of time length has been unloaded to watches and clocks, but if we do not have such a timepiece, we rely on the costly means. To study the innate sense of time held by the human mind, I need to consider the case of not having any timekeeping machine.

5.17   Indigenous Body Clock

Humans and animals have their own clock built into the brain and the body that sets a certain specific time period. There are two types of clocks. The first type is the species-independent circadian clock. In modern times, transoceanic airline travelers suffer from this clock setting until the body becomes accustomed to the time at the destination. This type of clock mechanism exists in creatures ranging from single-cell organisms to mammals and humans. The indigenous clock period of humans is slightly longer than twenty-four hours. The period is synchronized by the daily rhythm to exactly twenty-four hours.

The second type of clock mechanism depends on the species, and this type of clock controls the heartbeat period, the breathing period, the maturation period, the gestation period, and the life expectancy.

The ratio of any two such periods is independent of the species. The breathing period is about six times longer than the heartbeat period, and over the course of a lifetime, the heart beats two billion times. These time periods are proportional to the one-fourth power of the weight of the mature animal body. This is a very weak dependence. The *scaling laws* research on animal's mechanical features was the work of Professor Schmidt-Nielsen's group at Duke University.

Various attempts have been made to derive this one-fourth-power law. One way was to model the animal's body by a spring and relating the vibration period to the weight, assuming that an animal's body is designed to satisfy elastic *scaling law* (if body length increases m times, then the diameter of the vertebrae increases $m^{3/2}$ times; this is the requirement that the animal body shape must be mechanically similar). The elastic scaling law emerged in Renaissance times; Galileo Galilei's book mentions it. I propose my idea from the VLSI (very large-scale integration) technology to explain the one-fourth power time-scaling law.

If an adult animal's weight increases m times that of the standard animal, the length of the neuron axon from the brain to the body's control destination increases by $m^{1/3}$ times, and the signal transmission time increases by the same factor. This is because the animal body structure and the body material density are both about the same. This assumption is quite rational, but it gives an overestimate of the time. Why? Because the nervous system has mechanisms that expedite signal transmission speed, such as skipping action-potential conduction (section 3.28). For time, the simple scaling law does not seem to apply.

It is now well established that energy consumption per cell of animal is proportional to $m^{3/4}$, which is less than proportional to the weight. Energy consumed by the body's internal organs ultimately turns to heat, to raise the temperature inside the body. This law is to maintain the temperature rise within the body to a tolerable level. The source of the energy is the bloodstream coming from the heart through a narrow artery. An artery is the equivalent of the power bus of a VLSI processor chip. The chip designer's concern is how to select the width of the power bus to prevent voltage drop and noise generated by the power bus when the chip operates.

An animal body has the same problem. Blood flow through a narrow artery depends on the resistance created by the blood's viscosity. Let the average length of the artery be L and the diameter be D. Blood is a viscous fluid. Its flow rate is proportional to the pressure generated by the heart and to $L^{-1} D^4$ by the hydrodynamic Hagen-Poiseuille's law. If the animal size is m times, then L and D are both $m^{1/3}$ times, and the flow rate is also m times. Yet what the body need is only $m^{3/4}$ times more energy, the flow rate is $m^{1/4}$ times in excess. To match the energy need of the body, the heart must beat $m^{1/4}$ times slower. This means that the time that the animal's indigenous time is $m^{1/4}$ times longer. This is how the animal's quantitative subjective time depends on the weight of the animal.

An interesting question is whether or not the psychological time constant, indicating tolerance limit to confusing images that I discussed in section 4.16, is an indigenous clock like the heartbeat period. The time should decrease with animal size, yet I suspect it does not follow the one-fourth-power law, for the same reason the size scaling law does not lead to the correct time-scaling law.

There are several other indigenous clock periods determined by the mechanical structure of the body, such as a period of footsteps. Most of such periods are adjustable to the life's needs. An interesting feature of such adjustable mechanical periods is that the number of periods executed by the body can be counted *unconsciously.* Counting the footsteps while talking with a companion is possible. This feature indicates that the mechanism of adjusting the period provides the counting capability also.

5.18   EEG and EKG

EEG (electroencephalogram) is the simplest way to observe the brain's activity. When a person is in an alert state, an EEG observed from the forehead shows the β-wave, which has an average frequency of 20–25 Hz. In the deep sleep state, the EEG changes to the θ-wave, whose frequency is 8–10 Hz. Obviously the ratio of the frequency reflects brain's average clocking rate (section 5.20). An EEG's signal is the sum total of the brain's neurons' action-potential pulses that are filtered by the brain tissue, thereby making a smooth, random, pseudo sinusoidal waveform. An EEG reflects the level of consciousness of the person by its dominant frequency and by the wave amplitude. An EEG is like city noise heard from the suburbs, which provides an idea about the activity level of the city community. City noise is the EEG of *social self-consciousness*.

The β-wave represents the level of activity of the brain engaged in some sophisticated mental processes. This effect is most clearly observed by filtering the wave to remove the lower-frequency components (that is from the activity of supporting the body) by way of a band-pass filter. In my 2009 book, I confirmed that the amplitude of my filtered β-wave has clear correlation to the difficulty of the problem I am engaged with. So what does the average period of β-wave, which ranges from forty to fifty milliseconds, mean? This must be the time needed to display one basic unit of image in the internal image circuit. The wave's period and phase depends on the images; this is the mechanism creating the β-wave's randomness. During the sleep state, the period of θ-wave, 100–125 milliseconds, shows the average clock period to control the body functions. Chemical control of the body is slower than the brain's electrical image processing by that ratio. Compared with the complexity of thinking, body control appears amazingly involved. This is because the body has many organs to be controlled. The ratio 100(milliseconds) / 40(milliseconds) = 2.5 is the complexity ratio of the visual image and the body chemical image processing. In dreaming (REM) sleep, the β-wave reemerges, thereby indicating that the brain wakes up during REM sleep.

Observing an EEG while my brain is executing known image processing is a very meaningful experience. EEG observation is easy. If you make your own EEG machine, you can process the EEG wave with additional analog electronics and do many interesting experiments, such as removing the low-frequency components from the β-wave. As for the key design guidelines, I refer to my 2009 book (*Neuron Circuits, Electronic Circuits, and Self-Consciousness* [Vantage, 2009]). The book's appendix gives all the know-hows to build home EEG machine.

An EKG (electrocardiogram) is the simplest, most conspicuous body clock drive the heart. EKG observation is easier than EEG observation, since the pulse amplitude is in the range of a few millivolt everywhere in the body. The signal consists of repetitive spikes a few milliseconds in width with about 1 Hz repetition frequency, and this controls the heart operation. Since the pulse width is narrow, the EKG amplifier must have bandwidth up to several kilohertz to preserve the pulse shape.

Because of the EKG's pulse height, I suspect that the EKG pulses may affect the brain's operation. From the heart, the arteries carry blood, which works also as the conducting wire of the EKG's electrical signal. Arteries are the energy distribution network of blood, like the power bus of a processor, along with the electrical network of the EKG's clock signal distribution. Then EKG pulses must be able to affect the brain's activity. To excite the heart, the EKG pulse source has very low internal resistance and is able to drive the entire body. Then an EKG may affect neuron circuits, along with the pressure pulse from the heart that goes through the artery.

5.19   Dissipative Clock

The progression of quantitative time is sensed by energy consumption of the brain and body. When we do physical or mental work, the exercise consumes energy, and the spent energy is sensed as fatigue. Fatigue is the measure of quantitative subjective time, that is, the energy spent to execute the activity. A unique feature of fatigue is that it is the measure of subjective time *length*, indicating depletion of the stored energy. The body is able to integrate the energy usage rate to create the sense of fatigue. The body's fatigue is rather an accurate measure of the energy usage by physical work, that indicates the elapsed time of the work. Since the brain is supported by priority, mental fatigue is not so clear an indication of time. Mental fatigue is more the measure of nonproductivity of the current exercise.

The human brain and body derive their energy from food. To maintain life, energy must be periodically supplied from the outside.

The energy supply and the consumption of energy move the quantitative time's clock needle. Suppose that human life is the daily repetition of the same routine. When I wake up in the morning, I have free energy, *Em*. As objective time, *t*, progresses while I work, the energy is used at the rate proportional to the still available energy, *Em* − *E(t)*, where *E(t)* is the spent energy. Work vigor depends on the available energy at every moment. This process is described by a simple differential equation,

$$\frac{dE(t)}{dt} = \frac{\left[Em - E(t)\right]}{\tau}$$

where τ is the characteristic time that depends on tolerance to the physical work. The solution satisfying *E(0)=0* is given by

$$E(t) = Em\left[1 - \exp\left(-\frac{t}{\tau}\right)\right]$$

where *E(t)* is proportional to the subjective time *T* by the factor *r*, such as

$$T = rE(t) = rEm\left[1 - \exp\left(-\frac{t}{\tau}\right)\right]$$

T versus *t* is shown in figure 5.19.1. If *t* is small, *T* is approximated by a linear relation

$$T = (rEm/\tau)t$$

After the evening meal, the body has been supplied with energy from food, and during sleep, the food is digested and becomes usable energy. By the next morning, the available energy is again *Em*. If I take rest during a workday and supply energy by eating a sweet snack that becomes energy right away, the subjective time clock goes back as shown in the second day of figure 5.19.1.

This scenario indicates that the quantitative subjective time flows forward during the workday, and then backward during the night. The sense of the maximum quantitative subjective time length is limited to one day and cannot be longer. It is unnatural to imagine a continuous job that lasts more than one day. I am never able to guess when I may finish writing this book. It takes too many days.

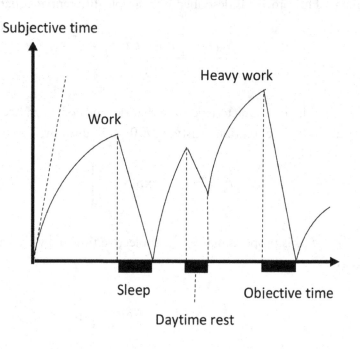

Figure 5.19.1 Dissipative clock

Such a long period of work is separated into parts. I can sense how long it takes to complete a day's quota of the work. Each sensible workload takes less than one day, and then I add the workloads to come up with an estimate of the time required. This is not an innate capability provided by evolution, since it requires arithmetic. This feature of quantitative subjective time is not convenient to get a perspective on the future. That is the reason why the advanced human brain created an alternative sense of qualitative subjective time. In many ways, quantitative subjective time is marginalized as a human sense of time.

5.20 Clocking of the Self-Conscious Brain

A brain is a digital system. The way the system operation is timed determines the sense of both qualitative and quantitative subjective time. A PC controls the entire system by a single central clock. A brain is an asynchronous system. There is no central clock generator that coordinates the entire system's operation. Instead, the brain has many local clocks. This is because the brain evolved from the primitive central nervous system of the Cambrian period animal, adding more and more neurons and retaining only the adaptive structures. The original structure had no central clock. Evolutionary development could not change such a basic, preexisting architecture. Three more reasons for not adopting the synchronous clocking system are (1) the reliability of the clock generator is too critical for life, (2) it is impossible to distribute the clock with a short enough delay time over the entire nervous system and (3) the data, images, do not have fixed size as required by a synchronous clocking system.

Yet the brain has many signals somewhat similar to the clock signal in an electronic processor. These clocks were acquired during evolutionary development when the evolving brain adopted images as its data. Images do not have a fixed data structure or size. Any brain's clock period is defined by the time required to display or process one image. The required time depends on the complexity of the image. Since any image has its own size, the clock cannot tick at regular intervals like in a PC. In figure 5.20.1, the excitation of previous image A fades away, and the current image, B, emerges. Then the current image B fades away and the next image, C, emerges. The time when image B occupies the internal image circuit is a period of the clock associated with the image B. The clock period depends on the image and also on other images closely associated with it to create its meaning. The displayed image remains some time before it completely fades away. The clock period that belongs to image B of figure 5.20.1 extends into the period of the clock of image C. The brain's clock overlap creates a significant advantage in the brain's capability, that is, to relate the earlier image to the later image as shown in figure 5.20.1(d).

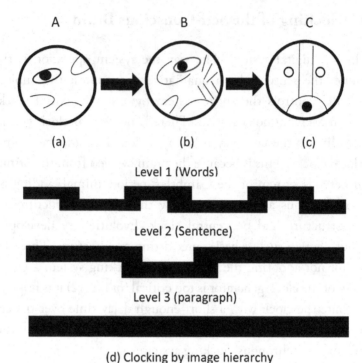

(d) Clocking by image hierarchy

Figure 5.20.1 Clocking images

This feature is quite important in sensing and understanding images as I discussed in section 4.25, and also for executing introspective observation (section 1.07). Each of these clocks is an image support-level control signal. Some of them are global or block global support control signals (section 3.27), and many others are image-specific support signals (section 3.19).

Each image of figure 5.20.1 (a)–(c) is an elementary image consisting of image elements like vectors and arcs, which carry the minimum meaning. In normal human life, most images handled by the brain are more complex than elementary images. Useful images are built from several elementary images connected together or are arranged into a hierarchical structure. In the language channel, a word is the elementary image that has the shortest clock. Yet what is useful in real life is a sentence or a message. A composite image such as a sentence has a longer clock period. So, the brain's clocks make a hierarchy as shown in figure 5.20.1(d). Each level's clock is unique to the brain's operation.

Can such a brain clock period be sensed? Sense of the clock is usually hidden behind the clear sense of the image. The clock that defines an event is still sensed, but the element images that make up the event do not have clearly sensible clocks. What is sensed as the clock is variation of the sensation associated with the images, or change of the support level. Because of this feature, the clock is sensed by the body, and the image is sensed by the brain. I think that the dominant EEG beta wave period, forty to fifty milliseconds, is the clock that displays a single image element (section 5.18) such as that of figure 5.20.1(a)–(c), or a word in language. Because image is more clearly sensed than sensation, progression of time is sensed not quantitatively but qualitatively, by sensing successively emerging images.

From this observation, the irregular-period, image-size-dependent hierarchical clock of the brain is well adapted to the objective of normal life in the natural or social habitat. A brain works asynchronously by the clock that specifies each internal image. Such a clock system is more flexible in handling extremely variable data structures such as images needed for life. Images processed in different parts of the brain by different local clocks can be assembled to make useful action images. Therefore, the highest-level clock that organizes the entire action comes not from the brain but from the actuator of the body.

The brain's clocks provide some key brain functions. By the overlapping periodic clock, images A and B can be displayed alternately. Then the brain can compare images A and B. The capability to determine if image A is the same as image B is the basic function of the brain in recognizing images. This is the basic mechanism creating the sense of understanding (section 4.25).

The support signal and the clock signal play the same role in the brain system. This is actually a new insight to be used when looking at electronic systems. Clocks are really the AC power supply of electronic digital circuits. This is an interesting way to look at digital circuits.

5.21 Brain Interruption

Our brain reacts immediately to any incoming image that may affect our welfare. Such an incoming image quenches the existing activity quickly, and the brain focuses on the new image. This is similar to interruption of a data processor, and such a capability is required for life. How is an interruption executed? The key is how to terminate the existing activity quickly and then to focus on the new image. Interruption changes the engaged image, so it executes the same function as clock.

Since an electronic data processor executes a long program, it is interrupted in an orderly fashion so as to continue with the processing later. This is not what a brain needs. Human and animal brain operation is primarily to watch and then respond to the emerging situation quickly. The external signal indicating any change is more important than the currently processed information. The human brain does not continue an interrupted process; such a process is re-executed afresh, from the beginning if necessary, except for the case of a multiple, inflated specious present (section 5.07).

Since the current activity of the internal image circuit can be extensive, terminating the activity must cover all the functional blocks of the internal image circuit. This can be effected by a sharp reduction in the support level, in both the block's support level and image-specific support. Figure 5.21.1, *right side*, shows the activity levels of the internal image circuit. When the incoming signal is processed, and if it is identified as important, the deep area's fear center directs the body-control area to sharply reduce the support level of the internal image circuit blocks for a short time.

Then the body-control area increases the support to its highest level to highlight the incoming image, so the incoming image-induced activities spread out quickly by the joint actions of all the functional blocks. The new activity establishes itself and deals with the emerging situation. In this process, the sensors, the analyzer, and the deep area supports are kept unchanged. The analyzer formats the incoming image during the interrupt execution and sends it to the assembly area so that the new image takes over the activity right away. If the new image turns out to be a false alarm, the support level returns to the normal level, and the brain resumes the terminated process from the beginning, if necessary. A particular case of interruption is when a sudden change happens in the external world. Then the interruption is initiated by the analyzer, and the activity spreads out rapidly downward to attend to the situation, similar to the process of the line-of-sight mechanism (section 4.15).

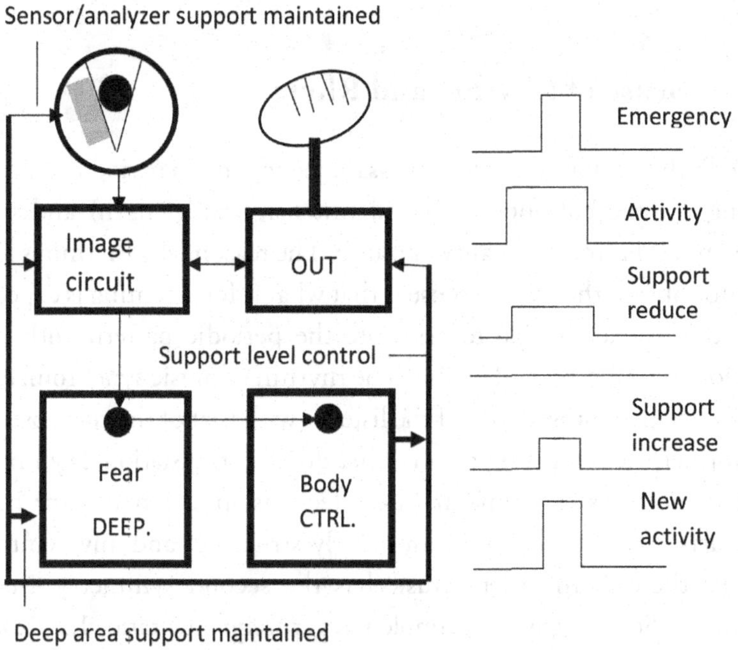

Figure 5.21.1 Brain circuit interruption

The brain executes the role of the body's sentry guard by this interruption capability, but the role of interruption is not limited due to the external cause. Interruption is a key mechanism to keep the brain operation continuous. Since the images make multiply connected web structures, image activation moves around the connected web continuously for some time. Then an interruption comes in, and a jump of active image to the new web location takes place.

In each of the states in which the brain is engaged with continuously related images, the SELF is in a single specious present. Thus interruption is a special type of the brain's middle-level clocking mechanism (figure 5.20.1[d], level 2). The brain's interruption may be initiated from the internal image circuit during its image processing, by discovering some risk features of the image that have so far escaped the attention of the SELF. Then the brain focuses on the image by interrupting the current process, displaying the image, and examining the feature.

5.22   Sense of Rhythm and Rhyme

The rhythm of music creates a pleasant feeling. It is a periodic, repetitive change of the envelope of sound (intensity and length) and is the element of the artistic quality of music. The reason why rhythm is felt as comfortable to the human sense is that what is forthcoming is expected, and the listener is able to associate the periodic pattern with body motion like tapping or dancing. The rhythm of music synchronizes the subjective time progression of the listener with that of the composer and performer. Repetitive rhythm is time-domain translational symmetry, and it produces the same artistic effects as spatial symmetry in the fine arts. We feel beauty in an orderly structure, and any symmetry means there is an order. Music has the second symmetry, that is, harmony. Sounds having a simple integer frequency ratio, 1:2, 2:3, …, are harmonious, and the pair of sounds are beautiful if they are heard together. Harmony carries as much variety as visible and language images of a poetic scene displayed in words. Why? Because music is actually a twelve-alphabet poem. The only difference is that each sound has no direct visible image connection. In songs, artistic resources are further enhanced by the words' visible images. Rhythm, harmony, and rhyme in music and poetry set the artistic quality of information presented in a time sequence. As such, they are the basic features of the human sense of subjective time.

A poem has the same time-domain symmetry as music. Its rhythm is created by a regular number of phonemes in a row or column, depending on the language, and this creates the musical features of a poem. As for the number of phonemes, five and seven appear most popular in the poems of Middle Ages Chinese and Japanese poetry. Although the two languages are basically different, the periodic structures induce the same effect, since one Chinese ideogram carries one phoneme, and one Japanese phoneme is a combination of a consonant and a vowel. Because of this rather accidental similarity, five or seven phonemes make up the preferred basic unit of poetic rhythm. Japanese poems consist almost entirely of five or seven phoneme units, 5-7-5, 5-7-5-7-7, or 7-7-7-5. Thus, both Chinese and Japanese poems' rhythms are set by five or seven phoneme clocks. In this poetic style, a certain pair of columns of Chinese poems must display a contrast of images. This is an additional symmetry in the poem, greatly adding artistic quality. In the poetry of the Tang dynasty, this rule and the rhyme rules were strictly followed.

Rhyme depends on the poet's language. In the subject (S)-verb (V)-object (O) type of language, such as most Indo-European languages and Chinese, the last word of a row or column is rhymed. This is because the last phoneme of an S-V-O language is not conjugated, and a rhyme can be placed there by choosing the word. In Japanese, the first phoneme of a column is rhymed because in the S-O-V language, the last word, the verb, is conjugated. Because of the character of Japanese language, some keywords within a column can be rhymed. An example is:

(A)saborake-(A)kashi no ura no-(A)sa guiri ni-(Shi)ma gakure yuku-Fune wo (Shi) zo omou.

Because of my limited literary background, I can appreciate only Japanese and Chinese poems. Not many Japanese poems are rhymed like this piece, but rhymed pieces are almost always superior ones. The rhymed first word of a column invokes expectation of the emerging poetic scene. What will come next is awaited with anticipation. The visual image following the rhymed word emerges as if from a thin mist. Yet how the poetic scene ends is uncertain, and that provides a lingering emotional echo. Emotional echo is the key artistic feature of Japanese poetry. Chinese poems, whose last word is rhymed, gives me the impression that each visual image of the column ends there sharply.

This displays the image clearly from the background. I love both types of poetry. One displays masculine, the other feminine, beauty.

Rhythm and rhyme are examples of the sense of quantitative subjective time creating artistic sense. Since rhythm is set precisely by the number of phonemes, it is the first-level clock. The rhyme sets the higher-hierarchy-level clock (section 5.20) and adds beauty to the poem. Poems are always recited many times so the listener may taste their artistic images by rhythm and rhyme. While reciting the first column, the image of the next column emerges and becomes clearer and clearer as if the mist is being lifted. Rhyme is the poetic art's clock that emerges in the human mind and creates a synchronized sense of the poet's image and emotion. By rhythm, the poet's heart rate, and by rhyme the breath rate is transferred along with the visible images. This is a great feature of the quantitative sense of subjective time.

5.23   Static Anthropomorphic Sense of the Past

As I remember my life's past and reexperience the times I've lived, I feel a real emotional, yet resigned, observer SELF within me, witnessing the drastic change of the world, from dominance of the British and French colonial empire to the emergence of China and Islam as the major political elements of world affairs. World War I was the war in Europe only, but World War II covered all the globe and terminated the entire colonial empire. The complex emotion of an old historian is more than the sense of survival in the harsh world. I feel an intense, gloomy prospect for humanity's future. I feel as if I were an old tree. This is one significant way of sensing qualitative subjective time.

Since trees live much longer than animals, and since grown old trees are magnificent, they are often anthropomorphically identified with an old sage who has survived history. In my backyard, there are a few oak trees whose lives are probably longer than U.S. history. Whenever I see them, I think that the trees have been alive since the time of de La Mettrie, whose three hundredth birthday was only a few years ago. I continued the work he started all through my life. Since his book was under the suspicion of Western rulers during the time of the Cold War, I didn't publicly share my work based on his materialistic philosophy until the Soviet empire collapsed and the stigma of this classic vanished. I always wondered why scientific truth had been so blindly mixed up with political ideology, both in the East and in the West. I am a firm Japanese right-winger, a devoted admirer of the Japanese emperors, as I remained even after my parents lost such sentiment. Yet I believe in Owen's utopian socialism, perfectly implemented by the twelve Inca emperors and brutally destroyed by the conquistadors.

I learned about Easter Island in World War II, when the Japanese extended their vision across the Pacific. I was determined to visit the island. When I finally visited and saw the spectacular Moai, I was struck with emotion. When they were erected, there were no colonial powers, with whom our generation of Asians fought. Each fallen and re-erected Moai of the island tells his own story, seeing this barren yet immensely holy island (they stand looking inland). The Moai are paired with the face of the island's great god MakeMake, whose face looks up the Moai from the foreground. There was a small Moai on the top of the hill of Orongo. The British carried the Moai away, but not the god's face. They did not realize that the god's face was the Moai's pair.

When I faced the lone god's face, I clearly saw the sorrow of the god whose people had become victims of colonialism. Yet, to be fair to the British, *The Golden Bough* by James Fraser was written based on similar historical emotion; the introduction describes the goddess of Lake Nemi and her priest. I feel such a great book will never be written in the twenty-first century, because such an emotional drive does not come from looking at the towers of New York City by modern people who regard any classic as out-of-date.

5.24 An Event's Gap in the Sequence

Suppose that I review my personal history by a sequence of events, A, B, C, … Each spatialized event carries no sense of time length by casual observation (section 5.10). Then how about the gap between A and B, B

427

and C, and so on? If my life's history is described by several events, A, B, C, …, the objective time length between any successive events was much longer than any one event. Because of this, the gap should give us a sense of subjective time length. Does this actually happen? If not, why?

Let us consider this question from the general character of image sequence. Consider a sequence of the alphabet, A, B, C … Is there anything between A and B? Nothing. The same is true for positive integers 1, 2, 3, … But, in this case, there is 1.5 between 1 and 2 as a rational number. Whether the gap of any sequence can be filled or not depends on the nature of the image of the sequence. Objective time is a mathematically continuous parameter, and there is always a time point between any pair of time points.

In the subjective time's event sequence A, B, C, …, A and B, and B and C, are qualitatively different, and there is no way to specify the element that fits in the gap between A and B. One way to see this sequence is as if there is nothing between A and B, but the other way is that A and B are qualitatively different, so they cannot specify any event to fit in there. The gap is open to be filled. Then it is possible to place any event between the consecutive pair, to enrich the sequence. The gap is not *inactive* but is *active* space, *waiting* to be filled by events. The gap is an expected event, and any number of any kind of event can be inserted. When a gap emerges between two events, I feel as if the time makes a discontinuous jump of unspecified length. Any gap creates the sense of discontinuity, which is like an end of an era or century, and this creates a real sense of time's progression. This is how the sense of qualitative subjective time emerges from the events placed discretely on the continuous time line.

By observing this feature from a different point of view, if A, B, C, …, are actually experienced real event sequences, then surely there must have been some event between A and B, but the memories were lost. This is the result of the brain's memory management (section 4.09). A qualitative sense of time by a sequence is developed by taking the brain hardware's capability into account. Loss of an event makes the sequence poorer, and addition makes it richer. Yet the sequence maintains its identity, the personal history. The sequential structure's identity is never lost by the addition or removal of any event.

Yet an interesting point is this: if the gap is filled by an almost continuous sequence of events derived from an intense recollection effort, the clear sense of time's progression fades away. The whole sequence is felt as a single spatialized event. As this experience shows, the sense of time is not as *robust* as the sense of space. Sense of space is robust and can be unconsciously (or automatically) recognized. The sense of time's progression is not so robust and is recognized only consciously. So it is easily spatialized, as in the way I show how an event of personal history is formed (section 5.06). Any event sequences that are quasi continuous are integrated into the spatialized event's image, in which the sense of time's progression ceases.

From this viewpoint, the sense of time is the conscious sense of discontinuity of the events. If the spatialized event is internally exercised and serialized, the sense of time reemerges; this is a conscious way of finding and sensing discontinuity. Here I notice that the sense of space is continuous in order to recognize the shape of any object. Space information does not display a discontinuous image. Yet the sense of time is the sense of *discontinuity*, or maybe even the sense of *surprise*, induced by the emergence of new images. Time measurement requires counting clock ticks, and each tick is a *surprise*. Clock ticks are the most basic discontinuity in time, and no time length can be measured without a sense of this basic discontinuity such as the clock tick (section 5.02). Continuous time is sensed by discontinuity, and discontinuous space is sensed by continuity. This is one of the mysteries of the sense of time.

5.25 Memory Connection to the Past

A peculiar feature of human self-consciousness is the role played by memory. The human brain cannot work with any information as it is received. As I described in chapter 2, the brain converts it to the usable form (consisting of vectors, arcs, phonemes, etc.) and memorizes it first. What is sensed by the brain is not the image that comes in but the preprocessed and memorized image. Even the present event's image must be converted and temporarily stored in the memory in a form that the brain is able to handle. The memory is read, and the image is recognized. Then what is recognized are all past images, including those of the immediate past.

Once an image is memorized in the brain, it becomes its asset. How it was memorized, and when it is read and used doesn't matter. Memorized images become the source of new images. Human imagination capability is limited, and any imaginative creation is based on the past images. An example is why an ET looks like a human? I have never heard any explanation that convinced me. ETs are created by artists who are exceptionally imaginative and defy common sense. If ETs should exist, they must have evolved with a very different body structure and a very different way of thinking from humans.

This is the case even with the greatest creative mind in human history. I admire Ludwig van Beethoven. He learned a lot from Niccolò Paganini. Darwin created his theory by altering the mechanism of transformation of species from that of his grandfather and of Jean-Baptiste Lamarck by incorporating the economics of Thomas Robert Malthus. Their products are absolutely spectacular, yet even such a great genius relies on inheritance. We all owe our cultural wealth to our ancestors, and amazingly, those who contributed most of all were our Neolithic ancestors. They were never naked barbarians.

Any event expected in the future is assembled at a specious present by the imagination, from the materials of the memorized images acquired in the past, by modifying, adding, and integrating them into a new image structure. Such image processing is mostly a conscious operation; that is, the SELF is involved in the process. This is always the case if the image is used for external action. The images we display and see are built entirely from the past images.

From this viewpoint, the human mind and images are firmly anchored in the past. As for the images of the past, not every detail is retained as it was, and when the images are recalled, the lost details are made up by other past images (section 4.13). In this way, our mind is quite tightly bound to what we once experienced and is never free from it. The past is the real source of everything. The images of the past and the future, real or imaginary, are all sensed in a specious present, and they are all built from the past images to fit the present needs of the SELF. Future images are those of the past, modified to fit the present SELF's intention and desire.

So to distinguish past and future as independent is, at least, misleading or maybe even superstition. Without having a past, we may not be able to understand anything. We humans share the same past with practically all the animals on earth. Therefore it is not impossible for us to understand the self-consciousness of bats, yet we are not even sure if we will be able to understand ETs, if they should arrive.

By extending this thought, any system that has no memory in it never carries self-consciousness. Self-consciousness is a specially developed mode of operation of memory that interacts with its supporting system, the body, and controls it. Self-consciousness's alternative definition is that it is the memory that supports the body, is supported by the body, and is able to steer the direction of the body's action for the benefit of life.

5.26 Most Events Do Not Have a Past, Present, and Future

I ask a simple question: Does the triplet phase of subjective time apply to all the events in our daily lives? Consider the experience of watching the evening news. Almost all the foreign events occur without any warning or anticipation. Political regime change, terrorist attacks, and financial collapse are all that way. One task of self-consciousness is future prediction and preparation. This fails most of the time. The chaotic natural or social habitat's state is totally unpredictable (section 1.12).

When an autocratic ruler dies, who will take over the power next is never known to outsiders. The last political succession in North Korea brought out a character who had not been anticipated by most Asian experts. This event had no future for most of us: it had the present, and then it became the past. The event might have been known by some insiders, and for them, the event had a future. The same is true of the events of September 11, 2001. Most people never expected the event, and so the event started at the present, and then it became the past. Could the rational expectation of economics have predicted the huge stock market crash of September 2008? It happened at the present as a real surprise since no economic forecast was made public. This event had no future, only the present, and it created a painful past memory.

The traditional belief that any future event is predictable is not true because of the basic unpredictability of a complex nonlinear system that shows chaotic behavior, as I discussed in section 1.12. Above all, any future event can never be defined precisely. If an event is defined absolutely precisely, then practically no prediction is possible. Future events that are expected to happen always have a vague definition, and that determines our future.

Similarly, certain other events never have a past. Any event forbidden by the basic laws of physics is of this type. Practically all the events having past, present, and future are subjected to the laws of nature or rules of the society. Some human events are similar to physical phenomena. My death is an event that has all three phases of time since the cells of my body cannot go through more than a certain number of renewals by splitting. Some events have no future, some others have no past, and the three time phases are ensured to exist only by the natural laws or social rules. In such a case, the triplet phase of past, present, and future has only limited validity to characterize qualitative subjective time.

5.27 Triplet and Doublet Categorization of an Image

We often imagine a paradise in the remote past or future. Utopia is in the future, and Eden is in the past. Are they real? No. Both of them are products of human imagination. Future prognosis is also imagination. Americans in the 1960s expected that someday in the future, Ted Kennedy would be a U.S. president. The expectation remained for forty years, and now, after his death, it has turned out to be a product of the imagination.

In the later part of the twentieth century, there was speculation that Polynesians reached South America before Columbus. This had been dismissed by historians as imagination, but in the early twenty-first century, hard archaeological evidence emerged, and the imagination became a historical event. At the same time, a theory emerged that Olmecs were Africans. Then their graves were discovered, and the anthropological tests showed that they were Native Americans.

From these examples, some past and some future events are indistinguishable from imagination. The only difference is that future imagination is purely speculation, but the past imagination can be scrutinized by historians and might turn out to be an historical event. Here is a great model: Herodotus described that in the seventh century BC, the Egyptian king Neco hired Phoenicians and let them circumnavigate Africa, and they found that Africa was a big island. This story had been dismissed as imagination. Then Alexander von Humboldt interpreted a detail of this story that Herodotus wrote without recognizing its significance, and proved that the expedition actually took place. Uncertain events of the past, because of lack of information, can be classified as imagined, similar to future prediction and religious prophecy.

As I have already shown, an event that has all three phases of time is ensured by some laws or rules. Prediction of a solar eclipse has all three phases of time; so does the election of Parliament in the future. Yet who will win the election is only imagination. Events that have the triplet phase are ensured by either natural or social laws, and because of this, they are destined to happen, independent of time. That is why some physicists try to eliminate time from physics, and why some philosophers consider that the triplet phase of time is logically inconsistent—so time is a mirage (section 5.31).

I feel these are attractive conjectures. Both arguments sound quite reasonable, but I am not ready to accept time's nonexistence, because history requires time. At the time of ideology, history was the study of the power relationships among the social classes. I hated this Marxist dogma. I held that history is the dynamics of the images carried by humans, which is similar to Thorstein Veblen's thought. Development of images by humans is so rich, so varied, and so colorful that history requires a milepost of their development, that is time.

Since not all the events follow the development of the triplet phase of time, then what is the proper categorization of an event? Here I state that experienced and securely memorized events are real, and events that are set up by imagination and not yet experienced are imaginary. This latter case includes expected but not yet experienced future events. So there are two clear categories. The present is a qualitatively different phase, so it is eliminated. Past and future must be reinterpreted. Any event can be classified into two kinds. The first kind of event has been *revealed* already, and either its memory or its record can establish its ensured existence. The second kind of event has not yet been revealed and is still in the domain of imagination. The first kind generally covers the past. The second kind covers expected future events, and the events that might remain as imagination. The second kind of event includes past events whose memory or record is lost, and therefore the self-conscious mind is unable to include them in the revealed category. In case the record is found, at that moment the event becomes a revealed event.

This doublet classification is natural to the subject SELF and contains no internal conflict of the triplet phase, which I describe in section 5.31. One additional key point is that an event that happens in a specious present is a revealed event, because the specious present accommodates the image's display and analysis, setting its meaning and memory formation, since the present covers a nonzero-length objective time period. The present is able to process the event's image and to place it securely in memory. Revealed events are firmly placed on the time line of history. The historical record is the marker of the time. This is why I believe in the existence of time. It is history that qualifies the revealed events. History is the reason for the existence of time.

5.28 Past-Future Asymmetry

Of the triplet phase of past, present, and future, past and future are both images, but they appear psychologically different. I need a close introspective observation of this difference. I prefer a life of eventless peace to one with high hopes and deep fear. In modern competitive society, one disaster is worse than many good fortunes. There are so many risks in life in modern society. If I focus on this feature, the future looks like a dark cloud on the horizon. Images of disaster keep emerging in my mind, and their relevance will end only at my death. When and how will my death come? This is the first and the deepest fear of the future. Since self-consciousness developed to delay this end, this fear is a built-in feature of the human mind.

Yet there are many other events before death. Since we all want more or less the same fortune in modern society, interpersonal competition is severe. With so many competitors, I am sure to be a loser. Expecting more and more personal disasters, I feel that the future carries little hope and beats me down under the dark shadow of failures. Every so often, I dream of the utopia image presented by a paisano guide when I visited the Sacred Valley, Peru, once ruled by the Inca. She told us—and I was struck by her sincerity—"There was no money, but there was no hungry man and no freezing woman under the Incas' rule." Very severe rule was exercised, yet there was no corruption by special interests, and the minimum quality of life was secured for everyone.

What is the fear of the future? The most dreadful phase of the future is waiting for disaster to come and not when I am struggling through a crisis. Practically all disasters arrive unexpectedly from nature or from a person in power. My mind's task is to anticipate and prepare for such unknowns all the time. As my brain searches for the future amid the meager clues of the present, the number of worrisome possibilities increases exponentially as the time in the future extends. Think, think, think, ... there is no end.

Finally I am completely exhausted by desperation. I end up cursing: Why do humans have to compete? A sense of deep misery occupies my mind, seeing those who won big at the time of my failure. Democracy has never eased anything but has worsened everything since the system has created hundreds of rulers instead of one. Everyone tries to be a ruler of something vital to life. Certainly I am not the one. I worry and feel afraid. Worry is the sense of fear that casts a long, dark shadow toward the future, to my death. This fear is shrewdly exploited by institutionalized religion. But what can God or Buddha do? They have no means to control the powerful rulers. In spite of this, I believe in the gods and goddesses in my image world. They were born with me, they suffer with me, they always tell me to behave honorably, they share my modest fortune with me, and they will someday die with me. So they are dear to me.

The ancient pagans knew this very well, but modern humans have lost their wisdom and exposed their ugly weakness in broad daylight. This is another reason why I believe that we are inferior to our Neolithic and classic ancestors. Achilles knew he would be dead in Troy, and he had no protection from that fate. Yet he chose to live eternity in human memory. Pagan heroes whom I admire, Odysseus, Siegfried, Leif Erikson, Naksitl Topiltzin Quetzalcoatl, and Hotu Matua, all lived such a life. Ancient pagans were born with their protector deities, who shared the honor and fate with the heroes. Such a viewpoint can still be gained from reading the classics, but modern practical education does not include any such subject.

If the dreaded event is still in the future, there is a mitigating effect, a faint hope that the worst may not come. Yet this is the most humiliating waste of time. It is wasteful to predict and prepare for all the possibilities.

When real disaster arrives, my SELF searches desperately for the way out. My SELF becomes a fighter; all the available energy is directed to find the solution, and the sense of fear eases. There is no energy to fear. In World War II, a Japanese foreign ministry agent went deep into China and Tibet and met with all sorts of risks. He wrote, "When I was struggling with hardships, I was most peaceful."[1] What a strong man! I admire him deeply. We pre–World War II Japanese boys were told, "Don't expect to die in the comfort of home. Be prepared to die on the battlefield." Now war is not for military honor but for survival.

As the feared event comes and then it becomes gradually the past, the impact of the event becomes known. Some worries are found useless, most of the hopes are not fulfilled, and the sense of satisfaction of

---

[1] Nishikawa Kazumi, *Eight Years of Secret Mission in the Mysterious Western Frontier* (Chuoh Koron, 1991), in Japanese.

survival gradually emerges. I was once almost laid off from my job because I objected to an idea proposed by my boss, who once dominated the technical community (the story is in section 2.08). The shock of this disaster has receded to the past. I need not be afraid of the past because its effect is already known. The desperation of the crisis heals by the passing of time. Then some small good fortune creates positive emotions of relief and peace. At the same time, I have learned what happened to the big winner at the time of my defeat, and I am shocked that he is in a much worse state than I am now. At first I feel a sense of revenge, then I feel deeply ashamed to have felt that way in front of my protector deities, who always tell me, "Behave honorably." I am grateful to my gods and goddesses. I wondered if I could help one of my former competitors in some way. Then, in my convoluted emotion, I realize that my offer of help might make him feel even more miserable. I remember the sad story of a very proud fellow who met misfortune after his big early success. He finally killed himself. Competition is never the way to heaven, but it is the expressway to hell, paved by modern society. Something is deadly wrong in modern society.

Fear of the future is the fear of the excruciating wait time for the unknowns. I give up the past with minimum satisfaction, but I fear the future. Thus, past and future are psychologically asymmetric. The asymmetry of the two emerges from the fear of future uncertainty. Since the future is frightening and the past is minimally peaceful, the human mind created the past and the future and added their dynamic boundary, the present. This is purely an emotional stage set. The three phases cannot be used to characterize subjective time objectively. That is why I replace it by the dual category: what has been revealed and what has not yet been revealed. My mind's search ends here. Fear created self-consciousness, and therefore the SELF fears the unknown future but feels peace in the past.

5.29 Past/Future and Real/Imaginary Images

The reader will agree that past events are real, but how about the relationship between future events and imaginary events? From the operation of the self-conscious brain, any future events and imaginary events are quite similar. An imaginary event may turn out to be a real event at an unspecified future time. The source material of both an expected future event's image and an imaginary event's image was experienced in the past and stored in memory. It is modified and assembled to build the future image or the imaginary image. To make one's own future is to build a sequence of future events' images by imagination, modifying the existing past images in the memory.

The dual classification of events into the category of what has been revealed and the category of what has not yet been revealed puts any event that has taken place already and that has a secure memory of its existence into the revealed category, and any future prediction and imaginary event into the not yet revealed category. This classification conforms to the unpredictable nature of both the self-conscious brain and the world and, because of that, is realistic and is rational.

This classification throws the present, the qualitatively different, phase away, and deals with the nature of the image only. An event that took place in a specious present is classified in the revealed category since the end of the present is when the image is accepted and memorized. Any not yet unrevealed event acquires probability to be revealed. Although the probability is subjectively set, this does not matter, since the probability exists even if its computation algorithm is unspecified.

In this classification, scientifically proven facts are revealed and religious prophecies have not yet been revealed. So far it is simple and natural, but close examination shows a few peculiar cases. Since qualitative subjective time can be created by the self-conscious subject SELF, the time need not be in the historical future. Subjective time can also be created in the historical past. Then confusion may arise. The most illustrative confusing case concerns one of our most precious cultural assets, the ancient myths. They appear to belong to the past, but they are still the product of imagination. As such, they belong to the yet to be revealed category.

By reviewing the myths of the world, we find that the origin of the human race has been variously described. Many myths begin with glorification of the mythmakers' ancestors, who are deified and worshipped. Pagans do not consider the myths to be the historical facts. The myths carry cultural, literal, artistic, and especially ritualistic values. The images of the myths were reproduced by the annual rituals to enrich the pagans' cultural life. They are the source of inspiration and high self-esteem, as if the ritual participants themselves had played the role of the heroes someday by themselves. I felt this strongly when I joined the *costumpre*, the Maya fire ceremony. Pious pagans wish to relive in the future like their glorious ancestors. This is to maintain high self-esteem in the struggle of the present hard life. Thus, classifying the ancient myths into the yet to be revealed category has proper justification.

The myths of Judeo-Christianity carry, from the general mythological principles, equal status as many of the pagan myths of the world and are the product of the ancient Semites' imagination. From mythology's general principles, the part of the myth that is earliest in the myth's own history was appended at the latest period of the myth's creation, to the body of the ancient legend that reflects some historical events. The Genesis stories are imaginary products.

I would expect a lot of objection to this view in the U.S. On this dispute, I do not argue from the natural scientist's position. Rather, I stand on my alternative background of ancient history and mythology of the world. The Judeo-Christian myth is no more than one myth among many different myths of the world, and I have no reason to choose that one as special. Domination of a single myth in modern society impoverishes the imagination, and that is a sign of cultural decadence. Myths must be created all the time to maintain the vitality of imagination. But they should not be confused as historical fact.

5.30 New Categorization and Event's Probability

I have shown that the past-present-future classification of subjective time has many irrational features. So in its place I proposed a new categorization into two phases, events that have been revealed and events that have not yet been revealed, including imaginary events. This was the time concept of one tribe of Native Americans of the Southwest, the Hopi, reported by B. L. Whorf in the 1960s. Their concept of time goes back to pre-Columbian pagan times. Once I had a chance to talk with one of them. I found him very intelligent, thoughtful, and introverted like me.

The dual categorization of events highlights the unpredictability of the future, and accordingly, it introduces a new feature that the triplet classification does not have, namely, the probability assigned to each event. Time does not change an event, but it changes the probability or its reality. For a past event that took place and was securely memorized, I assign a probability of 1. An imaginary event that has no chance of actually taking place has a probability of 0. An event such as someone's building a perpetuum mobile is sure to carry probability of 0. Probability setting can be somewhat subjective. The algorithm to compute probability is certainly the issue, yet this is the nature of any probability (section 6.14), and that does not affect the basic fact that any event carries probability.

The probability assigned to an event changes with time. The example I quoted before, "Ted Kennedy will be a U.S. president," was a quite well-expected event in the 1960s, so let me estimate the probability by my intuition. My probability estimate is as follows: In the 1960s, the probability was 0.8. As U.S. politics turned in the conservative direction, the probability dropped to 0.5 by the end of the 1970s. The probability dropped further as Kennedy aged in the 1990s, to 0.1, and a few years ago it settled at 0 because of his death. All the events, either personal or socially expected in the future, have a probability that changes with time like this.

Here I note that setting up probability depends on how precisely the expected event is defined. The death of a queen is a vaguely defined future event. The circumstance of her death is not specified. The death could be defined more precisely, for example, by heart attack, by an assassin, or by suicide. If her death is defined vaguely, it should happen someday, but if her death is more precisely defined, the event may remain imagination. Change of an event's categorization from unrevealed to revealed occurs at a specious present when the probability is set at 1 or 0, not to change any more. Yet if the memory of the event is lost, future people may assign new probability.

There are some confusing cases. Suppose that there is an accident and a man is on the scene. The casualty list has not yet been released. His relatives are anxiously waiting, and some of them pray to God. In this case, if the man is alive, there is no need to ask for divine help. If the man is already dead, God cannot help. Either way, God is useless. Is that so? My interpretation of this case is as follows: The man's death has not yet been revealed. Until the death list is out, his death is an imaginary event. Then asking for divine help is rational for those who are anxiously awaiting the news.

As I discuss more thoroughly in the next chapter, probability setting has a certain ambiguity to it, and some odd results may be concluded. A curious method of future prediction has been presented by J. R. Gott (*Time Travel in Einstein's Universe* [Houghton Mifflin, 2001]). Let the life expectancy of an organization be T. The organization exists now. Gott assumes that the probability of the organization's remaining lifetime is independent from the present age. He requires that the probability of the organization's existence in the future be 95 percent certain. Then the present age is either 97.5 percent of its lifetime or 2.5 percent of it. Then the remaining lifetime is $T/40$ minimum and $40T$ maximum. Gott showed that in AD 2000, Oxford University (est. 1249) would survive a minimum of 19 years and a maximum of 29,289 years with 95 percent probability. This logic sounds rational. Yet the probability estimate must be proper for each case, since the university certainly survived the minimum lifetime at the time of writing this book, *Self-Consciousness*. The unrealistic feature of this scheme is that the remaining lifetime of any organization depends on the present age of the organization (section 5.32).

5.31 Time's Paradox and Its Interpretation

The existence of time is taken for granted by most of us, but not by all of us. Those who suspect time's existence or question some of its features are thinkers such as philosophers, fundamental physicists, and cosmologists. So their skepticism cannot be dismissed easily. The basic physicists point out that the laws of physics are valid independent of time's chosen origin. Since the laws do not change with a different choice of the origin, time is irrelevant.[2] I believe that this opinion is valid only if the clock I defined in section 5.02 exists all through the history. This view implies that the *absolute time* referenced to be the universe's beginning is not relevant to physics and that the laws of physics and the universal parameters (such as the Planck constant) do not change as the universe ages. This possibility cannot be confirmed, since clocks are machines that operate according to the laws of physics.

Although my present issues are covered by objective time which I defined in section 5.02, it is almost certain that there are yet uncovered questions of objective time, and this is surely one of the problems of twenty-first-century physics. Yet I believe that the discovery and interpretation of time's features is within the domain of the presently established physics. There is no need to go overboard, to such exotic concepts as a *landscape universe*.[3] The source of this problem is that in the border region of general relativity and quantum physics, no physical model has been set up, and everything depends on mathematics. We need to recognize that there can be a perfectly self-consistent, yet unrealistic, mathematical theory. Beyond a certain limit, mathematics becomes the breeding ground of fantasy.

Philosophers focus on subtle logical inconsistencies in the statements involving time. An event is first in the future, then it becomes the present, and then the past. The future, the present, and the past are mutually exclusive categorizations, and the event remains unchanged. The meaning of the event remaining unchanged can be explained by

---

[2] L. Smolin, *Time Reborn* (Spin Networks, 2013).
[3] Jim Baggott, *Farewell to Reality* (Pegasus, 2013).

the example of junking my car in 2008. The event *junking* means the action of disassembling a car into parts to be sold as used parts. This action can take place anytime, and therefore it is independent from time. This happened actually in 2008. When I bought the car in 1993, the junking was an event in the remote future. In 2008, it became the present, and in 2019 it is the past event.

The event of junking the car does not change with time, but as the time passed, the event took all three, mutually exclusive categorizations. So the concept of time must have a logical flaw. From what I discussed in this chapter, I do not agree with this assessment, but putting that aside, this point cannot be refuted by restricting that the categorization should not be applied at the same time. That is because this restriction assumes, implicitly, that the categorization changes with time, and that is the point of dispute. This paradox is called *McTaggart's paradox*.

Where does this paradox come from? I believe that the triplet phases of time have so many logical flaws as I discussed before. As I discussed in section 5.27, events having all three phases share a common character, namely that the event is governed by natural laws or social rules. The event *junking my car* is meant to take place inevitably sometime. The event is not the six-hour action in the junkyard to disassemble the car. It is an integrated action that began in the Hyundai assembly plant at about the year 1992 and that ended in a New Jersey junkyard when the last parts were sold in about 2010. For the event of junking a car to occur, the car must be produced first, and then the used parts must be sold. So, the event of junking took eighteen years to take place. During that time, the event developed exactly following the laws of materials science (wear and tear, rust, etc.) and the social rule (the car must be inspected every year). Yet if the moment in 2008, when the disassembly work was done is defined as the event, its carried probability, which was 0 until 1992, gradually increased with time, reached 1 at 2008, and ever since has remained at 1. The probability is set by the natural laws of wear and tear and rust and the social laws that demand that the car must pass annual inspection.

This is a reinterpretation of the paradox. I reiterate the key point: any event that takes the triplet phases of time is controlled by a physical or social law, and the event spreads out over time and becomes a revealed event when the probability is set at 1 (or, depending the issue, 0). The dual categorization carrying probability is clean and rational and has no logical contradiction.

5.32   Subjective Time of Society

Human society, consisting of self-conscious individuals, has its own self-consciousness that resembles, in many ways, that of individuals (section 1.27). A dramatic display of social self-consciousness is witnessed at the time of national crisis, such as the 9/11 terrorist attacks. That is the time when all Americans became sensitive to the risk of death, and an unusual consensus was reached. This is functionally similar to an individual facing a personal crisis. Each individual of a society is equivalent to an image in a person's brain.

Social self-consciousness, a superstructure to the personal self-consciousness, has its subjective time, and that is observed in history. Social self-consciousness is as ancient as urban civilization. Because of the complexity involving many persons, intersociety relations, and economic conditions, the subjective time of a self-conscious society reveals peculiar features. Few, if any, political regimes have survived more than 250 years. The majority of regimes perished within a much shorter time. The lifetime of a political regime is defined, in the modern age, by the lifetime of a single constitution or any other rules that define the method of succession of power. In the premodern age, practically before the nineteenth century, the period of the time a single family ruled a country was the lifetime. By this definition, the maximum 250-year life time of a regime applies all through the history of China, Japan, and Hindu India without exception. In China, there has been no exception from the thirteenth century BC to the present. Notable exceptions are found in the Europe-Middle East boundary areas, with ruling families like the Ottomans, Hapsburgs, and Romanovs. They managed to keep a single ruling family, but their empire changed character drastically sometime before they expired. In the New World, the Copán dynasty of the Maya and the Inca Empire are exceptions. Yet the Maya holy calendar had a 260-year period, and the Maya people were aware that this was the regime's lifetime. The Itza tribe moved around the Yucatán Peninsula every 260 years and left a record of their belief.

The overwhelming majority of regimes perished earlier. As for any premature death of a regime, history shows either the preceding regime's problems were left unresolved, or the early ruler engaged in excess, such as with the first emperor of China. I am concerned because the U.S. reaches 250 years of age in 5 years, and the writing is on the wall. The gap between the haves and the have-nots is rapidly widening, and the vitality of the society has diminished significantly in the last 50 years. Declining vitality is most clearly felt as there are so many cases of apathy among the present young generation, many cases of substance use, and the emergence of autocratic rulers. A statement such as "Make America great again!" means that we think we are not great anymore.

A similar life span is observed in business and even in a single family, such as a playboy grandson of a self-made, successful grandfather. Why do dynasties, businesses, and families suffer a lifetime limit? The human thinking pattern makes a correlated chain from generation to generation. There is the accumulated effect of the way of thinking and of practice. During my lifetime, there has been a huge shift of the human value system in the developed world, such as dominance of female virtue over male virtue, and luxury over thrift. Such accumulated excess finally brings any society down.

Another cause of decline is the institutionalization of society. A political regime tends to concentrate power and wealth in the hands of a small fraction of the population, and operation of a family business becomes easygoing and wasteful. In either case, the resource usage becomes less and less effective, to an unsustainable level.

All such features of social self-consciousness emerged from the change in the evolutionary mechanism from Darwinian to Lamarckian. Social self-consciousness emerged when the change took place in the Neolithic age. During their early lives, human children acquire the already established social behavior, which is either positive or negative. In a liberal society, unfortunately, they get more negative values. The next generation generally becomes more easygoing, likes luxury, and has limited flexibility and less imagination. The trend can be reversed only by drastic social change, most of the time including bloodshed. World history is full of such cases; almost all the dynastic changes in China since 200 BC included bloody takeover by the successive regime. Then consider the French Revolution, the communist revolution in Russia in 1917, and the Nazi takeover of the Weimar Republic. This is human fate. There is no hope of changing this pattern. Darwinian evolution does not seem to define the clear lifetime of a species. There are a few Cambrian species still thriving with minimum change. Darwinian evolution retains adaptive features, but Lamarckian evolution of human society tends to accumulate negative genes in personal and social capital, setting the limits of regime, business, and family life.

Here is an interesting observation. Let the lifetime of an organization be T and the number of individuals of the organization be N. Then there seems to be an approximate relation, $T = cN^{1/8}$, where c is a numerical constant. This relation is approximately valid for a family (lifetime fifty years; six members), an institution (one hundred years; one thousand members), and a political regime (two hundred fifty years; one million members). This scaling law corresponds to the one-fourth-power law of an animal's body and lifetime (section 5.17). Maybe animal's body and human society evolve according to similar basic laws?

Human history shows, other than a regime's lifetime, several episodes of manic-depressive syndrome: in certain portions of prehistoric and historic periods, human creativity exploded for a short time: the prehistoric event of controlling fire, organization of society by building ceremonial centers, adoption of agriculture, invention of the calendar and writing system, emergence of science and philosophy at about 500 BC in the East and West, the new development in the Renaissance period, and rapid developments in science and technology in the twentieth century. Between any pair of consecutive active periods, human vitality was low, and a spell of dull cultural development and senseless political struggle continued. We are just at the beginning of another dark age. What I hope is that the coming dark age does not exterminate human culture altogether.

CHAPTER 6

SENSE OF MYSTERY

6.01 Human Mind Facing Mystery

My SELF senses itself, its world, and its history. In so doing, it must deal with uncertainty and mystery, not always by lack of, but often by excess of, poor information. Some such images show mysterious features that puzzle the SELF, its being unable to identify the image or explain it, or unable to manage because of its overwhelming complexity. In this chapter, I classify and discuss such images that the SELF has to handle. The mysteries are not only a burden but also a challenge to the active mind. Mystery is a qualitative uncertainty and, conversely, uncertainty is a quantitative mystery. Thus, the SELF's challenge to deal with them has two sides: one is to know why the images are mysterious, that is, to explain them qualitatively, and the other is to deal properly with the uncertainties, that is, to decide a proper quantitative response. This introduces probability, which controls the choice of action.

Probability was originally introduced to deal with lack of information, but in quantum physics, probability became the basic parameter characterizing any state. It shows the most predictable feature of the unpredictable microscopic world. A similar situation exists in a certain operation of the self-conscious mind, where again probability becomes the parameter to describe the predictable features of the unpredictable. Because probability is used to extract the predictable from

447

the unpredictable, a probability estimate algorithm carries probability. Thus probability is just as mysterious as time. Not only the probability of secular affairs, but also that of basic physics suffers from this mystery. How does the SELF deal with probability? This is one of the themes of this chapter.

My fear of future uncertainty has made me a lifelong amateur historian, and I have tried to learn from history the laws governing events' development. From 2017, I tried to see if the U.S. simulated Germany in the 1930s. The prognosis appears quite informative. Why did the ultra-right-wing movement reach the national scale? In both the U.S. and Germany, the respective ultra-right-wing leader wore a left-wing persona and mobilized a large frustrated population, and as the movement gained momentum, he put aside the persona. Quite often the Nazi Party is mistaken as an ultraright party, but as its German name shows, it was started as a labor (Arbeiter's) party, nominally. The present U.S. president's policy is definitely ultraright, but he appeals to the working-class people. Yet there is one historical difference: the U.S. leader put aside his persona in the early phase of the movement, and this is likely to affect his future development as of 2019.

Historical study made me more aware of the mysteries of humanity's past, along with those of the future. Why did human life become like this as we are now, with severe economic inequality and mutual hostility among the racial and religious groups? Why are there many more unhappy people now than in ancient times or in the Middle Ages? Why has the progress of physics created mysteries that are harder to solve than a hundred years ago? As an ex-physicist, I find that this last topic attracts my attention more than any of the others.

In my student days in the 1950s, I was deeply impressed by the book of quantum mechanics by P. A. M. Dirac, the most philosophically deep book (so famous that it needs no reference or quotation!). In this book, the respected author states that the task of physics is to define the system's observable parameters and to describe their development by mathematics. The role of a model, he writes, is to make the relationship between physics and mathematics persuasive, if such a model is available. Quantum physics developed spectacularly on this philosophy for the first eighty years. Yet in the twenty-first century, I suspect, what is going on in basic physics is not what Dirac expected. Physics developed to such a level that the theory is practically disengaged from observation or experimental check.

As a sideline of this trend, theories trying to explain human self-consciousness by quantum physics emerged. Thus my old profession and my new research theme crossed each other's paths. That is why I must investigate how the two areas are related. Since I have made the mechanical model of self-consciousness in this book, *Self-Consciousness*, I will try to make a similar model of the quantum world also and to show why they appear similar. This is another theme of this chapter.

As basic physics has reached the theory-only state, an imaginative model is required. A model is an image that appears rational to the self-conscious mind to explain the mystery. As a part of this chapter, I try to make a model of the quantum-mechanical world. Model making is not done entirely by logical reasoning; a certain artistic sense is necessary. This artistic sense emerges, more often than not, suddenly from the unconscious mind working in totally different work areas. To make a model is to polish up the unconsciously found material consciously. I love to give explanations of mysterious phenomena. This is emotionally quite rewarding for an introvert like me. The psychology of model making is an important task to clarify the mechanism of human imagination.

I believe that in every area now, we need more imagination. As an old storyteller, I show my image world. I talk about the problems that I handled in natural or anthropological studies, and I give my explanation that convinced me. Mystery and uncertainty are two severe burdens to my mind. I struggle to explain things that common-sensed people believe are not worth thinking about. I am aware of my Mephistophelean character, which has given me the reputation of a troublemaker in my immediate circle. Yet a small number of friends tell me that I am an interesting old fellow who never bores my listeners or causes them to yawn.

6.02 Mysteries of the Human Mind

Humans experience many events that cannot be explained, as long as they rely on their common sense. Belief in common sense is stronger among better-educated, socially mainstream people, because modern education makes everyone equal. Naturally, the more common-sensed individual is less imaginative (section 4.38). As the majority loses imagination, they explain mystery as the work of god or the devil and replace a mystery with an even deeper mystery. This retrogression is evidence of a defeatist mentality. I firmly believe that there is nothing in the universe that cannot be explained by the rational human mind after strenuous thinking. Yet that is a frightening prospect since the cost is high. Once a person, including me, experiences something unexplainable, the mind is stuck with an emotion of fear, including the fear of further thinking. The study of a subject such as self-consciousness costs one dearly in mainstream U.S. academia.

There are several types of mysteries. One is the type we meet in our ordinary lives. These basically psychological mysteries include phantoms, ghosts, and ESP. Phantoms are rare, unreproducible phenomena that are impossible to explain by simple thinking, but the observer does not feel he is morally involved. They are usually experienced at a certain place at a time of the day when the senses are weak, like dusk. Ghosts are similar, but the appearance of a ghost is implicitly attributable to a human who once lived or to certain objects capable of carrying human character, such as gods, angels, devils, and dead spirits. In this case, some sense of relevance or responsibility scares the observer. I am able to explain such psychological phenomena from my model rationally.

The other types of mysteries are real, and these demand explanation. There are a group of mysteries for which the object of the mystery cannot be properly defined. A general feature is that the definition of such a mysterious object refers to itself, and an easygoing explanation falls into infinite regression or tautology. A statement, "I am a liar," is the most popular undefinable object. Self-consciousness and a non-Cantorian set in mathematics are other examples. I discuss these mysteries in section 6.03. A somewhat related mystery is that a pair of characterizations of the objects support each other and become tightly consistent, and there is no *logical gap* to access. "Which came first, the chicken or the egg?" is the most popular case. Because the pair is so tightly consistent, there is no way to break into the core of the question. A pair of crime suspects proves the innocence of each other, and there is no other evidence that the judge can find. In quantum-mechanical entanglement, the law of spin angular momentum conservation becomes consistent with nonlocality of interaction, and that is why the phenomenon becomes mysterious, as I discuss in sections 6.28 and 6.29. The other kind of mysteries belong to the world that we cannot experience directly because the event happened in prehistoric times, the object is too small or too large to see, and the time is too short or too long to experience. The quantum-mechanical world is too small and the structure of our universe is so big that we cannot see either of these from the proper perspective.

Still another type of mystery emerges among human individuals. Although each individual has images of the same objects, the images' meaning, set by the connection to the other images, is unique to each individual. If two individuals have a significantly different image-to-image connection, then one can never understand the other. This is the mystery originating from the overwhelming complexity of the object's structure. As the last topic of my self-consciousness study, I include my views on these mysteries and show how our mind deals with them, relying on the mechanism of self-consciousness I described before and using the examples I experienced myself.

6.03 Mystery of an Object by Its Definition

There is a group of mysteries that share a common character, that is, the object's definition destabilizes the object itself. The definition that is supposed to specify a static object increases or decreases its size or alters its character indefinitely. Definition by language often creates such objects. A remarkable example is the non-Cantorian set of the set theory in mathematics. A set is an assembly of well-defined objects, such as *all the humans on earth*, which is quite numerous but still finite. Some set consisting of an infinite number of objects is *well-behaved*. The number of all the integers is infinite, but this infinity can be handled properly by defining *cardinal* aleph 0. Cardinal is the *number* specifying the rank of infinity. The cardinal of the set of all the real numbers (including π and e, and so forth) is the next level, infinity, called aleph 1. There is an algorithm to make a set that is larger than a given set. The set of all the subsets of a given set is larger than the original set.

Suppose there is a set that includes a set of all its subsets. This set automatically grows by itself. If the starting set is an infinite set, the way the set grows by itself is beyond any imagination. This is surely the largest object that the human mind can ever imagine. Mathematical logic excludes this from the set theory. I was once fascinated with this set in my youth, when I imagined the biggest object the human mind could conceive of, and I stumbled upon this set. Along with that, I was quite surprised to notice that humans were dealing with this set already. The set of images in a brain is a set of this kind, because a set of images is also an image. The human brain uses this monster. No wonder images are the most versatile information type! To make a sensible image of such an object is a task belonging not to mathematics but to psychology.

Set theory presents an interesting challenge to psychology. It is easy to imagine an aleph 0 (countable) set. An aleph 1 set, the *number* of all the real numbers, can be imagined as the number of points on a single continuous line. Yet an aleph 2 set is difficult to imagine, and any set higher than that is almost impossible. I believe it is a very rewarding task of psychology to make such a hard-to-imagine object imaginable. I cite another case of an unimaginable object, quantum foam, in section 6.31.

Any definition is supposed to specify a static object. Then, if the object changes by its own definition, it becomes unmanageable. Such an object demands a different definition. This is relevant to self-consciousness. One way to define a self-conscious subject SELF is to assume that there is a self-conscious subject inside it. If this is considered seriously, the subject becomes a Russian doll, whose size decreases indefinitely. To avoid this infinite regression is to follow the method of understanding an image as I discussed in section 4.26. The activity center of a pair of images is set up and replaces the infinite regression by the interacting image pair. This is to set up feedback loop between the pair. Feedback has been suspected to be the basic mechanism of self-consciousness, but before accepting that naively, we should define self-consciousness differently and expose its general character. Then the role of feedback will become clear. I use the definition that self-consciousness is the capability developed by evolution to protect the brain and body at the minimum cost. That definition is rational and productive and will never fall into infinite regression.

I made time's definition precise and specific, referring to the way the concept of time is used by humans. I inductively defined the existence of objective time and then separated subjective time, which is proper to a digital system, including the self-conscious human mind. Then I focused on subjective time and showed that there are many features that are not obvious.

6.04 Mechanism of Seeing a Nonexistent Object

Seeing a physically nonexistent object, such as a phantom or a ghost, is now considered to be the subject of literature and not of science, but it is impossible to deny that humans have such experiences even now. I, along with many of my friends and relatives, have had such experience. A *phantom* appears to be similar to a natural phenomenon, like a fireball or pillar of fire, and a *ghost* presents some human image. Ghost as a human image has survived throughout history to the present day. Why do we have such experiences?

My model of the human machine provides an explanation. The basic mechanism is that the image we see is, most of the time, a faithful copy of the objects of the outside world, but sometimes the image is fabricated by the brain in the same way as we see a dream or daydream. In a fully awake state, a talented person can produce the likeness of anyone whom he has seen only casually. The artist holds the person's facial features in his or her memory, and reproduces them on a piece of paper. The artist *sees* the memory's image and copies it on the paper. So it is not surprising that we can see an internally fabricated image under certain conditions.

Figure 6.04.1 shows the mechanism of seeing a ghost according to my model. Suppose that I am in an uncomfortable state, such as walking in a graveyard on a dark night while feeling a sense of guilt toward someone whom I made unhappy while he was still alive. Then the memories of the scene, including both of us, emerge one after the other in my mind. The world surrounding me provides a matching background where a revengeful person's image may appear.

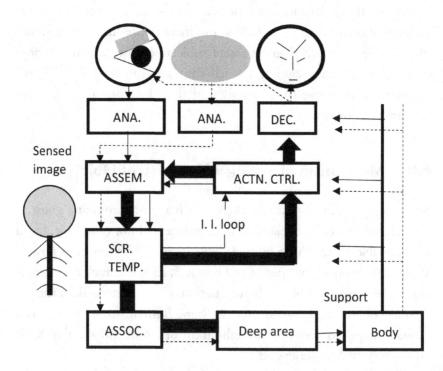

Figure 6.04.1 Mechanism of seeing a nonexistent object like a ghost

The person's image is excited internally. Because of the scary situation, the support level of the brain's internal image circuit is high, and the sensors are sensitized by the person's internal image by the mechanism I discussed in section 4.17. If the internal image circuit activity intensifies to the critical level, even a nonexistent object is caught by the hyperactive sensor, or any normal object caught by the eyes is misidentified by the internal image circuit as the image of the revengeful ghost. Any not so clearly visible round object may be seen as the face of the ghost. Such misidentification occurs only momentarily, yet a scared mind is stuck on the fearful image, and the panic state continues and intensifies.

The size of the emerging image depends on the level of internal tension, the level of fear, and the brain's support level. Usually a phantom is less menacing, and the image occupies only a small part of the vision frame, like observing a flying fireball. Such a small-scale image is created by a malfunction of the hyperactive sensor and analyzer, whose function includes pixel image differentiation to help increase the contrast. This process intensifies the noise of the image coming to the receptor. A phantom often invites curiosity, which mitigates the fear, but a ghost's image gives no way out, and I freeze in panic. A ghost's image is usually quite extensive, and it may occupy a large portion of the vision frame. It includes images of other senses, such as words of curses, or even an unpleasant smell that fills the air. In some cases, I've even felt the sense of something cold touching the exposed part of my body. A ghost is created by vision plus all the other sense channels' hyperactivity.

Figure 6.04.1 shows the internal signal flow in the functional diagram. The ghost's image is excited in the internal image circuit. It leaks to the mechanism of the eyes' direction control. The eye direction control moves by the directive of the internal image (the dotted line). This mechanism fabricates *image*. The fake image is sensed by the somatic sensors attached the line-of-sight control mechanism, is analyzed by its own analyzer (section 2.23) and returns to the internal image circuit. This positive feedback sensitizes the eyes and the vision channel, and the images of more nonexistent objects are created and picked up. The internal image circuit misidentifies any image associated with the expected ghost image. This misidentification process is aggravated since a ghost's image usually does not carry any color. To the fabricated and misidentified image, realistic features are attached, and the ghost's image expands in size and image content. Once such an image establishes itself, the brain misidentifies more images, such as the smell of rotten flesh, and hears words of curses. Everything goes out of control. In my childhood during wartime, I saw what ghosts really looked like.

If one gets into such a state, one should take whatever possible action necessary to reduce the fear. One frequent practice in the Buddhist cultural zone is to say a short tantra or sutra to appease the ghost's spirit. Yet, as a practical matter, doing even that is not easy in a tense state. As a small child at the time of World War II, I had such experiences, since so many people perished under the most hideous conditions. Some victims simply evaporated into thin air by way of nuclear explosion.

A ghost image from such a death is truly terrifying. Yet seeing a ghost is a normal function of the brain, developed to adapt to the hostile natural habitat while fighting for survival and often victimizing fellow humans. I think the image of a ghost could be the first and the most primitive form of human conscience and the origin of the sense of morality. "Thou shall not kill" is the most basic moral code of any religion. The worldwide experience of seeing ghosts and the telling of ghost stories, several of my own, confirms my point. Because of their archaic origin, phantoms and ghosts play a significant role in archetypal images. So ghosts should be given their proper place to enrich human cultural life.

I miss the late Professor Kathryn Josserand of Florida State University, who was an excellent teller of Maya ghost stories. Maya ghost stories are terrifying. Their image of the human is the skeleton, and flesh is simply its clothes. Ghosts are significant elements of every culture.

6.05 Mysteries by Memory Failure

It is impossible to define the failure mode of the brain. Yet, since I have a hardware model, it is possible to identify some special failures and their psychological effects. Some such cases create situations that appear mysterious. Our image memory has only limited capacity, and the incoming images have unlimited volume. Our brain is constantly throwing irrelevant images away. Then, if the lost information suddenly becomes necessary, it is not available. Such a situation may be mistaken as telepathy, the most popular topic of parapsychology. I believe the following story is not telepathy but a case of lost memory:

When I was still in Japan, I learned English conversation from a woman, Ms. L. H. Eight years later, in the U.S., I learned from a Japanese classmate what had happened with her. That being my most hectic period, I just dismissed the story. Eight more years passed. As I established myself in the U.S., I remembered her. So I asked the same classmate if he knew her whereabouts. He checked with all the then accessible classmates, but no one knew.

As I was thinking of Ms. L. H., a strange idea emerged, namely that she was at the national monument called Pipe Springs in Arizona. I have never been able to remember where the information came from, but I felt it so strongly that in 1978 I visited the national monument and asked if she was there. There were persons who knew a Ms. L. (but not the last name), and their stories generally checked out with the story I had heard from my Japanese classmate. When I went to Pipe Springs, Ms. L. had already gone, but I was sure that Ms. L. was the Ms. L. H. whom I was looking for. If I had never learned of her whereabouts before, this was a case of telepathy with incredible odds. Yet I believe I can explain this story as a case of memory loss. The circumstances of getting the information were completely lost, but the key information of her whereabouts survived. Since Pipe Springs was not a popular national monument, the information had not come from my personal investigation.

I struggled hard to recover the memory of the circumstances of the acquisition of this information. My search remains unsuccessful after forty years. From this scenario's simplicity, such a case could possibly be held up as evidence of telepathy. Yet I absolutely refuse to explain such a case by invoking something that is even more mysterious. This experience convinced me that the memory of the circumstance of the acquisition of the information is an integral part of a healthy memory. From what I explained in chapter 5, I should be able to recover the time of the day when I had gotten the information, but I cannot remember even that.

Ms. L. H. was an excellent teacher. I never forget great teachers. I still remember how Ms. L. H. kindly arranged for me to learn how to make a telephone call in English by inviting me to her residence in the Tachikawa air base. It is a characteristic of my hero and heroine worship that I never forget great teachers (section 4.10).

In my twenties, I was confident of my memory capability. This overconfidence costed me dearly. I forgot the name of a very important African American woman—Ms. E?—who was Dr. William Shockley's assistant and who assembled the first transistor for him. She was such a high-class, sophisticated woman, who smilingly told me, "Maybe I didn't do so well?" She admired Dr. Shockley. She was the key witness who helped me clear up the misunderstanding about Dr. Shockley, but somehow I lost her last name. I regret that (section 4.27). Yet in this case, I remember that my encounter with her was in Bell Laboratories building 2, on the third floor, at about 4:00 p.m. The memory of the circumstance of my acquisition of this information has survived.

Why did such memory loss happen? I remember Ms. L. H. and Ms. E. by their visual images, but the source information holding the whereabouts of Ms. L. H. and the last name of Ms. E. has been lost. As I showed in section 2.25, the vision and language channels communicate in the association area. Then the connection of the visible image and the language image identifiers is weak or indirect since they are from different sense channels. This is consistent with old-age memory loss. What is lost is more often the name of a person or object, whereas the visible image survives.

6.06 Dual Personality and Doppelganger

Perhaps the most mysterious mental phenomenon is dual personality. Reading the records of such cases, I am mystified because the behavior of the person is so far out of this world, yet still there are some suggestive features. That is, if person A and person B coexist in a single person, either A or B does not, or both A and B do not, know of the existence of the paired other. This can be the result of a neuron connection failure, that is, the breakdown of the connection from bidirectional to unidirectional, or complete disconnection of huge memory blocks. Since each character emerges alternately, this is a restorable connection breakdown of the memory circuit. Yet how this disconnection occurs is hard to explain by my model. In A or B state, both A and B must share the same basic images necessary for life maintenance. The volume of such images, C, is huge, and these images must exist as a complex, entangled web in the brain's image memory. Then why can't A and B communicate bidirectionally via such images?

Psychoanalysis' interpretation of double personality is that it is a growth of a complex to an unmanageable extent that takes over the ego. I find that this explanation is not easy to accept, since the connection breakdown mechanism is not explained. Suppose the complex is the image united by an emotion, X. Then both the complex and the ego can get into the state controlled by the emotion center X. Then the complex and the ego can be connected through the center X. I show the connection mechanism that should exist in figure 6.06.1. Do such connections disconnect and reconnect all at once? I cannot make a reasonable hardware mechanism of such an operation. Figure 6.06.1 cannot be separated simply. The character A and the character B cannot obviously be independent from each other.

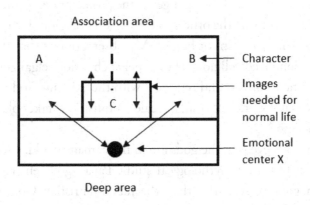

Figure 6.06.1 Connection of image identifiers required for explaining double personality

What is furthermore curious is that double personality cases have decreased in recent years, since about the 1950s. This is the time when precision mental testing methods such as the lie detector, EEG, and brain imager became available. In this stressful society, everyone, including me, wishes to live a different life. So I expect that some cases of double personality could be explained by the person's sophisticated acting.

Doppelganger can be explained by my model. The image of a person that makes up the missing part of the person's personality can be created in the image world of an intensely introverted character. Since it is a human image, it is enriched by adding more and more features, and finally it becomes quite real. Because doppelganger is a complementary personality, it can be an integral part of the self-conscious life, and more often than not it becomes the driving force of personal development. Specifically, it is possible, and is quite beneficial, to have an internal dialogue about highly personal issues, difficult personal decision-making, and resolution of personal conflicts.

Doppelganger emerges like a dear sibling, and since it is compassionate and accepting, it is able to persuade the SELF to make a hard-to-swallow decision. Often, a doppelganger appears as a protective deity who shows life's direction. From my personal observation, a truly religious person has a doppelganger as the protector deity. Such a person never tries to convert the others to the person's religion. He or she keeps the deity strictly to him or herself. My observation is that the practice of institutionalized religions is to expel such a doppelganger from the mind of a new convert and replace it with the existing God or Buddha. If that does not work out, a small-scale "Inquisition" takes place. I know of such a case.

Pagans believe that the gods are in their image world. I reached this conclusion from my mythological study. Pagan gods emerge in much more imaginative scenarios than the Judeo-Christian God, but at the same time, they come down to talk with us and help us realistically. This contradictory feature makes me believe that they are surely in the image world. Since their gods are more like close friends, pagans are more hesitant and more ashamed to behave dishonorably than non-pagans. Just read the

Greek hero stories of Homer. The Greek heroes held personal honor as the highest value. Honor became their basic value. The relationship between the SELF and the doppelganger is like the relationship between friends and not like the relationship between the ruler and the ruled. In the Greek hero saga, I am quite sure that Athena Parthenos emerged in Odysseus's mind as a noble doppelganger. In Buddhism, there are numerous stories of pilgrims going out to search for Buddha. When they come back home, they find the Buddha in their own mind.

6.07 Why Do Our Ancestors Look Mysterious?

Modern humans have the habit of evaluating ancient peoples' accomplishments by referring to the presently available capability. This trend emerges most dramatically when modern humans see the works of the people of thousands of years ago. Those people had no diesel engines or explosives. They never possessed a strong structural material like steel, and in the New World they did not even have any metal, wheels, or draft animals. If modern humans who hire mechanical contractors to do even minor house repairs look at such monuments as the Maya pyramid or Inca-Tiahuanaco stone edifices, they are naturally overwhelmed by the objects' size and craftsmanship. This trend has created a prosperous video/book industry, and these media highlight ETs as being responsible for building these structures.

Is this really fair to the builders of those spectacular monuments? Do we have to invoke an ET's brainpower to build the monuments? From my experience of actually seeing the magnificent hiero-megalithic ancient structures, I feel a deep sense of disgust toward the ET stories. Hidden behind this view is unfair racist disrespect for the capability of the ancient people, whose descendants now mostly live in poverty. Most of such monuments are now in countries that are not among the world's industrial powers, and the people who live there are poor in their living standard, but their ancestors were once great builders. On the side of the Sacrificial Cenote of Chichén Itzá, Mexico, I told our guide, Alfonso Escobeto, quoting the legend of King Hunac Ceel, "If they make me the king of such a great city, I am ready to jump into this cenote!" Alfonso's eyes sparkled as he said, "Me too!" I love and respect such a proud descendant of the great Itzá.

To build an object of such an enormous size required determination to accomplish the objective. Technology was only the secondary requirement. Their determination is what we no longer have. We never dare to try what our ancestors did.

How our ancestors built the spectacular monument is now mostly forgotten. Ancient Phoenicians circumnavigated Africa and found that it is a huge island. A detail of the story that Herodotus unknowingly wrote in his history was interpreted by Alexander von Humboldt. The Phoenicians' voyage, commissioned by King Neco of Egypt, actually happened in the seventh century BC. We should learn from the attitude of von Humboldt when we see great ancient monuments. Motivated by this story, I challenged the tough question: How were the Inca able to build almost a modern socialist empire in a short two-hundred-year period in the Andean highlands? My answer is simple: The Inca claimed that they were proud successors of Tiahuanaco, which had already been a socialist empire, and the Inca took over it. Tiahuanaco's ancestry goes back to 3,000 years ago, which means there was enough time to establish the system.

A spectacular accomplishment of the Polynesians was their arrival at South America and their return trip to Polynesia with some cultivated plants and a new cultural style. Since I read Thor Heyerdahl's *American Indians in the Pacific*, I compared the evidence he found on Easter Island with the Inca and Tiahuanaco. The ahu Vinap of Easter Island is built not in the style of the Tiahuanaco but of the Inca. The ahu is built from nearly the same-size rocks like in the Inca edifices. The time of high Polynesian activity was the thirteenth century, and not earlier than that. That was the time of the Inca.

Now, at the beginning of the twenty-first century, not only human society, but also the trend of the natural sciences, is going through a drastic change. As an insider of the scientific community, I feel we are becoming too easygoing by our dependence on expensive equipment and data processors. Natural science has become the task of financial elites. Even in the theoretical front, there is a trend of starting from basic equations, setting the initial and boundary conditions, and dumping them all into a huge data processor. Whatever the answer the processor spits out is physics, chemistry, or economics. There is not much struggle by the human mind involved. Such a culture deteriorates our thinking capability. The works of the physicists of the nineteenth century may soon become mysterious to us. Shouldn't we learn more from physicists of that time such as Rudolf Clausius, James Clerk Maxwell, Max Planck, and Albert Einstein?

Since I have read the original papers of Wilhelm Wien, Lord Rayleigh, Max Planck, and Albert Einstein, I learned how these physicists created quantum mechanics and special relativity. They started from very simple ideas and then got to the bottom of their ideas by way of the strenuous effort of thinking. Isn't it necessary for a college physics class to familiarize students with these originals?

With all that I've discussed about our ancestors' abilities, regarding the ancient peoples' works as mysterious is not a virtue of modesty but is the symptom of decadence. We need to revitalize the capability of thinking and doing.

6.08 Mystery of the Ancient Myths

The ancient world presents us with many wonders: hiero-megalithic monuments, amazingly high technology, and some very advanced scientific thoughts in astronomy and mathematics. Such accomplishments honor our great ancestors and remind us how great human thinking power can be. Instead of giving all the credit to ETs, we should humbly learn from our ancestors.

Yet as I study the ancient world, I feel that there are a few true surprises. Freedom of the movement of ancient peoples is one of these. From the extinction of large mammals in the New World, the speed of migration of the Native Americans from Beringia to Tierra del Fuego was estimated to be less than a thousand years. Then the yearly movement was 10 km. If one generation is twenty-five years, every generation moved 250 km. Is this impossible? I do not think so. As determined as they were in building spectacular hiero-megalithic edifices, I imagine it was hard but not impossible for them.

The north → south migration of Native Americans is, however, an easy puzzle to solve. There is yet another, deeper mystery in mythology that I have recognized but that has not yet attracted attention from the others, namely that there is a curious similarity between Greek myth and Japanese myth. In Greek myth, one popular story is the myth of Demeter and Kore, worshipped at the Eleusis shrine near Athens, Greece (section 2.07).

In this myth, the Greek sea god Poseidon appears as a violent invader. Poseidon is the god of the rough seas, and his totem is the horse. This god appears in Japanese myth as a carbon copy by the name of Susanowo. In the 1950s, when I was aspiring to be an historian, I recognized this similarity and did some investigation.

There is every reason to believe that the two myths were related, but by which route was the older Asia Minor version carried to the Far East? It is impossible that the myth had been carried by sea route. The myth must have been carried overland. The natural land route goes through the extremely unhospitable arid desert region of Central Asia, where there is no water that looks like sea. So how did the image of the violent sea god survive in the mind of the traveler and be carried so far away?

Suppose that a father of the travelers lived on the Mediterranean coast. If his son was born somewhere east of the Caspian Sea, the son has no idea of the formidable power of the rough sea. This man's son, born somewhere in Central Asia, could not even imagine any sea. The memory must be lost in one generation. When their descendant arrived in northern China and saw a real sea once again, how could he recover the myth of a violent sea god whose totem is the horse and who violated his own sister goddess?

This means that their movement was done within only one generation. From Japanese mythology, the myth must have come from the Jōmon period. The goddess Demeter's Japanese counterpart was from that period. So this travel must have taken place around 3,000 BC, when the travelers could not have been on horseback. The saddle and stirrup were invented much later. Remember the movie scenes of the

Trojan War. In about 1100 BC, Achilles and Hector rode in a chariot and not directly on horseback. Therefore the Asia Minor travelers must have walked ten thousand kilometers through the rough terrain in one generation. For what purpose? The neolithic people had not only great inventors and scientists but also great explorers. If that was their desire to know what the rest of the earth was like, they deserve high respect as explorers as well.

6.09 Sense of Complexity

When we look at an animal body or a complex machine built by system engineers, we are often mystified and ask ourselves, "How can such a complex structure be built by nature or by humans?" The building of an animal body is still one of the most complex and fascinating research subjects. How could such a structure be built automatically? A curious mind never fails to pose such a question. I have been eager to look into the mechanism of the human mind since my youth because it is complex.

The human sense of complexity is also cultural in the same way as the sense of time. From 1973 to my retirement in 2000, I worked as a semiconductor chip designer. In 1974, my first chip, an 8-bit D/A converter containing only seventy bipolar transistors, worked by its first design. A manager was surprised and said, "It is unbelievable that such a *complex* chip worked by the first trial." This was not unusual at that time: any manager who let his subordinate design an integrated circuit carrying middle-scale complexity was afraid about whether the complex task could be executed successfully or not.

Then, in 1977, I got a job fixing a mis-designed 8-bit microprocessor having about seven thousand MOSFETs (metal-oxide-semiconductor field-effect transistors). The circuit appeared absolutely impossible to me, and I struggled and struggled. It was a bad dream, even now. Thereafter, from 1979 to 1984, I designed the BellMac32A/B, a 32-bit microprocessor having about one hundred eighty thousand MOSFETs, after only three short yet hard years of struggle. I never felt that the processor was impossibly complex. It worked by the first trial. I was sure it would work, but our director (the same person who had commented on my seventy-transistor chip before) was not. He moved out of his position, presumably, afraid of taking the blame that he expected if the processor design failed. He must have thought that it would ruin his career. Then, one week later, the processor worked perfectly. Complexity was frightening to him, but not to me.

This immunity to the fear of complexity I have now is due to neutralization of the sense of fear of the object's complexity. If I become confident enough about a complex object, it does not scare me anymore. This is not a reckless confidence. Since a complex object casts a certain aura to the human mind, the one who can handle it gains pride and confidence, and that motivates one's challenge to tackle more and more complex objects. Such motivation is what created modern high-power processors. From my own experience, the mysterious feeling toward a complex object emerges from lack of experience and courage to deal with such objects.

This is interesting as technical history. Only 150 years ago, the most complex machine was the pipe organ. One hundred years ago, the most complex machine was the telephone switching machine. Now the most complex processors have a practically infinite number of MOSFETs in them. Yet the most challenging task of complexity still remains, namely, to clarify how an animal body is built by the genetic code.

Complexity and beauty mix in music. I am listening to Beethoven's Seventh Symphony right now. I am still mystified, how Beethoven ever managed to compose this piece. It is not only complex but also deeply philosophical and ultimately beautiful. I still feel complexity is a wide-open frontier of study by the human mind. Maybe this is the last frontier.

6.10   Trial and Error of Complexity

From my experience as a VLSI (very large-scale integrated) chip designer, I realized that the mystery of complexity originates from the lack of courage to squarely face a complex object. Instead of hesitation, a simple decision to directly confront a complex object dissipates the sense of mystery. When ancient humans had to solve a complex problem, they dared to try whatever they could think of, and the chance of success depended on their luck. The consequence of such an attempt ending up in success may be mysterious. Yet the secret is flexibility of strategy to attain the objective. The first blind trial never hits the objective, but we learn a lot about the peculiarity of the task. The second trial discovers an efficient way to execute the objective. Then, in the third trial, we execute the work using the efficient way by focusing all the energy to accomplish the objective. The crucial point is, unless we persevere to perform the first and second steps, we can never find the most efficient way using the available resources to complete the task. Once the best way is found, we should not hesitate to pour all the available energy into it.

As a realistic example of this trial-and-error attempt, I describe my experience with the BellMac32A/B microprocessor circuit design in 1979–84. My position in the design team was to accept the logic design from the architect, and to direct the circuit layout team. Since the logic integrity was ensured by the architects, my task was to make the processor work at 7 MHz clock, which was well above the state of the art in 1979. To accomplish this objective, the size of each of the 180,000 MOSFETs had to be properly set.

In the 1979–84 period, computer-aided design capability was in its infancy. A good circuit simulator called ADVICE was available, but the *gate-level simulator*, which is able to exercise the entire processor, had just emerged, and the simulator could not include resistance-capacitance delay time of long connection wires. The processing technology available at that time offered only one level of metal wire connection, so the delay time of wire crossover by the high-resistance polysilicon layer had to be estimated for each signal path by the circuit simulator. This was a huge task. What is more, the circuit layout had to be executed concurrently with the circuit design. If I could not provide timely design information to the layout team, the entire project could come to a standstill. How could I satisfy all the needs? My assistant, Bob Beairsto, and I, and most of my team members worked twelve hours day, seven days a week, from 1979 to 1983.

I looked at the delivered logic diagram and first designed the output drivers. The specification of the output drivers was set by the load capacitance and the output delay time, and that determined the size of the driver MOSFET. A signal-input circuit is simple, but any circuit that is connected to the chip's outside must be carefully laid out so that the voltage surge does not destroy the MOSFETs and also does not induce latch-up of the CMOS chip. Such layout is time-consuming. I delivered the design instructions to the layout team, and Bob and I got some breathing space to plan the next step. Since the output driver size is set, the processor's internal circuit must be able to drive the large driver MOSFETs in a short time. While we were doing the design, logic design sheets were arriving every day. I had to deliver the circuit designs so that the layout team would not be idle. What could we do? This was the critical period of the project.

After struggling to simulate and optimize the delay time of several long signal paths, I found that the delay time roughly depended on the number of signals combined. I hit on an idea: count the number of signals combined between a pair of clocking points, and classify all the signal paths. If a signal path consists of an inverter (1), a two-input NAND gate (2), an AND3-AND2-NOR gate (3 + 2 + 1), and a transmission gate (2), then the number of signals combined is $1 + 2 + (3 + 2 + 1) + 2 = 11$. I asked Bob Beairsto to go through all the logic diagrams to count the numbers. The number ranked the signal paths from about 4 to 15. This was not a complicated task, but Bob went through at an amazing speed and marked the complex signal paths with red pencil, with the number of signals combined in the path.

I checked all the paths higher than rank 10 and saw the generated signal by the path was really required within the same clock phase. If the signal was not required within the same clock phase, I returned the logic diagram to the architects with the suggestion to move some gates either to an earlier slot or a later slot in the clock phase, or duplicate some logic circuit to reduce the number of signals combined. As for a few signal paths that could not do this reduction, I instructed the layout team to keep enough space margin on the chip so that later MOSFET size adjustment would be possible without affecting the rest of the circuit structure. As for the signal paths of rank 7 or less, I instructed the team to lay out the circuit by using the standard-size MOSFETs. For anything above, I asked them to provide some extra, but not extensive, space margin to adjust the MOSFET size later.

After starting the layout operation, Bob and I began circuit delay simulation starting from the highest-ranked signal paths, and we sized the MOSFETs to satisfy the minimum 7 MHz clock requirements. Since by this time the actual layout diagram was coming back from the layout team, Bob and I were able to include all parasitic resistance and capacitance of the connecting wires to simulate all the signal path delay times accurately. Each signal path was simulated several times to minimize the signal delay time by adjusting all the MOSFET sizes. The revised MOSFET sizes were delivered to the layout team to finalize the circuit layout. As Bob and I finished and delivered the design of signal paths higher than rank 7, two stacks of the simulation printout became higher than average human height. Both of us personally had confidence that this was not a 7 MHz processor but a 10 MHz processor. As we finished the work, we were surprised to hear that our director had moved out from his position. He missed getting the credit for the success. One week later, the BellMac32A processor at 10 MHz clock emerged from the Bell Laboratories, Murray Hill, test center. The best processor worked at the top speed of 17 MHz clock and created a commotion in a processor workshop.

This was a task that appeared impossible at the beginning. Its success gave me confidence later to struggle with the complex mystery of human self-consciousness. For this project, we had a superb middle-level manager, Bob Krambeck. He protected me and my assistant from the high-level pressure to expedite the work. Without his protection, the project would never have been successful. The BellMac32A and its follow-up, the BellMac32B, were mass-produced and were used in the Blit terminal of Bell Labs' Computing Science Research Center. I used this terminal to write all my earlier books on CMOS digital circuit theory.

The processor experienced a sad fate. It was flushed down the drain by ATT's computer business failure. Since our new director (from a powerful political clan) moved the design team from Murray Hill to the Pennsylvania countryside, we lost over thirty well-trained designers, mostly to Silicon Valley. They were later quite successful there. I was already too old to move out. Yet the technical success of the project provided a lifelong memory of confidence to everyone. My coworkers who contributed to the project, Bob Beairsto, Brian Colbry, Alex Lopez, Mike Chung, Bob Krambeck, Mike Killian, Dan Blahut, Carry Garrenton, and Hing So, and many others on the layout team, were the best of the best engineers who executed the last megaproject of Bell Telephone Laboratories. It was a Wagnerian end.

6.11   Top-Down Approach to Complexity

Complexity is the first hurdle for those who attempt to break into brain research. I described my experience with complexity in sections 6.09 and 6.10, and I am at least no longer afraid of the brain's complexity. So how do I proceed? The last half century's history of complex data processor development showed how to do that. The method was skillfully applied to design more and more complex processors.

The method is the top-down approach. The system function is first described by the diagram showing the input-output relationship of the system, and then the system is separated, one level lower, into smaller-scale functional blocks and their connections. The connected functional blocks execute the same system's input-output operation. To do so, each functional block has a well-defined set of input and output signals that connect the blocks and the outside. Then each block is subdivided into connected subblocks, and the same process is repeated hierarchically. Each division simplifies the design problem.

I was familiarized with this method while working on the Bell Laboratories BellMac32A microprocessor project.[4] In the 1980s, AT&T wanted to break in to the computer business, and the first

[4] R. H. Krambeck, D. E. Blahut, et al., "Top-Down Design of a One-Chip 32-Bit CPU," VLSI81, Edinburgh, Scotland, September 1982; M. Shoji, "Electrical Design of BellMac32A Microprocessor," ICCC 82, New York, October 1982.

requirement was to have its own processor that ran AT&T's UNIX software efficiently. So I was scouted as a member of this project team.

A very important point of this technique that can never be overstated is that every time the design level goes down, the level issues specification of the lower level *precisely*, and if that cannot be done for any technical reason, the present-level design is redone. A well-designed level issues the lower-level specification. That is the key point.

My study of human self-consciousness is carried out by separating the self-conscious human brain into eleven well-defined functional blocks. Their names and functions are shown in figure 2.14.1. This was the third level after the previous two levels of separation (sections 1.08 and 1.20). By separating the complex brain into several blocks, I am able to simplify the complex brain operation into the interaction of less complex and more precisely defined lower-level functional blocks. A high-level psychological operation like self-consciousness is well reproduced by only a three-level hierarchical model of the brain. This is certainly a reductionist approach, but it is closely tied with the integrated function of the system.

The three-level decomposition of the brain is adequate since self-consciousness is so robust that it can tolerate brain damage caused by stroke, tumor, or invasive surgery. This suggests that its mechanism must be simple. If this is so, then the basic mechanism identification does not require a detailed mechanism of the individual neuron-level operation. If we consider the system function at the neuron level, we realize that there are too many possibilities—so many that I am never able to maintain an overall perspective. Yet if the brain is described by its input-output relationship only, there is no way to nail down the mechanism. This is the philosopher's and the psychologist's approach practiced until the last century.

There is a proper level of decomposition of the system to take advantage of simplification available. What will be the level of decomposition of the brain? This is the level that can handle the brain's data, the images, flexibly. This is mostly manageable by the three-level decomposition, but sometimes I need one more level, that is, the neuron level. This lower-level decomposition is necessary only to nail down the mechanism of sensation and the brain's analog operation.

Application of the top-down design method to build a complex system can be made quite efficient by an additional strategic choice: one level design execution sends out a *scout* to find the know-how of the still one level lower design, to get the general guidelines of that level's design. As the design reaches the lower level, the best way to design is known already. The top-down method is executed to be specific to go down the levels and to be general enough to accept the specification from the higher level.

Top-down system design finds its direct parallel in animal body structure building. After several splits of the egg, each cell has a definite body destination. The differentiation is directed by the structure already built by the earlier splitting. Then each cell splits and creates a structure, which directs the next-level structure. Genetic instruction is coded hierarchically. The carrier of the directive is the structure-sensitive chemical signal issued by the already built structure. The hierarchical process continues in a series-parallel fashion until all the design directives are executed.

Issuance of genetic instruction by the existing structure has been shown by the elegant polar coordinate model, which explains malfunction of grafted roach legs. The experiment showed that the existing body structure issues a directive to build the lost structure. Genetic information builds structure, and the structure directs the genetic information carrier to issue the next step's instruction. If the structure is not properly built, the next instruction is to undo the last step and repeat the step once again. There is close interaction between the information source and the result of its execution. Since the genetic code is thus structured, animal body construction is proper almost all the time. The go-between agents are macromolecules, whose chemical reaction is extremely structure sensitive. If this process is transcribed to structure the building of any complex system, the chance of making an error becomes quite small.

6.12 Uncertainty and Probability

From the time of our ancestors, we learned that our expectations are not always fulfilled. As human society developed, life became more complex, and life's uncertainty increased. A feature of Darwinian evolution by natural selection, that intraspecies competition is more severe than interspecies competition, was aggravated by the feature of Lamarckian evolution, by inheriting a winning strategy and desirable features of life from one generation to the next generation. This created the twenty-first-century brutal mass society.

In our modern life, success or even survival is a matter of *chance*, which is mistaken to be the matter of an individual's *choice* by philosophers and social scientists, because the basic information required to make a career choice is hidden by the social institution. A company hired a talented scientist and then declares bankruptcy only nine months later. The scientist never knew the company's financial basis. Here, the concept of probability is the general concern. After my graduation, I got offers from two major companies' research laboratories. I chose the lucky one, since the other one was never successful in the emerging field of integrated circuit technology. If I had chosen that company, I might have lost my job.

Probability is an analog parameter associated with a certain set of images that carry a different degree of impact and reality in life. As such, it is similar to sensation, but it does not cover all the images. Sensation specifies impact of image on life, and probability specifies reality of the expected event that has not yet been revealed. As sensation is the measure of fear, probability is the measure of worry and anxiety, which is fear projected onto the future. Like sensation, probability is sensed quantitatively by the body. High probability of forthcoming of disaster makes me feel a shooting cold running down my spine.

Some probability can be rationally estimated by mathematics as a number between 0 and 1, but the probability we deal with in secular life is sensed in the same way as sensation, as the bodily sense and not by a number. Even if a rational or objective estimate of probability is possible, often the algorithm of estimate may not be unique. This is the case of even a scientific probability such as in meteorology, predicting the chance of rain. Any method of computing probability carries its own probability. If the probability of an expected event is p, and if the probability of the algorithm and data used for the estimate is q, then at most what I can hope for is that the real probability is in the range of pq and p/q. If $p/q > 1$ or $pq \ll 1$, the estimate itself loses validity. Practically this limit is reached almost right away.

This feature of probability dictates that the method of calculation of probability requires a model as the backup position. Here arises a most bizarre situation. Secular probability of the lottery or gambling has a well-defined model, but not all the probabilities that emerge in natural science have a clear model. Probability in classical statistical mechanics has a clear model, yet quantum mechanics does not put weight on making such a model. Its objective is to define the measurable parameters of the quantum system and to establish mathematical relations among the probabilities of the physical parameters. Then something quite strange, such as negative probability (called a ghost), sometimes emerges.

Yet even more strange is that the probability given by established quantum mechanics is so accurate that we do indeed trust the theory. I feel the same mystery here, as very invasive brain surgery keeps self-consciousness almost intact. I give my interpretation of this feature in section 6.31. Yet isn't it time to create a model to guide theoretical developments? No popular book on string theory explains why the theoretical anomalies vanish if the string vibrates in ten-dimensional space-time. This is the reason why the string theory appears unrealistic. If they could show a model, I would trust it as a realistic theory, even if there was no experimental support. It is really a shame to see that the most secular application of probability (in gambling and the lottery) has a better-defined model according to the legal standard enforced by the attorneys. Attorneys are more precise than physicists? That hurts my pride as a physicist. I struggle to restore this pride in the rest of this chapter.

Probability is a mathematical concept, but it is something of its own, quite independent from information. If this parameter is regarded as information, many weird features emerge. Thus, its features must be studied not only from the point of view of mathematics and physics but also from the viewpoint of psychology.

6.13 Is Probability Information?

Does probability qualify as information? This question appears irrelevant in the probability of secular matters, but a precise observation in certain secular cases brings out its curious features. This feature becomes crucial in quantum physics: if it were information, the probability-setting signal could not propagate faster than the velocity of light. This has an impact on the interpretation of quantum mechanics and was a subject of controversy during the twentieth century.

Let us consider an information-transmission channel having a protocol defined as follows: A single channel sends $2n + 1$ binary bits (HIGH or LOW) in sequence, where n is a integer. If the majority ($> n$) is HIGH or LOW, 1 bit of HIGH or LOW *information* is transmitted through the channel, respectively. The HIGH-LOW sequence from the channel is perfectly random, and only the majority of HIGHs or LOWs determines the transmitted 1 bit.

Suppose that the first signal came. How much information arrived? In the channel, 1 bit is divided into its fractions. Until $n + 1$ bits are either all HIGH or all LOW, there is no chance of knowing what is to come. If that is the case, then $1/(n + 1)$ bit arrived by the first bit. If the first $2n$ bits are half HIGH and half LOW, then $1/(2n + 1)$ bit arrived. The volume of the information, I (bit), by the first bit is in the range $1/(n + 1) > I > 1/(2n + 1)$. As signals 1, 2, 3, … arrive, each bit carries successively more fractional information. But until signal 1, 2, 3, …$(n + 1)$ bit arrives, the chance of getting definite information remains zero. As signals $(n + 1)$, $(n + 2)$, … arrive, the chance of getting definite information begins to increase, and as all $(2n + 1)$ signals arrive, the set of signals defines 1 bit of information securely.

If we are given a probability of an event, we are in the same situation as this example, waiting for more signals to arrive. Without these *additional* signals, we cannot take action. Here I use the term *signal* to refer both to the carrier of definite information and to the fractional information. This scenario is relevant to neuron majority logic. This *wait and see* feature of neuron logic is one reason why neurons are used not to execute binary logic in the brain, but to build image structure. The brain cannot display a partial image, since any image is held by a subcritical oscillator. Until all the loop elements are fully excited, an image cannot be displayed. The brain can do this since it is not a synchronous logic circuit. The neuron circuit carries an analog parameter, the intensity of excitation, that is, sensation. Sensation reflects how confident the SELF is of the action directed by the image.

What can 1 bit of information do? It enables the making of one out of two choices, such as the choice of object A or B, on a secure basis. In the rigidly controlled society we live in, we are not allowed to take any action by chance. Attorneys are there to punish anyone who takes probabilistic action, and that is why secular probability is more precisely defined than probability in physics. Speeding on the highway and not being fined is a matter of chance, but the chance is at least predictable from the local government's policy. The probability computation algorithm of quantum field theory is a prescription set by mathematics without any model. It is really surprising that the algorithm gives such a precise answer!

If a system receives information, the system's operation is definite. If the system receives a set of signals, and if even one of these signals is probabilistic, the system's response becomes probabilistic. Since probability cannot be combined with information to create any definite response of the system, it is really not an information. If the analog value of probability is given, we can take action only after digitizing it to 0 or 1 by some means.

When I hear that there is a 50 percent chance of rain, I look at the western sky and decide what to do. In this case, the probability signal only initiates the action to get more signals. If there is anything that can direct definite action, it is information. That is why probability is not information. Information has a hierarchical structure. Down to the level of 1 bit, any information can be split into smaller and smaller chunks, and the chunks are still qualified as information. Similarly, a molecule can be split into atoms chemically. The reduced size of the object carries less information. As splitting reaches the atom's level, it cannot be split anymore chemically. Then even the information describing the object splits into probability. It is not surprising at all that probability describes the quantum world.

The macroscopic world begins at the molecular level, where classical parameters become proper. Why is that so? A single electron is able to be in one of two states, its spin being either up or down (section 6.20). An electron's state carries only 1 bit, the atom of information. Further splitting is impossible. The same is true for atoms also. Suppose that N of such atoms makes up a molecular structure, and its fraction, rN, is so tightly bound that these atoms cannot take on independent states. Then the structure carries $2^{(1-r)N}$ distinguishable varieties. For this number to be large, N must be the size of the molecules. This means that even if N is large, the structure may behave as a quantum object, if factor r is close to unity. An atomic nucleus consists of nucleons, but they are so tightly bound that the nucleus appears to be an integrated unit. An even larger object is the *buckyball*, which consists of tightly bound carbon atoms. Such a molecule appears to show the quantum effect, like the double-slit interference effect. A structure's distinguishability is the qualification of any macroscopic object.

An image is a very interesting object from this viewpoint. Since any image is generally connected to many other images, it can be split. Yet the brain cannot handle a split image as it is. The image must be requalified. This is the problem I discussed in section 3.21. The SELF and its functions are able to carry out qualification consciously by sending the image out, splitting it outside, taking the pieces back in, and memorizing. Since an image is an object comprehensible by the brain, if an image is split, the products may carry more information than the original image. Because of this, the simplistic explanation of brain function by quantum mechanics is not a proper approach, even if the two systems have many other similar features.

6.14 Characteristics of Probability

If the secular probability-setting process is precisely defined and closely observed, I find it always includes some process that cannot be executed, because it must be done instantly. Here the term *precisely* means that the same requirement may cover quantum-mechanical probability also. There, the probability-setting signal appears to propagate at infinite speed, and this is considered to conflict with the requirement set by special relativity. This pair of *impossibilities* suggests that the probability concepts used both in secular life and quantum mechanics have similar *executional impossibility* that stresses the human mind in the same way. I say, quantum probability is nothing special. Henri Poincaré wrote about such a feature in chapter 11 of *La science et l'hypothese*, as follows: "For any computation of probability to make sense, the starting hypothesis inevitably includes arbitrariness. Choice of the hypothesis can be done only by preponderance of rationality. Unfortunately, this guideline is quite vague." Probability stresses and confuses the human mind.

Probability refers to events. Any secular event carrying probability is always defined vaguely. Let us look at a simple example. I shall be dead someday. That probability is 1. But shall I be dead in 2020? Judging from my present health, that is not very likely, so the probability is 0.4. I shall be dead in 2025 in Russia. This is very unlikely, so the probability is 0.1. I shall be dead in New Jersey in 2034, struck by a meteorite. That probability is almost ensured to be 0. As the event is more precisely defined, the probability tends toward 0.

The original concept of probability refers to events in a small spatial locality and to instant execution of any required action. These are approximately satisfied at the gambling table or when playing the lottery. If the two requirements are strictly enforced, however, many strange features emerge, even in secular probability. Any secular probabilistic event consists of multiple participants and a single administrator. In a case where the participants are distributed over a wide spatial domain, and if the administrator requires some time to manage the event, curious problems emerge.

Of the problems of probability that I have so far pointed out, the first problem, the definition of the event, matters only to secular probability. Probabilities that emerge in quantum mechanics deal with such simple events as the existence or nonexistence of the particle at a location. This is free from such complication. It is the second problem of probability covering extended spatial area that conflicts with the locality problem of the special relativity and that is the most serious. The last problem of the administrator handling the operation matters to secular probability, but this feature shows some essential impossibility of probabilistic exercise, and this is related to the second problem that occurs in the quantum world.

HOW is the algorithm used to compute probability? Here, any secular probability has a better and clearer definition. If there are N participants of a lottery, and if each of them has an equal chance, then the probability of participant number n is given by $Pn = 1/N$. To select the winner, N numbered balls are set in a jar, and air is blown in from the bottom. The turbulent air flow randomizes the balls. After enough randomization, one ball is sucked up, and that ball's number is the winner's number. Most, if not all, of the secular probability problem assigns equal probability to the participants. This probability setting has a well-defined model. To make the chance uneven, a participant must buy more than one lottery ticket and thereby let the expense and the chance balance. That is considered to be fair. Probability in quantum physics is different; the probabilities of its *participants* (specified by the spatial coordinate of the particle) are uneven and are time dependent in a quantum state.

To simulate the uneven quantum probability feature by using the secular probability model, we consider a corrupted lottery business. The number of balls in the lottery machine is adjusted by the corrupt administrator. He gives, for participant n, Nnp positive balls and Nnn negative balls, such that the probability normalization condition

$$\sum_{i=1}^{N} \left(Nip - Nin \right) = N$$

is always satisfied. Then the probability for participant nn, Pn, is

$$Pn = (Nnp - Nnn)/N$$

This formula displays some strange features. If $Nnp < Nnn$, Pn becomes negative. Such a probability is called a *ghost* in quantum field theory. In the case of $Nnp - Nnn > N$, Pn exceeds unity. This situation was once expected, if the Higgs boson did not exist (actually it does exist). Precise observation of such cases shows that the quantum probability computation algorithm does not have a comprehensible model, and that is why these unrealistic situations cannot be explained convincingly.

If the corrupted secular probability scheme is used to simulate quantum physics probability, Nnp and Nnn depend on time. The normalization condition is still

$$\sum_{i=1}^{N} \left[Nnp(t) - Nnn(t) \right] = N$$

Can this condition actually be satisfied by the secular lottery administrator? The number of ball adjustments and lottery winner decisions are independent events; the *corruption* is going on all the time, and the latter may occur at any time. The decision time is not known to the corrupted administrator. To change the number of balls, so many balls must be taken out and added, and then they must be completely mixed. These operations take time. While the process is still at the halfway point, the lottery decision may be made. Then the probability calculation rules no longer make sense. To avoid this situation, the ball adjustment and randomization processes must be executed instantly. This is obviously impossible. Ball number adjustment requires observation of the balls and exchange of the balls, and randomization certainly takes time since the balls cannot move instantly. The balls carry information, so, they cannot move faster than the velocity of light. This observation shows that the secular probability model simulating quantum probability already includes a nonexecutable process. Time-dependent secular probability contains a process that is impossible for the administrator to execute. This is closely related to the quantum probability defined over the spread-out area that displays features not consistent with special relativity.

The mathematical hypothesis of quantum mechanics is that the probability of a particle's existence is proportional to the magnitude squared of its wave function. This conclusion comes out directly from the basic Schrödinger equation and the boundary condition. Because of that, preservation of the quantum probability is automatically derived. It is consistent, logically, to use probability in quantum mechanics. This *consistency* prevents one from digging into the depth of this problem. Then, as long as the probability interpretation is established both by theory and experiment in quantum mechanics, we need to admit that the probability-setting signal in the quantum world does indeed propagate at infinite velocity. Then the issue is to find the propagation mechanism that is least unnatural from the classical viewpoint and to see if the mechanism has a rational mechanical model.

6.15   Probability Signal Propagation Velocity

Propagation velocity of information is limited by the light velocity by special relativity. Why? To send information, a carrier is required. For the carrier to crick the signal receiver, it must have energy. Then the maximum velocity is set by the energy's velocity (or its equivalent, mass). Since probability does not qualify as information, there is a basic question about how fast the probability-setting signal can propagate.

From what I have mentioned, does the probability signal carrier need to crick the receiver? This question has a logical answer: if it does crick, definite information arrives, because that is how the regular communication channel is set up. Then a probability-setting signal need not, and does not, crick the receiver. Probability normalization in quantum mechanics requires, in case of wave function collapse, infinite speed propagation of the probability-setting signal. So far, this is a necessary conclusion from using probability in quantum mechanics, and the physical nature of the mechanism is quite tenuous. Is there any other interpretation of wave function collapse?

What appears to be the infinite propagation velocity of the probability signal may emerge from the way to set up the probability problem like lottery. Let's talk about the way to announce lottery results. The fair way is for the administrator to send the results simultaneously to all the participants in different locations. For fairness to make sense, all the participants must get the notice simultaneously so as to prevent cheating (such as exchanging a losing lottery ticket for a not yet certain ticket). The communications must be made by a signal of infinite speed if the participants are distributed over a wide area. This explanation also applies to the probability in quantum mechanics.

There is yet another way to explain the same feature. The lottery administrator creates N earths, in each of which there is one winner at his or her location, for all the participants. All the N earths are superposed before the decision. At the moment of the decision, one of the superposed earths becomes real. A more interesting explanation is, at the moment of decision, the superposed earth splits into N earths, and all the participants are on their own earth. This may sound strange, but this kind of interpretation of quantum probability is called the "many world interpretation."

Now it is time to reveal my preference: Isn't it more rational to accept that the quantum probability signal propagates instantly to maintain the integrity of the probability concept, and to search for the mechanism of the fast signal propagation? For this purpose, there is a hint I mentioned at the beginning of this section: look for the signal-propagation mechanism that *needs not* crick the receiver. This is not a firm reason, unfortunately, but it appears to be a rational starting point.

Figure 6.15.1(a) shows an array of inverse L-shaped touching dominoes set up on a table that can be tilted. All the pieces are identical. The table is carefully adjusted to a critical slope so that the dominoes are still standing, but even a minimal push of the first domino initiates fall of the entire chain of dominoes.

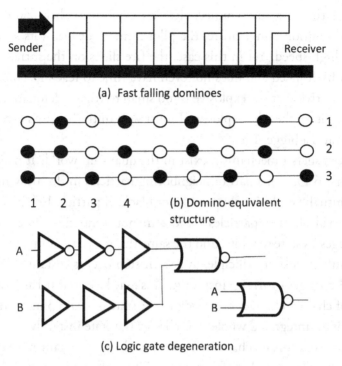

(a) Fast falling dominoes

(b) Domino-equivalent structure

(c) Logic gate degeneration

Figure 6.15.1 Infinitely fast, no-information-carrying signal

The dominoes fall at a very high speed. In simplistic thinking, the speed is infinity, but certainly it is not. What keeps the speed finite is, first, the dominoes must rotate at a nonzero angle, and second, the mass of each domino is not zero. Falling dominoes carry energy, and the last domino can crick the receiver. To make this cricking impossible, the dominoes' falling angle can be made infinitesimally small, and the dominoes can be made from hard material having no mass. Then the speed becomes infinity, but the domino chain cannot crick the receiver.

In the 1960s, I found that a similar signal-propagation mechanism actually existed in a certain semiconductor subjected to a strong electric field.[5] Actual speed of signal propagation was in the 10^8 cm/sec range, much faster than that of the saturated electron drift velocity in the semiconductor, which was of the order of 10^6–10^7 cm/sec. A similar

---

[5] Masakazu Shoji, "Theory of Transverse Extension of Gunn Domains," *Journal of Applied Physics* 41 (February 1970): 774–78.

effect is that if a fuse connected to an explosive is held close to the natural ignition temperature, the pilot flame propagates its surface at a very high speed. Yet in this case, the fire slides on the surface of the fuse at high speed and does not even have time to reach its core. Then the fire arriving at the explosive is too small to trigger detonation at the moment it reaches the explosive. I must wait until the fuse's core burns and creates a bigger fire.

Does such a mechanism exist in the quantum world? It may exist. In figure 6.15.1(b), a pair of neighboring particles in the array must be in a mutually exclusive state, white or black. If particle 1 changes from white to black, then particles 1 and 2 are not compatible. Then particle 2 changes its state to white, and the same thing repeats. This is to satisfy the Pauli exclusion principle, and each step occurs instantly. That is, array 1 changes to array 3 instantly. This may be explained as such: The state of chain 1 changes *as a whole* to the state of chain 3 instantly. The chain is an integrated whole that change the state instantly.

I propose this mechanism as the most likely mechanism to explain the probability signal's infinite speed. This infinite propagation speed has a curious twin *paradox* in digital circuit theory. Signal propagation along a digital gate chain makes sense only if there are capacitive loadings of all the nodes that make up the gate chain (section 6.23). If no node of a gate chain of figure 5.15.1(c) has capacitive loading, then the gate chain collapses into a single NOR gate that obviously responds instantly to the input signal. If the gate chain models the quantum space that transmits the probability-setting signal, then collapse of the gate chain to a single gate means that the space's structure changes. For me, this feature of the equivalent circuit model has its parallel to the quantum entanglement model, as I show in sections 6.19–6.31.

6.16 Physical and Psychological Misdirection in Nature

Let us consider the mysteries that have challenged physicists for the last eighty years and that still remain mysteries. Why are the definite physical parameters replaced by probability in the quantum world? Why does the wave function that describes the quantum state collapse instantly? And why does the quantum vacuum appear to *give away* so much energy to the universe by the Heisenberg uncertainty principle? Such features of quantum-mechanical phenomena appear deeply mysterious to the human mind. The observers are self-conscious physicists using various pieces of macroscopic equipment to observe the microscopic world. I consider their observation and their interpretation from a rather unconventional viewpoint; that is, I assume that the physicists are spectators of a sophisticated magician's performance. What the magician shows on stage is the display of quantum phenomena. This exercise has the merit of digging into the quantum mysteries from a psychological viewpoint.

The psychology of the spectators of a magician's performance is classified into two kinds. One is physical misdirection; that is, the magician misleads the spectators in the process of observing the performance. A floating ball (or even a floating girl) is an example of physical misdirection. The spectators are not seeing everything on the stage. The other is psychological misdirection; that is, the observed action is misinterpreted by the spectator's mind, and what is perfectly normal appears deeply mysterious. Much of the magic involving playing cards is of this latter kind. By looking for the two misdirection in quantum-mechanical observation and interpretation, I can classify quantum mysteries into two types.

Physicists use grossly oversized test equipment to observe microscopic objects. These pieces of equipment are at least 10 million times larger than the measured object, and they are the intermediary of the senses of the physicists. Because of this, the *quantum magic* can certainly be effected by physical misdirection at the time of observation. How can quantum theory explain such invasive test results so precisely? Isn't the quantum state very delicate, so that it is badly disturbed by observation?

Yet there are simple, noninvasive cases: radioactive decay of an unstable nucleus observed by placing a particle detector does not affect the object. Let us consider this simple case first, to get some idea. Why is the decay perfectly random, following the simple exponential decay pattern? What is the source of this randomness? Is there any effect that is similar to nuclear decay?

There is a model of this effect. The effect of a digital latch's metastability, which I discussed in section 4.29. In this case, the source of randomness is the thermal noise generated by the circuit's resistors. Field-effect transistors are equivalent to resistors, and they generate thermal noise. Resistor R generates thermal noise v, whose square average is given by the Nyquist formula,

$$\langle v^2 \rangle = 4kTRdf$$

where T is the absolute temperature, df is the frequency bandwidth of the noise measurement, and k is the Boltzman constant (1.38×10^{-23} joules/deg.). The noise is caused by the random thermal motion of the current carriers in the resistor, and the formula is quantitatively precise. This noise affects the lifetime of metastability of the latch. The average lifetime of the metastability depends on the detail of the latch circuit, as I showed in section 4.29, yet each episode of metastability lasts a random period, simulating the random decay time of an unstable nucleus.

Then what is the source of randomness of the unstable nuclear decay? As I search for the randomness source, I conclude the only probable cause is the fluctuation of the quantum vacuum, governed by the Heisenberg uncertainty relation. This is not pointed out explicitly in many of the popular books I read. So this is the physical misdirection of the quantum world by the human mind. We are not seeing everything involved in the experiment. I wonder if it is possible to reformulate quantum mechanics in the style of the thermal noise theory of the electronic circuit?

Another physical misdirection is this: Why does probability take over a definite parameter in the quantum world? I mentioned in section 6.13 that if an object is split, its information is also split. Therefore, at the ultimate limit, any definite information should become fractional information, that is, the probability. If four toothpicks cost three cents, there is no way to buy one of them. Let us see if this is the mechanism of emergence of the price's *probability*.

If a macroscopic object is split, the information carried by it is also split. How many steps of splitting can be executed? Neither the substance nor the information of the object can be split beyond a certain limit. The split of a substance has different limit, depending on the tool used to split. Let us consider a product development from wood. Splitting wood by a hatchet limits the size of the product to that of firewood. By knife, any wood can be split down to the size of a toothpick. By chemical reaction, a substance can be split down to atoms. By physical means using a high-energy accelerator, a substance can be split to nucleons and leptons. That is the limit of substance splitting. As for information (or character, as I refer to it later) splitting, its ultimate limit is 1 bit of information, such as the electric charges ($+e$ and $-e$) or spin ($+h/2$ or $-h/2$). What is interesting in nature is that both limits are reached at the same level of atoms, nucleons, or leptons.

I compare this limit with the limit of splitting wood. As I assumed before, four toothpicks sell at three cents. Can I buy one toothpick? No. There is no three-quarter-cent coin. At minimum, I must buy four pieces at three cents. A penny cannot be cut to retain its value. In spite of this, I insist to ask, "What is the *price* of a single toothpick?" In the conventional system of trade, it does not have *price*. The conventional trade rule does not hold for any object that has no definite price. Then, a new trade rule in this case is to set the price in one of the following three ways: One piece costs three cents and the rest are free (buy one, get three free); the first piece costs two cents, the second piece costs one cent, and the rest are free; or three pieces cost one cent each and the last piece is free (buy three and get one free). These are the three equivalent choices of setting the *price* of a toothpick. The price has three choices that the seller can set, and which one the seller offers to the customer depends on his *probabilistic* policy, or business hunch. This is what physicists are trying to observe in the state of the quantum world. If the substance is split, the information is split, and at the ultimate limit any parameter like *price* must become probabilistic. Therefore, it is not surprising at all that probabilities govern the quantum world instead of definite parameters.

But that is not all. Quantum mechanics is a self-consistent and very precisely verified theory that explains all the microscopic phenomena, yet its idea is not very natural to the human mind, accustomed to dealing with common macroscopic objects. Observed quantum objects display many more exotic features than the observers expect. One such feature is the indistinguishability of the same kinds of microscopic objects. Electron A at location 1 and electron B at location 2 of a quantum state is the same as A at 2 and B at 1.

By exchanging A and B, the state remains the same. Is this really a mystery? If the object carries definite identification, their exchange must alter the state. Yet isn't this also the case of splitting material, which results in splitting information and reducing the object's identification? If the two particles make a joint state, the state cannot be split any further.

Electrons A and B become distinguishable only if they are separated and identified individually. This question arose when I learned organic chemistry in my high school. A benzene nucleus is a six-member carbon atom loop consisting of alternating single and double bonds. So if a pair of hydrogen atoms that are spatially nearby are replaced by some other radicals, there should be two variations, one that has the carbon double bond between them, and another that has a single bond. The teacher told me that the pair is the same thing. I wondered why. Now I think that the electrons making the single and double bonds are not distinguishable. If the object is as simple as an electron, it does not carry any identification, if included in a tightly bound molecular nucleus.

Does such an object exist in the macroscopic world? Actually it does. It is money. Say we received a $40 refund from IRS, and I got one $20 bill and my wife got another $20 bill. If we exchange the bills, nothing changes as far as the money's function is concerned. Money is such a characterless, elementary object that it behaves like elementary particles. That is why some economics theories appear mysterious and screwy. This is a psychological misdirection to presume that any object is distinguishable.

6.17   Resolution of Mystery by Model

A sense of mystery emerges in the human mind when a person sees an object that he or she has never seen before, and whose features cannot be explained by common sense or past experiences. To resolve any mystery, one effective way is to make a model of the object. A model is a functional image of the object, built from familiar components. Non-Euclidian geometry was a mystery for almost a century between its inception and general acceptance.[6] It was finally accepted after a demonstration of its model: Nikolai Lobachevsky's version was the geometry of a saddle, and Bernhard Riemann's version was the geometry of a sphere.

Showing a model is a powerful way to persuade skeptical minds, but making a model is more like an artistic creation than a scientific work. Indeed, making a model of human emotion is a fine art such as sculpture, painting, music, and poetry. Copernicus's model of the solar system, Darwin's model of evolution by natural selection, Watson and Crick's double-helix model of DNA, and the standard model of elementary particles are as beautiful as the fine Renaissance arts of the maestros.

Related to my past profession, the model of the electron triode that Dr. William Shockley personally showed me (section 4.27), and the charge-controlled model of a transistor made by John Sparks (*Junction Transistors* [Pergamon, 1966]), were so simple and beautiful that they have inspired me throughout my whole life. Model making is the highest display of the interaction between superior intelligence and sensitivity to beauty. To study how that is executed is a serious theme of psychology.

This is one area where psychology is able to contribute to basic physics, because there has been a certain confusion at the forefront of physics since the twentieth century. Seeking consistency between quantum physics and general relativity sent people into a spooky maze that is too remote for experimental or observational checks. Since

---

[6] H. P. Manning, *Non-Euclidian Geometry* (Dover, 1963).

experimental evidence is most likely unavailable by using the resources accessible to humans, we do need a model. If a proper model is shown, conclusions of the mathematical theory can be evaluated.

Then where can I start? In the domain of physical science, there is a semi-systematic model covering practically all the simple physical phenomena, that is, the equivalent circuit model. This model is able to cover any physical phenomenon described by first- and second-order differential equations. Within its own limits, the model provides explanation of the phenomenon by relying on the well-developed and easy to comprehend electronic circuit theory. The linear equivalent circuit model covers many motion, diffusion, and wave propagation problems. The nonlinear equivalent circuit model explains oscillation and saturation phenomena in general. I worked out a digital equivalent circuit model to cover mechanical phenomena (*Dynamics of Digital Excitation* [Kluwer Academic, 1997]). This model is able to represent some classical and quantum-mechanical phenomena in a unique way. My attempt was motivated by the short self-consciousness research boom in 1990. Then a theory that self-consciousness is a quantum effect emerged. I have deep doubt about that view, so I intended to present my thinking in the aforementioned book.

I firmly believe that self-consciousness is not a quantum effect. A neuron is a logic device having micron size and operating at about room temperature. Its operation can be adequately described by including nominal quantum-mechanical features in classical physics. Here, *nominal* means only as much as elementary chemistry needs quantum concepts. Later, I show how some quantum phenomena can be explained by the digital equivalent circuit model, which is upgraded for this purpose. The similar neuron circuit model explains that the mystery of self-consciousness emerged from the neuron circuit operation. As such, the brain's operation is the same as the operation of an electronic processor. To connect the two, I now show how some quantum phenomena can also be explained by the equivalent circuit model upgraded for this purpose, in the last part of this chapter. A self-conscious brain is functionally similar to the quantum world but not physically similar.

The virtue of a model is validation of the proposed theory. In the history of astronomy, Prince Alfonso failed to persuade the world of his doubt about the geocentric model, but Copernicus succeeded, since he had a new model. Criticism of *math econ* in the 1970s failed since the critics failed to provide an alternate model.

There is a view that until an alternate model emerges, the existing model survives. It appears that democracy and capitalism will survive until their alternatives emerge. What would such an alternative be? I propose my expectation, namely, an enlightened, pagan, theocratic, socialist, hereditary monarchy. If some of us luckily survive the nuclear holocaust (unfortunately, I believe that such an event is inevitable), this system will become the realistic one to rebuild human culture again. Here I stress *theocratic*: humans eternally need religion to behave properly. Why? No god or goddess approves unlimited freedom in human life.

6.18   Image of Hyperdimensional Space?

In the world of ultramodern physics such as string theory, the theories are formulated in hyperdimensional space-time, having ten, eleven, or twenty-six dimensions. Since the theories have not yet been verified by any observation, we do not know if they are realistic physics theories or just permanently unproven conjectures. Popular books of string theory show the hyperdimensional space forcefully fitted into three-dimensional space. All such four-dimensional space images presented in the string theory books are so deformed in appearance as to be a turnoff to any further thinking.

The reason why hyperdimensional space has been adopted into the theory is that it is easy to describe such space using algebraic expressions. Notation specifying the location of a three-dimensional space point (x_1, x_2, x_3) can be easily extended to an n-dimensional point (x_1, x_2, x_3, ..., x_n). In n-dimensional space, the distance between a pair of points can be given by the extended Pythagorean theorem, and geometry can be set up by algebra. This easiness allows extension of the theoretical structure to hyperdimensional space without paying attention to its physical reality.

My basic question is, if the dimensionality of the physical space should be defined by the theorist or by the experimentalist. My choice is definitely the latter, since the experimentalists use macroscopic equipment to study the quantum world, and their equipment are all three-dimensional objects. Generally, n-dimensional equipment can measure only up to n-dimensional objects. So any theoretical conjecture referring to an object having more than three dimensions cannot be tested by any experiment.

In the quantum world, the concept of dimension becomes vague. Suppose that a particle is placed at location $x = a$, $y = z = 0$ at time $t = 0$. Since the particle is set at the definite location, after time δt, it can be anywhere within the sphere centered at $(a, 0, 0)$ that is within $(x - a)^2 + y^2 + z^2 < (c\delta t)^2$, where c is light velocity. The particle is no longer on the x-axis, and its location spreads out to the other dimensions. Yet the experiment is able to find it somewhere within the sphere. The particle never disappears. The Heisenberg uncertainty principle has the effect of mixing up the dimension, but only within three-dimensional space. This means, at least to me, that space does not have any extra dimension. The theory that explains the particle's behavior must conform to this basic requirement.

A particle has substance (mass or energy) and character (spin, charge, and color) as its internal dimension. String theory intends to explain a particle's character by creating the extra dimension in small hyper-dimensional space. To detect such a structure, the experimenters must build macroscopic equipment having the hyper-dimension. This is obviously impossible. Then any available evidence is not direct but is only circumstantial. Because of these reasons, I believe that all the physical theories must be formulated in four-dimensional space-time. It is not necessary to introduce an extra dimension into the theory. The string theorists' difficulty in *compacting* hyperdimensional space clearly reveals this problem. Thus hyperdimensional space is only a mathematical image and is not included in the physical mystery.

6.19   Model of the Quantum-Mechanical World

To describe the quantum-mechanical world, the required concepts are particles, states, and forces. Of the three, particles and forces are familiar in classical mechanics, except that a particle sometimes appears as a wave. State describes the activity of both wave and particle. Mode is the corresponding term familiar in classical physics. Mode is the operation of a system determined by its structure. In quantum mechanics, even a single elementary particle is described by a state. Force affects classical modes and induces transition among quantum states. A quantum state usually consists of multiple superpositions of eigenstates, and the force working on the state changes the proportion of the eigenstates building up the state.

To set up a model of the quantum state, I recognize that a particle is a carrier of its characteristics associated with its substance (mass or energy). When we work in classical mechanics, we regard that the two are integrated together, but when we work in quantum mechanics, we must recognize their differences. A character often behaves independent of the substance. An electron is a mass point, yet it has built-in angular momentum, the spin $h/2$, where h is the Planck constant $h = 1.06 \times 10^{-34}$ joules/sec. When this electron circles around a hydrogen nucleus (proton), it draws a circular orbit of 10^{-8} cm and carries spin, h. How can a size-less (point) particle have half as much angular momentum? Generally, any character is as different from the substance (energy or mass) in the quantum world as in this example. A particle has mass or energy, and it carries character such as spin, charge, and color.

The quantum-mechanical state carries uncertainty originating from the basic constraint, namely that a certain pair of variables like energy and time are complementary; if one of the pair is set, the other becomes completely uncertain. This Heisenberg uncertainty principle affects the substance and character differently. The character is quantized and is definite, and it comes as a plus-and-minus pair in elementary particles. Keeping this in mind, I am able to set up a model of the quantum-mechanical state using the equivalent circuit model. I introduced this model before (*Dynamics of Digital Excitation* [Kluwer Academic, 1997]), but I now revise the original model to more closely reflect the quantum features, and I add many details to cover the quantum world in the following sections. The objective of this exercise is to show the startling similarity between the working of the quantum world and the working of the binary digital system, which includes the human self-conscious brain. Yet we should not quickly connect the two.

I use the horizontal lines shown in figure 6.19.1(a) to represent an empty quantum state, which a particle can occupy. There are two basic types of elementary particles, fermions (such as the electron and the proton) and bosons (such as the photon and the meson). On an empty state line, a fermion is represented by a step function like that shown in figure 6.19.1(b). The height of the step function is set at unity to derive most of the qualitative conclusions of the model. The fermion is located at the step's location, and the base of the state line stretches to both sides. This is to accommodate the uncertainty principle.

If the fermion is moving at a definite velocity (or momentum), it can be anywhere on the baseline. The upper line of the step function belongs to the *particle world*, and the baseline belongs to the *antiparticle world*. The fermion is at the boundary of the two worlds and is connected to its source by the particle world line. Natural emergence of this connection is the key feature of this model, which explains many mysterious features of the quantum world. I call it the *umbilical cord*. From the step function waveform, it is impossible to put more than one fermion in a single state, that is, the baseline. This is the Pauli exclusion principle.

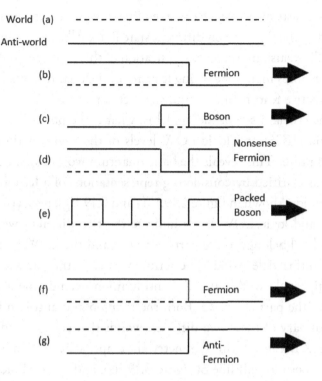

Figure 6.19.1 Particle and anti-particle

On an empty state line, a boson is represented by an isolated pulse as shown in figure 6.19.1(c). A boson carries no umbilical cord. The boson is a free particle that transmits force between fermions, so it must not be connected to its source. A boson exercises force on a fermion, which remains as a fermion, so figure 6.19.1(d) is meaningless (this is actually a fermion). Only one fermion is in a state, but any number of bosons, such as photons, can be put in a single quantum state as shown in figure 6.19.1(e). A closely packed boson state like a laser beam is called the *Bose-Einstein condensate*. The clear difference between a fermion and a boson is the basic feature of this quantum world's equivalent circuit model.

If the motion of the particle in space is considered, I assume that the step function and the isolated pulse move to the right as shown by the arrows. In the later sections, I transcribe the waveform of a fermion and a boson to the voltage profile of a chain of cascaded buffers, each of which consists of two-stage cascaded inverters. Particles moving to the left and to the right are on different state lines. All such features reflect the Pauli exclusion principle. Application of this principle to the circuit model exposes many interesting features of the quantum world. This is the attractive feature of this equivalent circuit model.

One crucial issue of the model is, what is the physical meaning of the logic HIGH and logic LOW levels of the step function and the isolated pulse? This reveals the basic quantum world's symmetry. This feature is clarified by considering representations of a fermion and an anti-fermion, shown in figure 6.19.1 (f) and 6.19.1(g), respectively. Logic HIGH and logic LOW levels indicate the two different worlds. The HIGH level belongs to the particle world, and the LOW level belongs to the antiparticle world. The fermion extends the particle world to the antiparticle world, and the anti-fermion extends the antiparticle world to the particle world. Both the fermion and anti-fermion are at the boundary of these two different worlds that coexist, and both are accessible. Because of this symmetry, the empty state of the anti-fermion is the upper (dotted) line of figure 6.19.1(a), and the umbilical cord is the connection made by the bottom line. A boson is a small speck of the particle world emerging in the antiparticle world.

In my model, the substance and character (like spin, charge, and color) of a particle propagate in synchronization in physical space, on different pair of lines, which are later modeled by CMOS buffer chains. Any particle carrying mass or energy cannot move faster than the velocity of light. Any character is a property associated with the substance. Any character carries no mass or energy of its own, and it can propagate at whatever the velocity. Yet it propagates in step with the substance. The character defines the type of force affecting the substance. If character alone is to propagate, its velocity is not limited by the velocity of light. The carrier of the character is the virtual particles associated with the propagating particle. Energy is carried by the real particle, but character is carried by the virtual particle. The virtual particle surrounds the *naked* particle and screens the particle. This is like a popular singer is surrounded by admirers; their admiration spreads out instantly among the crowd. Similarly, virtual particles carry a character not by moving but by handing the character from one to the next by the mechanism of falling dominoes discussed in section 6.15. This virtual process allows the probability signal to propagate at infinite speed.

In my model, I am building a structure that cannot be observed directly. Any such propagation path is not accessible experimentally. When the wave function collapses, a probability-setting signal propagates the path once, and then the path is destroyed. Then the empty quantum space reemerges. The character propagation path is similar to the fermion's umbilical cords: the HIGH level carries positive character, the LOW level carries negative character, and an indefinite level between the two definite levels carries character that is set probabilistically (section 6.29).

6.20 Spin and Character

In the previous section, I introduced the pair of attributes of any elementary particle, that is, substance (mass or energy) and character. Spin, electric charge, weak charge, and colors are the characters. They determine the force working on the substance. They have distinctly different features in the quantum world. If they are measured, they take definite absolute value. Any character takes a pair of positive and negative values, and sometimes zero. Elementary leptons and quarks have only positive-negative pair of values. This feature suggests that positive and negative characters cancel out as a whole.

Let us consider the feature of spin. Spin is angular momentum. If mass m rotates around a center with radius r at velocity v, then angular momentum H is given by $H = mvr$. Here is the first mystery: H is the similar dynamic variable to momentum $P = mv$, which takes any value. Why is spin angular momentum different? I asked this question in quantum-mechanics class, and the answer was, "That is what it is." The only conceivable reason I could think of at the time was that the spin direction reflects the lost degree of the freedom of motion of a small ball, whose size is shrunk to zero.

A classical Bohr hydrogen atom is in a nonrelativistic regime. Its ground state electron's angular momentum is $h = 1.053 \times 10^{-34}$ joules/sec. An electron is, theoretically, a size-less point. Yet it carries spin angular momentum $h/2$. How could a point rotate to create that much angular momentum? Spin emerges if relativistic effects are included in quantum theory. If an electron were an infinitesimally small ball, its surface velocity must diverge to infinity. Even if there were a difference between relativistic and nonrelativistic effects, the velocity divergence would be hard to swallow. Furthermore, the lightest neutrino and the heavier electron carry the same angular momentum, $h/2$. That was also a mystery to me. After fifty years, I still wonder why.

As for my question in the quantum-mechanics class, since I was an electrical engineering student and not a physics major, I took the wise advice of "Shut up and just calculate," and I got a passing mark. I thought, *Maybe an angular momentum is special, because it can be confined within a narrow space. Maybe, fundamentally, we still do not understand what rotation of any object in space really means!* (section 4.22). Going a little ahead, to section 6.27, I show how the particle moves in space by way of the carrier replacement mechanism. There, a particle is surrounded by virtual particles, and they become the agent to move the particle. They *screen* the *naked* particle. *Perhaps the spin is the by-product of the screening mechanism?* I wondered ever since.

Is spin not angular momentum? This possibility is eliminated, since the spin of photons from a laser beam exercises torque. As for the hyper velocity, it appears that there are other suspicious cases that involve such velocity, such as electrons going through the tunnel barrier. Even if such velocity exists, it is impossible to take it out and use it. Information can be carried only by energy or mass (the substance), since otherwise the signal may arrive at the receiver but cannot crick it (section 6.15). Yet if the signal carries no information, it need not crick the receiver. Maybe in nature, there is unobservable infinitely high velocity. If not observable and not usable, infinite velocity does not violate the relativity's restriction.

Furthermore, such velocity seems to emerge when the quantum effect is *finagled* classically, as I just did in the last page. When an elementary particle is observed in an experiment, we are actually *finagling* the quantum object classically. Such a velocity is observed by the equipment that operates on a classical physics principle, such as Bell's inequality test. It appears that infinite velocity emerges at the border region where the quantum world meets the classical world, or if the quantum effect is interpreted by classical physics, either theoretically or experimentally. When definite classical physics parameters are replaced by probabilities in the quantum world, such an anomaly seems to emerge. In section 6.16, I explained the problem of setting the *price* of a toothpick. There, some toothpicks become free. This is a similar kind of anomaly.

I continue asking this question from a different viewpoint: How can spin be packed into a size-less point? To say this in casual words, how can I attach a handle to rotate a sizeless point to supply angular momentum? Here I notice that any character emerges only as a pair of positive and negative values. So I look into the process of making elementary particles by splitting material. I place the material on an anvil (as shown in figure 6.20.1[a]), set a chisel on it, and beat it as shown in figure 6.20.1(b). By this splitting operation, the separated pieces rotate in mutually opposite directions as shown in figure 6.20.1(c). Splitting always creates rotation. Rotation of an object is an inevitable consequence of any splitting operation, which I always experience when I make firewood. If many pieces are split, an equal number of pieces rotate clockwise and counterclockwise. When a pair of such pieces rub against each other, their rotation cancels. Such pieces are split again and again. The rotation acquired by the final split remains as the spin of the particle. By this last split, the pieces that appear like rods acquire their own angular momentum $h/2$ shown in (c).

This model explains why even a point particle can rotate. The final product of the splitting appears like a rod and not like a sphere. The rod can rotate around its own long axis, but it cannot rotate by itself around the axis that is perpendicular to the rod's axis as shown in (d). To rotate the direction of the spin axis, it is necessary to apply external force, which is shown in the figure by a handle. Another interesting conclusion is that there must be equal numbers of clockwise and counterclockwise rotating particles in the quantum world. If the ultimately split particles stick together to add to or to cancel the spin, the resultant angular momentum becomes either zero or a multiple of *h*, that is, a boson emerging from a pair of fermions.

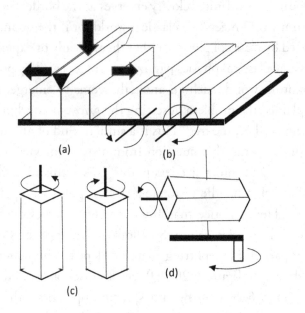

Figure 6.20.1 Model of spin generation

In section 6.14, I suggested that if material is split, the information it carries is also split. How much can the substance be split? Until the information becomes its unit, 1 bit. That is why the spin of an elementary fermion is ± *h*/2, which can be specified by 1 bit of information. Therefore, the character's state is defined by a single binary parameter. This is the reason why the character propagates in space like a fermion.

Spin is only one characteristic of elementary particles. There are other characteristics, such as electrical, weak, and color charge, that are distinct from each other and different from the substance of the particle's mass or energy. A substance responds to the force defined by the character, and the energy or the mass keeps changing all the time. The spin's direction can be altered by applying an external magnetic field, but its magnitude does not change. The electrical, weak, and color charges are immune to any applied forces, and they retain their constant value (the unit of electrical charge cannot be altered by applying a strong electrical field). The order of susceptibility to external force is substance-spin-charge, and there is a clear difference between the substance and the character. Spin is halfway between the substance and the charge, since at least, its direction can be flipped. This is rational since spin is originally a dynamic parameter like momentum.

If I take one more step of imagination, I can make a convenient model to visualize the elementary particles, as shown in figure 6.20.2. The substance of the particle and spin are integrated into a single rod. Between two such rods, gravitational force works. The electrical, weak, and color charges are the rings fitting to the rod. An electric charge ring pops out from the rod by electrostatic interaction, and if positive and negative rings meet, both vanish and create a new rod without any ring, a photon. As for weak charge, its reaction is chiral and is related to the spin direction. So the weak charge ring fits to the rod by a screw. Figure 6.20.2 shows all the common elementary particles.

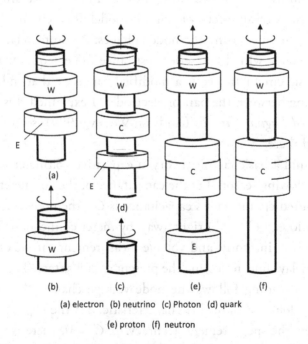

(a) electron (b) neutrino (c) Photon (d) quark

(e) proton (f) neutron

Figure 6.20.2 Visual model of elementary particles

If a quark's color ring is removed and the electric ring is widened, it becomes an electron. If the electric ring is removed, it becomes a neutrino. Protons and neutrons are quite similar, both carrying the three color rings to cancel the colors, but a neutron has no electric ring. This model may appear curious, but it is convenient to memorize the various elementary particles.

Two fermions fit in one quantum state if their spin is opposite. In my quantum state diagram, the two fermions are in the state created by providing a pair of V_{DD} lines above and below the groundline. If a boson has a spin of +1, 0, or –1, then three independent V_{DD} lines are arranged symmetrically around the central ground. The model accommodates all such quantum world features.

6.21   Equivalent Circuit Model of the Quantum State

In the following sections, I develop an equivalent circuit model of the quantum world. Before going into the model, I explain the basic characteristics of an electronic circuit model. The circuit's operation is observed by measuring the node voltages. A commercial voltmeter is an ammeter with high series resistance. The required voltmeter in the basic circuit theory is a modified capacitor that indicates the force acting between the pair of electrodes. I explained this choice in *High-Speed Digital Circuits* (Addison-Wesley, 1996), so more details are found there.

To build a basic circuit theory, a capacitive voltmeter is required for the following reason: Let the capacitance of the voltmeter be C_V. If the measured circuit node's capacitance is C_N, the node voltage drops by the ratio $C_N/(C_N + C_V)$ right away, by meter connection. The node voltage settles instantly, and voltage measurement can be carried out without delay time, reflecting the present circuit's state. The capacitive voltmeter's reading follows the node voltage change. A commercial voltmeter does not have this characteristic. Yet the capacitance ratio C_V/C_N sets the measurement accuracy. If $C_N = 0$, there is no way to measure the node voltage. As soon as the meter is connected, the node voltage drops to zero. Therefore, the nodes of the circuit having no capacitance are not accessible for measurement. The equivalent circuit model I use in the following sections includes such circuit nodes in order to model the quantum world. The quantum world is so simple, basic, and exotic that such a feature is required in the equivalent circuit model.

Any node in the circuit model whose voltage is not measurable indicates that the quantum information represented by the node is not accessible. Such a node's physical meaning can be defined by the theory, but it cannot be accessed by any experimental means. In the process of equivalent circuit model building, if an electrically inaccessible node emerges, the node carries physically inaccessible information. This is a clean correspondence between the circuit model and the quantum world, unique to this model. If a circuit node has no capacitance loading, the signal that goes through the node propagates instantly, that is, at an infinitely high speed. Any capacitance loading reduces the speed to a finite level. All measurable nodes must be capacitively loaded, and the signal needs the minimum time to go across the node.

Figure 6.21.1(a) shows the equivalent circuit model of the quantum state of a particle, shown in section 6.19 by a pair of lines that are identified as the power supply line (V_{DD}) and the ground line (GND) of the CMOS buffers that I use in my model. CMOS technology is now well established in digital electronics, and many references are available. One is my own, *CMOS Digital Circuit Technology* (Prentice-Hall, 1987).

This technology offers an ideally clean, pullup-pulldown symmetrical equivalent circuit model. Each CMOS buffer consists of two-stage cascaded CMOS inverters shown in figure 6.21.1(a) and 6.21.1(b). The CMOS buffer can be loaded by capacitance C_0. The capacitance is required if the node voltage is measurable; a node having zero capacitance can be defined in the circuit model, but does not carry any accessible information. Only a *physically accessible node at the accessible time* is loaded by a capacitor. A voltmeter terminal is connected to the node, and the other terminal is connected to ground or V_{DD}, depending on particle or antiparticle, respectively. Power supply voltage

V_{DD} determines the height of the waveform as I discussed in section 6.19.

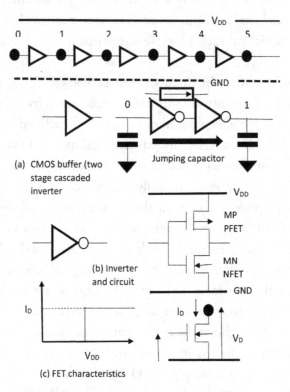

(a) CMOS buffer (two stage cascaded inverter

Jumping capacitor

(b) Inverter and circuit

(c) FET characteristics

Figure 6.21.1 Equivalent circuit model of the quantum-mechanical world

For most of qualitative study, V_{DD} can be set at unity. Each CMOS buffer is made of an N-channel MOSFET (metal-oxide-semiconductor field-effect transistor) MN and a P-channel MOSFET MP, as shown in figure 6.21.1(b). The character of MOSFETs is realistically quite complex, but to model the basic quantum world, the simplest version is required. Let the power supply voltage be V_{DD}. The N-channel MOSFET current is zero, except when the gate voltage V_G equals V_{DD} as shown in (c). If V_G equals V_{DD}, the NFET carries current I_D. The P-channel MOSFET has its *mirror image* characteristic to the power supply lines. Both FETs have a *conduction threshold voltage* equal to V_{DD}

and no leakage current. Then the inverter has an uncertain output node voltage, except when its gate voltage V_G equals 0 or V_{DD}, since then both FETs are turned off. Such a node represents an uncertain, probabilistic quantum state. By this idealized characteristic, many key features of the quantum world are modeled.

The inverters are cascaded as shown in figure 6.21.2(a). Let the node n voltage be V_n, and let the N- and P-channel MOSFET of inverter n be MN_n and MP_n, respectively. At the beginning, node 0 voltage V_0 is 0, node 1 voltage V_1 is V_{DD}, V_2 is 0, V_3 is V_{DD}, and so on. At time t = 0, V_0 makes stepwise increase to V_{DD}. MP_1 turns off, MN_1 turns on, and current I_D draws the first node voltage V_1 down to 0 instantly as shown in figure 6.21.2(b), because node 1 has no capacitance load. At that moment, MN_2 turns off and MP_2 turns on. Node 2 is now capacitively loaded. MP_2 current I_D charges capacitance C_0, and node voltage V_2 goes up linearly with time, as shown in figure 6.21.2(b). When V_2 reaches V_{DD}, MP_3 is already off, but MN_3 turns on, and since node 3 is not capacitively loaded, node voltage V_3 drops down instantly to 0.

At this moment, V_0 goes down to 0 instantly. This is a special (extra) condition set for this example, to show the mode of propagation of a photon. At this moment, capacitor C_0 (which is not charged) emerges at node 4. As node 4's voltage goes up, node 2's voltage goes down. As V_2 reaches 0, node 2's capacitor C_0 (no longer charged) disconnects, and the uncharged capacitor jumps to node 6. Capacitor's instant jumping is possible because the capacitor carries no energy. This capacitor jumping is a unique feature of this model, and it is explained step-by-step in the following sections. This process is electrically equivalently described by the current generator I_D shown in figure 6.21.2(a), which transfers the charge and energy that was in node 2 to node 4 to node 6, and so on. The charged capacitor represents the substance of the photon, that is the energy the photon carries. The jumping capacitor is a new feature of the model. I explain this step by step in the next sections.

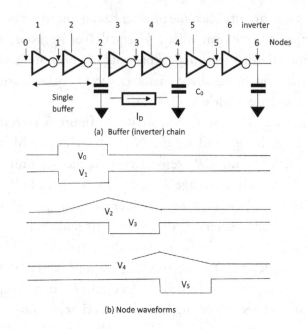

(b) Node waveforms

Figure 6.21.2 Boson propagation in buffer chain

By this mechanism, the photon's energy moves from node 2 to node 4, then to node 6, ... The number of capacitors remains at 2. Since there are only two capacitors on the chain, the energy stored in them, $C_0 V_{DD}^2/2$, is the photon's substance, that is, its energy. By repeating the same process, the delay time of photon propagation per buffer stage T_D is determined from the waveform of nodes 1, 2, 3, 4, ... By comparing the node waveforms, $T_D = C_0 V_{DD}/I_D$. We find that if a single stage of the buffer occupies spatial length L, the velocity of pulse propagation is given by $v = c = L/T_D$ where c is the light velocity. This is the velocity of the photon, a boson. Velocity v diverges to infinity if $T_D \to 0$ as $C_0 \to 0$. The maximum velocity of information is the light velocity $c = 3 \times 10^8$ m/sec. In this case we have $c = LI_D/C_0 V_{DD}$.

This model does not exclude infinite velocity signal transmission, although it is impossible to use such velocity for signal transmission purposes. Signal transmission faster than light velocity indicates the breakdown of the locality of interaction (any effect reaches from the source to the destination by light velocity, at the fastest). Propagation of the probability-setting signal can be instantaneous as I discussed in section 6.15. Probability does not qualify as information, so its propagation velocity can be faster than light velocity. Such a state can be modeled by the unloaded chain of buffers of the equivalent circuit model. This is one of the key points of the quantum world model.

One issue is how to set the length, L, occupied by a single buffer. From quantum mechanics, the de Broglie wavelength may appear proper, but the model does not lead to this conclusion. When a particle image is derived from a wave image, the standard procedure is first to determine the dispersion relation of the wave. Then, from the relation, the group velocity of the wave packet is derived. This procedure involves many mathematical details not covered by this simple equivalent circuit model. This model is not for the analysis of physical parameter values of elementary particles. Rather, the model reveals a certain hidden structure of the quantum world that is not obvious from the more precise mathematical model. To gain insight into the quantum world's structure, I do not need to set the length at L. Yet later I will show some choices for setting L, in section 6.30.

6.22 Boson Model

Figure 6.22.1(a) shows an empty quantum state. It consists of buffers that are two-stage cascaded inverters. To test the state of a node, the capacitive voltmeter is connected to the node and the bottom closed circle, the ground, if the object is a particle. If the object is an antiparticle, the voltmeter is connected to the node and the top closed circle of the figure. In figure 6.22.1(a), the output node of a buffer shown by the closed circles is loaded by a capacitor only when the location is occupied by the particle.

The empty quantum state of a particle is set by keeping node 0 at ground. The voltage profile of the buffer chain is shown in figure 6.22.1(a) by the zigzag wave of the solid line. If it is the empty state of an antiparticle, node 0 is kept at the V_{DD} voltage level. The antiparticle empty state voltage profile is the zigzagging dotted lines in the same voltage profile. Closed circles show the nodes whose voltage can be made measurable, if the particle is there and is capacitively loaded. In the empty state without capacitor loading, the closed circle nodes are still measurable, since the pair of terminals of the capacitive voltmeter are connected to the same node, and the voltmeter does not draw any charge or energy from the node.

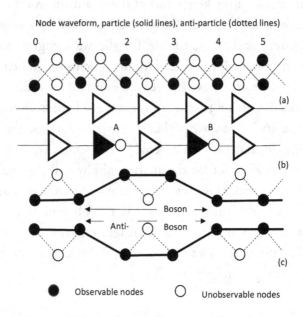

Figure 6.22.1 State of boson and antiboson

This capacitive loading has tricky features, as I suggested in the previous section. This represents the moving particle in quantum space. I explain this feature step by step in the following sections. The capacitor is the holder of the substance of the particle (mass or energy). Because of this, in the empty state in figure 6.22.1(a), no node is capacitively loaded. The capacitors jump into the buffer chain at the moment when the particle is launched from the source. The source supplies energy or mass and the capacitor, and they move to the right as the particle moves. Since this dynamic case is complicated, let us first consider a stationary boson shown in figure 6.22.1.

To create a stationary boson in the empty state, I add an inverter in series to buffer A and buffer B as shown in figure 6.22.1(b). Nodes 2 and 3 move from the antiparticle world to the particle world. The pair of nodes are now capacitively loaded, and the capacitors carry the electrostatic energy, that is, the boson's energy. The node becomes accessible, and also the entire boson waveform becomes accessible (the nodes outside the boson's feature are all accessible, since the voltmeter does not draw energy). The boson energy is supplied by the process of adding inverters to the buffer chain. Similarly, to place an anti-boson in its empty state, nodes 2 and 3 are pulled down by adding inverters, and the nodes are capacitively loaded. The capacitors carry the anti-boson's energy. A boson and an anti-boson carry the same amount of energy. The waveforms of the boson and the anti-boson are shown in figure 6.22.1(b) and 6.22.1(c), respectively. What do these wave profiles really mean? Since the bosons are assumed to be not moving, the boson can be anywhere on the horizontal line according to the Heisenberg uncertainty principle. Then the profile is a snapshot of the particle whose location is unspecified.

By observing figure 6.22.1(a) and 6.22.1(b), we come to an alternative interpretation of boson creation by shifting the phase of the zigzag waveform of the original empty state by 180 degrees in the phase at the location of the boson. If I consider the zigzag wave of (a) as the basic rhythm of nature, then I see the effects of shifting the phase is to create a particle or an antiparticle. The role of the inverter is to shift the phase of the nature's basic rhythm. Inverters are tricksters that execute jump between the particle and the antiparticle world at the respective particle's location. What drives the tricksters is the energy supplied by the operation of inserting the inverters. This means that if the particle moves in the space, the charged capacitors move with the particle, and when the capacitor moves, it is not charged (a charged capacitor cannot move instantly, since it carries energy). In other words, if a particle passes a node, the uncharged capacitor vanishes and then reemerges at the moving front. The capacitor guides the energy. This is a new, essential feature added to the simple equivalent circuit model I described in my 1997 book, to simulate the quantum world realistically.

6.23 Fermion and Fermion Space

Continuing from the previous section, figure 6.23.1 shows the motion of a fermion in the buffer chain whose components, the inverters, are explicitly shown. The fermion moves to the right. First, node 1 is held at logic LOW level, and then it is pulled up to logic HIGH level. A fermion is launched. As the particle moves to the right, the original down-up profile changes to the up-down profile behind the front (gray-colored nodes are HIGH in the down-up profile and LOW in the up-down profile). At the step function location where the fermion is located, the moving up-down profile returns to the preexisting down-up profile. By connecting the observable nodes (the closed circles), the moving fermion's step function profile is shown by the thick line segments. The fermion pulls the particle world (upper line) from the source to its present location, and beyond the front, the preexisting antiparticle world remains as the lower line. The capacitance C_0 exists at the fermion's step function front. All the nodes behind the fermion's location lose the capacitor as the particle moves ahead. The particle's substance, energy or mass, is sent to the front at each step forward, and thus the energy of the fermion is conserved.

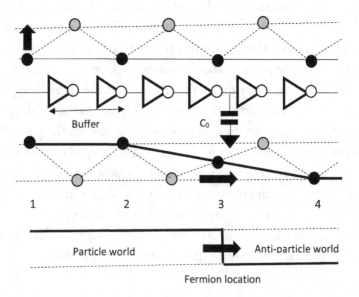

Figure 6.23.1 Fermion propagation

The velocity of energy transport is set at a finite level less than the light velocity because the capacitor charge-up requires time. As this mechanism shows, the phase shift from the up-down to down-up profile at the location of the fermion can be effected only if the capacitor load exists there, and if the propagation velocity is set at a finite level. No real particle carrying mass or energy can move at infinite velocity. What the physics and the circuit theory require becomes consistent. This is a nice feature of the equivalent circuit model. The phase shift of nature's basic rhythm is created by the capacitor's charge-up time.

From this model, we see that the fermion is the boundary of the logic HIGH level, which is the particle world, and the logic LOW level, which is the antiparticle world. As the fermion moves to the right, it extends the particle world by dragging it. This means, physically, that the fermion is creating its own space by invading into the antiparticle world. Since the space left behind the moving fermion is its own creation, it carries the fermion's character and is different from the empty quantum space. The space has a structure modeled by the buffer chain, whose nodes are logic HIGH level that is maintained by the fermion's source. Including the source, none of the nodes are capacitor loaded and therefore are not observable. The capacitor that once existed there has moved ahead to the fermion's present location.

In figure 6.23.1, nodes 1 and 2 are held at logic HIGH level by the fermion's source. The fermion is bound to its source by the buffer chain whose nodes are logic HIGH level, which maintains the fermion's state (by its connection to the source). The state includes the fermion's source, which is also unobservable after sending the fermion out. This structure, consisting of the unobservable buffer chain and the fermion's source, is something new. This structure emerges naturally in the equivalent circuit model, and is consistent with the Pauli exclusion principle. This structure is called the fermion's *umbilical cord*. Quantum particles are not size-less points, as is imagined by some physicists, such as string theorists, but the structure is not accessible. That is some spatially extending yet unobservable structure. My umbilical cord model is like the relationship between mother and child: they are connected by a real umbilical cord first and then by an emotional umbilical cord later in life.

This rather remarkable feature originates naturally from the step function representation of a fermion, which is required to accommodate only one fermion in a state by the Pauli exclusion principle. That only one fermion can be in a state means that the fermion's state must occupy its state's spatial domain. The fermion does so, by building the umbilical cord in quantum space. It occupies the state's space and prevents the other fermion from coming in. The cord is not maintained by the real force and is therefore unobservable. The quantum-mechanical interpretation of this feature is that the particle is actually everywhere, where the wave function is not absolutely zero, and the umbilical cord is sustained by its probability amplitude drive. This retention mechanism is essentially the same as the brain's memory retention mechanism. By occasionally recalling the image, the image memory is kept connected securely for a long time. An umbilical cord connection cannot transmit an information-carrying signal. As the quantum state collapses, the umbilical cord transmits a probability-setting signal once and then collapses. A structure similar to the umbilical cord should support any quantum state, but it is so fragile that it is destroyed by any observational access.

In the foregoing discussion, I did not explain how the node capacitor moves as the particle space expands. Figure 6.23.2 shows the mechanism. Node n, $n + 1$, and $n + 2$ voltage waveforms are shown on the bottom. When node n's voltage V_n reaches V_{DD} at time T_A, an umbilical cord from the fermion's source to node n has been formed. At that moment, node capacitance $C_0(n)$ becomes a part of the power supply, and an uncharged capacitor $C_0(n + 2)$ emerges at node $n + 2$. Node $n + 1$'s voltage V_{n+1} drops instantly to 0 since node $n + 1$ is not loaded by capacitor. Then capacitor $C_0(n + 2)$ begins to charge, making use of the charge returned from previously charged capacitor $C_0(n)$. How and why is that possible? Since the P-channel MOSFET of inverter 0 (just left of node n) has infinite differential conductance as its characteristic (section 6.21), the charge of capacitor $C_0(n)$ can move back to the power supply quasi statically. This occurs while $C_0(n + 2)$ is charged up.

Since this is a reversible process, the energy returns to the power supply without entropy increase. While the charge is returned to the power supply and $C_0(n)$ vanishes, the node n loses its capacitor and becomes unobservable. A new, uncharged capacitor $C_0(n + 2)$ emerges at node n + 2 to make the node observable, while $C_0(n + 2)$ is being charged. The charge-up time of $C_0(n + 2)$ determines the delay time of the fermion front-moving from node n to node $n + 2$ and the fermion's velocity. While the charge-up of $C_0(n + 2)$ is going on, the channel of the P-channel MOSFET of inverter 2 consumes as much energy as the capacitor gets, that is, $C_0 V_{DD}^2/2$. This energy is consumed by generating heat in the PFET channel. So it appears that the free energy is lost by the power supply (that is, by the quantum vacuum). The question is, does the vacuum spend free energy just to move the fermion? Actually it does not. Since it is impossible to extract any free energy from the quantum vacuum, its absolute temperature must be zero. Then the heat created in the PFET channel to the vacuum is 100 percent converted back to free energy by the second law of thermodynamics, and entropy does not increase. By this mechanism, the model's rational feature, namely that the quantum space does not spend any free energy to move the fermion, emerges.

So far, I have not explained the nature of the circuit's power supply. Any power supply is a charged capacitor that is able to supply charge and energy instantly to the circuit. For this requirement to be satisfied, the capacitor must be close to the switching inverter, since otherwise the charge and energy are not available in time. Capacitor $C_0(n)$ serves that purpose to charge $C_0(n + 2)$. The quantum vacuum at absolute temperature zero converts the heat back to free energy locally as well. Now all the circuit mechanisms are consistent with the physics.

As a fermion pulls the particle world out, an anti-fermion pulls the antiparticle world out from its source. As for a boson, it is a small speck of the particle world in the antiparticle world, and similarly an anti-boson is a small speck of the antiparticle world in the particle world. They are not connected to their source, and they are free to move in the quantum space and exercise force on any fermion they meet. Yet one of the crucial features of the equivalent circuit model is that not only the substance of the particle but also its characteristics such as spin, charge, and color make their own spaces. Since any character emerges as a positive-negative value pair, a buffer chain for each character makes their umbilical cord, in the same way as with a fermion, except that they are nowhere capacitively loaded. To observe a character without affecting the particle's substance is not possible.

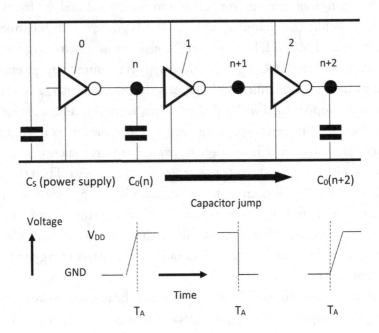

Figure 6.23.2 Jump of node capacitor

I have introduced the concept of the umbilical cord of a fermion from the source to the particle. Actually, an umbilical cord must have another connection structure from the fermion back to the source. This connection is required by the same reason as that required for a biological umbilical cord, so blood can be sent to the fetus and then returned to the mother for recycling. The fermion must send an unobservable signal back to the source to erase the umbilical cord, as soon as the present quantum state collapses. I show this feature in the next section. Another unique feature of the equivalent circuit model is that the model describes quantum space not as mathematical continuum but as a structure assembled from discrete elements, the inverters. A few more interesting features emerge from this (section 6.31).

6.24 Model of Fermion State

Fermions and bosons have their substance, mass or energy, and their characteristics, spin, charge, and color. These characteristics make their own space. The spaces that they make by themselves have their own characteristic *structure*. I place the term in italics because such structures must exist to support any quantum state, but I cannot observe them. What is discussed in this and the following sections are the model that reveals such *hidden* structure. The buffer chain model provides a natural starting point, but it must be made self-consistent. To do this, I must append a signal path from the fermion back to its source, to the structure I described in section 6.23.

The first question is whether the fermion and its source connection is only from the source to the fermion, or should it include the reverse connection, from the fermion back to the source? By simple consideration, the connection must be bidirectional because the fermion is eventually affected by some force and changes its state. Then the connection from the source to the fermion must be erased. The umbilical cord is not to be left over in the quantum vacuum after the state collapse. To erase the cord, a signal from the fermion to its source must report that the current state has been terminated. The fermion-launcher circuit is a set-reset latch that is the source of the umbilical cord, shown in figure 6.24.1(a). Figure 6.24.1(a), the fermion-launcher circuit, is a set-reset latch, which includes a narrow pulse generator consisting of the short delay circuit and exclusive OR gate. This circuit generates an infinitesimally narrow pulse. The pulse width is of the order of the minimum time unit (of the order of the Planck time 10^{-43} seconds).

Because the latch circuit is nowhere capacitor loaded, the narrow pulse is able to set the latch. In figure 6.24.1(b), if the set terminal S of the fermion launcher makes the LOW to HIGH level transition, the latch is set by a narrow pulse, and a fermion is sent out to the buffer chain. The launcher must supply energy to the fermion to be sent out. The buffer output Q is loaded by capacitor C_0 that holds the energy or mass of the launched fermion. The capacitor and energy jump from the fermion, whose state was terminated at the launcher's input, S. This circuit mechanism satisfies the rule that the number of fermions must be conserved. Then, as the fermion leaves the launcher, the whole node of the launcher is no longer capacitor loaded.

One crucial detail is the buffer at the output of latch B, shown in figure 6.24.1(a). By this buffer, the latch can be set or reset by an infinitesimally narrow pulse. The charged capacitor that arrived at input S of the launcher (the substance of the terminated fermion) jumps to buffer B's output to launch the new fermion to the upper buffer chain of figure 6.24.1(b). I may say that buffer B is part of the new fermion's umbilical cord, and the capacitor jump is from the old to the new umbilical cord.

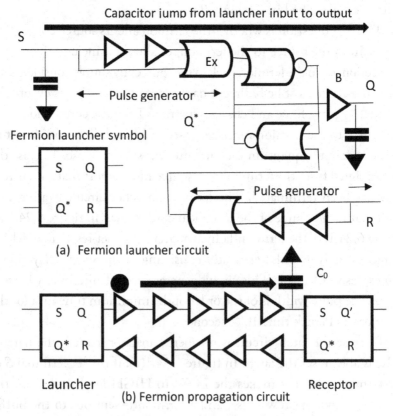

Figure 6.24.1 Fermion launch and propagation

The fermion is launched to the upper buffer chain of figure 6.24.1(b), and as the particle moves, the capacitor C_0 from the launcher moves along the buffer chain to the right, as I explained in the previous section. The velocity is set below the light velocity by C_0 and by the MOSFET current I_D. The nodes behind the fermion are maintained at logic HIGH level by the launcher, which has no capacitor loading and is unobservable. The fermion travels and is acted upon by the external force. By that, the fermion goes into a new state, and the new fermion is launched from the receptor of figure 6.24.1(b) (this is the same circuit as the launcher). The receptor emerges at the moment when the fermion's state is changed. The latch of the receptor was originally reset so that Q' is LOW and Q^* is HIGH. This HIGH level matches the empty state of the anti-fermion that is the particle making the lower buffer chain (this is explained in detail in section 6.27). Then the receptor's latch is set by the incoming fermion's step function, and sends the new fermion out from Q', as Q' makes a LOW-to-HIGH transition, along with that Q^* makes a HIGH-to-LOW transition, and sends out a virtual anti-fermion back to the launcher.

The lower buffer chain is made in step with the upper chain as I describe in section 6.27. This chain is built by the virtual anti-fermion, which moves by making a rocking backward motion toward the direction of the launcher by repeating generation and annihilation, as I discuss in section 6.27. Then the nodes are originally logic HIGH level, that is, the empty state level of the anti-fermion (section 6.19). At the very moment of the receptor's emergence, Q^* of the receptor is HIGH level, so the levels of the buffer chain and of the just-emerged receptor match. Yet as soon as the new fermion is launched from the receptor, Q^* of the receptor makes the HIGH-to-LOW transition, and the virtual anti-fermion is launched from Q^* of the receptor. This is a virtual particle that carries an unobservable signal. Since no node of the lower chain is capacitor loaded, the step function propagates instantly to reach R terminal of the launcher, where it resets the launcher's latch, and Q of the launcher makes a HIGH-to-LOW transition. Since the upper buffer chain is no longer capacitor loaded, all the buffer nodes are pulled down instantly. The latch of the receptor is not affected when the upper umbilical cord is erased, since the receptor's latch was set before, and by that time, a new fermion has already left from the receptor.

This is a complicated process. I reiterate the mechanism of erasing the umbilical cord. As I show in section 6.27, the particle that builds the lower buffer chain from Q^* of the receptor to R of the launcher is a virtual anti-fermion. This chain is built by the virtual anti-fermion repeating a rocking motion along with the moving fermion of the upper buffer chain (section 6.27). At each rocking step, the virtual anti-fermion annihilates to give away the energy. Then the nodes of the lower buffer chain are the anti-fermion's empty state, that is, in the logic HIGH level with no capacitor loading. That level matches Q^* logic level of the receptor at the moment of the receptor's emergence. Then Q^* of the receptor makes a HIGH-to-LOW transition and launches a virtual anti-fermion, that travels the unloaded lower buffer chain instantly. As it arrives at R, the reset terminal of the launcher, the signal resets the launcher, node Q of the launcher makes a HIGH-to-LOW transition. Since the upper buffer chain is not capacitor loaded, the umbilical cord is wiped out instantly. Since the receptor latch has been set before, another signal from the vanishing upper umbilical cord does not affect the receptor's state. The lower buffer chain nodes are all at the LOW level, holding the virtual antiparticle. When the fermion launched from the receptor is terminated, the receptor latch is reset. Q^* of the receptor makes a LOW-to-HIGH transition, and the lower umbilical cord is wiped out also. Given this, the digital circuit model operation is consistent with the fermion's propagation mechanism. As this scenario describes, the fermion leaves its traces behind, and they are kept moving while erasing the track step by step, like a wise fox erasing his footsteps by wagging his tail. This *track-erasing function* occurs instantly since the chain of unloaded buffers transmit signal instantly. The chain of buffers collapses to a single buffer by losing the loading capacitor (section 6.15). This may be interpreted as a change of the structure of the quantum space made by the motion of the fermion.

In this section, I described the unobservable structure built by the motion of the fermion that carries its substance (mass or energy). Yet an elementary particle carries characteristics. From their close association, they also build their own space along with the substance. Any such character creates an unobservable structure in quantum space, that is, the buffer chain not loaded to any capacitor. So a single particle may carry more than one umbilical cords. Any umbilical cord, be it one of the substance or of the character, ensures satisfaction of the conservation laws. I note here an important feature of the quantum space built by these characteristics. Some character space inverter chain switches to HIGH or LOW logic level, but some others do not switch, remaining in an indefinite state representing the probabilistic quantum state.

6.25 Particle Creation and Interaction

Since a fermion and a boson are modeled by digital waveforms, their creation and interaction are executed by logic gates. Launching a particle is effected by triggering the launcher. Figures 6.25.1(a) and 6.25.1(b) shows the circuits that launch a fermion and a boson, respectively. The source of a fermion is a set-reset latch shown in figure 6.25.1(a). The diagram is simplified to highlight the latch: the small closed square boxes show the narrow pulse generators in figure 6.24.1, which consist of a short signal delay circuit and an exclusive OR gate. The circuit generates the minimum width set or reset pulse when the signal to the launcher changes the state. Since the latch is not capacitively loaded, the narrow pulse is able to control the latch. This idealized feature originates from the compactification of a not capacitively loaded digital circuit chain (section 6.15). An unloaded digital circuit is an instantly responding circuit that executes the specified logic function. The elementary particle world is so simple that such idealized digital circuit is used to model the state. Since a fermion is always connected to the source, the umbilical cord must be erased if the fermion's state is terminated. This requires a bidirectional, infinitely fast connection between the source and the particle.

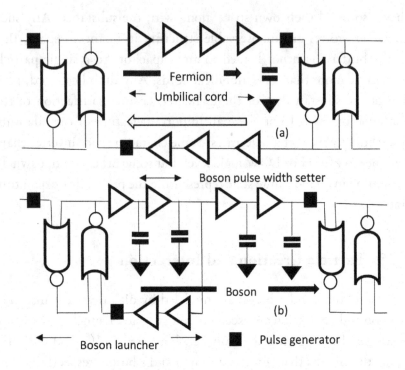

Figure 6.25.1 Fermion and boson launcher and propagation circuit

As for a boson, the launching circuit is a monostable trigger circuit, shown in figure 6.25.1(b), that generates pulse, having the specified width by using the capacitors which are transferred from the boson's energy source terminated at the launcher (which is either boson or fermion). At the beginning, a few stages of the buffer chain, which are then capacitively loaded, create the delay time. The delayed signal turns the set-reset latch off to set the boson's pulse width. The first several stages of the umbilical cord become a part of the monostable trigger circuit of the boson source. The monostable trigger boson launcher turns off when the boson leaves its launcher. As the boson moves to the right, the capacitors move with the boson (section 6.21). Since the launcher has already turned off, the unloaded buffer chain behind the boson returns to the empty boson state, and the boson flies freely away from the source while maintaining its own space only at the present location. However, the launcher can be triggered again and again to send many bosons out in sequence. Then all the bosons are made mutually coherent like the photons in a laser beam. The bosons are packed in a single state of the Bose-Einstein condensate.

Since a boson has no umbilical cord, it is free to move, but it carries its own character, such as spin or charge. As a boson propagates, the character's path is created by the boson's substance. The character connection path back to the boson source is required in order to satisfy the character's conservation law. When a boson meets a fermion, it gives its energy, momentum, and character away. This is possible since a boson's substance is not connected to its source, and it is free to terminate anywhere. The boson's characters are transferred to the new fermion, or to the fermion and the reaction's by-product, to satisfy the conservation laws, and the fermion's and the reaction by-product's umbilical cords are rearranged.

In figure 6.25.1, the particle's substance is determined by the parameter of the buffer chain. The energy of a fermion is set by the electrostatic energy stored in the capacitor, which depends on the power supply voltage and the loading capacitor. The velocity of the particle is determined by the capacitor and the inverter's drive current I_D, defined in section 6.21. As for the boson, there is one more adjustable parameter, the pulse width. For quite general reasons of circuit theory, isolated pulses are unstable unless special conditions are satisfied. The lifetime of the pulse is proportional to the exponent of the pulse width.[7] The model predicts that bosons are basically unstable except for a special case, photons (sections 6.21 and 6.30).

The state change of a fermion is effected by emission or absorption of a boson. The pair of processes is shown in figures 6.25.2(a) and 6.25.2(b), respectively. Since the particles are represented by digital waveforms, their interaction is modeled by the logic gates. Since a fermion is bound to its source, the logic gate is followed by another fermion launcher. As for the boson, it is a free particle, and therefore the launcher may not be necessary. Boson absorption and emission may occur in succession. Figure 6.25.2 shows that conservation of energy

---

[7] Masakazu Shoji, *Theory of CMOS Digital Circuits and Circuit Failures* (Princeton University Press, 1992).

is satisfied by the way that the capacitor is transferred across the logic gate, effecting the interaction.

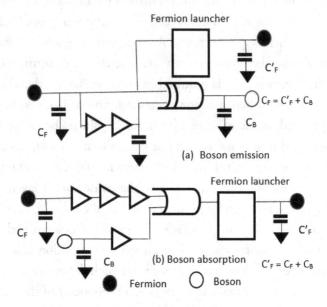

Figure 6.25.2 Particle to particle interaction

Momentum is also conserved as I show in section 6.30. The fermion is a particle bound to the source, and the boson is a free-force particle affecting the fermion. This is why a number of fermions in a nuclear reaction are conserved (here, one fermion counts 1, and one anti-fermion counts –1). Boson numbers are generally not conserved. The model reproduces such features.

6.26 Electron-Positron and Electron-Hole in a Semiconductor

I have shown a digital equivalent circuit model of quantum particles moving in space. The next problem is to show what is modeled by the equivalent circuit, especially to determine the physical meanings of the element, the inverter and buffer. This model carries a new feature, namely, to build quantum space from discrete elements. I need this model in order to explain the quantum particle's behavior, called the entanglement, which is related to ESP according to some authors. My principal objective is to disprove the idea and thereby free self-conscious research from the psychic phenomena like ESP.

Entanglement appears to suggest that a moving elementary particle leaves behind itself a trace of communication path. The path appears to transmit an infinite-speed probability-setting signal to effect the wave function collapse. This feature of a quantum state annoyed Einstein and many other physicists.

I never had any doubt of Bohr's Copenhagen interpretation, which includes apparent action at distance. That is because I regard that the quantum-mechanical probability is the same as lottery probability, which includes a similar *impossible process*, as I showed in sections 6.13–6.15. This is the *mystery* of probability that emerges on many life occasions. That is why I went off the track of systems science and psychology, to build a nonlocality model of the quantum world in my way.

An insight into the mechanism of the quantum particle's motion is gained from the now well-established model of semiconductor physics. Figure 6.26.1(a) shows the mechanism of electrical conduction in a pure semiconductor, including the long high-purity silicon bar. The energy band structure of pure silicon consists of the filled valence band and the empty conduction band at absolute temperature zero. At higher temperatures, some electrons in the valence band are excited to the conduction band, and the valence band states vacated by the electrons, which are called "holes," behave as if they were positively charged particles. They are both able to move in the silicon crystal bar if the electric field is applied to the bar, as shown in figure 6.26.1(a). For more details of semiconductor physics, I refer to the classic of my respected mentor, W. Shockley, *Electrons and Holes in Semiconductors* (Van Nostrand, 1950), as the best.

Because of thermal vibration of the crystal lattice, the electron-hole pair is kept created and is destroyed. The silicon crystal lattice vibration is described by the quantum of sound, the phonon, which plays a similar role as a photon. A phonon is involved in the electron-hole pair generation and recombination, as shown in figure 6.26.1(b). Pair generation and recombination occurs concurrently as the electron moves to the positive electrode and the hole moves to the negative electrode. The electron reaching the positive electrode is not the first excited electron but the last excited electron as shown in figure 6.26.1(a). The same is true for holes. This multicurrent carrier replacement process creates current fluctuation through the silicon bar above and below the average current, which is called the generation-recombination noise. My PhD thesis was about observation of this type noise in silicon-junction field-effect transistors at low temperatures (thesis at the University of Minnesota, 1965).

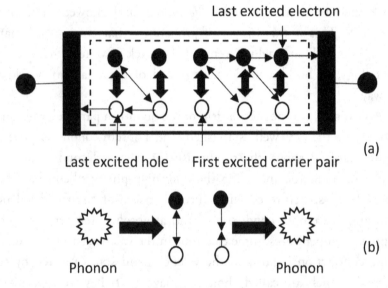

Figure 6.26.1 Carrier replacement in
semiconductor, and particle-wave duality

An electron-hole pair is kept excited by absorbing a phonon, and the pair recombines by emitting a phonon. A phonon makes the carrier pair, and the pair makes the phonon, as shown in figure 6.26.1(b). The process occurring in the silicon bar is a model of electron-positron creation and recombination mechanism by γ-ray photon. What is going on in silicon

is a model of the elementary particle world. In the quantum vacuum, a virtual particle-antiparticle pair is kept created and destroyed. The total energy of the vacuum created by this generation-recombination process is so large that it rejects any explanation at present.[8] This is yet another mystery of the quantum vacuum (section 6.31).

The two differences between the pure silicon and the quantum vacuum are, first, that the particle motion in the quantum vacuum is ballistic; that is, no friction is exercised. In silicon, the lattice vibration creates friction, and the electric field must be maintained to keep the electron and hole moving. This means that the energy derived from the electric field creates heat and raises the temperature of the silicon crystal above absolute temperature zero. In the case of the quantum vacuum, there is no such energy exchange to and from the quantum vacuum, so its temperature remains absolute zero, as I discussed in section 6.23. Yet for my present purposes, only the constantly going on carrier replacement in crucial. The second difference is this: the holes in silicon are real particles whose properties can be measured, but their equivalent in the quantum vacuum, the virtual antiparticles, is not accessible for observation. This does not matter either. With these differences in mind, I have shown that the role of the inverter in the quantum vacuum model is the agent of carrier replacement, or the pair creation-annihilation operator.

6.27 Physical Meaning of the Model

The carrier replacement model in an intrinsic semiconductor can be transcribed to a moving particle-antiparticle model in the quantum vacuum. Since this is a complicated process, I show it by a pair of diagrams, figures 6.27.1 and 6.27.2, each of which highlights a feature of umbilical cord formation. First, I show in figure 6.27.1 how a fermion, 0, of figure 6.27.1(a) moves to the right and builds the cord. The fermion is shown by closed circles, and the anti-fermion is shown by open circles. The fermion 0 makes a virtual fermion pair, 1 and 2, in the direction of

[8] Kaku Michio, *Physics of the Impossible* (Doubleday, 2008).

its motion, where particle 1 is a fermion and particle 2 is an anti-fermion as shown in figure 6.27.1(b). This is the first step of structure building in the quantum vacuum. Referring to figure 6.27.2(ab), this process builds up a structure in the vacuum, represented by a pair of inverters. The inverter above develops the umbilical cord from the fermion source to the fermion, and this represents the motion of the real fermion. The inverter below develops the umbilical cord from the fermion back to the source and represents the rocking motion of the virtual anti-fermion, accompanied with the real fermion motion. Neither process is observable, so the inverters are not capacitively loaded. The capacitor holding the fermion's substance, energy, is still at the starting node N_0 of figure 6.27.2(ab).

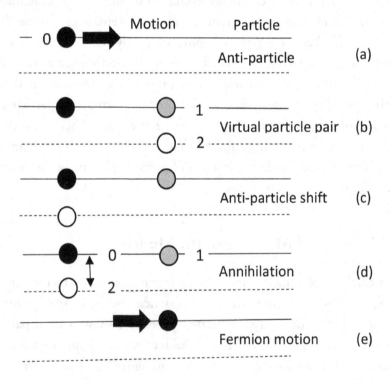

Figure 6.27.1 Particle motion by replacement mechanism

The next step, shown in figure 6.27.1(c), is the shift of the virtual anti-fermion 2 to the left, to the location of fermion 0 by their mutual attractive force, by the opposite charges working between the pair. This shift is actually a rearrangement among the virtual particles relying on the mechanism of figure 6.15.1(b), which occurs instantly. This process is also unobservable. Then fermion 0 and the shifted virtual anti-fermion pair annihilate, as shown in figure 6.27.1(d), and release the energy. The energy is received by the virtual fermion 1, and that converts the virtual fermion into a real fermion as shown in figure 6.27.1(e). This process creates a pair of inverters as shown in figure 6.27.2(cde').

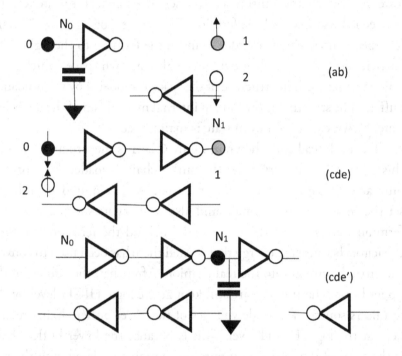

Figure 6.27.2 Umbilical cord construction

In this process, the anti-fermion motion and the pair annihilation are not observable, and therefore the inverter in the lower chain is not capacitively loaded. As for the inverter of the upper chain, the energy released by the pair annihilation must move from particle 0 location to particle 1 location (or node N_0 to N_1). It takes time to move energy, and the velocity is less than the light velocity. Then the inverter that created by the real particle 1 of figure 6.27.1(e) must be capacitor-loaded as shown in figures 6.27.2 (ab)-(cde'). Node N_0 capacitor returns the charge to the power supply, while the capacitor that emerged at node N_1 is charged (section 6.23) as the fermion moves from node N_0 to N_1. The capacitor charging time determines the velocity of the particle's motion. By the process of figures 6.27.1(a)–(e), the fermion moves by way of the distance occupied by the buffer (which is the pair of inverters). The node capacitor at N_0 does not exist after the particle moves ahead from N_0 to N_1, as I explained in section 6.23. Then both the upper and lower inverter chains transmit an unobservable signal at infinite velocity between the source and the fermion. The process of figures 6.27.1(a)–(e) repeats many times in order to move the fermion to the right. The particle moves, and while moving, it makes its own space, which has a unique structure. The structure of the space is modeled by the unloaded buffers. The structure is the hidden internal mechanism of the quantum state, by which the quantum state is maintained.

The umbilical cord shown in figure 6.24.1 is the structure built by this process. In the structure, the buffer chain is loaded by capacitor only at the fermion's location. The capacitor is required in order to set the velocity of the fermion and also to carry its substance. As the fermion moves to the right, the nodes behind the fermion lose their capacitors because the energy that existed there has been used to convert the virtual fermion into the real fermion. After that, the voltage of the upper buffer chain nodes are still kept at the logic HIGH level by the fermion's source. The node voltages of the lower buffer chain are also kept at the logic HIGH level. This is because the lower buffer chain is the trace of the virtual anti-fermion motion associated with the real fermion of the upper chain. The anti-fermion is created and then is annihilated to move the real fermion.

Then the lower chain represents the empty anti-fermion state that is in the logic HIGH level. Both buffer chains' nodes become inaccessible to any observation. If the fermion is accessed for observation, the umbilical cord transmits the probability-setting signal and immediately vanishes. The umbilical cord and the wave function live and die together. The fermion's wave function is spread out and has nonzero amplitude along its track. The particle's motion is going on everywhere along its track probabilistically. This *virtual* activity maintains the umbilical cord's structure. If the wave function collapses, this *probabilistic support* ceases, and the umbilical cord is wiped out.

The equivalent circuit model highlights that repetition of the conversion of the fermion to the virtual boson (virtual fermion–anti-fermion pair) back to the fermion moves the fermion in the quantum vacuum. The conversion process creates the umbilical cord step-by-step. In the upper buffer chain, the fermion moves left to right. The lower buffer chain is created by the rocking motion of a virtual anti-fermion. As the fermion state collapses, a virtual anti-fermion moves from the receptor to the launcher, resets the fermion launcher, and wipes out the upper umbilical cord.

Fermions are the carriers of information. The location of a fermion in space is the information, but it also carries other information, such as spin or charge. Each of the particle's characteristics creates a similar pair of umbilical cords consisting of the go-return pair of the buffer chain. These characters' umbilical cords are constructed keeping step with the particle's motion. Then their structures behave similarly to the fermion's umbilical cord upon interruption of the state by observation.

This model of particle's motion is physically a dynamic version of the screening of a fermion by its associated virtual particles. From this feature, I suspect, some curious features of the character such as spin (section 6.20) may possibly emerge. Where to assign the origin of the characteristics was the difficult issue of string theory also. By the cooperation of the screening virtual particles, some still unexplainable features of the character may emerge, and the umbilical cords are built by the activity. To dig into the mechanism is beyond my simple equivalent circuit model.

This explanation has a hidden question. Virtual fermion pair 1 and 2 in figure 6.27.1 might be thought to exist in any direction, looking from fermion 0. How is the virtual pair in the direction of motion selected? The answer to this question is, the structure built by the process is actually the *state that preexists in the quantum vacuum* that supports such straight-line particle motion. Such a state should already exist as the *matrix* of the quantum vacuum, and the fermion actually selects one of these states and rides on it, like a train runs on the already laid-out railroad track. The fermion's initial state selects one of such states, and once this selection has been made, the fermion is kept riding on the state's track. A quantum vacuum is built from such states.

An empty quantum vacuum is the matrix built from such empty quantum states, in the same way as the brain's template and the association area are built. This feature of a particle's activity is analogous to the brain's neuron circuit activity. A neuron circuit absorbs action potentials, which are bosons, and connects neurons in the matrix. Fermions actually do the same thing. This is another similarity between the quantum world and the brain. An interesting feature of such a quantum state is that not only definite state, such as a particle moving in a direction, but also indefinite state can ride on the state, and the state becomes definite when the state collapses. This is actually the case of quantum entanglement that I discuss in sections 6.28–6.30. Similar structure building occurs in the brain.

6.28 Quantum-Mechanical Entanglement

Suppose that an electron-positron pair is created by a single source, and they fly away in different directions. Such a particle pair shares a common wave function until either one is observed. At the time of particle creation, the pair's total spin angular momentum is 0. Although the combined electron-positron system's spin is 0, the spin of each particle is unknown as shown in figure 6.28.1. After some time, the spin of the positron is measured and it is $h/2$. Then, at the very same moment, the spin of the electron, which is some distance away, is changed from the unknown to $-h/2$, so that the law of spin angular momentum conservation is satisfied. The distance between the two particles can be long, allegedly even light years away from one another. This effect is symmetrical: the spin determination of the electron has the same effect on the positron. This is a characteristic of the quantum state deducted from the Copenhagen interpretation. This strange phenomenon is called quantum *entanglement*.[9] I explain this effect in the next section, using the model I set up in this chapter.

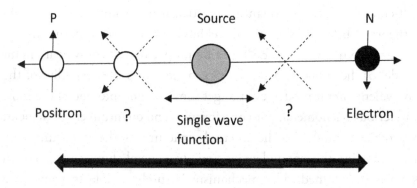

Figure 6.28.1 Quantum-mechanical entanglement

In the late twentieth century, this effect was confirmed by the experiments that used photons. The entanglement effect appears to violate the basic physical principle of locality stipulating that any state change at the source is transmitted to the destination at most by the speed of light. It appears as if signal transmission velocity faster than the speed of light exists between the pair of particles to set the spin states. Yet by this effect, it is impossible to send information. Even if I want to send a signal with logic HIGH level from location P to N of figure 6.28.1, the result of the measurement at point P can be either HIGH or LOW level because of the unknown result of the spin direction measurement at point P. There is no control over the information to be sent from point P to N. Therefore, the effect does not violate the relativistic constraint.

This effect suggests that the structure of the quantum state is maintained by an as yet unknown structure, and the structure allows transmission of the probability-setting signal by infinite velocity. As I discussed in section 6.14, this is not surprising according to the mathematical definition of probability, yet there are sustaining doubts and questions since there is no physical model. I am concerned with this

---

[9] K. W. Ford, *101 Quantum Questions* (Harvard University Press).

mystery because some influential authors think that the mechanism of self-consciousness is quantum mechanical and that entanglement is the mechanism of telepathy (ESP). I intend to disprove this idea and to free self-consciousness from quantum mysticism and paranormal effects. As a theory of basic physics, my model has not yet reached maturity.

I try to disprove the ESP idea by proposing the equivalent circuit model of the entanglement. This example shows the versatility of the equivalent circuit model, even to get some insight into one of the most mysterious phenomena, self-consciousness and quantum entanglement. I provide a model of the internal structure of the quantum state that explains the entanglement and, in general, how any quantum state is maintained. The mechanism is surely unable to transmit a telepathy signal by itself since the entangled structure is so fragile and unpredictable that it cannot carry any definite information in the noisy human living space.

6.29 Model of Quantum Entanglement

I set up an equivalent circuit model of quantum entanglement of the previous section. At the center of figure 6.29.1, an entangled electron-positron pair, which shares a single wave function, is created. The positron and the electron fly away to left and right, respectively. Both particles are described by a joint wave function, and their states are correlated. This means that if one of the particles is subjected to an observational test, the state of the other is set. The lower *pair* of buffer chains models the particles' substance, which creates the particles' space to the left and to the right. Both particles are connected to their common source by their umbilical cords.

The lower buffer chain's upper umbilical cord models the motion of the particles' substance, and the lower cord models the rocking motion of their companion, the virtual antiparticle, as I explained in section 6.27. On the left side, the particle is a positron, and the associated antiparticle is a virtual electron. On the right side, the particle is an electron, and the associated antiparticle is a virtual positron. The upper cords are loaded by capacitor only at the location where the particles presently exist. At the time of observation of the spin direction, only the left end and the right end are capacitor loaded. The other parts of the umbilical cords are made of buffer chains that are not loaded by capacitor, and therefore the nodes are not accessible.

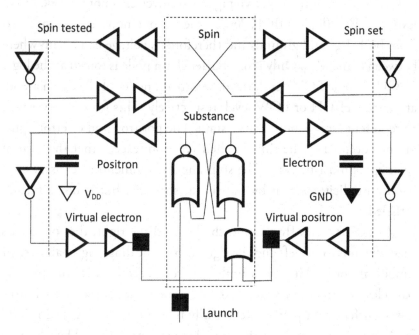

Figure 6.29.1 Equivalent circuit model of quantum entanglement

The upper buffer chain *pair* carries the spin direction information: the left chain for the positron spin, and the right chain for the electron spin. Similar to the substances' umbilical cords, the upper cord carries the spin information of the particle, and the lower cord carries the spin information of the companion virtual antiparticle. At the location of the particles' source, the spin buffer chains cross over: the lower virtual electron spin buffer chain from the left side connects to the real upper electron spin chain to the right, and vice versa. If spin is up ($+h/2$), the digital level is HIGH, and if it is down ($-h/2$), the level is LOW. When the particle is created, its total spin is zero, but the direction of each particle's spin is not set. Their spin states remain unknown until one particle is observed.

The CMOS buffer model described in section 6.21 can be used to model such a quantum state. The buffer chains are built from inverters consisting of MOSFETs having the simplest characteristic described in section 6.21. If the input voltage of an inverter is not 0 (logic LOW level) or V_{DD} (logic HIGH level), the output node is disconnected from both V_{DD} and ground, and therefore its voltage can be anywhere between 0 and V_{DD}. Only if one buffer chain node is forced at the logic HIGH or logic LOW level, the downstream nodes of the chain are set at definite HIGH or LOW level, respectively. This feature serves well to represent a probabilistic spin state. The positron and electron spins are not defined at the time of their creation, except that the sum of their spins must be zero. The spin angular momentum conservation is only implicitly meant by the circuit structure but is not explicitly satisfied.

As the particles fly away to the left and the right, the spin state's space extends to the left and the right also, while dragging a pair of their umbilical cords. The spin's umbilical cord accompanies the moving particles, but there is a difference. The state of the substance chain (the lower buffer chain pair) switches fully between the LOW and HIGH levels since they represent the particle's mass or energy. Their leading buffers are loaded with capacitor to hold their energy and to set the velocity. The space of the spin (the upper buffer chain pair), however, carries no definite state. The spin buffer chain is not loaded by capacitor, and the chain stretches the same length as the substance buffer chain. The substance chain makes a spin chain. This state resembles a fully conscious man pulling a zombie.

Suppose that both the electron and positron reach the point shown on their respective right and left ends of figure 6.29.1. On the positron side, the spin state observation is executed, and the test finds the spin either up (logic HIGH level) or down (logic LOW level). This is a test that applies a magnetic force. The force applied to the positron sets its previously undefined spin state to either up or down state. At the same time, the spin of the positron's shadow companion, the virtual electron, is set at the opposite direction at the same location. This is to conserve the local spin angular momentum on the left end. This spin inversion is indicated by the inverter set at the end of the positron spin buffer chain. The enforced virtual electron spin level is instantly transmitted through the unloaded lower spin buffer chain to the location of particle creation.

Here the spin buffer chain of the virtual electron from the left side crosses over and connects to the real electron spin buffer chain of the right side. The spin-setting signal then goes to the right side, to the present location of the electron, via the buffer chain of the real electron spin state. This spin-direction-setting signal sets the real electron spin to the direction opposite that of the real positron. The spin of the real electron sets its shadow virtual positron's spin in the opposite direction, which is also shown by the right-end inverter. The virtual positron's spin signal goes to the particle's creation location, crosses over to the real positron spin buffer line on the left side, transmits the signal through the left positron spin buffer chain, and confirms the positron spin set by the test that has been executed there. The signal flows first from the left to right and then from the right to left and holds the definite state of the spin pair. Now the spin conservation law is explicitly satisfied. The task of the umbilical cords is over. They all vanish. The electron and the positron become independent particles.

Since the circuit is symmetrical, setting the electron spin by its observation sets the positron spin to its opposite direction. At the moment of testing, the entire state changes to satisfy the spin conservation law explicitly and instantly. Before the test, the law is only ensured to be satisfied by building the umbilical cord structure. It appears that nature requires only assurance that the conservation law is satisfied, by building an unobservable structure in the quantum vacuum. The spin direction setting occurs instantly since the probability-setting signal propagates at infinite velocity through the unloaded buffer chain.

As it is observed from this scenario, instantaneous interaction within a quantum state is mediated by the hidden structure built behind the moving particle. There, the relativistic limit does not apply. All the quantum states have such a hidden structure, which is created to maintain the state. It is supported by the wave function of the quantum state. Once the wave function collapses, the structure passes the probability-setting signal only once at infinite speed to change the probabilistic state and ensures that the implicitly satisfied conservation law is explicitly satisfied. The hidden binary logic circuit executes conversion of the previously not set probability to the definite value and then vanishes.

A crucial feature of this model is that a particle, which carries energy, is unable to move faster than the velocity of light, but the particle's character is an independent entity, and if the character alone is transmitted in the quantum space, its velocity is not limited by the relativity. This feature is neatly consistent with the collapse of a buffer chain to a single-gate direct connection by removal of all the capacitor loading (section 6.15). In an electron, its substance, which carries mass and energy, cannot move faster than the velocity of light, but its spin and charge are the characteristics that can follow wherever the substance goes. Spin cannot exist without substance (mass or energy). Spin is bound to move with the substance. The velocity capable of any character must be faster than the substance's velocity, because sometimes an electron's virtual velocity can be infinite, for instance, in tunnel barrier penetration. If the characters are arranged in such a way that they can be transmitted separately, their velocity can be infinite, but the signal is only for probability setting. No real information can be carried.

Figure 6.29.2 shows a simplified schematic of how the entangled spin states are separated by setting both spins to the definite state, thereby making the particles mutually independent. The probability-setting signal circulates the closed path, setting the spin to the definite state, thereby separating the two entangled particles into a pair of independently recognizable particles. The entangled state is really a single elementary state. I showed the same features of brain operation in section 3.21 by the example of splitting a template. A single integrated template is like an entangled pair of the pair of the component templates. This is another functional similarity between the quantum world and the brain's operation.

This spin entanglement model can be explained by a simple metaphor. Twin sisters have red and blue dresses. In total darkness in their home, each of them picks up a dress and puts it on, and then they walk out right and left in total darkness.

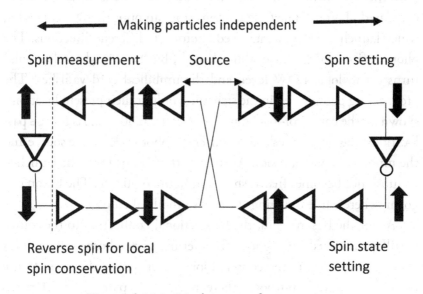

Figure 6.29.2 Mechanism of spin setting

The only information available is that their dress colors are red and blue. Which woman wears which color dress remains unknown until one of them emerges under a streetlight. Here are two different interpretations of entanglement: In the *hidden variable interpretation*, their dresses were dyed before they were worn. This is not a correct explanation of quantum entanglement. The right interpretation is that their dresses were originally white, and cans of red and blue dye were with the dresses. At the moment when the streetlight hits one of the women, a can of dye, either red or blue, flies from the twins' home and splashes color on the dress. The other can of dye, the different color, flies to the other woman and colors her dress. Indeed, this is really strange!

6.30 Quantum Vacuum Model

After showing the entanglement mechanism of fermion, I now show how the entanglement of a photon (boson) works. Figures 6.30.1(a)–(c) show the equivalent circuit model. The photon launcher creates a pair of correlated photons. They use photons from an optical down converter, which launches a pair of entangled photons in different directions. The photons first make their umbilical cords, but then the launcher pulse turns off to logic LOW level, and the umbilical cord vanishes. The propagating photons retain the structures only at their present locations, shown by the capacitor-loaded nodes of figure 6.30.1(b). As for the past locations, the activity ceases soon after the photons leave the source and the umbilical cord vanishes. As soon as the bosons leave the launcher, its substance becomes free as shown in figure 6.30.1(b). The boson can go anywhere while dragging the spin's umbilical cords.

As for the boson's spin, the bidirectional connection to the source is still maintained throughout the lifetime of the boson's state. This is necessary to secure the conservation law of spin as shown in figure 6.30.1(c). For that purpose, there must be a pair of signal paths connecting the spin state to the source. Any character is specified by a single binary parameter. The parameter is carried by a pair of go-and-return buffer chains as shown in figure 6.30.1(c), and this is the same as the case of the fermion in the previous section.

As the pair of photons are apart and some significant distance away, a spin measurement of one of them is carried out. A photon's spin is directed either in the up or down direction. If one photon's spin is measured and it is in one direction, then the paired photon's spin is set to the other direction instantly. That is, if the photon spin is set to one direction at the location of the closed circle of figure 6.30.1(c), then its virtual companion's spin at the same location is set to the opposite direction. What follows is the same as with the case of the fermion that I discussed in the previous section.

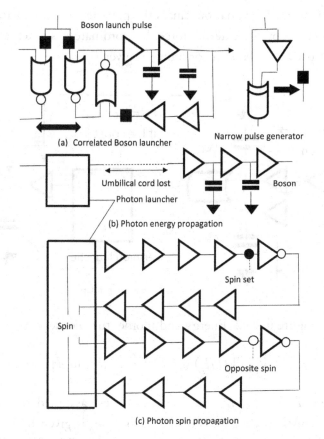

Figure 6.30.1 Entangled photon

The photon entanglement effect has been confirmed by several experiments in which the paired photons are apart many kilometers away from each other. Interaction within a single quantum state is definitely not local.

Going back to the basics of the equivalent circuit model of the quantum world, the model of a quantum state contains parameters such as V_{DD}, I_D and C_0, as I introduced in section 6.21. Because these parameters are not for quantitative analysis, I discuss only their physical meanings and their relations by a bit of mathematics. V_{DD} is a parameter common to most cases. $C_0 V_{DD}^2/2$ is the energy of the particle, $T_D = C_0 V_{DD}/I_D$ is the delay time per buffer stage, and L/T_D is the particle's velocity, where L is the buffer's spatial size. I_D is the parameter that characterizes the state of particle motion. I_D's variation causes the particle's velocity change, that is, acceleration by the external force. If coordinate x is taken along the particle's path, acceleration constant g is given by

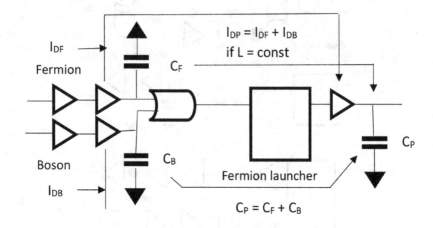

Figure 6.30.2 Energy and momentum conservation

$$g = [L\, I_D^2/(C_0 V_{DD})^2]\ (L/I_D)\ (dI_D/dx) = (L/T_D^2)\ (d/d\xi)(\log I_D)$$

where $T_D = C_0 V_{DD}/I_D$ and $\xi = x/L$. Here I assumed that L is the model's constant. Rest mass of the particle m_0 is given by the energy divided by c^2, where c is the light velocity, as $m_0 = C_0 V_{DD}^2/2c^2$. These are the model parameters in terms of the classical interpretation.

  L is a structural parameter that is required in the model, but its real value is not relevant to the qualitative consequence of the model. To gain qualitative insights is the only objective of this model. Thus I assumed that L is a constant. As a model constant, it must be shorter than the distance of the particle's travel during the time of the particle excitation, set by the Heisenberg uncertainty principle. For an electron, the energy is $m_E c^2 = 0.82 \times 10^{-13}$ joules, where m_E is the electron's mass. Then I have $L < v_E(h/m_E c^2)$. If the maximum electron velocity v_E is light velocity c, then I get $L < 4 \times 10^{-13}$ meters. This is the absolute maximum limit allowed for L to be consistent within the model. Actual L must be much smaller than that.

Figure 6.30.2 shows when a fermion absorbs a boson, the energy and momentum are conserved. First, I assume L is a model constant. Then the capacitor C_0 and the MOSFET-driving current I_D are transferred across the interaction gate and launcher as they were. For the fermion and boson, I show their values by subscript F and B, respectively. The velocity is $v_{F,B} = LI_{DF,B}/C_{0F,B}V_{DD}$, the energy is $E_{F,B} = C_{0F,B}V_{DD}^2/2$, and the mass is $m_{F,B} = E_{F,B}/c^2$. Then their momentum is $p_{F,B} = LV_{DD}I_{DF,B}/2c^2$. If the fermion and boson collide, then I_{DF}, I_{DB}, C_{0F}, and C_{0B} are transferred across the interacting OR gate as shown in figure 6.30.2. Then the total energy $(C_{0F} + C_{0B})V_{DD}^2$, and the total momentum $LV_{DD}(I_{DF} + I_{DB})/2c^2$, are both conserved before and after the collision. If I assume that L is given by the de Broglie wavelength, the energy is conserved as before, but as for momentum, the post-interaction $I_{D(post)}$ is given by $I_{D(post)} = (I_{DF}^{1/2} + I_{DB}^{1/2})^2$. Parameter I_D is modified after going through the interacting logic gate.

Figure 6.30.3(a) shows a single fermion in a long buffer chain at location A. To convert the fermion to a boson, I cut the buffer chain at the location shown in figure 6.30.3(b) and insert an extra inverter B there. Then I get an anti-boson. Similarly, to convert this anti-boson back to a fermion, I cut the buffer chain once again and insert another inverter, C, as shown in figure 6.30.3(c).

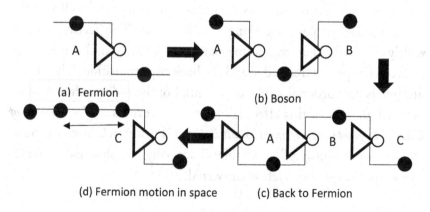

(a) Fermion   (b) Boson

(d) Fermion motion in space   (c) Back to Fermion

Figure 6.30.3 Fermion-boson-fermion
conversion moves a fermion in space

If I observe the upstream (to the left) of the resultant waveform, I find that the pair of inverters A and B are equivalent to adding a single buffer stage. Then the resultant fermion appears as shown in figure 6.30.3(d). The closed circles show the location of the observable nodes of the buffer chain. In tracking the conversion by locating the observable nodes 1, 2, 3, ... shown by the closed circles, we find that the fermion → boson → fermion conversion moves the fermion by three buffer lengths. This feature suggests that motion of the fermion explained in section 6.27 may be interpreted by converting a fermion to a boson and then back to a fermion. This is one feature of supersymmetry.

Since the structure of a fermion and the structure of a boson are basically quite different in the equivalent circuit model as I discussed, I do not feel comfortable with the supersymmetry conjecture. Yet this model has a curious feature of reproducing its expectation. The motion of a particle is translational, or an external symmetry exercise, and conversion of a fermion and a boson is the particle's internal symmetry exercise. The equivalent circuit model mixes the two essentially different symmetries.

Yet another curious feature of this model is this: it implies that bosons are essentially unstable. There are only two stable elementary bosons—photons and gravitons—but there are many stable elementary fermions. This feature emerges by a generalization of instability of the isolated pulses propagating along a buffer chain. This feature is quite widely observed in nature. The mechanism is the result of the interaction between the pulse's front edge and the back edge transition. The pulse's lifetime is proportional to the exponential of the pulse width. A more detailed analysis of this effect is in one my previous works (*Theory of CMOS Digital Circuits and Circuit Failures* [Princeton University Press, 1992]). Are bosons really unstable? Then why are photons so stable? These are the questions left unanswered.

6.31 Quantum Vacuum Model—Conclusion

I now come close to the end of my road. I believe that the conclusion of a technical work should give some *imaginative* future perspective. Events that become a source of mystery are not limited to incidents of personal or social affairs. Nature presents deep mysteries. The progress of physics has resolved most of the mysteries experienced in normal daily life, but many as yet unresolved physics mysteries appear quite formidable. These mysteries are in the realm of quantum physics. Why do definite classical parameters become probabilities, why does established quantum mechanics give such accurate probability estimates that are confirmed by severely invasive observation of the microscopic objects, and why does a quantum state collapse instantly? I've attempted to *finagle* my answer to such questions in this chapter from the side of psychology. Yet there are more.

A quantum vacuum is powerful, but is singularly quiet. It generates virtual particles, whose energy is δE and whose lifetime is δt, that satisfy the Heisenberg uncertainty relation $\delta E \times \delta t = h$, where h is the Planck's constant 1.05×10^{-34} joules/sec. During the short time δt, the physical world is able to borrow energy $\delta E = h/\delta t$ from the quantum vacuum. I can borrow 1 billion joules of energy for the time period of $\delta t = 10^{-43}$ seconds. What is the nature of this energy? If this energy emerged as heat, it is enough for me to cremate myself. So, in what form does the energy emerge from the quantum vacuum? Does it emerge as a harmless particle having mass? Then the doctors would be able to find it by doing an autopsy on my body?

Suppose that 1 billion joules of energy emerged somewhere in my body for 10^{-43} seconds. For this energy to destroy my body, its effect must spread out. How large an area would be affected? About 10^{-33} cm from the energy source—and that area must be destroyed. This area is very small. To cremate my body, the energy must be kept working in my body long enough. Is this the reason why I am not cremated by this energy?

There is a hard problem of astronomy from this same effect. Energy per unit volume contained in the space by this mechanism is said to be 10^{120} times larger than that estimated from the astronomical observations, and there is no explanation of this huge discrepancy at present.[10] I challenge myself by stretching my wild imagination to finagle an answer to this question, so that I might feel safe living in this world. With this bizarre question in my mind, I take a second look at my equivalent circuit model from a different viewpoint. In the equivalent circuit model, there is a capacitor that is charged to store energy. The capacitor is ale to convert some, but not all kinds, of the energy to the voltage, which affects the circuit until the energy is dissipated. Strong magnetic energy does not affect my body if I sit down quietly. That is, magnetic energy cannot charge the *capacitor* if the body does not move. So the energy from the quantum vacuum may not have the equivalent of a capacitor to exercise its effect? The capacitor's role is to extend the effects of energy in time so that energy can do the work.

From this viewpoint, the interesting feature of the equivalent circuit model is that the model distinguishes *energy* and the *energy acceptor*, that is the capacitor. Even if energy is available, some energy may not create any effect since there is no energy acceptor. One obvious case is electromagnetic energy. Electrostatic energy does not affect an insulator whose dielectric constant is unity. Nonmagnetic material is immune to strong magnetic field. That is why a patient can be pulled safely into the tunnel of the strong magnetic field of an NMR imaging machine.

Let us consider quantum entanglement from this viewpoint. In the experiment, the pair of particles are a long distance away, alleged to be light years away. Then why are their umbilical cords not affected by the fluctuation of the quantum vacuum? One explanation by the equivalent circuit model is the same as the noise immunity of CMOS logic circuits used to model the effect. If the effective noise voltage in the circuit from the quantum vacuum fluctuation is less than the model's power supply voltage V_{DD} (which can be chosen arbitrarily in my model), then the equivalent circuit is not affected. Yet this explanation is too arbitrary to consider seriously.

---

[10] Kaku Michio, *Physics of the Impossible* (Doubleday, 2008), 270.

Couldn't we think of this problem in a different way? What affects the CMOS circuit operation is the *noise voltage* and not the *energy* from the outside. Some energy charges the capacitor and creates the noise voltage, which affects the equivalent circuit operation. In the entanglement model, there is only a pair of two capacitors at the terminal ends of the particle's umbilical cords. Observation of the particle affects these capacitors. The umbilical cords themselves have no capacitor. Does this mean that "the node capacitor is zero" and "there is no capacitor to accept energy to the nodes" are two different things? This is quite an interesting possibility to consider, one that affects the structure of the umbilical cord.

In the basic circuit theory, any circuit node that has nonzero size has parasitic capacitance associated with it. If a node has small capacitance, even a small amount of electrical energy deposited on it creates high voltage, which should affect the circuit operation. In my model, I may imagine the following. The buffer chain not only *loses* the capacitor but also compacts into a single buffer (section 6.15) so that the structure has only one capacitor at each end of the line, such as shown in figure 6.29.1. Such an equivalent circuit can be affected only at the two ends, where the capacitors exist. Other nodes are immune because they are *capacitance-free,* or because the node itself is *nonexistent* in the *compacted gate* configuration (section 6.15). The observational access or the quantum vacuum fluctuation can dump charge only to the capacitors at the end of line, and that terminates the entangled state. The other nodes of the umbilical cords have no capacitor to accept the external effect. Is this too much of a stretch of the imagination?

Collapse of the logic gate chain to a single gate (section 6.15) means that somehow the space between the entangled pair of particles collapses, in the same way as the digital circuit not loaded by any capacitor collapses to a single gate. This is required to make sense for the pair of statements "the node has zero capacitance" and "the node has no capacitance," carry different meanings. The difference may suggest that the quantum space structure changes. According to Sabine Hossenfelder in *Lost in Math* (Basic Books, 2008, 229), Juan Maldacena and Leonard Susskind hold the opinion that the space between a pair of entangled particles becomes a *wormhole*. My equivalent circuit model describes how that process actually takes place. Such a feature makes the equivalent circuit model unique.

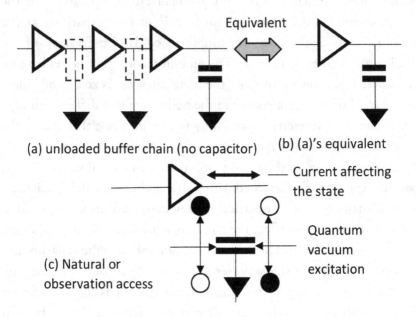

(a) unloaded buffer chain (no capacitor)   (b) (a)'s equivalent

(c) Natural or observation access

Current affecting the state

Quantum vacuum excitation

Figure 6.31.1 How the entangled state is affected by natural or observational access

The structure of the umbilical cord is functionally equivalent to a compacted single buffer, as shown in figure 6.31.1, and as I discussed in section 6.15. From the logic circuit theory, the two circuits are functionally same. Then, only the pair of capacitively loaded terminal nodes of the pair of the buffer chain is accessible by the external influence. The umbilical cords are immune because of this reason. Is this really the case?

If this is really the valid explanation, then the only capacitors that work as energy acceptors are at the ends of the umbilical cords, and they are certainly susceptible to any external access like observation. If there is no energy acceptor, then the huge amount of energy emerging from the quantum vacuum or anything else cannot affect the equivalent circuit. It cannot affect my body and also cannot destroy the extensive umbilical cord. As a consequence, quantum vacuum fluctuation is ineffective to cremate me, and it cannot create the huge astronomical effect. If such were the case, then this would be an interesting science fiction subject!

Then how about the structure of the quantum vacuum? The equivalent circuit model should be applicable to any quantum state as well. As the capacitor moves around the localized state structure, its energy may be affected by any external access, including the quantum vacuum fluctuation. Thus the quantum vacuum fluctuation determines the lifetime of the unstable nucleus. The Schrödinger equation predicts its probabilistic consequence. For external observation, the equation gives the emerging state's probability.

What is the structure of the quantum vacuum where all the quantum effects are displayed? The inverters, buffers, and logic gates are the functional agents that display the quantum effects. They exist in the quantum vacuum as its building blocks, waiting for a real particle to ride on them. A quantum vacuum consists of these functional agents. I explained in section 6.27 that the particle builds the state. Now I reinterpret this to mean that the particle selects and rides on the already existing state's structure.

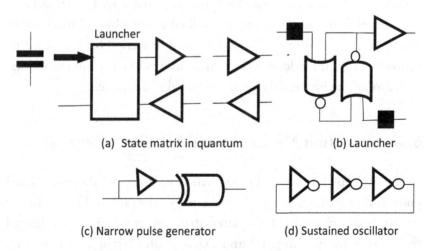

(a) State matrix in quantum   (b) Launcher

(c) Narrow pulse generator   (d) Sustained oscillator

Figure 6.31.2 Quantum vacuum model

A quantum vacuum model is the matrix of the states built from the gates that are not yet assembled, or partially assembled, as shown in figure 6.31.2. The quantum vacuum is a huge matrix of quantum states, such as those shown in figure 6.31.1(b), which further includes a fermion launcher, (c) a narrow pulse generator, and (d) a self-excited oscillator, and their combination. The matrix also includes particle interaction gates. The motion of particles simply connects the inverter and buffer to build the invisible umbilical cords. To initiate structure building, a charged capacitor carrying the particle's substance, energy, rides on the node, as shown in figure 6.31.2(a) by the thick arrow. This is quantum-mechanical transition. As the capacitor moves in the structure, the path which is made of many buffers, collapses to a single gate. Thus, infinite speed signal transmission becomes possible.

The matrix structure is similar to the neuron matrix of the template and the association area, discussed in sections 3.23 and 3.24. Its mode of excitation is also similar. Excitation of the subcritical oscillator begins by activation of the loop neurons by action potential, that is, bosons.

I described a quantum vacuum as an assembly of inverters and logic gates. They are convenient to describe quantum effects by the simple circuit diagram. As the standard practice of using any equivalent circuit model, these gates are the symbols of the activities of particles and virtual particles. They are transcribed to the physical mechanism by the same procedure as the one I showed in section 6.27. I built this equivalent circuit model as a convenient means to represent the hidden structure of the mysterious quantum world's backstage.

6.32   Quantum Mechanics and Self-Consciousness

In my attempt to explain human self-consciousness, the one crucial point is that humans live both in the physical world and in the image (or information) world. This paired structure of worlds is not limited to covering human internal and external life, but it also covers all objects, including living and lifeless objects. Among them, human mental activity clearly shows how the two worlds interact. This is easy to see in the quantum world, but not in the macroscopic world.

In the physical world, energy is the working agent. In the image world, the agent is information, carried by energy, as I discussed in sections 6.13–6.15. What is the role of energy in the information world? For information to move from one location to another location, energy is required as its carrier. Fractional information, probability, is carried without energy cost. In lifeless objects of macroscopic size, the two worlds are closely integrated. Yet, as I showed in this chapter, they split in the microscopic world, into the substance and the character of the particles. Although the human brain is a macroscopic object, its operation reveals the split of the two worlds and simulates the features of the quantum world, because the information in the brain and the physical action by the body are separated but interact—and this interaction is clearly observable from the mechanical model.

Let us paraphrase this basic viewpoint. In the human brain, the template memories belong to the physical world, and the identifiers in the association area belong to the information world. Templates are spatially spread-out structures, and identifiers are compact point-like objects that maintain their meaning by their extensive mutual connections. Templates are sent out to take action in the external world, and they are the directive to control the energy of the physical world. Identifiers are connected or disconnected to organize the images, and they are the carriers of information. Their connection and disconnection is the movement of information, which consumes energy, and that energy is sensed as sensation. Identifier's activities belong to the information world that uses the energy as its carrier.

In a similar manner, the wave of a quantum object spreads out over the space and specifies the action in the physical world. In the quantum domain, the particle carries the event's information. The wave's and particle's roles are distinct. The two worlds are different, but their difference becomes less and less clear as the size of the object increases. Therefore, the quantum world and the human mind appear similar. This similarity had a historical consequence in self-consciousness research.

In the 1990s, self-consciousness research enjoyed a short period as a tolerable theme of research in academia. During that time, several theories were proposed asserting that the mechanism of self-consciousness was quantum-mechanical. The brief period of academic tolerance ended before a final consensus was reached. This trend had a curious prehistory. Around the 1970s, Cold War tensions eased. A direct consequence of this was a huge reduction in basic physics research support in the U.S. Suddenly, many physicists lost their field of activity. Some such physicists in California set up an alternative semiprivate work group and thought over the basic physics problems such as the measurement problem in quantum mechanics, which had not, and still has not, been resolved. These were the first people who connected self-consciousness to quantum mechanics. Their activities are summarized by David Kaiser in *How the Hippies Saved Physics* (W. W. Norton & Co., 2011).

This prehistory may have been somehow taken over, or perhaps independently rediscovered, by several prominent physicists in the 1990s, and this created a new trend during the short period of academic tolerance. Because I firmly believe that self-consciousness is a feature of a digital circuit's attributes and that the 1970 California physicists were misled because digital systems and quantum systems have close functional (but not physical) similarities, I published a part of my earlier works during that time (*Dynamics of Digital Excitation* [Kluwer Academic, 1997]).

I am particularly concerned that ESP (extrasensory perception) is naively connected to the quantum phenomena, the entanglement. I personally respect the lifelong devotion of J. B. Rhine, since science needs a character like him. Yet, objectively, I believe that Rhine proved that ESP is not a reproducible phenomenon, and there is no evidence of its physical mechanism. This *negative conclusion* is what he accomplished, and that I appreciate. Humans encounter mysteries of the mind, but there is always some alternative explanation. Quantum entanglement cannot deliver any information.

Future of Psychology Research

I wish to propose some promising subjects of psychology. Psychology is now heading toward mental pathology. Is this the only way to the future? Psychologists should look for the forefront of the natural sciences. I discussed the psychological reaction of the human mind facing complexity in sections 6.09–6.11. Those who face the enormous complexity of society, biology, and new data-processing systems require a psychologist's insights. Another area is the psychology of model making, which is an entangled process of rational thinking and artistic sensitivity.

Yet another area is the psychology of seeing or sensing those objects that cannot be seen or sensed by ordinary means. At the smallest size and in the shortest time limit, 10^{-33} cm and 10^{-43} seconds, respectively, in the so-called "quantum foam" world, objects have no shape. How can such a world be imagined? Can any psychologist extend his or her imagination and create the *image* of such a world? Such work is sure to inspire physicists to think through the basic issue more realistically and will stimulate them to make a realistic model. I believe the role of psychology is not limited to plugging the bottom leak of the human mind but is meant to break open its top cover.

CONCLUSION

The conclusion of this book, *Self-Consciousness*, is short. Self-consciousness is a valid theme of scientific research based on honest, unbiased observation of our own minds by introspection. Self-consciousness is the product of evolutionary development and is shared by all developed animals. The difference from species to species is only in the image-handling capability. All the vertebrates, and some invertebrates, are self-conscious. Self-consciousness emerged in the long history of the evolutionary development of animals, guided by the naturally set objective of thriving at the minimum cost. In the recent past, the evolutionary mechanism changed from Darwinian to Lamarckian, and many positive, along with many more negative, features emerged. These might ultimately lead to the destruction of human culture.

The mechanism of self-consciousness can be clarified by tracking the process of its Darwinian evolution in the animal's brain and body structure and operation, by conceptually designing a mechanical model of the brain and body, and exercising it. This methodology and its basic thought, namely that self-consciousness is the subject of study of an emerging systems science, is the most important conclusion of *Self-Consciousness*. Different from traditional science, systems science relies heavily on the synthetic method, which is easier to use when studying the complex human brain and mind than the traditional analytic approach. My objective is, above all, a proposal of the methodology of self-consciousness research. I have shown an example of its actual execution in *Self-Consciousness*. According to this study, self-consciousness is shown to emerge from the brain's neuron circuit's activity. The sense of existence of the elusive subject SELF, and various modes of its operation, are effected by the neuron circuit's excitation. The SELF is the sum total of such mode of excitation.

This method is focused on the basic capability of self-consciousness, such as acquisition, assembly, recognition, and manipulation of internal images. These can be integrated to create a higher brain capability of symbolic thinking, such as solving geometrical problems as shown in section 4.08. Self-consciousness need not be explained starting from the highest capability of mind, as traditionally done by philosophers. This is another major conclusion of this research.

The conclusion derived from this study will have a direct application on psychology. The new systems science approach will provide a realistic model of the self-conscious human mind. A necessary prerequisite is elimination of the traditional religious and ideological bias to the human mind, and also liberation from the simplistic trend of trying to connect self-consciousness to subconsciousness or quantum mystery.

To put things into historical perspective, humans are now in the last phase of the Enlightenment period that began during the Renaissance. If no active effort is made, then we will go back to another dark age. Human imagination has withered very considerably during the last fifty years. Now is the time when everyone should take a deep look into his or her own mind and revitalize imagination to find new directions. To do so, it is necessary to remember the now forgotten words of Thorstein Veblen: the most important cultural progress comes from idle curiosity and not from money or business-driven activity.

The next dark age will be global and will be intolerable to anyone who has a free spirit. What's more, this dark age may return the earth to the Mesozoic era by extermination of the human race and human culture. A historical conclusion of *Self-Consciousness* is that the future of humanity is no longer determined by Darwinian evolution. Therefore, its basic mechanism, competition for survival, should not be carried over as the basic merit of the social system. We should aim for a society in which competition of individuals is not required for survival. Competition in the present degenerate social culture is the sure way to ensure the ultimate doom of all humanity.

Printed in the United States
By Bookmasters